Comparative Law as Critique

Günter Frankenberg

Professor, Goethe University in Frankfurt, Germany

ELGAR STUDIES IN LEGAL THEORY

Edward Elgar
PUBLISHING

Cheltenham, UK • Northampton, MA, USA

Cover: 'Tischgesellschaft' ('Company at the Table'), 1988. Thirty-two figures made of polyester, table and benches made of wood, partially painted, color printed and bleached cotton. Artist: Katharina Fritsch, born 1956 in Essen (DE), lives in Düsseldorf (DE). Photographer: Axel Schneider, Frankfurt am Main. On permanent loan from Commerzbank AG, Frankfurt am Main, Inv. Nr. 1989/1L.1-36.

Published by
Edward Elgar Publishing Limited
The Lypiatts
15 Lansdown Road
Cheltenham
Glos GL50 2JA
UK

Edward Elgar Publishing, Inc.
William Pratt House
9 Dewey Court
Northampton
Massachusetts 01060
USA

A catalogue record for this book
is available from the British Library

Library of Congress Control Number: 2015957873

This book is available electronically in the **Elgar**online
Law subject collection
DOI 10.4337/9781785363948

FSC
www.fsc.org
MIX
Paper from
responsible sources
FSC® C013056

ISBN 978 1 78536 393 1 (cased)
ISBN 978 1 78536 394 8 (eBook)

Typeset by Columns Design XML Ltd, Reading
Printed and bound in Great Britain by TJ International Ltd, Padstow

Comparative Law as Critique

ELGAR STUDIES IN LEGAL THEORY

Series Editor: Wojciech Sadurski, *Sydney Law School, University of Sydney, Australia*

Elgar Studies in Legal Theory is a new series designed to cultivate and promote high quality works of scholarship on all aspects of legal theory. The focus of the series is on the development of original thinking in legal theory, with topics ranging from law and language, logic and legal reasoning, morality and the law, critical legal studies, and transnational law. Innovative work is encouraged from both established authors and the new generation of scholars.

Titles in this series include:

Understanding the Nature of Law
A Case for Constructive Conceptual Explanation
Michael Giudice

Comparative Law as Critique
Günter Frankenberg

Contents

Preface

Comparison happens all the time. Common wisdom suggests it is inevitable. By the same token, professional wisdom proclaims that comparison is impossible,[1] at least in an ideal form. What appears to be a contradiction (taken at face value), may be only a matter of perspective. Let's turn to *Hamlet* for assistance:

HAMLET:	Do you see yonder cloud that's almost in the shape of a camel?
POLONIUS:	By th' mass, and 'tis like a camel indeed.
HAMLET:	Methinks it is like a weasel.
POLONIUS:	It is backed like a weasel.
HAMLET:	Or like a whale.
POLONIUS:	Very like a whale.[2]

Hamlet, or rather Shakespeare, uses analogies and metaphors of likeness, so he compares. And Polonius follows suit. From this short dialog we may infer that comparison happens – on stage and, since the world is not always a theater, very likely also off stage. But comparison has its pitfalls whether performed by mainstream comparatists in the spirit of innocence[3] to demonstrate understanding of the foreign or, as in *Hamlet*, to test and demonstrate honesty and loyalty.

In the everyday as in legal studies, the comparatist has to decide how to compare, what to compare and, especially, what to look out for – similarities or dissimilarities. So comparatists have a choice how to deal with the foreign. More importantly, comparing laws is quite different from comparing clouds with animals, the results of your math homework

[1] Evans-Pritchard, Edward Evan (1965) 'The Comparative Method in Social Anthropology' in *The Position of Women in Primitive Societies and Other Essays in Social Anthropology*, London: Faber & Faber, 13–36.

[2] Shakespeare, William (1602) *The Tragicall Historie of Hamlet, Prince of Denmarke*, Act III, scene ii, ll. 392 *seq.*

[3] The varieties of the spirit of innocence are discussed in Chapter 3 in this volume.

with what your friend figured out, or the data of two empirical studies about climate change.

Legal comparison is a social construction. Comparatists bring a thing – a law, institution, ruling, etc. – into a relationship with another. Comparing and contrasting laws means setting up and *representing* the law, legal situation, event or idea in one cultural context as *similar to* or *different from* another. What is more, legal comparison, rather than briefly looking at a natural phenomenon (cloud) and drawing whimsical conclusions, is a *performance* which involves investigating, selecting, perceiving, interpreting and evaluating data on the basis of one's reading about unfamiliar, strange, foreign legal phenomena.

The Foreign

This performance is precarious because of the co-presence of the foreign in the comparative space. How we deal with and understand foreign laws and foreign legal cultures is not only a matter of theory and method but has ethical and political implications.[4] To begin with, it makes a difference whether the foreign is treated as a phenomenon in its own right or is domesticated and assimilated as basically similar, a member of the same legal family or derived from one's 'own' law. If the familiar ways of law take center stage, the comparatist yields to 'the unconscious spell that holds us to see others by the measure of ourselves.'[5] In consequence, legal regimes, ideas and practices that resist domestication because they are quite different, tend to receive only marginal attention or are allocated an inferior status in the comparative study of the world of laws. Thus, comparative law supports the reproduction of geo-political and economic hierarchies as well as cultural asymmetries.

Critique

Critique may help uncover and dismantle those hierarchies and asymmetries: it may deconstruct hegemony by unsettling settled knowledge. Critique may help us see through the posture of innocence and bring to the fore hidden assumptions and biases, interpretive frameworks and ideological predispositions that privilege the familiar legal ideas and practices. It may demonstrate that there is nothing virginal, natural

---

4 As will be shown in Chapter 4 in this volume.

5 Frankenberg, Günter (1985) 'Critical Comparisons: Rethinking Comparative Law' 26 *Harvard International Law Journal*, 411, 414.

and inevitable about the ways and means of comparative law's mainstream schools and scholars – in particular, about their similarity disposition.

When critique has finished deconstructing the dominant paradigms and delegitimizing their ideologies, when it has finished showing that comparison is a social construct and unraveling cognitive structures,[6] it neither 'help[s] us decide which social constructs to retain and which to replace,'[7] nor offers us a blueprint for 'good comparative practice.' At best, it suggests that comparatists keep an eye out for intersubjectively 'available cues,' 'shared context[s] of understanding,' 'socio-cognitive context[s] and the likes.'[8] That is as difficult as it sounds and errors have to be reckoned with.

Comparative Law as Critique is intended to challenge the routines of mainstream legal comparison. Rather than presenting a systematic treatise, complete textbook or comprehensive introduction, I try out various approaches and move to diverse venues of critique. Bereft of a single unified guiding theory, I explore critical methods and ideas and hope my project supports attempts to deconstruct Anglo-Eurocentrism in comparative law and provincialize Western law, civil and common. Since I had to rely on trial and error, I probably committed elementary mistakes that I submit to critical scrutiny. What else?

Support

Critical thought is a fragmented terrain with an uneven topography. What is more, in the field of comparative law, critique does not come wholesale. So, writing about comparative law in the mode of critique is enhanced by contexts amenable to intellectual experiments and companions generous enough to supply comments and suggestions. *Comparative Law as Critique* enjoyed both kinds of support and drew inspiration from many sources. I am indebted to various settings, projects and approaches, which have animated the critique of comparative law and helped me

---

6 See Legrand, Pierre (1996) 'European Legal Systems Are Not Converging' 45 *International & Comparative Law Quarterly*, 52, 60.

7 With regard to philosophy, see Rorty, Richard (1995) 'Feminism, Ideology, and Deconstruction: A Pragmatist View' in Žižek, Slavoj ed. *Mapping Ideology*, London and New York: Verso, 227–234.

8 For references, see Grosswald Curran, Vivian (1998) 'Cultural Immersion, Difference and Categories in U.S. Comparative Law' 46 *American Journal of Comparative Law*, 43, 52.

rethink 'Critical Comparisons.'[9] While 'Critical Comparisons' was inspired particularly by discussions in the context and spirit of Critical Legal Studies (in the old times), this book was developed in the environment of New Approaches to Comparative and International Law (NAIL) and, more recently, the IGLP network.[10]

Discursive contexts are not free-standing but constituted by people who are willing to share ideas. There were many versions of the different chapters, and there were many colleagues and friends who helped me rewrite them. For their generous comments and encouraging ideas along the road to the final text, I thank, in particular, Helena Garcia Alviar, Claudia Baumann, Jorge Esquirol, Priya Gupta, Ratna Kapur, David Kennedy, Maria Rosaria Marella, Giovanni Marini, Lena-Maria Möller, P.G. Monateri, Horatia Muir Watt, Anne Orford, Nikolas Rajkovic, and Larissa Vetters. Claudia Baumann, Jana Gawlas and Eric von Doemming helped me get the manuscript ready for print. As always Edward Elgar Publishing provided a very professional and supportive team: Elizabeth Clack and Stephen Gutierrez encouraged me to go on with this book project. Nick Bromley and Nicky Crane did a fantastic job of copy-editing the text and preparing it for publication respectively. I also thank Katharina Fritsch for allowing me to use her 'Company at the Table' ('Tischgesellschaft'), for the cover of this book. So it is fair to say that *Comparative Law as Critique* has been an exciting cooperative venture. Nevertheless, albeit unfortunately, all mistakes, misreadings and misunderstandings are private property.

Content

Comparative law is introduced as a discipline (Chapter 1) in the light of the self-interpretations of comparatists. The Cinderella complex and fantasies of comparative law as queen of the legal sciences compete as

---

[9] See the overview of critical approaches in Chapter 2 in this volume.

[10] IGLP (Institute for Global Law and Policy at Harvard Law School) has, for several years, organized conferences and workshops attended by young scholars from all over the world and provided an institutional basis and forum for transnational debates on global legal thought, comparative and otherwise. The 2015 participants in an Advanced Writing Workshop in Cambridge discussed an earlier draft of the first two chapters in this volume. I presented Chapters 3 and 4 at the IGLP Workshop in 2014 and also at the Inter-University Center in Torino, and Chapters 5 and 7 at the University of Perugia and Melbourne University School of Law. Research fellows from the Max Planck Institute for Social Anthropology in Halle (Germany) provided comments on the lecture version of Chapters 3 and 4 in this volume.

constitutive elements of the discipline's imaginary. Thereafter, critical approaches are reviewed, albeit briefly (Chapter 2). The review concentrates on diverse concepts of and possible criteria for critique. Whether they have any purchase in comparative legal studies and how they might actually enhance a good comparative practice will be tried out in the following chapters.

To achieve some distance from the official narratives and to identify their characteristic features, notably a shared view of the tools, concept, and purpose of comparative law at a given time, I focus on the major schools and styles of legal comparison (Chapter 3) and their rhetoric, methods, and theories as variations of innocence. The ethical and political dimensions of the mainstream 'tracks' of comparative work are represented by means of a 'grid' that allows one to capture and discuss the dilemma of interpretation (*similarity/difference*) and the problem of positionality – whether the comparatist recognizes that she is always already anchored in her 'own' legal culture and how she relates the familiar to the foreign (*detachment/commitment*) (Chapter 4). Turning from academic discourse to the practice of dealing with normative pluralism and the negotiation of differences, and shifting the attention from cognitive to visual phenomena, the grid is then applied to the legal-judicial discourse on Muslim veiling (Chapter 5).

The last part of the book concentrates on a comparison of human rights narratives – discussing, first, human rights law in general and its narratives of justification (Chapter 6) and then Kafka's story of the human right of access to justice (Chapter 7). Narrativity is considered in the closing remarks (Chapter 8) as a possible ingredient of 'thick comparison.'

PART I

Discipline and critique

1. Comparative law as discipline

1. FROM CINDERELLA TO QUEEN

Comparative law has been suffering for quite some time, in the Western comparative community,[1] from what can be accounted for as an inferiority syndrome. Comparatists feel (or, at least, felt) neither adequately recognized by their academic peers nor sufficiently represented in the law school curriculum. Comparative law, some argue, 'has enjoyed so little prestige in the inner circles of the academy';[2] colleagues 'see our work as peripheral.'[3] Their field of research and study, some complained, continued to be 'a subject in search of an audience'[4] and was treated, as others imagined with mild disdain, as the 'Cinderella of the legal sciences.'[5]

In the meantime, a participant observer diagnosed that '[c]omparative law is moving swiftly from a long infancy to teenage maturity ... This is the nature of a healthy adolescence.'[6] A decade later two comparatists turned to psychology again and, noting the growing popularity of the discipline, stressed that it was still 'fraught with internal contradiction, uncertainty, and a sense of mid-life crisis.'[7]

---

[1] Comparatists from Japan claim that comparative law has always played a leading role in Japanese legal academia – a princess all along, rather than a stepdaughter and maidservant hidden in the attic.

[2] Fletcher, George (1998) 'Comparative Law as a Subversive Discipline' 46 *American Journal of Comparative Law*, 683.

[3] Gordley, James (1998) 'Comparative Law in the United States Today: Distinctiveness, Quality, and Tradition' 46 *American Journal of Comparative Law*, 607, 615.

[4] Markesinis, Basil (1997) *Foreign Law and Comparative Methodology*, Oxford: Hart Publishing, 3.

[5] Gutteridge, Harold (1949) *Comparative Law*, 2nd ed., Cambridge: Cambridge University Press, 26. For the more recent development see Reimann, Mathias (2002) 'The Progress and Failure of Comparative law in the Second Half of the Twentieth Century' 50 *American Journal of Comparative Law*, 671.

[6] Watson, Alan M. (1974) *Legal Transplants. An Approach to Comparative Law*, Edinburgh: Scottish Academic Press.

[7] Harding, Andrew and Örücü, Esin (2002) *Comparative Law in the 21st Century*, London: Kluwer Academic Publishers, xii.

Over the years, the feeling of marginalization has developed into a Cinderella complex,[8] which has only become more knotty and perplexing, one might say. It combined the reality of curricular marginality with the fantasy of liberation from the 'atmosphere of hostility … at best the chilly environment of indifference'[9] and, ultimately, the hope for the well-deserved invitation as princess to the sciences' academic dance. Some comparatists entertained the grandiose idea that the princess would marry the prince and become queen of all the legal sciences in the end.

To these visions and diagnoses we have to add today the rare predicament of late puberty and adolescence combined with mid-life crisis. And there is more: comparative law, a.k.a. Cinderella, has always been accompanied by a twin sister, unheard of in the fairy tale. Where the former complained about her ancillary role and her lack of appreciation, the latter leaned toward the pretentious and was liable to overestimate the powers of legal comparison.

> [T]oday comparative law studies are admitted to be a necessary part of any legal culture and training.[10]
>
> Comparative law manifestly has a crucial role to play in the development of legal philosophy.[11]
>
> Comparative law is useful in gaining a better understanding of one's own national law and in the work of improving it.[12]
>
> Comparative law is helpful in the understanding of foreign peoples; it thereby assists in the creation of a healthy context for the development of international relations.[13]

Oh, comparative law! The self-aggrandizing comments are succinctly summed up in Esin Örücü's observation: 'Such important things have taken place in Europe recently [that is, the process of convergence] that

---

[8] Regarding the complex, see Frankenberg (1985) 'Critical Comparisons. Re-Thinking Comparative Law' 26 *Harvard International Law Journal*, 411, 416–418.

[9] Lepaulle, Pierre (1922) 'The Function of Comparative Law' 35 *Harvard Law Review*, 838.

[10] David, René and Brierley, John (1985) *Major Legal Systems of the World Today*, 3rd ed., London: Stevens & Sons, 3.

[11] *Ibid.*, 5.

[12] *Ibid.*, 6.

[13] *Ibid.*, 8.

comparative law is now referred to as the science of the 21st century.'[14] *Voilà*, comparative law after its coronation as queen!

Over time, things – the ancillary status of comparative law, its collateral reputational damage and crises – have changed. One may conclude, on a more sober note, paraphrasing Rodolfo Sacco's opening statement in 2000 as to the state of the discipline one hundred years after the Paris Congress: '*Les nouvelles sont meilleures*.'[15] After a century of muddling through, in attics and royal coaches, comparative law has firmly established itself as a genuine field of study. What is more, it has generated a series of mainstreams, which in turn have represented comparative law with vigor, though not always with theoretical and methodological rigor.

Arguably, comparative law was founded as a discipline during and with the 1900 Congress in Paris, where it experienced its mythical moment.[16] Although it had taken shape gradually, here and there, and with a heavy private law accent, throughout the nineteenth century, it was only then, at the *fin de siècle*, that the mainstream began to flow. 1900 saw legal comparison beginning to move on two contrasting tracks. First, the speculative orientation, energized by history, philosophy, and anthropology, continued the nineteenth-century preoccupation with origins and evolution. Second, comparative law's somewhat traditional and philosophical orientation soon had to compete with, and was superseded by, a basically positivist interest in legislation that focused on more mundane, present matters. While the first group was preoccupied with the construction of law's universal history or a universal jurisprudence, the members of the second compared legislation and legal solutions to social problems. They routinely assumed the laws of diverse countries, 'systems,' 'families,' 'circles,' 'styles' and 'traditions' to be factually 'out there,' ready and only waiting for comparative scrutiny. Where methodologically rigorous analysis was avoided, legal comparison settled for juxtaposition, classification, structural accounts or functionalist appraisal. Furthermore, comparatists regarded the legal vocabulary and grammar as an autonomous body of rules and decisions, arguments and doctrines.

---

[14] Örücü, Esin (2007) 'What Next in the Convergence Process in Europe?' in Bussani, Mauro and Mattei, Ugo eds *Opening Up European Law: The Common Core Project towards Eastern and South Eastern Europe*, Bern: Stämpfli, 175.

[15] Sacco, Rodolfo (2000) 'One Hundred Years of Comparative Law' 75 *Tulane Law Review*, 1159; see also Reimann 'The Progress and Failure,' 671.

[16] For a less enthusiastic view of the Paris Congress (than is prevalent): see Michaels, Ralf (2002) 'Im Westen nichts Neues? 100 Jahre Pariser Kongreß für Rechtsvergleichung' 66 *Rabels Zeitschrift für Rechtsvergleichung*, 97.

Undaunted by the charge of epistemological *naïveté*, they were able to pursue (with considerable success and relative ease) what they believed to be an 'objective' access to the reality of foreign law.

Mainstream comparative law embraced the formalist notion of legal validity entertained by legal positivism as well as its unlikely ally, the anti-formalist style. This combination betrays the impossibility of what positivists are desperately trying to do: to neutralize, albeit analytically, all extralegal incursions – notably politics, ethics, culture and the economy – on law-making and law-deciding.

Textbooks and treatises have always affirmed the spirit of the mainstream and have spread the traditional canon that was basically constructed on the foundations of the Anglo-European concept of common/civil law and its entrenched ideology of law-rule (rule of law, *Rechtsstaat*, *état de droit*). Legal comparison tended to start from the West, and it would invariably return there, leaving little cognitive and imaginative space, in this circular movement and intellectual round-trip, for recognizing the other – foreign legal systems, cultures, institutions – in its own right and therefore genuinely *appreciating* differences. Critical insights came from some mainstream authors whose explorations into the territory of anthropology may have sensitized them to the ethnocentrism infecting 'good comparative practice':

> Ethnocentrism means that the researcher uses his or her own bias while problematizing, concluding, reasoning, or systematizing the study of another culture. Comparative law can claim no special immunity from this virus [of ethnocentrism].[17]

> So it must be asked how does an external observer, despite the best will in the world, ever escape from his or her own framework of imbedded conceptions and looks outward with a detached eye (*l'œil agnostique*) that does not superimpose these conceptions onto the object under observation? ... The comparative investigator must hope to keep a certain distance from his own culture and prejudice, from the society under study, and from the biases of his informants.[18]

Undaunted by doubt and self-reflection (reflecting the Anglo-European legal self), navigators of the mainstream comfortably accept the traditional object-subject conception of comparison, which of course would

---

[17] Fikentscher, Wolfgang (1995) *Modes of Thought: A Study in the Anthropology of Law and Religion*, Tübingen: Mohr Siebeck, 117.

[18] Palmer, Vernon (2005) 'From Lerotholi to Lando. Some Examples of Comparative Law Methodology' 53 *American Journal of Comparative Law*, 261, 264.

grant them, free of charge, permanent subject status, and the idea that 'complete objectivity' is impossible to achieve, which justifies, they firmly maintain, their lack of self-criticism.[19] With their cultural return ticket safely stowed away in their pocket, they are likely to follow the directions of an ethnocentric compass. And it takes a critical perspective to uncover comparative law's dark side.

2. COMPARATIVE LAW'S DISCIPLINARITY

Disciplinarity

Tradition and convention have it that studies and research, to gain recognition as academic science, need to be constituted as a 'discipline.' Scholars and researchers have to demonstrate that knowledge is acquired in an orderly fashion and then integrated into some kind of systematic order. The production of knowledge in academic institutions by professionally trained scholars in disciplinary form is widely considered to be 'so natural that we tend to forget their historical novelty and fail to imagine how else we might produce and organize knowledge.'[20] As academics produce disciplines, so disciplines produce 'disciplinary' practitioners. They are disciplined in their world-making by the established criteria and conventions of 'normal science'[21] that scholars are expected to meet and conform to in their work. They learn to recognize the borders of their field of study and its topography. They are trained to apply the methods introduced in every discipline to establish and protect the 'order of things.'[22]

Why would scholars bow to the yoke of a disciplinary regime? Because disciplines lend protection: they cover up 'the historically contingent and adventitious way in which various ideas and practices' are assembled and ordered into (and in) fields of study and research and essentialized there as 'philosophy,' 'medicine' or 'law.' Also, and more importantly, because only disciplines, as institutionalized formations,

---

19 *Ibid.*

20 Messer-Davidow, Ellen, Shumway, David R. and Sylvan, David J. eds (1993) in their 'Preface' to *Knowledges: Historical and Critical Studies in Disciplinarity*, Charlottesville and London: University of Virginia Press, vii.

21 Kuhn, Thomas (1970) *The Structure of Scientific Revolutions*, 2nd ed., Chicago: University of Chicago Press.

22 Foucault, Michel (1970) *The Order of Things: An Archeology of the Human Sciences*, New York: Pantheon Books.

organize the procedures and communication for the production of knowledge in a way that lends itself to according the label 'truth,' which then may become the basis of power.[23] Disciplines organize and account for the constitution of knowledges, discourses, objects and strategies of research, they privilege theories, methods and objectives for study. Furthermore disciplinary regimes are accepted because they 'produce economies of value.'[24] Most importantly, in an immediately practical sense, they provide jobs, offer professional identities, secure funding for study and research, and, if all goes well, generate prestige.

Methods play a crucial role in the constitution of disciplines insofar as they organize the way knowledge is produced and information for study, research and education is processed. They organize schemes of perception and concepts of interpretation, and provide tools of cognition and translation.

Methods comply with and, by the same token, reproduce 'scientific standards' and the accepted conventions of an epistemic community. Methods that come across as ways of doing science are quite powerful tools: they define and distinguish academic disciplines more than, say, explanatory theories. Jointly, methods and theories, however, promise to guide scientific analysis of a discrete subject-matter or field of thought and investigation, like law or, for that matter, comparative law. In addition, they usually provide both scholarship and (university) education, based on and structured by a curriculum, with a disciplinary orientation ascertaining the reproduction of knowledge within a given domain, and they sustain the 'illusion of disciplinary unity.'[25]

For research, study and education to be externally perceived and internally understood as being governed by methods and theories pertaining to a specific discipline, they need to be distinguishable from other fields of inquiry, thought and teaching. Boundary-work is crucial for disciplinary activity, because it ascertains that the scientific practice in a bounded field is performed by professionals and, more so, specialists. Therefore, what this practice, like comparing law, is 'about' has to be protected (and limited) by boundaries on the outside and structured by routines within, that is, the subject-matter.

---

[23] Foucault, *The Order of Things*; Foucault, Michel (1980) *Power/Knowledge. Selected Interviews and Other Writings 1972–1977*, New York: Random House, 109.

[24] Messer-Davidow et al. *Knowledges. Historical and Critical Studies in Disciplinarity*, vii–viii.

[25] Messer-Davidow et al. 'Introduction: Disciplinary Ways of Knowing' in *Knowledges. Historical and Critical Studies in Disciplinarity*, 12.

Over time the standards practiced in research and education, the borders limiting a field of study, as well as the internal and external perceptions, tend to establish a disciplinary identity, which lends a name to the field, the practitioners working there and their projects. As a result, the disciplinary identity provides the criteria for defining who is in and who is out and, if reified, forms the core around which the orthodoxy of thought and practice may crystallize. Orthodoxy tells its followers (and also curious visitors) that, at a time, only one method or theory or an established set of them is considered legitimate. It mandates a (serial) kind of intellectual monogamy that looks down upon pluralism and mandates for eclecticism to be integrated, as far as possible, in a unitary framework.

The orthodoxy of comparative law – or rather the sequence of orthodox approaches, their rhetoric, methods and agenda – will be discussed below as 'mainstream.'[26] I attempt to map and submit to critical review the varieties of disciplinarity by stressing the historically contingent forms and rhetoric of 'doing' comparative law.

Comparative Law as a Discipline

Most comparatists take it for granted that their field of research and study qualifies as an academic discipline, even if it may still be incoherent, of a 'piecemeal nature,' and in need of theoretical-methodological overhauling.[27] Arguably, the (re-)production and ordering of comparative knowledge has been elevated to the level of science since the end of the nineteenth century. The authors of the widely read *An Introduction to Comparative Law* express the mainstream's consensus when they endorse the scientific nature of the discipline, albeit insisting rather too much:

> It is beyond dispute that the scholarly pursuit of comparative law has several significant functions. This emerges from a very simple consideration: no study deserves the name of a science if it limits itself to phenomena arising within national boundaries. For a long time, lawyers were content to be insular in this sense, and to some extent they are so still. But such a position is untenable, and comparative law offers the only way by which law can become international and consequently a *science*. ... [I]t is clear that the

---

[26] See Chapters 3 and 4 in this volume.

[27] See Reimann 'The Progress and Failure,' 671; Palmer 'From Lerotholi to Lando,' 261.

> *method* of comparative law can provide a much richer range of model solutions than a legal science devoted to a single nation ...[28]

From this statement one may infer that comparatists no longer mix neglect with contempt, nor do they treat foreign laws 'more like objects of simple curiosity than of real science'[29] – even if faint echoes of this complaint can still be heard today.[30] And despite the porous boundaries that demarcate the subject-matter and methodological problems, comparatists no longer appear as 'intellectual nomads,'[31] bereft of a genuine field of research. Many would indeed subscribe to the conclusion 'that comparative law has developed into a respectable body of actual knowledge.'[32] Moreover, the typical genres of literature covering fields of research, their genealogy and tools – encyclopedias, handbooks, monographic studies and elaborate introductions[33] – as well as intensive debates about theory and method[34] provide comparative law with the widely recognized credentials of science. It comes with a peculiar feature, though, because many comparatists argue that, in comparative law, method and subject-matter are coextensive. In other words: there is only method – a claim that will have to be discussed in detail later.

---

[28] Zweigert, Konrad and Kötz, Hein (1998) *An Introduction to Comparative Law*, 3rd ed., Oxford: Clarendon, 15 – emphasis added. See also Reimann 'The Progress and Failure,' 677.

[29] Escarra, Jean (1933) 'The Aims of Comparative Law' 7 *Temple Law Quarterly*, 296.

[30] See Mattei, Ugo (2006) 'Comparative Law and Critical Legal Studies' in Reimann, Mathias and Zimmermann, Reinhard eds *The Oxford Handbook of Comparative Law*, Oxford: Oxford University Press, 815, 832–835.

[31] Grosswald Curran, Vivian (1998) 'Cultural Immersion, Difference and Categories in U.S. Comparative Law' 46 *American Journal of Comparative Law*, 657.

[32] Reimann 'The Progress and Failure,' 672. One wonders about the 'actual,' though.

[33] See the 17 volumes of David, René et al. eds (1972 seq.) *International Encyclopedia of Comparative Law*, Tübingen: Mohr Siebeck; and Smits, Jan M. ed. (2012) *Elgar Encyclopedia of Comparative Law,* Cheltenham, UK and Northampton, MA, USA: Edward Elgar Publishing; Bussani, Mauro and Mattei, Ugo eds (2012) *The Cambridge Companion to Comparative Law*, Cambridge: Cambridge University Press; Reimann and Zimmermann, *Oxford Handbook of Comparative Law*; Örücü, Esin and Nelken, David eds (2007) *Comparative Law. A Handbook*, Portland: Hart Publishing.

[34] See only Monateri, Pier Giuseppe ed. (2012) *Methods of Comparative Law*, Cheltenham, UK and Northampton, MA, USA: Edward Elgar Publishing; Zweigert and Koetz *Introduction to Comparative Law*, 8; Palmer 'From Lerotholi to Lando,' 261.

What is more, aside from the receding Cinderella complex, the profession seems to be grappling with an identity problem, if only a minor one. Scholars express concern about the accurate label for their work. The majority, which will be referred to as 'mainstream,' clearly favors comparative *law*, whereas a significant number of dissenters privilege comparative *legal studies*.[35] Sure enough, not everyone associates dissimilar programs with this semantic distinction. Generally speaking, however, the 'law' faction tends to follow approaches, such as formalist taxonomies and surveys, functionalist searches for better (legal) solutions, structural analyses, and factual accounts geared towards legal harmonization projects, which by number and institutional influence qualify as mainstream. From a critical perspective these attitudes and the practices of comparison they generate have been characterized as (a) featuring 'Comparative Nomoscopy,'[36] (b) seeking to describe other legal systems as fact,[37] (c) propagating a 'legocentric'[38] style of positivism, narrowly focused on laws, appellate court decisions, legal doctrines and legal institutions, and finally (d) being preoccupied with perceptual and conceptual tidiness and, above everything else, similarities.

As paradoxical as it may seem given that one would expect comparatists to be extolling the value of diversity – and the virtue of appreciating it – much about comparative legal studies – or rather, comparative law – has been written, and continues to be written, as Pierre Legrand put it, from 'Uncle Theo's' theocratic point of view: commonalities *envers et contre tout*, no matter how much manipulation of data must intervene in the process.[39]

In contrast, the comparative-studies faction is disposed to reject traditional comparative law, some members take the studies orientation to be an alternative to the 'armchair' manner of legal comparison. They call for (and, at times, practice) a shift from law-in-books to law-in-action, more interdisciplinary research, a widening of the legocentric lens to

---

35 Nelken, David (2007) 'Comparative Law and Comparative Legal Studies' in Nelken and Örücü *Comparative Law*, 3.

36 Wigmore, John H. (1928) *A Panorama of the World's Legal Systems*, Vol. III, St. Paul: West Publishing, 1120.

37 *Ibid.*

38 Frankenberg 'Critical Comparisons,' 411, 438, 445.

39 Legrand, Pierre (2001) 'The Return of the Repressed: Moving Comparative Legal Studies beyond Pleasure' 75 *Tulane Law Review*, 1033, 1036.

bring text *and* context into focus.[40] They invite their fellow comparatists to transgress the 'really fuzzy' borders of the discipline.[41] Accordingly, studies-persons lean toward treating norms, cases, and institutions as artifacts of culture. They base comparison on contextual analysis to include the social struggles behind the law and to develop 'a consciousness of difference.'[42]

Even if taken to designate diverse comparative agendas and not only signifying a more or less contingent shift in perspective or expressing the narcissism of the small difference, these labels as such do not argue against a disciplinary status, but only for lively internal debates (if that is what they are) and divisions over theory and method not uncommon in other disciplines. As a matter of fact, this semantic distinction and the theoretical-methodological orientation that comes along with it, bring to mind the 'positivism debate' in the social sciences.[43]

Disciplinarity, or what constitutes a disciplinary identity, also has a bright side. It actually has two. First, its constraints and burdens provoke (some?) scholars, particularly in comparative studies, to test the permeability of disciplinary boundaries, try out collaborative research, borrow insights from neighboring disciplines, and so forth – in short: to rethink 'the way we think about the way we think.'[44] Second, disciplinarity brings forth criticism. One might even argue that disciplinarity presupposes critical thought. I will take up this argument again, which is suggested by the title of this book, in the next chapter.

Disciplinarity means quite practically that it may serve as a point of departure for interdisciplinary enterprises. Interdisciplinarity[45] logically presupposes disciplinarity. Boundaries need to be there so that they can be crossed, fields of study need to be defined and segregated before they can be combined or deconstructed. However, there seems to be some

---

40 Hirschl, Ran (2013) 'Editorial: From Comparative Constitutional Law to Comparative Constitutional Studies' 11 *International Journal of Constitutional Law*, 1.

41 Menski, Werner (2007) 'Beyond Europe' in Nelken and Örücü *Comparative Law*, 189, 194.

42 Foster, Nicholas (2007) 'Comparative Commercial Law' in Nelken and Örücü *Comparative Law*, 279–280.

43 I will return later to the positivism controversy.

44 Geertz, Clifford (1982) 'The Way We Think Now: Towards an Ethnography of Modern Thought' 35 *Bulletin of the American Academy of Arts and Sciences*, 14.

45 See Thompson Klein, Julie (1990) *Interdisciplinarity: History, Theory, & Practice*, Detroit: Wayne State University Press; Moran, Joe (2010) *Interdisciplinarity (The New Critical Idiom)*, 2nd ed., New York: Routledge.

confusion[46] (at least no consensus) about what 'interdisciplinary' means. For all intents and purposes it is here defined, in rather general terms, as a specific modality of scientific interaction and, more specifically, as the exchange of scientific tools and the exchange of insights.

Comparative law, one might assume, offers the perfect platform – and is a 'natural' – for border-crossing travels not only to other countries, systems and laws but also to other disciplines, such as history, philosophy, anthropology and political science. However, the standard 'good practice' informs us otherwise. Originally, notably in the post-1900 era, which will later be referred to as the immensely productive 'golden era,' the comparison of laws and legal systems was open to information from the neighboring sciences, especially philosophy, history and anthropology. During the nineteenth century, comparative constitutional law started quite straightforwardly as political science.[47] As will be shown below, throughout the twentieth century, the interdisciplinary predisposition of comparative legal scholars got lost in the mainstream(s). The discipline became known for its 'entrenched ahistoricism'[48] and the loss of the speculative dimension, rather than a yearning for interdisciplinary adventures. Interestingly enough, the very comparatists who reduce comparative law to a method are especially likely to keep research intra-disciplinary.

3. MAINSTREAM AS ORTHODOXY

Comparative law looks back on a venerable academic tradition. Neither ethnocentrism, that is, the focus on the Anglo-European legal hemisphere and its privileged position in comparative studies, nor the preference for cognitive control[49] – ordering the phenomena under comparison rather than providing a genuine learning experience – undermined the mainstreams' disciplinary success.

'Mainstream' does not denote a monolithic camp or homogeneous comparative practice but is made up of a series of diverse schools of

---

[46] Thompson Klein *Interdisciplinarity*, 12–14.

[47] Emphasizing the study of political institutions: Crane, William W. and Moses, Bernard (1884) *Politics: An Introduction to the Study of Comparative Constitutional Law*, New York: G.P. Putnam; and Burgess, John W. (1890/2000) *Political Science and Comparative Constitutional Law*, Getzville, NY: William S. Hein & Co. See also Hirschl, Ran 'Editorial,' 3.

[48] Legrand 'The Return of the Repressed,' 1037.

[49] Frankenberg 'Critical Comparisons,' 416 seq.

thought committed to divergent purposes of legal comparison and to different comparative methods and theories. Each phase or era, dominant school or trend was characterized by a paradigm[50] of legal comparison privileging a specific tool-kit (method/theory), distinct goals and a peculiar interpretive framework. Justified by the prevailing discourse, each paradigm shaped the nature, style and purpose of 'good comparative practice' and congealed into an orthodoxy or mainstream.[51] The orthodoxy came with the trinity of a disciplinary identity, institutional power and mechanisms of exclusion:

> Beyond fashionable designations … the pertinent research and teaching enterprises remain infused by one abiding concern, which is a determination to extol the value of the foreign in terms of what is relevantly legal locally. As is no doubt the case with every other field, 'comparative law' boasts an orthodoxy. I have in mind established comparativists, those who edit the journals, are called upon by leading academic publishers to assess book proposals, secure large budgets to launch major research projects or fund new postgraduate programs, and direct centers or institutes. These comparativists function in a structuring capacity in that they uphold an identifiable regime of knowledge and information. On account of the institutional positions they hold, they defend what they regard as good comparative practice, that is, good comparative manners … [52]

In other words, the orthodoxy (or mainstream) of the discipline, institutionally influential or not, prefers not to take help from outside (say, Derrida) or inside (internal crits) but steers unflinchingly its legocentric, positivist and Anglo-Eurocentric course.

Good comparative practice looked different in the different ages of the discipline, though. It is striking, how each mainstream or orthodoxy domesticated and 'othered' the foreign whose co-presence in the comparative space haunts any 'good comparative practice.'

In the days of Aristotle, the comparative imagination had concentrated on ideal legal or constitutional orders. Based on a contextual analysis of climate, religions, mentality and other factors, Montesquieu distilled the spirit of the laws out of the real existing diversity. In the founding years of the discipline, towards the end of the nineteenth century, comparatists

---

50 See Kuhn *The Structure of Scientific Revolutions.*

51 See also Palmer 'From Lerotholi to Lando,' 261; and, as regards to the mainstreamer as one of the archetypical comparatists, Frankenberg, Günter (1997) 'Stranger than Paradise: Identity and Politics in Comparative Law' 2 *Utah Law Review*, 259.

52 Legrand, Pierre (2011) 'Siting Foreign Law: How Derrida Can Help' 21 *Duke Law Journal*, 595, 597.

first followed Hegel and the general trend towards codifications and focused on comparing legislation. Later, they picked up the spirit of globalism (that was soon to triumph disastrously in World War I) and constructed the comparative framework for a universal history of law or at least a universal jurisprudence. Thereafter the profession changed the register from code to system, from philosophy/history to taxonomy/geography and classified legal systems, usually from the vantage point of Western law, relegating the foreign, which should have been of primary interest, to the residual category of 'other' (minor, derivative, affiliated, radically different, etc.) and incorporated it into systems, traditions or families.

Since the middle of the twentieth century, the discipline's modernist phase has coincided with the triumph of functionalism, complemented by structural analyses and factual accounts. Mainstream comparatists set out to find the optimal legal system producing or providing for better, if not the best possible, legal solutions to the problems arising from conflicts in organized societies. Needless to say, once again (very much as previous generations defined the 'universal') what counted as a 'problem' or 'better solution' happened to be defined from the vantage point of the West, that is in Anglo-European civil/common law terms. Until today, the functionalist paradigm has proven viable (because of its institutional power rather than its intellectual sophistication) in withstanding criticism and accommodating moderately alternative approaches, like structuralist functionalism or functionalist factualism, as will be shown below.

Comparatists have done their 'good practice' in a variety of spirits, reaching from noble humanism to straightforward instrumentalism, from lofty idealism to humble pragmatism. They have compared the law as philosophers, historians, anthropologists, and social scientists, as legal scholars and legal engineers, as reformers and defenders of the status quo, mostly, though, as legal positivists bent on determining what the law *is* in another country, *the law* as contained in statutes and court decisions and accompanied by scholarly commentary.[53]

Therefore, 'mainstreaming' comparative law, like all reductions in complexity, does not capture the variety of motivations, spirits, and practices but encompasses the general drift of the discipline and, for starters, records who is in and who is out. What is more, the heterogeneity and vastness of the subject-matter dooms to failure any attempt to

[53] For a definition and critique of positivism, see Frankenberg 'Critical Theory' in *Max-Planck Encyclopedia of International Law*; and Legrand 'Siting Foreign Law,' 598, 602.

identify and trace the various rivulets and strands and then to render a detailed, accurate picture of the past and present of comparative law. So, concentrating on mainstreams or, if you prefer, dominant paradigms representing different modes of comparative *bricolage* will have to do. The 17 volumes of the *Encyclopedia of Comparative Law* (with a focus on private law!) demonstrate the futility rather than the utility of reaching out and comparing the laws of *all* countries at *all* times. Instead of attempting to (mis-)narrate 'the true and comprehensive story' of comparative law and getting lost in its maze of indeterminacy and global reach, I want to lay out and submit to critical scrutiny dominant styles and practices. Distorted and selective as this endeavor will be, it is intended to highlight crucial features of what the mainstream has considered to be, over and over again, 'good comparative practice.'

2. Critique and comparison

Disciplinarity[1] denotes the collection and ensemble of insights and information within the boundaries of a specific field of research type. These insights and this information are then brought into relation with one another, systematically or otherwise. Any discipline, including comparative law, is historically contingent, constituted by dispersed elements, delineated by porous and shifting boundaries. More often than not, it bases its authority on a seamless subject-matter and works with awkward tools. Therefore, 'good disciplinary practice,' one may conclude, needs constant scrutiny, introspection and systematic doubt. To keep their ensemble of insights and information together and to establish and sustain intra-disciplinary knowledge relations, disciplines have to rely on critical practices and ideas that turn on and probe the boundary-work and world-making done in the name of this or that science. Critique has to dust off the tools (theories and methods), de-essentialize the subject-matter, de-privilege the disciplinary perspective and disrupt the formation of main streams. That would be the optimistic conclusion, which underestimates the disciplining effects of academic disciplines.

1. CRITICAL APPROACHES

Comparative law has not made its mark as a discipline boosting doubt and introspection, even though a comparative attitude, more than a non-comparative approach, one would assume, would lend itself to practicing (or arguably presupposes) a modicum of self-reflection and critical thought. During the more recent past, however, numerous critical approaches and in particular 'post-modern critiques'[2] have finally sprung

[1] See Messer-Davidow, Ellen et al. eds (1993) *Knowledges. Historical and Critical Studies in Disciplinarity*, Charlottesville and London: University of Virginia Press.

[2] Different perspectives are provided by Legrand, Pierre and Munday, Roderick eds (2003) *Comparative Legal Studies: Traditions and Transitions*, Cambridge: Cambridge University Press; Mattei, Ugo (2006a) 'Comparative Law and Critical Legal Studies' in *The Oxford Handbook of Comparative Law*,

up, moving in different directions, especially after the non-mainstream response to the 1900 Paris Congress – the Utah Symposium celebrating 'New Approaches to Comparative Law.'[3]

Whereas mainstream comprises a heterogeneous ensemble of schools, works and scholars, united under the umbrella of cognitive control,[4] 'critical' has come to signify methodological and other opposition to or deviance from the mainstream way of comparing legal norms, decisions and regimes. Critical approaches, based on new or divergent analytics and vocabularies, boldly or modestly counsel the epistemic community of comparatists to do a lot of re-thinking – that is, to re-think the methods, theories, and masters of the discipline;[5] to re-view the genealogy of the privileged Western tradition; to confront its colonialist legacy and hegemonic services;[6] to re-evaluate the proclaimed ideological

---

Oxford: Oxford University Press; and Merino Acuña, Roger (2012) *Comparative Law from Below. The Construction of a Critical Project in Comparative Legal Studies*, Saarbrücken: Lambert Academic Publishing. For a critical analysis from the rather difficult vantage point of a post-modern universalism, see Peters, Anne and Schwenke, Heiner (2000) 'Comparative Law Beyond Post-Modernism' 14 *International and Comparative Law Quarterly*, 1. For a sketchy summary of post-modern critiques, see also Reimann, Mathias (2002) 'The Progress and Failure of Comparative Law in the Second Half of the Twentieth Century' 50 *American Journal of Comparative Law*, 671.

[3] Kennedy, David W. (1997) 'New Approaches to Comparative Law: Comparativism and International Governance' 2 *Symposium Utah Law Review*, 255–663.

[4] Comprising legocentrism, formalism and positivism, see Frankenberg, Günter (1985) 'Critical Comparisons. Re-Thinking Comparative Law' 26 *Harvard International Law Journal*, 416 seq.

[5] The re-thinking started in 1985 and has not come to an end yet: Frankenberg 'Critical Comparisons,' 411; Riles, Annelise ed. (2007) *Rethinking the Masters of Comparative Law*, Lake Mary, FL: Vandeplas Publishing; and Yu, Guanghua (2013) *Rethinking Law and Development*, New York: Routledge. Radical critiques of method and theory were advanced, notably by Legrand, Pierre (1995) 'Comparative Legal Studies and the Commitment to Theory' 58 *Modern Law Review*, 262 and Esquirol, Jorge 'At the Head of the Legal Family: René David' in Riles *Rethinking the Masters of Comparative Law*, Chapter 8.

[6] Monateri, P.G. (2000) 'Black Gaius: A Quest for the Multicultural Origins of the "Western Legal Tradition"' 51 *Hastings Law Journal*, 479 (deconstructing the cult of Roman Law); Twining, William (2000) 'Comparative Law and Legal Theory: The Country and Western Legal Tradition' in Edge, Ian ed. *Comparative Law in Global Perspective*, 47; Baxi, Upendra (2003) 'The Colonialist Heritage of Comparative Law' in Legrand, Pierre and Munday, R.J.C. *Comparative Legal Studies: Traditions and Transitions*, Cambridge: Cambridge University Press, 46; Frankenberg, Günter (1997) 'Stranger than Paradise: Identity and Politics in

agnosticism;[7] to re-consider the ethnocentric and nationalist framework of the discipline and meet the challenges of globalization;[8] to submit to 'close reading' the operations of the legal consciousness in foreign systems, the styles and mentality they shape;[9] to revise the exaggerated concern with private law;[10] to reject the assimilation between law and rules, law and state, law and the West;[11] to reassess the preoccupation with and privileging of similarity;[12] to re-orient comparative studies to the analysis of legal transfer, its contexts, risks and side-effects;[13] to analyze the relationship between comparative and international law;[14] to produce not only 'reliable information' but critical-comparative insights into projects of governance and legal harmonization – and much more. If

---

Comparative Law' 2 *Symposium Utah Law Review*, 259; Mattei, Ugo (2003) 'A Theory of Imperial Law: A Study on US Hegemony and the Latin Resistance' 10 *Indiana Journal of Global Studies*, 383.

[7] Kennedy, David (2003) 'The Methods and the Politics of Comparative Law' in Legrand and Munday eds *Comparative Legal Studies*, 345.

[8] Muir Watt, Horatia (2006) 'Globalization and Comparative Law' in *The Oxford Handbook of Comparative Law*, Oxford: Oxford University Press, 579; Kennedy, Duncan (2006) 'Three Globalizations of Law and Legal Thought: 1850–2000' in Trubek, David and Santos, Alvaro eds. *The New Law and Economic Development*, Cambridge: Cambridge University Press, 19.

[9] Lasser, Mitchel de S.-O.-I'E. (1995) 'Judicial (Self-)Portraits: Judicial Discourse in the French Legal System' 104 *Yale Law Journal*, 1325.

[10] Reimann, Mathias (1998) 'Stepping out of the European Shadow: Why Comparative Law in the United States Must Develop Its Own Agenda' 46 *American Journal of Comparative Law*, 637.

[11] Muir Watt 'Globalization and Comparative Law,' 584; also Legrand, Pierre (1997) 'The Impossibility of Legal Transplants' 4 *Maastricht Journal of European and Comparative Law*, 111 (criticizing the equations law = rule and rule = propositional content). See also Ruskola, Teemu (2013) *Legal Orientalism – China, the United States, and Modern Law*, Cambridge: Harvard University Press (criticizing the association of 'law' with the West which relegates lawlessness to the East or South).

[12] Zweigert, Konrad and Kötz, Hein (1998) *An Introduction to Comparative Law*, 3rd ed., Oxford: Oxford University Press, 59; Dannemann, Gerhard (2006) 'Comparative Law: Study of Similarities or Differences?' in *Oxford Handbook of Comparative Law*, 383; Legrand, Pierre (2003) 'The Same and the Different' in Legrand and Munday *Comparative Legal Studies*, 240.

[13] Frankenberg, Günter (2013) 'Constitutions as Commodities: Notes on a Theory of Transfer' in *Order from Transfer: Comparative Constitutional Design and Legal Culture*, Cheltenham, UK and Northampton, MA, USA: Edward Elgar Publishing, 1.

[14] Kennedy 'New Approaches to Comparative Law,' 545.

there is a motto connecting the disparate approaches it might be Samuel Beckett's 'Ever tried. Ever failed. No matter. Try again. Fail again. Fail better.'[15]

And the mainstream? The mainstream reacts as one would expect a mainstream to react. In general, it has not shown more than polite (?) interest in interacting with its critics on any terms and has always preferred the critics' critics. The *Oxford Handbook* has to be singled out as one of the notable exceptions to the rule of silence or the communicative principle of disdain.[16] While some critics were informed 'they had a point,' most critiques were dismissed as 'overdone,' 'contradictory,' 'too polemical,' 'not relevant' or 'not practicable.'[17] It comes as no surprise then that the network of critical approaches has not been able to dry out, redirect or open up the mainstream. Zweigert and Kötz mention a few critical pieces in the bibliography, while abstaining from discussing (or even rejecting) any of them.[18] Folklore rather than dialog.

Still, critical ideas about comparative law, both well- and mis-guided ones, have managed to grow and diversify over the years. They spread the message that critique does not harm comparative law but, on the contrary, may make for a healthy discussion and a lively discipline. A 'sympathetic' critic observed – in the privileged location of an *Oxford Handbook* – that the Critical Legal Studies brand of critique of comparative law (obviously there are many others) is 'remarkably influential' because of its 'highly privileged position at the centre of the Western world'[19] but that it 'takes on the features of a mere [post-modern] *divertissement*, played by ultra-theoretical scholars.'[20] Turning the Cinderella complex, one might say, against the 'crits,' he was concerned that this brand of critique may therefore 'deteriorate into mere aestheticism

---

[15] Beckett, Samuel (2009) 'Worstward Ho' in *Company / Ill Seen Ill Said / Worstward Ho / Stirrings Still*, New York: Faber & Faber, 79.

[16] Mégret, Fred (2009) 'That "Springbreak" Feeling: Pragmatism, Irony and Belief in the Age of Human Rights' (paper presented in December 2009, unpublished, on file with author).

[17] For references, see Palmer, Vernon (2005) 'From Lerotholi to Lando. Some Examples of Comparative Law Methodology' 53 *American Journal of Comparative Law*, 261; Peters and Schwenke 'Comparative Law Beyond Post-Modernism,' 800. In both articles critical approaches are discussed thoroughly.

[18] See e.g. Zweigert and Kötz *Introduction*. For a different treatment (too recent to be adequately discussed here) see Kischel, Uwe (2015) *Rechtsvergleichung*, München: C.H. Beck.

[19] Mattei, Ugo (2006) 'Comparative Law and Critical Legal Studies,' 833.

[20] *Ibid.*

and entail the risk that all serious political struggle is abandoned.'[21] While there is always that danger, the new approaches may claim that addressing and challenging the ways of the mainstream, its entrenched ideologies and hidden political agendas, for starters, *does qualify* as a political intervention – at least in intra-disciplinary terms – whether the tone is serious, ironic or other.[22] The critical critic had apparently overlooked this aspect.

Moreover, difference-oriented approaches to the comparison of foreign laws stand a good chance of recognizing the ethical dimension that opens up with the appearance of the other in the comparative space. At any rate, new approaches to comparative law – whatever their venue and goal – have managed to produce a body of interesting literature that students of comparative law can (or should) no longer disregard. One might very well say that they have become inserted into the disciplinary DNA. No need then for critics to develop a critical Cinderella complex, and mainstream scholars might contemplate the comparative advantage of critical discourse for the discipline.

Comparative Law as Critique is inspired by the diversity of critical approaches and the variety of genres of critical texts that I believe make for a lively discipline. Critical thought does not occupy a unified space. The ensemble of critical approaches creates an uneven and complex field of study. From the many diverse critical projects I pick up, it is the non- or even anti-mainstream orientation, the irreverent, subversive spirit that I have come to meet and appreciate in my legal education and comparative work.[23] Some of those approaches will be briefly discussed as illustrations of the diverse modalities of critique. I submit this book to my readers not as a project to define what critique 'is' but merely as an

---

21 *Ibid.*

22 Regarding irony and the critique of law: Frankenberg, Günter (1988/1989) 'Down by Law: Irony, Seriousness, and Reason' 83 *Northwestern University Law Review*, 360.

23 I am indebted to conversations I had with many of the metropolitan and non-metropolitan members of Critical Legal Studies (in the old times) and the IGLP (Institute for Global Law and Policy at Harvard Law School) network. IGLP has, for several years, organized conferences and workshops attended by young scholars from all over the world and provided an institutional basis and forum for transnational debates on global legal thought, comparative and otherwise. The first two chapters of this book have been thoroughly discussed by the 2015 participants in an Advanced Writing Workshop in Cambridge, who commented on the first draft. I am deeply grateful to all friends and colleagues who helped me write this text.

experiment in how it can be done. I draw on some of my previous work[24] not because it deserves to be remembered but because it needs to be submitted to critical revision.

2. MODALITIES OF CRITIQUE

The terms 'critique' and 'critical' do not turn an easily readable face to their readers. They are charged with a heavy baggage in the overhead compartment that is filled with layers of meanings and (not always illuminating) misunderstandings. They are informed by an assortment of diverse, eccentric, disparate traditions and orthodoxies. Avoiding 'critical,' as far as possible, is not really a way out of this conundrum, because possible counter-concepts, like heterodox, non-traditional, etc., are related, albeit asymmetrically, to the same logical household. They pose similar problems of indeterminacy and interpretation. And, what is more, heterodoxy taken as a disciplinary term of art, while being at variance with mainstream thought in some usages, remains within the dominant tradition as far as it comes with its own claim to truth.

Commonly, 'critique' and 'critical' are understood to characterize thought processes or activities like separating, selecting, judging or deciding a controversy.[25] However, depending on the context, they may also refer to cognitive properties and capabilities; to criticize may mean having good judgment or being learned. Contrary to a widespread understanding, the specificity of critique is not fault-finding. Raymond Williams was right to worry that critique or criticism is often unduly restricted to 'the habit (or right or duty) of [negative] judgment.'[26] And what he called for instead was a more specific kind of response, one that did not generalize too quickly:

---

[24] In particular, Frankenberg 'Critical Comparisons'; 'Stranger than Paradise'; (2007) 'How to Do Projects with Comparative Law. Notes of an Expedition to the Common Core,' in Bussani, Mauro and Mattei, Ugo eds *Opening Up European Law. The Common Core Project towards Eastern and South Eastern Europe*, Bern: Stämpfli Publishers, 17; and (2013) 'Constitutions as Commodities: Notes on a Theory of Transfer,' in Frankenberg, Günter ed. *Order from Transfer, Comparative Constitutional Design and Legal Culture*, Cheltenham, UK and Northampton, MA, USA: Edward Elgar Publishing, 1.

[25] Liddell, Henry G. and Scott, Robert (1977) *A Greek-English Lexicon*, 9th ed., Oxford: Clarendon.

[26] Williams, Raymond (1976) *Keywords: A Vocabulary of Culture and Society*, New York: Oxford University Press, 75–76.

> [W]hat always needs to be understood, is the specificity of the response, which is not a judgment, but a practice.[27]

This critical practice could be 'boundary-work,' in a certain sense, both demarcating borders between fields of knowledge and attacking and rescinding or transgressing them.[28] It could also be actual field work, at a desk or otherwise. Generally, it is (or should be distinguished as) open-ended, discursive, dialogical, dissident or even heretical.

As concerns their modality, critical approaches can be descriptive or prescriptive.[29] They may intend to show what a good practice would look like or demystify or deconstruct the way legal comparison is 'done.' Critique does not have to be constructive or normative in the sense of prescribing the way good comparison ought to be practiced. The motivating force of an alternative project, a better (more thorough, in-depth, theoretically informed) practice or positive counter-image should not be underestimated, though.[30]

With regard to perspective, one distinguishes generally between *internal* and *external* critiques. There are projects that address what is under scrutiny from an inside point of view. A norm or argument may be found semantically indeterminate, structurally contradictory or logically inconsistent, or a comparison methodologically unclear. So the perspective is *internal.*

External critiques come with an outside perspective or are characterized by a non-legal point of reference, as happens when one criticizes a court decision or a legal provision as *politically* conservative, a legal principle as *economically* dysfunctional or a comparative analysis as violating *ethical* norms. Whereas internal critiques seem to be securely grounded, external observations and evaluations have to cope with a nagging doubt because the observer neither sees the whole picture nor stands on an epistemologically firm ground.

Critique, in its most common usage, denotes judgments or evaluative statements, often unfavorable ones, regarding the quality of human

---

27 *Ibid.*, 76.

28 See Gieryn, Thomas (1999) *Cultural Boundaries of Society*, Chicago: Chicago University Press.

29 For a primarily descriptive usage, see Kant, Immanuel (1781/1999) *Critique of Pure Reason*, Cambridge: Cambridge University Press, xii; Al-Jabri, Mohammed Abed (2010) *The Formation of Arab Reason: Text, Tradition and the Construction of Modernity in the Arab World*, London: I.B. Tauris.

30 For a skeptical view see Rorty, Richard (1995) 'Feminism, Ideology, and Deconstruction: A Pragmatist View' in Žižek, Slavoj ed. *Mapping Ideology*, London and New York: Verso.

products and actions. One criticizes, for example, bad political decisions, non-transparent legal procedures, ethnocentric comparison, a corrupt judge or a painting as *kitsch* but not – at least not in the same way – the weather, an avalanche or the risk implied in gambling.

3. THE POLYSEMY OF CRITIQUE

The polysemy of the term invites diverse readings and strongly suggests there is no canon of generally recognized or widely considered acceptable modalities of critique. Who or what one submits to what kind of critical scrutiny and for what purpose, resists authoritative definition and remains basically a matter of choice, information, subject and temperament.

What are we talking about when we talk about critical legal thought or critical approaches to comparative law? Are there standards or criteria that help us identify critical ideas and practices? Or is critical simply a matter of random (self-)definition, uncontrollable attribution, political or aesthetical preference? Recognizing the indeterminacy of the term and baggage of meanings it comes with, I approach critique – how it is conceptualized and operates within and outside comparative law – from four different angles: as a matter of self-definition, attribution, criteria and, finally, practice.

Critical by Self-Definition

To define one's work as critical has its risks, because the label is edgy, quite demanding, and comes with asymmetrical, problematic counter-concepts. A critical approach to law, comparison or whatever, logically presupposes the existence of a *non*-critical or *un*-critical specimen. The neighbors of a self-defined critic might wonder whether, by innuendo, they are disqualified from being critical. And they may turn on the critic and submit her proclaimed criticality to critical scrutiny. Not surprisingly, authors prefer to abstain from proclaiming that their work is critical and from exposing themselves as critics. As always, there are exceptions to the rule, though.

The Critical Legal Studies movement (CLS) apparently had no problem with the label. Initially, at least. Since the early 1970s, CLS has shaken up legal academia in the United States (and, to a lesser degree, elsewhere) with its rhetoric, its theoretical-methodological rigor and political radicalism.[31] The network of authors was united by a strong oppositional stance vis-à-vis mainstream liberal-legal thought and traditional legal education:

> The invitation to the first annual Conference on Critical Legal Studies in 1977 gave little hint as to what the organizers thought 'critical legal studies' (CLS) was or might become. It seems that the organizers were simply seeking to *locate* people working either in law schools or in closely related academic settings (legal sociology, legal anthropology) with a certain vaguely perceived, general political or cultural predisposition and a relatively better defined relationship to ordinary academic life. At the general level they sought something akin to the New Leftist ...[32]

From the perspective of a participant, Mark Kelman went on to describe CLS as follows:

> ... egalitarian, in a more far-reaching sense than those committed to tax-and-transfer-based income redistribution, culturally radical, or at least unsympathetic to the furious New Right assault on permissiveness, [repelled by legal education, in particular] the routine Socratic discussions of appellate court decisions, repelled by their sterility and thorough disconnection from actual social life ... repelled by the supposition that neutral and apolitical *legal* reasoning could resolve charged controversies ...[33]

Most commonly, scholars affiliated with CLS challenged, indeed targeted, the self-image and ideas of liberalism. With their methods – especially 'doing doctrine,' 'trashing' or the 'method of contradictions' – they pinned down pervasive, internal contradictions, rifts and gaps in liberal legal reasoning, often appearing in the guise of sets of paired rhetorical arguments or principles (public/private, form/substance, etc.),[34] which resolve cases in opposite, incompatible ways, render court decisions unpredictable and incidentally demystify Dworkin's theory that

---

[31] In his programmatic speech, Roberto M. Unger outlined the different trajectories of the movement: Unger (1986) *The Critical Legal Studies Movement*, Cambridge: Harvard University Press; see also Kairys, David ed. (1980) *The Politics of Law. A Progressive Critique*, New York: Pantheon.

[32] Presenting a self-critical assessment: Kelman, Mark (1987) *A Guide to Critical Legal Studies*, Cambridge: Harvard University Press, 1.

[33] *Ibid.*

[34] For a later echo, see the contrasting critiques of international law analyzed by Koskenniemi, Martti (2005) *From Apology and Utopia. The Structure of International Legal Argument*, 2nd ed., Cambridge: Cambridge University Press.

there is 'one right answer' to all legal conflicts.[35] All in all, CLS stands for a non-traditional practice of critique, which continued the Legal Realists' attack on mainstream legal reasoning[36] by radicalizing the internal critique and undermining the belief that law can be cured from its indeterminacy if only supported by knowledge and methods imported from the (social) sciences.

Ultimately, the corrosiveness of CLS thought, especially the critique of rights,[37] also eroded the cohesion of the movement. Once the movement came to a halt and disintegrated and the annual conferences were discontinued, CLS underwent several metamorphoses that were signaled by shifting political agendas, theoretical orientations and methodological practices. While many of the 'crits' stayed on board, the protagonists' self-definition changed and gave notice of the fragmentation of the all-encompassing CLS into FemCrits (feminist legal theory), RaceCrits (critical race theory), Queer Theory and others.[38] When NAIL (New Approaches to International Law)[39] and TWAIL (Third World Approaches to International Law)[40] appeared to replace, or rather side-step, the CLS tradition, the precarious self-definition (critical) was

---

[35] Dworkin, Ronald (1978) *Taking Rights Seriously*, Cambridge: Harvard University Press.

[36] Horwitz, Morton (1992) *The Transformation of American Law, 1870–1960: The Crisis of Orthodoxy*, Oxford: Oxford University Press; Leiter, Brian (2004) 'American Legal Realism' in Edmundson, William A. and Golding, Martin P. eds *The Blackwell Guide to Philosophy of Law and Legal Theory*, Oxford: Blackwell, 50.

[37] The controversy over the critique of rights is documented in Brown, Wendy and Halley, Janet eds (2002) *Left Legalism/Left Critique*, Durham: Duke University Press; see also Kennedy, Duncan 'The Critique of Rights in Critical Legal Studies' in Brown and Halley *Left Legalism/Left Critique*, 178.

[38] E.g. Brown and Halley *Left Legalism/Left Critique*; Frug, Mary Joe (1991) *Postmodern Legal Feminism*, New York: Routledge; Halley, Janet (2006) *Split Decisions*, Princeton: Princeton University Press; Williams, Patricia (1991) *The Alchemy of Race and Rights*, Cambridge: Harvard University Press; Danielsen, Dan and Engle, Karen eds (1994) *After Identity. A Reader in Law and Culture*, New York: Routledge; Kennedy, David (2004) *The Dark Sides of Virtue. Reassessing International Humanitarianism*, Princeton: Princeton University Press; and Koskenniemi, Martti (2001) *The Gentle Civilizer of Nations. The Rise and Fall of International Law 1870–1960*, Cambridge: Cambridge University Press.

[39] Kennedy, David and Tennant, Chris (1994) 'New Approaches to International Law. A Bibliography' 35 *Harvard International Law Journal*, 417.

[40] E.g. Anghie, Antony (2005) *Imperialism, Sovereignty and the Making of International Law*, Cambridge: Cambridge University Press; Anghie, Antony and

casually dropped and temporarily replaced by postmodern, later post-colonial and finally heterodox – or whatever came after post-CLS and proceeded without a theory label.

CLS had little, if any, interest in comparative law. Contracts, torts, labor law and family law, and even legal history or constitutional law were privileged areas of critique.[41]

In the early CLS days, comparative law did not generate much enthusiasm as a field of critical inquiry, possibly because it *seemed* too academic, too far away from any social controversy, and politically agnostic. 'Critical Comparisons'[42] was an attempt to link comparative law to CLS in the mid-1980s and, more significantly, to carry the virus of critical thought into the discipline. The text with its innocently presumptuous title only preceded by a few years the move from CLS to a series of new approaches, each signaled by a different acronym. It was consciously meant to invoke the label 'critical by association' (with CLS) and was recognized and criticized as such.[43]

While CLS ignited remarkable legal and political controversies and even provoked McCarthyite reactions in US legal academia,[44] the recent self-definition of a 'Critical Systems Theory of Law' (miles, times and styles apart) is likely to remain an academic affair with little political import despite the leading protagonist's political intentions.[45] So far the self-labeling has raised some questions and led to an interesting, not yet concluded, theoretical debate. Tapping the tradition of the original 'Critical Theory', also named the 'Frankfurt School', could be an

---

Chimni, B.S. (2003) 'Third World Approaches to International Law and Individual Responsibility in Internal Conflict' 2 *Chinese Journal of International Law*, 77.

41 Later, Annelise Riles' work and, after the demise of CLS, Kennedy, Duncan (2006) 'Three Globalizations of Law and Legal Thought: 1850–2000' in Trubek, David and Santos, Alvaro eds *The New Law and Economic Development*, Cambridge: Cambridge University Press, 19, and David Kennedy's analysis of the politics of comparative law became the notable exceptions.

42 Moreover, the title 'Critical Comparisons' weakens the strong self-defining claim by allowing for a certain ambiguity. See also Zumbansen, Peer (2005) 'Comparative Law's Coming of Age? Twenty Years after *Critical Comparisons*' 6 *German Law Journal*, 1073.

43 E.g. the critique by Peters and Schwenke 'Comparative Law beyond Post-Modernism' and Mattei 'Comparative Law and Critical Legal Studies.'

44 E.g. Carrington, Paul (1984) 'Of Law and the River' 34 *Journal of Legal Education*, 222 – charging CLS with legal nihilism.

45 Fischer-Lescano, Andreas and Amstutz, Marc eds (2013) *Kritische Systemtheorie. Zur Evolution einer normativen Theorie*, Bielefeld: transcript.

intelligent move away from underneath the shadow of the general systems theory masterminded and dominated by Niklas Luhmann.[46] One wonders, however, whether the patricidal connotation was intended. It remains to be seen how the empiricism and realism, undeniably the strengths of systems theory, can be preserved in a normative environment and whether, having invoked Theodor W. Adorno as godfather of the new project, the original Critical Theory's cultural pessimism can be avoided and its transformative vision preserved.

In general, theories are work in progress, in fact *bricolage*. They need (and often have) to be modified, reoriented or even completely overhauled. In the case of critical systems theory, it is not easy to anticipate how much *bricolage* is required to rein in the divergent theoretical orientations. And it is almost inconceivable that the critical systems-theoretician will manage to integrate the individual and individual agency, that is, the perspective of action theory, into the abstract systems theoretical framework.

Critical by Association

A short step away from random, arbitrary self-definitions, critical by association denotes a practice where critical becomes a matter of *attribution*. Accordingly, an author and her work are labeled by virtue of their affiliation with a critical tradition or school. The major difference from the previous category (self-definition) seems to be that now the 'reasonable' or 'fair-minded' 'observer,' so prominent in legal doctrine, attaches the label to card-carrying members – or associates – of a certain brand of criticism, thus sparing authors the embarrassment of having to anoint themselves as critics.

Critical Theory capitalizes on both self-definition and attribution. It is widely understood to have originated in, or rather as, the Frankfurt School (or *vice versa*) where it formed the intellectual basis and informed the curriculum of philosophical and sociological theorizing about the dialectics of enlightenment, instrumental reason, bourgeois mass culture, and the authoritarian personality.[47] The School's principals were Max Horkheimer and Theodor W. Adorno, supported by Herbert Marcuse,

---

[46] From the vast œuvre, see only Luhmann, Niklas (2004) *Law as a Social System*, Oxford: Oxford University Press.

[47] Frankenberg, Günter (2004) 'Critical Theory' in *Max Planck Encyclopedia of Public International Law*.

adding the more rebellious 1968 spirit, and Walter Benjamin, delivering the mysterious 'Critique of Violence.'[48]

In a famous article, the theoretical program was defined by Horkheimer in *opposition* to traditional theory and to 'scientistic' theorizing.[49] Traditional theory, according to Horkheimer, was characterized, among others, by thinking in a departmentalized way that corresponded, in an often utilitarian style, to the immediate tasks scientists set for themselves, and amounted often to nothing more than systematically linked propositions and unitary projects. It brings to mind, as will be shown, the comparative practice of the more recent mainstreams of comparative law. By contrast, critical theory is understood as a function of the existent society. It is directed against the status quo, taking its cue from capitalist exchange economy and class society. It defines its role in constant, subversive conversation with the way things are in order to generate the necessary transformative energy. In short, to qualify as critical, a theory has to make social life (also law) intelligible and, possibly, better.

Critical Theory was meant to characterize the project to identify and scandalize the mechanisms, structures, and relationships which impede human beings in realizing their potential. As such, it was leveled against practices of exclusion and forms of alienation, and what Jürgen Habermas later referred to as the 'colonization of the life-world' by systems imperatives, like the routines of bureaucracy, the mechanisms of market exchange, and the abstract rules of juridification, which undermine or destroy the possibility of achieving mutual understandings.[50] In addition, Critical Theory developed its tenets within an explicit transformative perspective taking up central themes of Marxist thought by voicing the plight and needs and political interests of dominated classes, marginalized groups and all those excluded from dominant discourse.

---

[48] See Marcuse, Herbert (1964) *The One-Dimensional Man. Studies in the Ideology of Advanced Industrial Society*, Boston: Beacon Press; and Marcuse, Herbert (1965) 'Repressive Tolerance' in Marcuse, Herbert, Wolff, Robert P. and Moore, Jr, Barrington *A Critique of Pure Tolerance*, Boston: Beacon Press, 95; Benjamin, Walter (1921/2004) 'Critique of Violence' in Bullock, Marcus and Jennings, Michael W. eds *Selected Writings Volume 1, 1913–1926*, London: Belknap Press of Harvard University Press.

[49] Horkheimer, Max (1972) 'Traditional and Critical Theory' in Horkheimer, Max ed. *Critical Theory. Selected Essays*, New York: Continuum Publishing Company, 190.

[50] Habermas, Jürgen (1987) *The Theory of Communicative Action Volume Two. Lifeworld and System: A Critique of Functionalist Reason*, Boston: Beacon Press.

With regard to legal thought, the linking of 'critical by association' to Critical Theory does not work all too well as the *legal* played only a marginal role among the founding members of the Frankfurt School. Franz Neumann and Otto Kirchheimer would have been possible candidates who deserved attention, yet remained marginal figures in the Frankfurt School. Horkheimer and Adorno were clearly preoccupied with philosophy and sociology, late capitalism and mass culture. They seemed to have discounted law as a phenomenon of lesser importance, arguably under the influence of the Marxist basis-superstructure theorem. Neither Franz Neumann's monumental study of the National-Socialist regime, *Behemoth*,[51] in which he analyzed the destruction of the rational, almost Hegelian state by the Führer-Principle and the will of the people during the Nazi regime, nor his seminal article 'Change in the Function of Law in Modern Society,'[52] defending general law's formal rationality, was adequately recognized within the inner circle of the Frankfurt School's first generation. By the same token, Otto Kirchheimer's study of the political instrumentalization of legal procedures and institutions in *Political Justice*[53] received little attention. The Frankfurt brand of critique concentrated on grander themes, the principals may have found, like instrumental reason, its eclipse, and negative dialectics. The critique of law – in good Marxist tradition – was put on the back burner. As if receiving compensation for their marginalization, Neumann and Kirchheimer's influence increased later and became topical when the Frankfurt School was already in the process of being historicized.

Critical Theory's tradition was later carried on, notably by Rudolf Wiethölter's political theory of law. Published under the unassuming title *Rechtswissenschaft* (Jurisprudence or legal science) in 1968, his main programmatic work qualifies also as being critical by association.[54] Learned, ironic and serious about tracing the discontent about law,

---

[51] Neumann, Franz (1942) *Behemoth. The Structure and Practice of the National Socialism*, Oxford: Oxford University Press.

[52] Neumann, Franz (1937/1996) 'Change in the Function of Law in Modern Society' in Scheuermann, William ed. *Rule of Law under Siege. Selected Essays of Franz Neumann and Otto Kirchheimer*, Berkeley: Berkeley University Press, 101–141.

[53] Kirchheimer, Otto (1961) *Political Justice*, Princeton: Princeton University.

[54] Wiethölter, Rudolf (1968) *Rechtswissenschaft*, Frankfurt: Fischer.

Wiethölter's ideal of the 'political jurist' and his project of a 'disenchanted jurisprudence'[55] reverberated legal realism and Critical Theory and foreshadowed, on the other side of the Atlantic, the agenda of the early CLS and the political radicalization of legal realism. Later, his political jurisprudence turned into a complex and complicated edifice built on the foundations of – aside from Critical Theory – legal realism, critique of ideology, systems theory and discourse theory combined with a crisp doctrinalism.

Critique by Criteria

So far the schools of thought and some of the authors mentioned above suggest that relying on self-definition or on labeling (based on association) defeats, at least does not really support the purpose of getting a clearer picture of what 'critique' and 'critical' might actually mean – not only to those in the know.

Standards or criteria might be the answer then. However, as one moves onto that level one should be wary of what is on offer there as being 'universally consented to' or at least 'widely accepted.' Critics (and in particular the targets of their critique) are likely to disagree that there can be a consensus on standards or criteria. It is the special charm of critical thought that pluralism and relativity seem to be its natural allies.

Instead of embarking upon an elaborate discussion of the question, 'What makes (legal) theory critical?' I simply pick up some of the clues recognized in past and ongoing debates and introduce them as pieces of evidence for what may count as critical in the context of comparative law. The clues are: non-scientistic theorizing; non-traditional theory; oppositional spirit; and, if possible, transformative vision. I avoid 'heterodox' that has the charm of eruditeness but is often understood as coming in company with a (hidden) counter-claim to truth.

4. CRITERIA OF CRITIQUE

Critique means more than the random and vague expression of doubt, dissent or discontent. And while 'critique' and 'critical' resist strict definition, the practice of criticizing is not simply a matter of self-definition or affiliation with a school of critical thought. However,

[55] Wiethölter, Rudolf (2013) 'Politische Rechtstheorie Revisited' in Joerges, Christian and Zumbansen, Peer eds *ZERP – Diskussionspapier*, No.1, Bremen: University of Bremen.

convincing criteria are hard to come by. Theories could possibly help. As a matter of fact, there are different theories[56] that elucidate what these terms mean or could mean (also related ones like heterodox, unconventional or discriminating, and so on). They certainly help avoid the impression that anything goes as long as it expresses a negative feeling or thought that is not blatantly apologetic.

To start with: Critical Theory as developed in the halls of the Frankfurt School. From their works one may infer that 'critical' is best defined as *non-traditional*, which shifts the burden of definition but does not solve the problem. Non-traditional in comparative law would mean anti-positivist and non-legocentric. A critical approach to comparative law is to be expected as moving comparative analysis beyond cognitive control and strategic comparison that establishes or sustains the hegemony of the 'own' legal culture.

Classical Critical Theory characterized the enterprise to identify and scandalize the mechanisms, structures and relationships of alienation and reification. The program was focused on the pathologies of modernity and industrial capitalism. It contained a *transformative* vision, which resonated with central themes of Marxist thought. Accordingly, to be rated critical requires that theory is not merely descriptive, that it look out of the ivory tower and, even in general terms, consider the social-economic and cultural-political context. In comparative law, one would not seriously expect a critical approach to show class consciousness or revolutionary spirit, though.

However, critique *can* be expected to transgress the routines of normal science and of scientistic theorizing and to set out to explore what can be changed in a person's thinking by trying out new and foreign knowledges. Seen from this perspective, approaches to comparative law can be distinguished as critical if they reject the recurrent (often unfounded) claims to 'science' or 'scientific method,' 'knowledge' and 'truth' and start to dismantle the epistemological order established by mainstream approaches.

According to Michel Foucault, critique expresses the desire not to be governed. The critic '*se donne le droit d'interroger la vérité … à ses*

---

[56] In the following, I draw from Jaeggi, Rahel and Wesche, Thilo eds (2009) *Was ist Kritik?* Frankfurt: Suhrkamp; Horkheimer, Max 'Traditional and Critical Theory'; Foucault, Michel (1997) 'What is Critique?' in Foucault, Michel and Lotringer, Sylvère eds *The Politics of Truth*, Los Angeles: Semiotext(e), 41; Butler, Judith (2002) 'What is Critique? An Essay on Foucault's Virtue' in Ingram, David ed. *The Political. Blackwell Readings in Continental Philosophy*, Malden and Oxford: Basil Blackwell, 212; and Williams *Keywords*.

effets de pouvoir,' and expresses 'the will not to be governed thusly, like that, by these people, at this price.'[57] He considers critique a practice of virtue that shows how knowledge and power join forces to produce a more or less systematic order of the world or one of its segments. While this theory of critique as practice stresses *disobedience* and *resistance* (qualified as virtues), Judith Butler gives the concept a slightly different twist. In order to be and remain possible, critique needs to keep a *distance*:

> Critique is always a critique *of* some instituted practice, discourse, episteme, institution, and it loses its character the moment in which it is abstracted from its operation and made to stand alone as a purely generalizable practice. But if this is true, this does not mean that no generalizations are possible or that, indeed, we are mired in particularisms. On the contrary, we tread here in an area of constrained generality, one which broaches the philosophical, but must, if it is to remain critical, remain at a distance from that very achievement.[58]

Without that distance, critique loses its character, and critical intentions are engulfed in the dominant discourse.

Critique of comparative law creates an anarchic moment in knowledge production by disrupting the established routines and, in particular, what is considered 'good comparative practice.' At the same time, it requires discipline to accomplish the task of exposing bias, prejudice, constellations of power, etc., to 'apprehend the ways in which categories are themselves instituted, how the field of knowledge is ordered, and how what it suppresses returns, as it were, as its own constitutive occlusion.' Judgment may impede a practice that needs to question 'the occlusive constitution of the field of categories themselves.'[59]

5. CRITICAL COMPARISONS

The plural is intended to convey that there are various critical approaches to comparative law, some even under this label,[60] but not one critique nor

---

[57] Foucault 'What is Critique,' 75.

[58] Butler 'What is Critique?,' 212.

[59] *Ibid.*, 213.

[60] Örücü, Esin (1999) *Critical Comparative Law: Considering Paradoxes for Legal Systems in Transition*, Deventer: Kluwer – the project can also be seen as a mainstream approach. For further references see Siem, Mathias (2014) *Comparative Law*, Cambridge: Cambridge University Press, 108. Less directly:

a generally recognized canon of critiques. The various approaches and the diverse projects discussed here also show that a lot of critical work can and needs to be done, be it methodological reflection, legal analysis, political analysis or ethical considerations. Taking their cues from Critical Theory, CLS, Foucault, Williams and Butler, the critiques of comparative law presented here, in one way or another, attempt to qualify as non-traditional, confront mainstream's authority, question its certainties, methods and categories, uncover its ethics and politics – and thus keep their distance from any orthodoxy as well as illustrate 'the art of voluntary insubordination.'[61] Critical comparatists don't want to be governed by the dominant discourse.

Halley, Janet and Rittich, Kerry (2010) 'Critical Directions in Comparative Family Law' 58 *American Journal of Comparative Law*, 753; Zumbansen, Peer (2012) 'Transnational Comparisons: Theory and Practice of Comparative Law as a Critique of Governance' *Osgoode Hall Law School Research Paper Series*, No. 1.

[61] Foucault 'What is Critique,' 47.

PART II

Charting the comparative space

3. Navigating the mainstreams

The diverse vocabularies and grammars of comparative law are traced, for a first take, in their diachronic sequence.[1] By navigating down the mainstream, I treat the Anglo-European discourse as a peculiar feature of Western-style modernity, as it is gently historicized. The different kinds of rhetoric and grammars are submitted to critiques that concentrate on the central, or at least a characteristic, theme: that comparative law is nothing but – or not much more than – a scientific method and, in consequence, a rather 'innocent' and narrow cognitive operation that is liable to foreclose discussion of why studying the foreign might have ethical implications and raises political concerns. As an exercise in critique, miscellaneous techniques of comparison and the postures of innocence they favor will be submitted to critical scrutiny. This exercise may help demystify and provincialize[2] Western law and legal tradition, celebrated by textbooks and treatises as the natural hegemon of the comparative world.

1. SCIENCE/METHOD: TECHNIQUES AND VARIETIES OF INNOCENCE

That comparative law is nothing but a *method*, a cognitive path leading to good comparative results, appears to be one of the dominant themes, which actually cuts across the diversity of approaches and leads directly

[1] In this chapter, I draw on my article: Frankenberg, Günter (2014) 'The Innocence of Method – Unveiled' 9 *Journal of Comparative Law*, 222, which I modified and extended considerably. Earlier versions of this text were presented as lectures at two conferences of the Institute for Global Law and Policy and the project 'Law in Context' of the Wissenschaftskolleg Berlin. For their close reading of this (also of the next) chapter and the many suggestions they made, I am immensely grateful, in particular to Priya Gupta and Lena-Maria Möller.

[2] On provincializing Europe as an anti-hegemonic strategy, see Chakrabarty, Dipesh (2007) *Provincializing Europe. Postcolonial Thought and Historical Difference*, 2nd ed., Princeton: Princeton University Press.

to orthodoxy's core. Harold Gutteridge appears to have, if not inaugurated, at least, forcefully told the comparative-law-as-method narrative when he held that comparative law could not be regarded as a distinct subject-matter because comparison does not produce binding law. Therefore, the distinguished positivist concluded, the discipline had to be a method and nothing else:[3] '[T]he phrase "Comparative Law" denotes a *method* of study and research …'[4]

From a semantic perspective, Vernon Palmer added with caution that the discipline 'incorporates the idea of comparison into its name and this alone suggests that its method is somehow special or distinguishable from what comes naturally.'[5] This 'somehow' gets lost in the mainstream translation of the narrative, though:

> Comparative law is not a body of rules and principles. It is primarily a *method*, a way of looking at legal problems, legal institutions, and entire legal systems.[6]
>
> [Comparative law is] a variety of methods for looking at law.[7]

Other mainstream authors did not join the 'what is comparative law?' debate but practiced comparative law, first and foremost, as a method[8] or settled for the position of comparative law being, more or less, nothing but a method.[9]

The theme of comparative-law-as-method or of a discipline defined by its techniques is almost invariably complemented by tales of its *scientific* nature:

---

[3] Gutteridge, Harold (1949) *Comparative Law: An Introduction to the Comparative Method of Legal Study and Research*, 2nd ed., Cambridge: Cambridge University Press, 1 seq.

[4] *Ibid.*, 26 and 72–87 – emphasis added.

[5] Palmer, Vernon V. (2005) 'From Lerotholi to Lando: Some Examples of Comparative Law Methodology' 53 *American Journal of Comparative Law*, 261.

[6] Schlesinger, Rudolf et al. (1998) *Comparative Law: Cases-Text-Materials*, 6th ed., New York: Foundation Press, 2.

[7] Kahn-Freund, Otto (1960) 'Comparative Law as an Academic Subject' 82 *Law Quarterly Review*, 40, 41.

[8] Zweigert, Konrad and Kötz, Hein (1998) *An Introduction to Comparative Law*, 3rd ed., Oxford: Clarendon, 2.

[9] Merryman, John (1999) *The Loneliness of the Comparative Lawyer*, Boston: Kluwer Law, 4 ('clearly more a process or a method'). Similarly de Cruz, Peter (2007) *Comparative Law in a Changing World*, 3rd ed., New York: Routledge ('predominantly a method of study').

> [T]he development of comparative law, as a science, is rather more recent. Only in the last century was its importance recognized, its method and aims systematically studied, and the term itself *comparative law* (*droit comparé*) received and established in usage.[10]

Other jurists, however, have held that comparative law is not simply a method but a science with its own distinctive province. But there is no agreement as to what the province is, and the debate as to whether comparative law is a method or a science has turned into a debate over language.[11]

At times, comparatists justify the scientific nature of their work with reference to other natural or social sciences:

> [J]ust as the biologists draw the great line between invertebrates and vertebrates, and again between animals and humans, so the legal scientist must recognize and set apart the higher forms of socio-legal phenomena, viz. those which represent a body of rules consciously connected and developed as a whole.[12]

Conjoined, the formula of a – exclusively, primarily or predominantly – methodological control of the scientific production of knowledge, distinguishing 'higher,' that is, Western legal forms of socio-legal phenomena from lower, marginal, other ones, has shaped the profession's understanding of 'good comparative practice,' even though it is called into question today:

> [W]hen leading scholars considered comparative law merely a method, their view may have been justified because back then the discipline consisted mainly of a particular way of looking at law and of a research agenda. Yet,

---

10 David, René and Brierley, John E. (1985) *Major Legal Systems in the World Today: An Introduction to the Comparative Study of Law*, 3rd ed., New York: Simon & Schuster, 2 seq. For a thorough discussion of this theme see Watson, Alan (1974) *Legal Transplants: An Approach to Comparative Law*, Athens: University of Virginia, 1–9.

11 Watson *Legal Transplants*, 2. He adds that 'theories that Comparative Law is a science now seem to lack support' (which may have been the case in the 1970s) and further suggests that comparative law is 'the study of the relationship of one legal system and its rules with another' from a historical perspective. Similarly, de Cruz argues in *Comparative Law in a Changing World* that comparative law is 'becoming a branch of social science in its own right,' 4.

12 Wigmore, John H. (1928) *A Panorama of the World's Legal Systems*, Vol.III, St. Paul: West Publishing, 1126.

> when leading scholars today continue to subscribe to this view, that actual knowledge accumulated in the meantime makes their position indefensible.[13]

Unless guided by theoretical considerations, method is often identified with the techniques used for the comparison of the legal phenomena at hand. When reduced to a mere technicality, comparative law leans toward the mindset of legal engineers. The comparatist-as-engineer is likely to avoid critical methodological self-reflection or tone it down as superfluous, if not as a sign of disciplinary weakness. When informed by knowledges from other disciplines, like history, anthropology or political science, the scientific reflection of method mirrors a more academic mindset.[14]

The science/method formula may also have contributed to the abovementioned Cinderella complex. Comparative law's emaciated condition, its (once) 'rather modest position in academic curricula'[15] as well as comparatists' sense of feeling marginalized in legal education, not adequately appreciated in a 'chilly [academic] environment,'[16] and their

---

[13] Reimann, Mathias (2002) 'The Progress and Failure of Comparative Law in the Second Half of the Twentieth Century' 50 *American Journal of Comparative Law*, 676, references omitted.

[14] Watson *Legal Transplants*; John Wigmore distinguished *Comparative Nomoscopy* (description of various legal systems), *Comparative Nomothetics* (study of the merits of the legal systems) and *Comparative Nomogenetics* (study of the development of the world's ideas and systems of law) in Wigmore *Panorama*, 1120–1130.

[15] Zweigert and Kötz *Introduction to Comparative Law*, 3; Gutteridge *Comparative Law*, 5, 23. Critical: Twining, William (2000) 'Comparative Law and Legal Theory: The Country and Western Tradition' in Edge, Ian ed. *Comparative Law in Global Perspective*, Ardsley, NY: Transnational Publishers, 21. See Frankenberg, Günter (1985) 'Critical Comparisons. Rethinking Comparative Law' 26 *Harvard International Law Journal*, 411, 418–421.

[16] For almost a decade, it seems, the Cinderella image and complex have been fading and weakening, as more robust (critical) approaches and self-confident publications have established the discipline relatively firmly in legal education. See Reimann, Mathias and Zimmermann, Reinhard eds (2008) *The Oxford Handbook of Comparative Law*, Oxford: Oxford University Press; and Nelken, David and Örücü, Esin eds (2007) *Comparative Law. A Handbook*, Oxford: Hart Publishing. Recently, critics have challenged the orthodoxy of the discipline, e.g. Riles, Annelise (2001) *Rethinking the Masters of Comparative Law*, Oxford: Hart Publishing.

'ubiquitous angst about the disciplinary identity,'[17] is likely to have been informed by the ubiquitous comparative-law-as-method narrative.

Science/method favors postures of scientism and objectivism on the part of comparatists, which are described here as varieties of professional innocence. The form of innocence hinges upon the theoretical-methodological orientation. Comparatists with a speculative predisposition are likely to proceed – some as cosmopolitans, others as humanists – on the macro-level of world law or the evolution of law towards universal ends, oblivious to the Western[18] bias of universalism. Taxonomists classified '*Grands systèmes*' of law on the basis of a thin layer of humanism. Functionalists, factualists and structuralists had a more pragmatic mindset and aimed lower as, for instance, at legal solutions for social problems or Common Cores of contract law in Europe.

More importantly, the narrow conception of comparative law as science/method tends to foreclose discussion of the ethical and political implications of locating, studying and comparing the foreign – under whatever guise it may appear: legal system or institution, statute or decision, culture or argument. Moreover, the combination of scientism and belief in method is prone to cover up, rather than make explicit, the relations between knowledge and power,[19] as well as the violence[20] of definitions and classifications in comparative practice.

Various techniques of comparison and the postures of innocence they privilege will be submitted to critical scrutiny in this chapter. I address the ethical and political underpinnings of the production of comparative knowledge and argue that the 'comparative space' is constituted by the intricate connection between theory and method, ethics and politics with regard to the comparative study of the co-present other/foreign. To

---

[17] Riles *Rethinking the Masters*, 3. Jean Carbonnier describes comparative law as a 'collateral science' – Carbonnier, Jean (2002) *Droit civil: Introduction*, 27th ed., Paris: Presses Universitaires de France, 78. Palmer 'From Lerotholi to Lando' mentions comparative law's 'cloistered existence in the academy' and refers to the 'underdeveloped and emaciated state of our discipline,' 262.

[18] For a straightforward defense of Western legal culture, see Berman, Harold J. (1983) *Law and Revolution: The Formation of the Western Legal Tradition*, Cambridge, MA: Harvard University Press, 1–10.

[19] Foucault, Michel (1972) *Power/Knowledge: Selected Interviews and Other Writings 1972–1977*, New York: Pantheon, 78–108, 109–133.

[20] Cover, Robert M. (1986) 'Violence and the Word' 95 *Yale Law Journal*, 1601; Derrida, Jacques (1992) 'The Force of Law. The Foundation of Authority' in Cornell, Drucilla et al. eds *Deconstruction and the Possibility of Justice*, London: Routledge.

address this connection I introduce, or rather, revisit[21] in the final section of this chapter the twin operations of *distancing* and *differencing* I consider essential for a genuinely 'good comparative practice' – 'good' insofar as they are guided by self-criticism, inspired by curiosity about the foreign (law) and based on genuine interest in understanding unfamiliar/foreign/strange legal norms and practices, institutions and cultures in their own right.

In the following, I try to explore how *distancing* and *differencing* (*d/d*) can be put to work, and whether and how mainstream comparative law avoids or circumvents their challenge, comparatists stay comfortably settled in their armchair, look out of the window with its ethnocentric frame and make the – necessarily distorted – foreign familiar, thereby domesticating its foreignness and levelling diversity.[22]

2. COMPARATIVE LAW AND THE SPIRIT OF THE UNIVERSAL

Historically, the heroes of the *belle époque* of comparative law came first. Although there is always a 'before', the 1900 Congress in Paris marked the foundation of the *discipline* of comparative law, which is not to say that the nineteenth century was not interesting and crucial for later developments. *Belle époque* or *golden era* express the admiration and respect comparatists earned for their immense creativity and visionary style. In the spirit of the nineteenth century, they introduced and applied historical and ethnological methods as well as philosophical speculation. And some of the framers of the discipline did not shy away from a political agenda: namely to put legal comparison to the task of translating into treatises and monographic studies the dream of a better world – where there would be peace, not war, and harmony, not hatred. If one were to describe their vocabulary and mindset as innocent, one would have to focus on claims to ethical neutrality and political agnosticism that came with their turn to tradition, philosophy, jurisprudence and method.

---

[21] The operations of distancing and differencing introduced in Frankenberg 'Critical Comparisons,' 414–416 are revised here.

[22] See also Ainsworth, Janet E. (1996) 'Categories and Culture: On the "Rectification of Names" in Comparative Law' 82 *Cornell Law Review*, 19, 25 and Crapanzano, Vincent (1986) 'Hermes' Dilemma: The Masking of Subversion in Ethnographic Description' in Clifford, James and Marcus, George E. eds *Writing Culture: The Poetics and Politics of Ethnography*, Berkeley: University of California Press, 51 seq.

Many of the prominent contemporary comparatists invoked the venerable tradition of the discipline. In the founding years of the discipline (and occasionally thereafter), members of the epistemic community imagined their profession as inaugurated by Aristotle, then re-energized by Montesquieu and inspired by such diverse but eminent scholars as G.F.W. Hegel and his disciple Eduard Gans, by Henry Sumner Maine and Max Weber. Together, these forefathers (and others) also account for the philosophical and historical-anthropological, the sociological and juristic accents of early comparative legal studies.[23]

After the Paris Congress these traditions disembogue into the delta of attempts to recapture the pre-modern and early modern concepts and ideas of a universal jurisprudence, embedded in and informed by European culture, that might provide a 'moderate [natural law] compass ... for the whole groundwork of law,'[24] as well as to re-imagine them as an updated framework for comparative law. The universal-minded comparatist aimed high and far:

> [If] universal jurisprudence is to vitalize, it needs to compare the laws and legal practices of other nations at all times and places, the most like and the most different.[25]

Against the predicament brought on by the age of codification, comparatists, in the spirit of naïve enthusiasm or unaware of its implications for comparative research, embraced what may be called the *méthode Montesquieu*. They set the highest possible standards for the scope and complexity of the comparatists' task to both recognize the singularity of all items and sustain their comparability, which committed them to an endless search for phenomena related to law:

---

23 For the diversity of orientations: Lambert, Édouard (1905/1978) 'Conception générale et définition de la science du droit comparé, sa méthode, son histoire; le droit comparé et l'enseignement du droit' in Zweigert, Konrad and Puttfarken, Hans J. eds *Rechtsvergleichung*, Darmstadt: Wissenschaftliche Buchgesellschaft, 30.

24 Regarding the natural law pedigree: Pufendorf, Samuel (2009/1660) *Two Books of the Elements of Universal Jurisprudence*, Miami: Liberty Fund; Riley, Patrick (1996) *Leibniz' Universal Jurisprudence: Justice as the Charity of the Wise*, Cambridge, MA: Harvard University Press; and Thomas, John Penford (1828) *A Treatise of Universal Jurisprudence*, London: Longman.

25 Feuerbach, Anselm von (1810) *Blick auf die deutsche Rechtswissenschaft*, München: Fleischmann.

> The student of the problems of law must encompass the *law of the whole world*, *past* and *present*, and *everything* that affects the law, such as geography, climate and race, developments and events, shaping the course of a country's history – war, revolution, colonization, subjugation – religion and ethics, the ambition and creativity of individuals, the needs of production and consumption.[26]

However, comparatists seemed to have forgotten Montesquieu's insight that different societies produce different legal regimes and laws:

> Laws, in their most general signification, are the necessary relations arising from the nature of things. In this sense all beings have their laws[27] [and] a greatness of genius consists rather in distinguishing between those cases in which uniformity is a requisite, and those in which there is a necessity for differences.[28]

Instead, many of the illustrious comparatists showed little regard for diversity and context. They pursued unitary projects with what they thought to be a universal reach. The French school of comparative law became known for propagating a *droit commun législatif*, working toward '*l'unification du droit privé*' (UNIDROIT in 1926), and classifying *Les Grands Systèmes de Droit Contemporains* (René David).[29]

By contrast, the German language and frame of mind appears to have privileged the vision of a 'world-historical development' or the idea of a 'world law' (*Weltrecht*).[30] At any rate, it inspired both a historical orientation and philosophical speculation in the service of comparative law. Only legislative comparative law allowed for an easy French-German crossover.

The innocent spirit, instructed by the political naïveté of the all-male members of the academy of 'masters,'[31] is etched into relief against the

---

[26] Rabel, Ernst (1925) *Aufgabe und Notwendigkeit der Rechtsvergleichung*, München: Hueber, 3 – emphasis added; also see Kötz, Hein (1999) 'Comparative Law in Germany Today' 51 *Révue internationale de droit comparé*, 753, 754. In a similar vein: Kocourek, Albert and Wigmore, John H. (1915) *Sources of Ancient and Primitive Law*, Boston: Little, Brown & Co.

[27] Montesquieu *The Spirit of Laws*, 1.

[28] *Ibid.*, xxix, 18.

[29] For references see Fauvarque-Cosson, Bénédicte (2006) 'Development of Comparative Law in France' in *Oxford Handbook*, 35.

[30] For references see Schwenzer, Ingeborg (2006) 'Development of Comparative Law in Germany, Switzerland, and Austria' in *Oxford Handbook*, 69.

[31] Riles *Rethinking the Masters*. The gender implication is intended since the epistemic community was all-male during the first generations.

backdrop of the greedy 'scramble for Africa' and other ugly colonial-imperial adventures of European nationalisms – not unrelated to comparative law. Rather than addressing and confronting the law's impact on and comparatists' role in sustaining or at least facilitating colonialism and imperialism, most of the heroes of the discipline invoked what they understood to be a faultless program: celebrating humanism and – some of them – cosmopolitanism. Of course, they neither directly assisted the governments in preparing warfare nor in subjugating tribes, countries and continents. And they did not justify the civilizing mission of European nation-states. Instead, *fin de siècle* comparatists preferably set out to look at the bright side of life. They perceived legal phenomena through the lens of history, ethnology or philosophical speculation for the purpose of 'feel[ing] the pulse that trembles through all peoples.'[32] Their primarily academic enterprise was guided by a clean-handed humanitarian rhetoric of truth and objectivity; and their scientific project was based on the assumption that 'the general spirit of humanity reappears in the special spirit of each people.'[33]

The spirit of humanity elevated them above conflicts and wars, and incidentally elevated the own above the foreign. Informed by the Hegelian idea that legal phenomena should be contemplated in the spirit of philosophical speculation,[34] the German branch of the school of truth, under the leadership of the astoundingly productive Josef Kohler, focused many of their comparative legal studies on writing the universal history of law.[35]

By contrast, members of the French founding generation, in particular Raymond Saleilles, Édouard Lambert and Louis Josserand, upheld a politically moderate, reformist orientation and placed on the agenda what they considered a (blameless) search for a *droit commun législatif* or, more ambitiously, for universal legal principles.[36]

---

[32] E.g. Hegel's student Gans, Eduard (2005/1836) *Naturrecht und Universalrechtsgeschichte*: *Vorlesungen nach G.W.F. Hegel*, Tübingen: Mohr Siebeck; Kohler, Josef (1914) *Philosophy of Law*, London: Macmillan Publishers.

[33] Kohler *Philosophy of Law*.

[34] Gans *Naturrecht und Universalrechtsgeschichte*.

[35] Kohler, Josef (1904) 'Rechtsphilosophie und Universalrechtsgeschichte' in von Holtzendorff, Franz ed. *Enzyklopädie der Rechtswissenschaft Vol. I*, 6th ed., Leipzig: Duncker & Humblot; Kohler, Josef and Wenger, Leopold (1914) *Allgemeine Rechtsgeschichte*, Leipzig and Berlin: B.G. Teubner.

[36] Lambert 'Conception générale,' 35; see also Zitelmann, Ernst (1888) *Die Möglichkeit eines Weltrechts*, Berlin: Duncker & Humblot.

Innocence was conveyed by the aspiration for a more human and just society and world, promoted by a rhetoric and endeavor tapping '*un certain nombre de grands courants juridiques … auxquels [le comparatiste] ne saurait résister impunément.*'[37] Comparative law was geared toward the discovery of the spirit that informs the laws of all civilized nations. What could be more laudable, against the backdrop of war, nationalism and colonialism, than searching for '*l'élément d'unité ou rapprochement [des solutions données] par les diverses legislations*'?[38] Accordingly, comparative law was widely understood as '*un instrument du dégagement d'un fond commun.*'[39]

An innocent spirit was also transmitted by the disciplinary program, supported not only by French and German, but also other European protagonists of the '*école de vérité.*' What could be more innocuous than the virginal search for inspiration in other countries? Whether driven by humanism or reformism, it was invariably guided by the – untainted, it seemed – ambition to promote comparative law to a science, thus linking comparative legal studies with the overall nineteenth-century project of scientism.[40] By striving for a universal science[41] and jurisprudence – '*restituer au droit le caractère qu'il n'aurait jamais dû perdre, d'une science universelle*'[42] – comparatists sought to establish their field of thought and research as an academic discipline, distinguished by strict methods that could measure up to mathematics and the natural sciences. And they gave it a peculiarly twentieth-century twist: the seemingly innocent – because scientific – preoccupation with method[43] that permitted most of them to remain silent over politics.

---

[37] Louis Josserand, quoted by Lambert 'Conception générale,' 36.

[38] *Ibid.*, 45.

[39] *Ibid.*, 47.

[40] See Schröder, Jan (2010) *Rechtswissenschaft in der Neuzeit*, Tübingen: Mohr Siebeck.

[41] Del Vecchio, Giorgio (1909) *Sull'idea di una scienza del diritto universale comparator*, Rome: Fratelli Boca. See also Kocourek and Wigmore *Sources*; Kocourek, Albert and Wigmore, John M. (1915) *Primitive and Ancient Legal Institutions*, Boston: Little, Brown & Co.; and Riles' persuasive analysis of Wigmore's universal philosophy: 'Encountering Amateurism' in Riles ed. *Rethinking the Masters*, 94.

[42] David, René (1950) *Traité élémentaire de droit civil comparé. Introduction à l'étude des droits étrangers et à la méthode comparative*, Paris: Librairie Générale de Droit et de Jurisprudence, 214.

[43] Epitomized by the contributions of Kohler, Lambert, Rabel and Langrod in Zweigert and Puttfarken *Rechtsvergleichung*, see also Michaels, Ralf (2006) 'The Functional Method of Comparative Law' in *Oxford Handbook*, 339; and

While the ideas of the *belle époque* faded away and were certainly overtaken by pragmatic approaches, the echo of humanist idealism, for what it is worth, can still be heard from time to time. In 2006, Konstantinos Kerameus, the President of the Association, opened the Congress of the International Academy of Comparative Law in Utrecht proclaiming:

> [W]e look over the fence of our neighbor in pursuit of the common fate: to identify and grasp the human nature; indeed, to share the human destiny and to unite the human forces.[44]

To this overdose of humanity other authors added an equally strong dose of peace and community, arguing that 'the com-paring of laws is fundamental for peaceful co-existence,' in 'the process of globalization and in the pursuit of peaceful relations between peoples,'[45] and further claiming that comparative law can show:

> [T]here is something that can be done by the international community in response to genocide, crimes against humanity and other massive, state-sponsored violations of fundamental human rights during civil wars or by tyrannical governments abusing their own people.[46]

In their normative hyperbole, latter-day comparatists – with an evolutionary perspective or philosophical mindset – changed the disciplinary register from national to international comparison and its modality from analysis to confession.

3. AFTER UNIVERSALISM – TAXONOMY: MAPPING THE LAWS OF THE WORLD

After World War II, the vocabulary of universalism appeared to be exhausted, as if the atrocities of global warfare had infected or extinguished cosmopolitan and humanitarian ideas. At any rate, the discipline

---

Dannemann, Gerhard (2006) 'Comparative Law: Study of Similarities and Differences' in *Oxford Handbook*, 383.

44 Thus spoke Konstantinos Kerameus, the President of the Association, Opening Address at the XVIIIth Congress of the International Academy of Comparative Law, 16–22 July 2006.

45 Glenn, H. Patrick (2007) 'Com-paring' in Örücü, Esin and Nelken, David eds *Comparative Law: A Handbook*, Portland: Hart Publishing, 91, 93.

46 Roberts, Paul (2007) 'International Criminal Justice' in Nelken and Örücü ed. *Comparative Law*, 339, 346.

went through a phase of significant re-orientation, which had been prepared in the 1920s. While reproducing the rhetoric and continuing some of the themes of the founding generation, comparatists were no longer predisposed to dream of a better world. The geographer's imagination[47] replaced the philosopher's speculation. Charting the comparative space to provide an overview, demarcate families and relations, and serve as a 'guide to the terrain'[48] stepped in to replace cosmopolitan and universalistic conjecture and contemplation.

In the 1930s, Nazi fascism liquidated the transnational perspective and introduced its ethnic-racist and nationalist point of view instead. The golden era was destroyed and superseded by the dark age of anti-cosmopolitanism and anti-universalism. In Germany, eminent scholars of comparative law, like Max Rheinstein and Ernst Rabel, were forced by the Nazi regime to leave the country and seek exile.[49] This is how it sounded in the clinical cynicism of barbarism:

> Professor Rabel, whose merits are recognized by the Ministry, has to resign from his position as head of the Institute. It is intolerable for the State that a person presides over the Institute who must be superannuated as a result of the Nuremberg Laws.[50]

The regime ousted the scholars of Jewish-German origin and, by the same token, liquidated the high reputation of the German profession of comparative law.

Gradual recovery after the war soon led to a reorientation away from earlier historical-ethnological studies and philosophical speculation to the sober and pragmatic assessment of what the law *is*. On the macro-level, comparative law's mainstream focused on the classification of *grands systémes* or legal families or cultures.[51] On the micro-level, comparative

---

47 Gregory, Derek (1994) *Geographical Imaginations*, Oxford: Blackwell.

48 Twining, William (2000) *Globalisation and Legal Theory*, Cambridge: Cambridge University Press, 233–9.

49 See Schwenzer, 'Comparative Law in Germany, Switzerland, and Austria,' 82–4.

50 Statement of the representative of the Ministry of Science and Education, minutes of the meeting of the institute's governing council, quoted by Kunze, Rolf Ulrich (2004) *Ernst Rabel und das Kaiser-Wilhelm-Institut für Ausländisches und Internationales Privatrecht 1926–1945*, Göttingen: Wallstein.

51 Ehrmann, Henry W. (1976) *Comparative Legal Cultures*, Englewood Cliffs: Prentice Hall.

functionalism triumphed, until the end of the century, with its search for better legal solutions for social problems.[52]

Thus, comparative law lost its universalistic bearings in German academia and turned global (taxonomies) and general (functionalism) instead. While the functionalist-style micro-comparison, as will be shown below, set out on its worldwide career, in France comparatists managed to retain the grandiose gesture of universalism by comparing nothing less than *Grands Systèmes*.[53] In 1950, two French publications highlighted the move to taxonomy and classification.[54]

Regardless of the methodological orientation, comparatists tended to move from theory to practice and subscribe to moderately reformist projects. In terms of psychology, the profession oscillated between the Cinderella complex, which was expressed in laments about comparative law as an 'ancillary discipline' and narratives of decline on the one hand,[55] and a sense of comparative law's grandeur and importance on the other hand:

> Although there has been a rich comparative law tradition, the discipline has not been treated as a major subject in French universities. Many leading academics still consider it simply an exoticism. As a result, comparative law found itself limited to an ancillary function, not only in legal academia but also among judges and other practitioners.
>
> This marginal status has also been linked to a double identity crisis. After the two world wars, comparatists lost their belief in universalism and found themselves vexed by the question 'Who are we really?' ... Since the teaching of French law remained overwhelmingly positivistic and legicentric throughout the twentieth century, it should not come as a surprise that comparative law was considered a marginal field in French law faculties.[56]

Despite (or because of) their marginalization, a few French authors doggedly pursued, at least on the side, the concept of a universal

---

[52] See Twining, William (2000) *Globalisation and Legal Theory*, 174–193, Chapter 7.

[53] David, René (1964) *Les Grands Systèmes de Droit Contemporains (Droit Comparé)*, Paris: Librairie Dalloz; see Esquirol, Jorge (2001) 'At the Head of the Legal Family: René David' in Riles ed. *Rethinking the Masters*.

[54] David, René (1950) *Traité élémentaire de droit civil comparé: Introduction à l'étude des droits étrangers et à la méthode comparative*, Paris: Librairie Générale de Droit et de Jurisprudence; Arminjon, Pierre, Nolde, Boris and Wolff, Martin (1950) *Traité de droit comparé*, Paris: Librairie Générale de Droit et de Jurisprudence.

[55] See Fauvarque-Cosson 'Comparative Law in France,' 37, 48–55.

[56] *Ibid.*, 48, see also 45–47 regarding the '*grands systèmes*'.

jurisprudence[57] and claimed to explore the possible contribution of comparative legal studies to a better understanding among nations.[58] In particular, René David's taxonomy of legal systems echoed the universalistic spirit of the founding era. The universalism of taxonomies came reduced to the legal geographer's mindset, though, and with a bow to the functional approach:

> [a] serious comparison between systems of law is often possible only if a 'functional approach' is adopted, considering how the various systems deal with a particular problem; comparison of rules and concepts is meaningless unless it deals with systems of identical structure.[59]

Undaunted by most of his colleagues' loss of faith in law's universal history and theory, René David inspired a group of comparatists with his cartography based on the taxonomic method, which responded to the 'desire to facilitate knowledge of the law by putting it in order.'[60] Focusing on ideology and legal techniques, he 'presented the law in an orderly fashion'[61] by classifying the world's legal systems into 'legal families,' not by coincidence beginning with the Romano-Germanic family, the common law family (originally 'Western systems'), and the socialist law family (recently renamed as the 'Russian family'). The leaders were trailed by a motley group of other systems, constituted by Jewish law, Hindu law, the law of the Far East, African legal regimes, and Malagasy law. Even though David's taxonomy brought to mind Borges' list[62] and Foucault's Order of Things,[63] his 'mechanics of law' withstood criticism and the change of times as a monument representing a global frame for legal positivism, certainly bereft of the universal ideas that animated comparatists during the *belle époque*.

---

[57] David, René (1978) 'Le droit comparé – Enseignement de culture générale' in Zweigert and Puttfarken eds *Rechtsvergleichung*, 205.

[58] Tunc, André (1978) 'La contribution possible des études juridiques comparatives à une meilleure compréhension entre nations' in Zweigert and Puttfarken eds *Rechtsvergleichung*, 334.

[59] David, René 'Introduction' in David et al. eds (1972 seq.) *International Encyclopedia of Comparative Law, Vol. II: The Legal Systems of the World: Their Comparison and Unification*, 3, 6.

[60] *Ibid.*, 7.

[61] *Ibid.*

[62] Borges, Jorge Luis (1964) 'The Analytical Language of John Wilkins' in Borges, *Other Inquisitions*, Austin: Texas University Press.

[63] Foucault, Michel (1970) *The Order of Things: An Archeology of the Human Sciences*, New York: Pantheon Books.

His *Grands Systèmes de Droit Contemporains* still entitle law courses in France. Critics have not been able to discourage other comparatists from pursuing taxonomic projects with a similar[64] or divergent[65] underlying purpose and design:

> Taxonomy and legal families have the task or objective of separation and distinguishing, whereas legal traditions have the task only of supporting their own forms of normativity. This usually involves more art than science, more attempting to do justice than attempting to build and classify systems.[66]

Shifting the taxonomic framework from families to traditions begs critical questions rather than coping with them. From an internal point of view one would expect to learn how traditions (or families) can be identified and defined, what the information obtained from any classification can tell the readers, what the talk of 'scientifically chosen boundaries'[67] actually means, and so forth. The contradictory classifications of Japanese law, invariably from the unmarked Western perspective, illustrate the random results obtained with this 'method:'

> René David saw Japanese law as a legal system of the Far East and in the same group as Chinese law. In contrast, Léontin Jean Constantinesco treated Japanese law as part of the Western legal system, and John Merryman, David Clark and John Haley consider it part of the 'Civil Law Tradition.' Konrad Zweigert and Hein Kötz take an intermediate position and see Japanese law transforming from an Asian to a Western legal system. According to all these views, however, the identity of Japanese law is apparently to be judged by Western standards.[68]

How does a comparatist who can speak from the position of a participant observer feel about these classifications? Japanese comparatists recognize that 'their system successfully received and assimilated Western law. Yet, they are reluctant to consider Japanese law as part of the Western

---

[64] E.g. Glendon, Mary Ann et al. (1994) *Comparative Legal Traditions*, Eagan, MN: West Publishing; Merryman, John (2007) *The Civil Law Tradition: An Introduction to the Legal Systems of Europe and Latin America*, Palo Alto, CA: Stanford University Press.

[65] Glenn, H. Patrick (2004) *Legal Traditions of the World.* 3rd ed., Oxford: Oxford University Press.

[66] Glenn, H. Patrick (2006) 'Comparative Legal Families and Comparative Legal Traditions' in *Oxford Handbook*, 420, 425–426.

[67] *Ibid.*, 421.

[68] Kitagawa, Zentaro (2006) 'Comparative Law in East Asia' in *Oxford Handbook*, 237, 245.

tradition and have thus considerable reservations vis-à-vis the views summarized above.[69]

Taxonomies or classifications on offer today, operating with bounded entities (like systems, families or traditions) in the era of globalization and transnational legal transfers[70] appear to be obsolete, despite their impressive design and collection of material.[71] They bear witness to jurists' yearning for order and comparatists' recurrent attempts to dignify their asymmetrical, geographical vision with borrowings from the natural sciences and mathematics. It is true that mainstream scholars have moved beyond 'these relatively crude models,' have come to understand classifications as approximations, 'have learned to look beyond legal systems and families as static and isolated entities' and have developed a sense for historic contingency and the interaction between families, traditions and even cultures.[72] However, the practice of taxonomic mapping law and legal systems, despite having added nuances, dynamism and a relational view, still suffers from the vice of ethnocentrism.

4. FUNCTIONALISM: THE TRIUMPH OF COMPLEXITY REDUCTION

With melancholy one recalls the noble commitment to the discovery of 'universal innate legal ideas,'[73] natural laws or a universal jurisprudence in the golden era; even David's *Grands Systèmes* evoke nostalgic feelings in the face of the pragmatism that saw the light in 1920s (Ernst Rabel) but blossomed and proliferated after World War II. Despite the varieties of the functional method that have developed since then,[74] *the* spirit of this method is expressed in the categorical imperative of comparative reason:

---

69 *Ibid.*

70 See Muir Watt, Horatia (2006) 'Globalization and Comparative Law' in *Oxford Handbook*, 579; Frankenberg, Günter ed. (2013) *Order from Transfer. Comparative Constitutional Design and Legal Culture*, Cheltenham, UK and Northampton, MA, USA: Edward Elgar Publishing.

71 In particular, Glenn's taxonomy and narratives of the world's *Legal Traditions*.

72 Reimann 'The Progress and Failure,' 671, 675.

73 Del Vecchio *Sull'idea*, 24.

74 See Michaels 'The Functional Method'; and Graziadei, Michele (2003) 'The Functional Heritage' in Legrand, Pierre and Munday, Roderick eds *Comparative Legal Studies: Traditions and Transitions*, Cambridge: Cambridge University Press, 100.

> The basic methodological principle of *all* comparative law is that of functionality.[75]

> Today, we understand that when we compare rules, we *must* take a functional approach, i.e., analyze not only what rules say but also what problems they solve in their respective legal systems.[76]

The pragmatic turn to functionalism, which dominated the better part of the twentieth century, was characterized by a disciplinary shift from a more theoretical or academic orientation (search for origins, grand systems) to applied comparative law, and from legislation to (appellate) court decisions. Generally speaking, function-oriented comparatists concentrate, first, on legal systems rather than sources[77] or operate with a very broad concept of what counts as a source: 'For the purpose of comparative studies a legal source is everything that shapes or helps to shape the law.'[78] Second, they are more interested in finding legal solutions for social problems (on the micro-level) rather than the always elusive origins of law. Third, where Raymond Poincaré, in the founding era, believed in observing '*la culte de France et de la humanité*'[79] and a student of the German school might have been impressed by the scope of universalistic speculation about 'the natural laws which obey these manifestations of the social life,'[80] today's mainstream functionalists demonstrate their quite modest program, which is 'to consider rules in context, i.e., at least within the existent procedural and institutional frameworks' and to 'observe not only the law on paper but also the law in action.'[81] While function and context are said to be the central categories of functionalist comparison, on closer scrutiny the latter comes in an emaciated gestalt:

> Function is the start-point and basis of all comparative law. It is the *tertium comparationis* ... For the comparative process, this means that the solutions we find in different jurisdictions must be cut loose from their conceptual

[75] Zweigert and Kötz *Introduction*, 34 – emphasis added. Critical of the standard functional approach: Michaels 'The Functional Method,' 343.

[76] Reimann 'The Progress and Failure,' 675 – emphasis added.

[77] Concerning the importance of sources for comparative studies, see Vogenauer, Stefan (2006) 'Sources of Law and Legal Method' in *Oxford Handbook*, 869.

[78] Zweigert, Konrad (1960) 'Zur Methode der Rechtsvergleichung' 13 *Studium Generale*, 193, 196.

[79] Quoted by Rabel 'Aufgabe und Notwendigkeit,' 96.

[80] Lambert 'Conception générale,' 36.

[81] Reimann 'The Progress and Failure,' 675 with further references.

> context and stripped of their national doctrinal overtones so that they may be seen purely in the light of their function, as an attempt to satisfy a particular legal need.[82]

So, rather than indulging in the social, political, economic and cultural context of law, the functionalist radicalizes de-contextualization by 'cutting loose' and 'stripping' the solutions generated by the diverse legal regimes and very often focuses on concepts. She reifies 'function' as a principle of reality and totalizes it as *the* container of reality, and does not take it for what it is: an analytical device introduced by comparative functionalism to order and construct the real world from, and within, a peculiar perspective and subject it then to cognitive control.

The reorientation of the mainstream was foreshadowed in Ernst Rabel's seminal article on the aim of comparative law and later taken up in Konrad Zweigert's keynote address on comparative law as a universal method of interpretation.[83] In the guise of the modern law-maker, the universal spirit returned and was put to work as the comparative method to close the gaps of national laws.

Aside from function, *knowledge* and *information* were to become keywords for this new orientation: 'The primary aim of comparative law, as of all *sciences*, is *knowledge*.'[84] These keywords underscored the repeated claim to method/science[85] and sustained a widespread belief that the production of comparative knowledge was ethically neutral and unrelated to power. In this vein, comparatists followed the objectivist and positivist trend in the social sciences at the time,[86] which reflected the rise of the natural-science paradigm and the corresponding fall of the philosophical-speculative orientation.

---

82 Zweigert and Kötz *Introduction*, 36–37.

83 Rabel 'Aufgabe und Notwendigkeit,' 1; Zweigert, Konrad (1949/1950) 'Rechtsvergleichung als universale Interpretationsmethode' 15 *Rabels Zeitschrift für ausländisches und internationales Privatrecht*, 5.

84 Zweigert and Kötz *Introduction*, 15 – emphasis added; similarly Gutteridge *Comparative Law*, 5.

85 Gutteridge *Comparative Law*, 1, 72–87. See also Lasser, Mitchel (2003) 'The Question of Understanding' in Legrand and Munday *Comparative Legal Studies*, 197. See also Glanert, Simone (2012) 'Method?' in Monateri, P.G. ed. *Methods of Comparative Law*, Cheltenham, UK and Northampton, MA, USA: Edward Elgar Publishing, 61.

86 For a critical perspective see Habermas, Jürgen (1972) *Knowledge and Human Interests*, Boston: Beacon Press; *Habermas* (1988) *On the Logic of the Social Sciences*, Cambridge, MA: MIT Press; Adorno, Theodor W. ed. (1976) *The Positivist Dispute in German Sociology*, New York: Harper & Row.

After a phase of ataraxy during which comparatists were stoically indifferent to the intense debates on methodology in the neighboring sciences, they woke up innocent (again) – now with a functionalist tool-kit. The functionalist method or, if this should be a 'misnomer,'[87] the f-method, indicated a novel orientation for comparative law. It helped 'applied comparative law'[88] to leave behind the old and distinctly theoretical paradigm of the founders of the discipline and to bypass the *Grands systèmes* approach. Rather than addressing philosophers, jurists, and the global audience, functionalists developed a more practical and instrumentalist mindset and put themselves to the task of producing knowledge that would increase the supply of (legal) solutions for whatever problem might arise in society. Mainstream scholars, at least a considerable number of them, aligned themselves to the narrow purpose of comparative legal problem-solving on the level of doctrine and legislation.

Variations on the functional method[89] proliferated globally over the next decades.[90] Arguably, the success story may have to do with the circumstance that, in terms of theory, functionalism traveled light and, in terms of method, came with a simple design:

> Comparison traditionally requires an invariant element. In theory, a functional method could set either problems or institutions as invariant; in reality, as

---

[87] In his otherwise thoughtful article, Ralf Michaels qualifies the 'functional method' as a 'triple misnomer' because there are many of them, some not functional at all, and some not even a method: see Michaels 'The Functional Method,' 342. While all this may be true, as a *mainstream* functionalism has been and still is quite alive, dominant and successful, indeed on a rather underdeveloped methodological basis.

[88] Rabel (1925) 'Aufgabe und Notwendigkeit,' republished in Zweigert and Puttfarken *Rechtsvergleichung*, 85; Gutteridge *Comparative Law*, 9.

[89] The functional – or, actually, functionalist – method was arguably introduced by Ernst Rabel. See also Lepaulle, Pierre (1922) 'The Function of Comparative Law. With a Critique of Sociological Jurisprudence' 35 *Harvard Law Review*, 838; and Michaels 'The Functional Method' offering a detailed analysis of the varieties of functionalism.

[90] See Monateri, Pier G. (1999) 'Critique et difference: Le droit comparé en Italie' 51 *Revue Internationale de Droit Comparé*, 989, 991 seq.; Kitagawa, 'Comparative Law in East Asia' in *Oxford Handbook*, 250–253; Reitz, John (1998) 'How to Do Comparative Law' 46 *American Journal of Comparative Law*, 617; Schlesinger *Comparative Law*, 48; further references are provided by Michaels 'The Functional Method,' 339.

> long as institutions are non-universal, only problems can play the role of the invariant ...[91]

Mainstream functionalism either operated with fairly vague and abstract societal needs or limited the concept of more concrete problems to societies at similar stages of socio-economic development to circumvent the challenges of definition (what counts as a social problem?) and difference (not only in detail). In addition, the technical vocabulary and the spirit of legal engineering were geared toward sustaining the value-neutrality of functionalist analyses. This way, the innocent posture of functionalist scholars came in a different guise. The focus on (social) problems and their legal solutions generated a '*neue Sachlichkeit*,' a kind of legal realism without a critical edge. In a similar vein, some authors tagged their comparative practice, more recently, as a 'factual approach'[92] but followed functionalism insofar as they presumed similarity, while allowing for differences, concentrating on solutions to problems, and aimed at regional convergence to overcome fragmentation (in the European member-states).

Functionalists rearranged comparative law's veil of innocence. Their rhetoric shifted from universalistic hyperbole and cosmopolitanism to the jejune vocabulary of an artless pragmatism and objectivism. Their instrumentalism and moderate reformism, adopted by scholars and legal consultants alike, re-oriented their comparative projects. Overall, utility justified cognitive control and led the comparatist from the world of ideas to solutions:

> [T]he problem being studied must be set in the context of the *solutions* obtained in the *most significant* legal systems; then one must make a critical appraisal in order to determine which solution is *best suited here and now* to the national society as it is.[93]

Unlike universalism, taxonomy and classification, functionalism appears to be the only comparative practice which has gained prominence as a *method*. Method generally connotes a way of doing things or, in legal contexts, the proceeding on the path (of application) from a source of law

---

[91] Michaels 'The Functional Method,' 367.

[92] Michaels 'The Functional Method,' 339; Sacco, Rodolfo (1991) 'Legal Formants: A Dynamic Approach to Comparative Law' 39 *American Journal of Comparative Law*, 1–34, 343–401; see also Monateri 'Methods in Comparative Law,' 7.

[93] Zweigert and Kötz *Introduction*, 23 – emphasis added.

(statute) to a (court) decision[94] guided by rules of interpretation and good reasons. It is generally recognized that this is a creative process, in which new law is created.[95] It is further – at least widely – accepted that laws' meanings, connotations, and bindingness change when they are taken out of one context, transferred and re-contextualized in another.[96] Functionalists, however, often ignore that 'there is difference across laws' and that 'it is not a matter of whether difference is there or not, for it exists,[97] because foreign laws are generated in a context which differs from the familiar own. Functionalists are not likely to either recognize or respect, let alone relish, significant differences:

> [O]ne can almost speak of a basic rule of comparative law: different legal systems give the same or very similar solutions, even as to detail, to the same problem of life, despite the great differences in their historical development, conceptual structure, and style of operation.[98]

At first glance, one might think that functionalists are recognizing differences – great ones even – after all. Yet, that impression is deceptive because historical, conceptual and stylistic diversity is of no import for mainstream functionalist analysis and what happens in the process of transfer is virtually ignored because what counts is only the similarity of problem solutions, that is, results:

> If law is seen functionally as a regulator of social facts, the legal problems of all countries are similar. Every legal system in the world is open to the same questions and subject to the same standards, even countries of different social structures or different stages of development.[99]

---

94 See Vogenauer 'Sources of Law and Legal Method,' 885.

95 *Ibid.*

96 Frankenberg 'Constitutions as Commodities: Notes on a Theory of Transfer' in *Order from Transfer*, 1 seq.

97 Legrand, Pierre (2011) 'Siting Foreign Law: How Derrida Can Help' 21 *Duke Journal of Comparative and International Law*, 595, 601. For the recognition of diversity (before functionalism): Montesquieu *The Spirit of Laws*, I, 3, 8–9. See also the critiques of functionalism presented by Gutteridge *Comparative Law*, 8–9; Frankenberg 'Critical Comparisons,' 441 seq.; Damaška, Mirjan (1986) *The Faces of Justice and State Authority. A Comparative Approach to Legal Process*, New Haven: Yale University Press, 181; Legrand, Pierre (2003) 'The same and the different,' in Legrand and Munday eds *Comparative Legal Studies*, 240.

98 Zweigert and Kötz *Introduction*, 39.

99 *Ibid.*, 46.

From an internal perspective one can criticize functionalist method for not providing a comprehensive system of analysis but delivering only fragments, which, in addition, raise many questions functionalists usually leave unanswered. To begin with, the concept of function is vague or, as Ralf Michaels put it, the functions of function are manifold.[100]

Furthermore, it is remarkable that functionalists do not (sufficiently) discuss what counts as a social problem or legal solution nor who is entitled to define either one or both – the participants in the foreign 'system' would certainly be entitled and so would the observer but functionalists, quite naturally, privilege the observer. By the same token, they say very little (if anything) about benchmarks or standards they rely on when they distinguish 'better' from good results or solutions.

It is quite telling what advice the standard textbook offers if the heuristic does not work as expected but produces unexpected (!) differences:

> [If the researcher] finds that there are great differences or indeed diametrically opposite results, he should be warned and go back to check again whether the terms in which he posed his original question were indeed purely functional, and whether he has spread the net of his researches quite wide enough.[101]

Rodolfo Sacco, usually not listed among the mainstream scholars of functionalism, advised an exorcism of difference:

> [Conceptual] categories are different in various countries and lawyers in these countries do nothing to free themselves from these differences. The contrasts we have before us exist in taxonomy qualifications, languages, descriptions, explanations and concepts. They do not exist however in the operating rules. The task of the scholars is then that of comparing, and then banishing and exorcising these absurd conceptual contrasts.[102]

Considering that diversity is likely to provide some intellectual excitement in comparative legal studies (which is not to say that similarities can be disregarded), Sacco's advice should rather be turned on the method (or 'methoid') he tries to defend. It is a sorry comfort as one of the leading functionalists conceded recently:

---

100 Michaels 'The Functional Method,' 363.

101 Zweigert and Kötz *Introduction*, 40.

102 Sacco, Rodolfo (2001) 'Diversity and Uniformity in the Law' 49 *American Journal of Comparative Law*, 171, 188.

> [The functional approach] also has the disadvantage that it sometimes distracts from the truly interesting and important questions. For it can be compared with a 'black box,' into which the 'problem' is inserted [at] the one end, and which spits out the 'solution' at the other. What really happens within the 'black box' receives little attention, and is not particularly important for the principle of functionality. However, sometimes the solutions are not as interesting as the procedure by which they are generated.[103]

Therefore one is tempted to rethink whether functionalism should indeed be rated as 'comparative law's principal gift to the twentieth century'[104] (unless that gift can be qualified) at least as long as functionalists use a streetcar named similarity and refrain somewhat from elaborating their presuppositions, preoccupations and frames of comparative practice.[105]

5. FROM FUNCTIONALISM TO FACTUALISM: IN SEARCH OF COMMON CORES

The success story of functionalism does not end in textbooks and monographic studies but spills over into legal consulting and legal engineering. From the very beginning in the 1920s, some of the functionalist – Ralf Michaels characterizes them as teleological functionalists[106] – supported projects for the unification or at least harmonization of laws. The search for common concepts, transnational rules, a world law even, dates back to the 1900 Paris Congress. And while functionalism has not always dominated unitary legal thought and programs, it has been a 'factor' since the 1920s,[107] notably in Europe but also in Restatement projects in the United States.

Recurrent attempts in Europe to unify first and foremost private law, lately also criminal law and administrative law, testify to a significant functionalist influence, starting with *UNIDROIT* and continued under the auspices of the European Union by the *Lando Commission*, the *von Bar*

---

[103] Kötz, Hein (1998) 'Abschied von der Rechtskreislehre?' 6 *Zeitschrift für Europäisches Privatrecht*, 493, 505.

[104] Quoted by Palmer 'From Lerotholi to Lando,' 270.

[105] See Geertz, Clifford (1983) *Local Knowledge: Further Essays in Interpretive Anthropology*, New York: Basic Books.

[106] Michaels 'The Functional Method,' 376; see also Dannemann 'Similarities and Differences,' 402.

[107] Palmer 'From Lerotholi to Lando,' 270; Dannemann 'Similarities and Differences.'

Study Group and the *Trento Group* to name only some of the more influential endeavors.[108]

The Trento Group was constituted in 1993 and has since moved to Torino. In 2005, it became part of the 'network of excellence.' Ever since the early days, the members of the group have been untiringly searching for a Common Core of European private law, first in the legal regimes of the initially thirteen and today 27 member-states.[109] The group deserves special attention because of its endurance, productivity, visibility, and especially its methodological claims, based on a peculiar combination of functionalism, structuralism and factualism.

Quite strikingly, the Trento Group combined functionalism with Rodolfo Sacco's structural approach that became known as the analysis of 'legal formants,'[110] and with the factualism they borrowed from Rudolf Schlesinger's Cornell Project *Formation of Contracts. A Study of the Common Core of Legal Systems.*[111] Schlesinger and Sacco were appropriately named their godfathers:

> As from our origins we many times stated in very simple, almost naïve terms, the 'Common Core' research, developed at Cornell back in the nineteen sixties and applied to European Private Law seeks to unearth the common core of the bulk of European Private Law, within the general categories of

[108] For an overview of the different study groups, commissions, and committees, see Zimmermann, Reinhard (2006) 'Comparative Law and the Europeanization of Private Law' in *Oxford Handbook*, 539.

[109] An interesting account of the early Common Core search is given by Vernon Palmer, who had been the coordinator of the group at that time, together with Mauro Bussani; later Ugo Mattei became his successor. Palmer 'From Lerotholi to Lando,' 267–270. See also Bussani, Mauro and Mattei, Ugo eds (2000) *Making European Law. Essays on the Common Core Project*, Trento: Università degli Studi; Bussani, Mauro and Mattei, Ugo eds (2002) *The Common Core of European Private Law. Essays on the Project*, The Hague: Kluwer; and Bussani, Mauro and Mattei, Ugo eds (2007) *Opening Up European Law. The Common Core Project towards Eastern and South Eastern Europe*, Bern: Stämpfli Publishers.

[110] In particular Rodolfo Sacco's analysis of legal formants: Sacco, Rodolfo (1991) 'Legal Formants. A Dynamic Approach to Comparative Law' 39 *American Journal of Comparative Law* 1, 343. See also Mattei, Ugo and Bussani, Mauro 'Preface: The Context' in Bussani, Mauro and Mattei, Ugo eds *The Common Core*, 2.

[111] Schlesinger, Rudolf (1968) *Formation of Contracts. A Study of the Common Core of Legal Systems*, Dobbs Ferry, NY: Oceana.

> Contract, Tort, and Property. The search is for what is different and what is already common behind the various legal forms of European Union Member States.[112]

Rudolf Schlesinger once described his Common Core Project as a program to seek to 'redirect the emphasis of Comparative Law toward similarity rather than difference.'[113] Considering that the Trento founders stated that Schlesinger's methodology is 'encoded in the cultural DNA of each participant,'[114] their desire for difference should not be overrated. On the contrary, the obvious dissimilarity between the US context of Schlesinger's project and the European context of their Common Core search – plurality of legal regimes and languages, national histories and systems of governance, and so on – argue against the applicability or easy transfer of Schlesinger's method to the European setting. And the little critical reflection dedicated by the Trentoes to this contextual difference betrays an 'ideology of similarity' on their part[115] rather than skepticism and a keen interest in difference, notwithstanding their reverse proclamations:

> We do not wish to force the actual diverse reality of the law within one single map to attain uniformity ... While we believe that cultural diversity in the law is an asset, we do not wish to take a preservationist approach. Nor do we wish to push in the direction of uniformity.[116]

> The end product is not a set of rules but a potentially rich collection of parallels, partial correspondences and puzzles.[117]

By contrast, what Rodolfo Sacco called the 'ideology of difference' quite apparently has to be rejected by a group of legal advisors or consultants

---

[112] Bussani, Mauro (2007) 'Preface' in Bussani and Mattei eds *Opening Up European Law*, xiii, xiv.

[113] Schlesinger, Rudolf (1995) 'The Past and Future of Comparative Law' 43 *American Journal of Comparative Law*, 477, 479.

[114] Bussani, Mauro and Mattei, Ugo (1997) 'The Common Core Approach to European Private Law' 3 *Columbia Journal of European Law*, 339.

[115] I herewith reverse Sacco's 'ideology of difference'; Sacco 'Diversity and Uniformity,' 180. See also Grosswald Curran, Vivian 'On the Shoulders of Schlesinger: The Common Core of European Private Law Project' in Bussani and Mattei eds *Opening Up European Law*, 1, 3.

[116] Bussani and Mattei 'Preface: The Context,' 2; Bussani and Mattei 'The Common Core Approach to European Private Law'; Frankenberg 'Critical Comparisons,' 416–426.

[117] Gordley 'Mapping Private Law' in Bussani and Mattei eds *Making European Law*, 61.

pursuing a law-making project: constructing a Common Core for EU private law. They have to insist that the way (legal) things are in the various member-states of the EU are communicable, translatable, understandable. Or they have to claim, as do the Trentoes, that their project is scholarly rather than legal-political.

As a matter of fact, this is what can be inferred from the structure of the group – individual rapporteurs from the member-states were and are supervised by editors who report to the chief coordinators – and, more significantly, from what was presented as the Common Core method by one of the coordinators of the 'first hour' concerning one of the first studies 'to emerge under the banner of the Common Core in Trento, Italy … entitled 'Pure Economic Loss in Europe' (and has been confirmed in many later publications by others):

> The research was undertaken in 1996 by an international team of 20 scholars. The study was coordinated and edited by Mauro Bussani and Vernon Palmer and examined the subject from the standpoint of 13 systems within the European Union. Generally the individual rapporteurs were nationals of the country they reported upon and were specialists in the field of torts. They were in most cases comparative lawyers or at least familiar with other systems and well aware of the pitfalls of ethnocentricity. … In initial meetings at Trento, the entire team acted as a committee of the whole draft and devised a series of twenty hypotheticals which became the basis of the Questionnaire. The specific cases explored diverse angles of pure economic loss, but neither the words 'pure economic loss' nor any equivalent term was ever employed in the hypotheticals. This is in accordance with the Schlesinger–Cornell factual method which attempts to gather comparable answers to identical questions by developing, as far as possible, neutral, culture-free cases that allow an opportunity for each rapporteur to frame the solution in term of his or her national legal system … The significant merit of the factual approach is that it eliminates, or at least reduces, the distortion which occurs when normative terminology of one system is allowed to take over the framework of the enquiry. Instead of theory determining data, the Trento projects permits data to be extracted with minimal interference from preconceived theory. Of course, it still may be said that in the election of the facts, that is, in the selection of the problem itself, normative assumptions are inevitably made. Indeed, it can be claimed that the legal representation of fact is normative from the start.[118]

---

[118] Palmer 'From Lerotholi to Lando,' 268–269.

Neutrality and objectivity, facticity and reliability form the Common Core's magic quadrangle. From a critical perspective it is like a 'Bermuda Quadrangle,' where methodological insights get lost. This quadrangle delineates both the project's mantra and the members' creed. They hope to secure neutrality by a basically non-prescriptive and, they claim, politically agnostic practice. In the spirit of innocence, Rodolfo Sacco framed the neutrality principle rather broadly: 'With regard to the unification of the law, comparative science is neutral.'[119] Objectivity is to be secured by a narrow focus on concepts, categories and their interrelations; in short, on knowledge. Facticity characterizes the philosophy underlying the factual approach: the relentless search for and compilation of facts and nothing but facts. On the basis of the 'factual nature of the method' the Trento Group then proceeded to uncover the 'complex tensions and interplay between various legal formants … Operative Rules [how judges decide a case], Descriptive Formants [asking for reasons given by lawyers in support of operative rules], and Metalegal Formants [referring to broader elements, such as policy considerations, philosophical premises, social values etc.].'[120]

Reliability figures repeatedly as the Common Core searchers' ultimate standard for the production of information and knowledge.

> [They want to] obtain at least the main lines of a *reliable* geographical 'map' of the law of Europe. … This project seeks only to analyze the present complex situation in a *reliable* way. … In order to perform such a *reliable* drafting, we need the more sophisticated tools of comparative law.[121]

Hence, they trust that the 'magic four,' as an integrated, interconnected system of theoretical-methodological principles, complemented by the researchers' good intentions, will chill any desire to participate in the rush towards a European *ius commune* for contracts, torts and property.

By focusing on (hypothetical) cases they follow the tracks of Sacco's structuralist positivism and appear to be aware of the limits of their factual method:

> [A] list, even an exhaustive one, of all the reasons given for the decisions made by the courts is not the entire law. Neither are the statutes the entire law,

---

119 Sacco, Rodolfo (2000) 'One Hundred Years of Comparative Law' 75 *Tulane Law Review*, 1159, 1162.

120 *Ibid.*

121 Bussani and Mattei 'The Common Core Approach to European Private Law,' 340 – emphasis added. For an incisive critique of the map metaphor see Michaels, Ralf (2001) 'Common Core?' (unpublished, on file with author).

> nor the definitions of legal doctrines given by scholars. In order to know what the law is, Sacco's reasoning continues, it is necessary to analyze the entire complex relationship among what he calls the 'legal formants' of a system ... All these formative elements are not necessarily coherent with each other within each system. Only domestic jurists assume such coherence. To the contrary, a system's legal formants are usually conflicting and can better be pictured in a competitive relationship with one another.
>
> For example, we must not only know how courts have acted but we must also consider the influences to which the judges may be subject. Such influences may have a variety of origins. They may arise because scholars have given wide support to a doctrinal innovation, but they may also concern the judge's individual background. A judge appointed from an academic position will likely tend to put more stress on scholarly opinion than a judge who has always practiced law. The actual text of a statute is another of these influences ... All this, however, may still be insufficient to understand the law in a given system.[122]

The Trento Group reacted to such complexity with a 'factor analysis,' which consists in an effort

> ... to ascertain the factors that affect those solutions. This clarifies the weight that interpretive practices (grounded on scholarly writings, on legal debate aroused by previous judicial decisions etc.) have in moulding the actual outcomes.[123]

They address the obvious problem of identifying and weighing all the relevant 'factors' with resort to their 'Instructions About how to Answer the Questionnaires' that distinguish 'General Guidelines,' 'Level I. Operative Rules,' 'Level II. Descriptive Formants' and 'Level III. Metalegal Formants' without establishing a retraceable relationship between these levels.[124] While these levels are meant to structure the research process, the researchers fail to address, let alone solve the problem of weighing and interpretation and therefore cannot make the impression of reductionism disappear.

More importantly, they do not answer the more general question about whether and how they go about the management of differences, notably the transfer of concrete diversity to abstract commonality such as 'problems' or 'solutions.' Their non-functionalist rhetoric may very well correspond to the factual approach, however, it is incompatible with the

---

122 Bussani and Mattei 'The Common Core Approach to European Private Law,' 339–340.

123 *Ibid.*

124 *Ibid.*, Appendix 1.

'operative rules' and 'legal formants' geared toward finding solutions in a given legal system.

The notion of 'fact' constitutes the centerpiece of the Common Core search. It is here that critical approaches[125] find a lot to do:

> The place of fact in a world of judgment, to tack now for a while in the jural direction (as well as to abuse a famous title), has been something of a vexed question since the Greeks raised it with their grand opposition of nature and convention; but in modern times, when *physis* and *nomos* no longer seem such unmixed realities and there seems somehow so much more to know, it has become a chronic focus of legal anxiety. Explosion of fact, fear of fact and, in response to these, sterilization of fact confound increasingly both the practice of law and the reflection upon it.[126]
>
> [L]aw functions as much within the world of facts as within the world of law and it is this dual role that endows it with its capacity to create virtual facts. Lawyers, like scientists, do not work directly on reality but construct rationalized models of this reality, and it is these models that become the 'objects' of legal discourse.[127]

While the Trentoes bravely plod through what they consider 'natural' facts and grasp the factual world out there, they resort to what Geertz would have called the 'sterilisation of fact,' oblivious to their own fact-making. They start their fact-making mission with a questionnaire, their 'key tool,'[128] plus guidelines for answering the questionnaires. Like in the above-mentioned project on 'pure economic loss,' these questionnaires are composed of hypothetical cases, some based on court decisions, complemented by questions, variations and explanatory notes.

> This method should guarantee that rules are formulated in an identical way (by using an identical code provision, for instance), but which may produce

[125] Regarding fact-making see only Latour, Bruno (2002) *La Fabrique du Droit: Une Ethnographie du Conseil d'Etat*, Paris: La Découverte; Riles, Annelise (2006) 'Comparative Law and Socio-Legal Studies' in *Oxford Handbook*, 801, 804–812; and Samuel, Geoffrey (2004) 'Epistemology and Methodology of Comparative Law: Contributions from the Sciences and Social Sciences' in van Hoecke, Mark ed. *Epistemology and Methodology of Comparative Law*, Oxford: Hart Publishing.

[126] Geertz, Clifford (1983) *Local Knowledge: Further Essays in Interpretive Anthropology*, New York: Basic Books, 170–171.

[127] Samuel 'Epistemology and Methodology of Comparative Law,' 74.

[128] Bussani, Mauro (1998) 'Current Trends in European Comparative Law: The Common Core Approach' 21 *Hastings International and Comparative Law Review*, 785.

> different applications, or even different commentator rhetoric, that will not be regarded as identical. It should also identify the elements that may play an official and declared role in one system yet work in a more cryptic, unsystematic and unofficial way in another system.[129]

The Common Core method is illustrated, for instance, by the 'Questionnaire on Personality Rights in European Tort Law.' It lists, under No. 8, the famous case of Caroline, Princess of Monaco, whose personality rights were at the heart of a string of decisions leading up to the German Federal High Court of Justice and later to the German Federal Constitutional Court as well as the European Court of Human Rights:

> With a strong telephoto lens, a paparazzo took a photo of a famous princess, sitting in the garden of her private villa together with her new lover and her little son. The picture was published on the cover of a tabloid, under the heading: 'The Princess' New Family.'
>
> a) Can the princess skim off the profits the magazine earned due to the publication of her photo? If yes, is the magazine under a duty to disclose the necessary information?
> b) Would it make a difference if the princess was not sitting at home, but in the back garden of a countryside restaurant?[130]

The *Caroline* case and the questions relating to its private law substance are *designed* to guide the participants and reporters into the jungle of the (German) torts regime where the legal formants concerning personality rights will then be duly investigated. The fabricated 'elements at work' – norms, precedents and doctrinal-legal reasoning – are then 'unearthed.' The researcher will ultimately either qualify them as part and parcel of the Common Core of European tort law or consider them as peculiarities of the German tort regime.

The fabrication of fact works as follows. Very much like its siblings listed in this and other questionnaires of the Common Core Project, Case No. 8 (*Caroline*) of the altogether 19 cases covering the 'Personality Rights in European Tort Law' was first taken from the tort jurisprudence, then stripped of its complex narrative and skeletonized for the questionnaire to bring to the fore what the researchers regarded as the relevant (tort) aspects – rules, principles, precedents and doctrines. Finally, in the further process of the project work, the case was re-introduced into the

---

129 *Ibid.*

130 Brüggemeier, Gert and Colombi Ciacchi, Aurelia (2002) *Common Core of European Private Law: Torts. Questionnaire on Personality Rights in European Tort Law*, September.

various regimes of tort law via the questions posed in the questionnaire to stimulate the identification of similarities and differences. If one follows the questionnaire rationale, it comes as a surprise that crucial facets or 'factors' of the 'case,' even if narrowly construed – in particular Princess Caroline's status as a member of Monaco's 'ruling family' and her public function as representative of that family regime or a public welfare institution – are not included in the questionnaire. Without prior knowledge of the doctrinal concept of a 'relative public persona' or 'absolute public persona' one would not be able to answer how she could be protected against paparazzo attacks.

So the factual method's fabrication and sterilization of fact confounds the practice of law and reflection upon it. For the questionnaires reduce facts to legal facts and, in a second step, 'to the genre capacities of the law,' that is, to legal provisions and cases, doctrines and commentaries. While part of this reduction of complexity may be 'unavoidable and necessary,'

> it grows increasingly tenuous as empirical complexity ... and the fear of such complexity grows, a phenomenon that has rather seriously disquieted a number of prominent legal thinkers ... and a far larger number of plaintiffs and defendants made suddenly aware that whatever it is that the law is after is not the whole story.[131]

Aside from the fragmentary nature of the Common Core stories, their conception of what constitutes a fact is even more problematic. Their programmatic texts proclaim that the research focuses merely and exclusively on 'raw facts' as generated, in the context of a case, by courts, scholars, legal institutions, etc. One may infer that the members of the group know for a fact what is a fact and that they locate facts in a reality they find fairly easy to read because they translate it (without ever using that word) into questionnaires. The Common Core researchers believe they *participate* in the *real*, rather than constructing, representing and translating the *possible*. Thus, the philosophical twin peaks of facticity and objectivity make them fall prey to an epistemologically all too innocent vision of their Common Core research and prevent them from realizing 'that legal facts are made, not born, are socially

---

[131] Geertz *Local Knowledge*, 172–173. See also Frank, Jerome (1930) *Law and the Modern Mind*, New York: Brentano's Publishing; Noonan, John T. (2002) *Persons and Masks of the Law: Cardozo, Holmes, Jefferson, and Whyte as Makers of the Masks*, Berkeley and Los Angeles: University of California Press.

constructed,'[132] in particular by legal traditions and styles, judicial techniques, conventions of legal reasoning, the scholasticism of legal education, and, quite apparently, also by the paradigms of comparative law and research designs for comparative legal studies.

For this conclusion to be proven wrong, one would have to expect the Trentoes not only to match fact-situations with norms, rules or principles but rather to state clearly that 'fact-configurations are not merely things found lying about in the world and carried bodily into court, show-and-tell-style, but close-edited diagrams of reality the matching process itself produces.'[133] They could do so, according to Clifford Geertz, by acknowledging that they deal with representations calling for interpretation rather than brute facts:

> It is, of course, not sleight-of-hand, or anyway not usually, but a rather more fundamental problem, the one in fact upon which all culture rests: namely, that of representation. The rendering of fact so that lawyers can plead it, judges can hear it, and juries can settle it is just that, a rendering: as any other trade, science, cult, or art, law, which is a bit of all of these, propounds the world in which its descriptions make sense ... [T]he point here is that the 'law' side of things is not a bounded set of norms, rules, principles, values, or whatever from which jural responses to distilled events can be drawn, but part of a distinctive manner of imagining the real. At base, it is not what happened, but what happens, that law sees; and if law differs, from this place to that, this time to that, this people to that, what it sees does as well.[134]

To be able to recognize this as a *problem* and then cope with it, the Trentoes would have to expand Sacco's theory of legal formants and shift from their philosophy of facticity and objectivity to a constitutive or formative theory of law. There is not much evidence in their programmatic manifestoes, however, of their willingness to embark upon such a theoretical-methodological enterprise. Nor do they appear to be prepared to part with their rather tenuous prescriptive/descriptive distinction nor would they admit that '[t]he legal representation of fact is normative from the start'[135] and then address the problem of how such representation of fact can itself be adequately represented. To mention in passing, the 'post-modern condition' and to acknowledge the 'renewed consciousness' concerning the impossibility of neutrality and of a 'merely descriptive'

132 Geertz, *Local Knowledge*, 173 also concerning the following passages.
133 *Ibid.*
134 *Ibid.*
135 *Ibid.*, 174.

comparative approach[136] hardly suffices to immunize the project against critique. As will be shown in the following chapter, the Trentoes come with an *always already* toned down reformist agenda (politics!) that complements and contradicts the seemingly empirical and non-political 'cartography.' To quote one of their godfathers first:

> Those who compare legal systems are always asked about the purpose of such comparisons. The idea seems to be that the study of foreign legal systems is a legitimate enterprise only if it results in proposals for the reform of domestic law.[137]
>
> [T]he 'common core' research *may be a useful instrument for legal harmonization*, in the sense that it provides *reliable* data to be used in devising new common solutions that may prove workable in practice. Be that as it may, the latter goal has nothing to do with the common core research in itself, which is devoted to produce *reliable* information, *whatever its policy use may be*.[138]

Contrary to evidence, the leaders of the group made sure the Common Core Project would not be understood as an attempt to force the private law systems of the EU member-states into the Procrustean bed of harmonization:

> In using at the beginning of our journey the metaphor of cartography we have certainly tried to convey a message of neutrality and skepticism, locating our comparative work in the domain of the 'is' rather than of the 'ought.'[139]

Still, the modest claim that by searching for and digging out (method!) the Common Core, all they want is to 'obtain at least the main lines of a *reliable* geographical 'map' of the law of Europe,'[140] appears like a rather

---

[136] Bussani and Mattei, *Preface: The Context*, 2.

[137] Sacco 'Legal Formants,' 1–2.

[138] Bussani and Mattei 'Preface' in *The Common Core*, 4.

[139] Bussani and Mattei 'Preface' in *The Common Core*, 4 – emphasis added; also: 'The "Common Core" Project *has been requested* to apply its methodologies of factual approach and dissociation of legal formants to the results of [the] "legislative activity" [sponsored by the European Commission], in order to assess the operational impact such Principles [on European Contract Law] might have on legal outcomes in the different European legal cultures.' ('Preface,' viv [Fn. 3]). One of the other influential members stated the obvious: 'The Trento Common Core Project is an ambitious search for unity in private law.' Gordley, James (2000) 'Mapping Private Law' in Bussani and Mattei *Making European Law*, 61.

[140] Bussani and Mattei 'The Common Core Approach to European Private Law,' 340; Bussani and Mattei eds (2003) *The Common Core – Essays*;

empty gesture. The strategies of producing reliable information and gaining more knowledge 'whatever its policy use may be,' etc. point toward the false modesty of a comparative enterprise whose members have yet to call into question objectivity and neutrality, facticity and reliability, and have to consider the political context of their work.

Neither driven by a headhunters' rage[141] nor the treasure-hunters' greed, the Trentoes only (?) demonstrate the cognitive cannibals' appetite for 'reliable information.' What is more, unlike conquistadores, they are willing to share their spoils with the academic community to found a European law school.

6. STRUCTURING THE COMPARATIVE SPACE: DISTANCING AND DIFFERENCING AS METHOD

Comparatists study and compare foreign laws. How can the fallacies of the diverse approaches, in particular Anglo-Eurocentric 'othering' of the foreign, false universalisms, and strategic comparison, be avoided? The twin operations of *d/d* may help. In the following I argue that *d/d* structures the dialectic of learning[142] by comparing.

Distancing

In legal comparison *distancing* deals with the foreign from the comparatist's position and perspective.[143] It is an attempt to recognize what is not addressed to one-self and therefore remains foreign, strange, other, but is situated in the same comparative space. *Distancing* requires that the comparatist gives up the traditional armchair-approach as observer and undertakes the paradoxical task of bringing the other very close 'without

---

Frankenberg, Günter (2007) 'How to Do Projects with Comparative Law. Notes of an Expedition to the Common Core' in Bussani and Mattei eds *Opening Up European Law*, 17.

141 Rosaldo, Renato (1993) 'Introduction: Grief and a Headhunter's Rage' in *Culture and Truth. The Remaking of Social Analysis*, Boston: Beacon Press.

142 Learning about foreign legal regimes and cultures as well as one's own legal regime and culture.

143 For a different but related concept of distance see Butler, Judith (2002) 'What is Critique? An Essay on Foucault's Virtue' in Ingram, David ed. *The Political Readings in Continental Philosophy*, London: Basil Blackwell, 212.

becoming any less far away.'[144] This epistemological 'move' acknowledges and respects the foreign-ness of the foreign and abstains from its mindless domestication. To put it somewhat cryptically, distancing accepts the otherness of the 'other' without *othering* it:

> Distance is needed to gain a vantage on who we are and what we are doing and thinking. Distancing can be described as an attempt to break away from firmly held beliefs and settled knowledge and as an attempt to resist the power of prejudice and ignorance. From a distance old knowledge can be reviewed and new knowledge can be distinguished as it is in its own right. Distance de-centers our world-view and thus establishes what might be called objectivity.[145]

A comparatist trained in and committed to distancing will not simply subsume the information about the foreign to the old and settled knowledge but try to see it in its 'untranslated form'[146] so as to emulate 'the vision of the participants.'[147] Thus, distancing addresses the dilemma of understanding foreign cultures of law without being able to completely transcend the hermeneutic framework and cognitive matrix provided by the domestic culture. 'This dilemma can neither be resolved by 'going rational' nor by 'going native''[148] but possibly by always approaching and never 'pinning down' the other and by constantly repositioning the self: The comparatist 'must render the foreign familiar and, *uno actu*, preserve its very foreignness.'[149] In Chapter 5 of this volume the analysis of the (legal) discourse on Muslim veiling is meant to illustrate the multitasking it takes to bring the other very close 'without becoming any less far away' and thereby to suspend the othering power of the sovereign self.

---

[144] Geertz, Clifford (1983) 'Found in Translation' in Geertz ed. *Local Knowledge*, 36, 48.

[145] Frankenberg 'Critical Comparisons,' 414.

[146] Grosswald Curran 'Cultural Immersion,' 43.

[147] Methodological slogan of the Leyden School of Anthropology, quoted by Palmer 'From Lerotholi to Lando,' 266. See also Geertz, Clifford (2000) 'Thick Description: Toward an Interpretive Theory of Culture' in Geertz ed. *The Interpretation of Cultures*, 2nd ed., New York: Basic Books.

[148] Frankenberg 'Critical Comparisons,' 415.

[149] Crapanzano, Vincent (1986) 'Hermes' Dilemma: The Masking of Subversion in Ethnographic Description' in Clifford, James and Marcus, George E. eds *Writing Culture: The Poetics and Politics of Ethnography*, 52.

Differencing

By contrast, *differencing* brings the comparatist as interpreter of the foreign into the picture. It recognizes the hermeneutical problem of comparison. This strategy copes with the pull of settled knowledges and sabotages the yen to see similarity. It is a necessary condition for perceiving the (legal) other at eye-level and in its own right, which means as an empirically different phenomenon, and accordingly 'do[ing] justice to the singularity of the laws that are other than one's "own."'[150]

> Mere distance, however, neither opens our eyes nor makes us see clearly. As long as foreign places only look like or unlike home, as long as foreign legal cultures only appear to be un-common or uncivil, and as long as they are treated as same or other, they do not speak for themselves. In order to break the unconscious spell that holds us to see others by the measure of ourselves without abandoning the benefits of criticism, traveling as well as comparison has to be an exercise in difference.[151]

By *differencing* comparatists take on the fact that they do not view the phenomena they study from 'nowhere in particular.'[152] Instead, due to their education and training, they are intensely preoccupied with the systems and families, concepts and norms of the local legal culture and experience they have been accustomed to consider domestic or (misleadingly) 'own.'[153] In other words, comparatists operate and observe within the boundaries of a *particular* context and interpret what they see within a *particular* matrix provided by a specific cultural context that constitutes law and is also constituted by law:

> It is no mystery that law is part of culture, but it is not uncommon for those who, by profession or context, are deeply involved in a given legal system to act as if 'The Law' is quite separable from other elements of cultural life.[154]

---

[150] Legrand 'Siting Foreign Law,' 600.

[151] Frankenberg 'Critical Comparisons,' 414; see also Grosswald Curran 'Cultural Immersion.'

[152] In a fascinating study of our divided nature, Thomas Nagel distinguished our ability to transcend interest and our own experience from our subjectivity and context-dependence: Nagel, Thomas (1989) *The View from Nowhere*, Oxford: Oxford University Press.

[153] Obviously, the connotation of possession is misleading.

[154] Rosen, Lawrence (2006) *Law as Culture: An Invitation*, Princeton: Princeton University Press, 6.

> The comparative investigator must hope to keep a certain distance from his own culture and prejudice, from the society under study, and from the biases of his informants.[155]

As a matter of consequence, comparatists do not describe and compare neutrally or objectively what they see and read but come to the foreign with a bias, pre-understanding and purpose informed by the 'own' (or self). In general, the 'how compare' is shaped by a 'why compare': purpose infiltrates perspective. Often utility takes the lead: let's compare how the other can help improve the domestic law or deepen the insights of law students at home. Or legal comparison may be guided by a more mundane and practical concern. What kind of comparative law course-book sells best in the West? Authors whose textbook was included in the 'American Casebook Series' found that

> [their West European colleagues] quite *naturally* have tended to focus on those elements of these three legal traditions [civil law, common law, and socialist law] that are of interest from the perspective of the European scholar, [whereas] our course-book is written from and for the viewpoint of the American trained lawyer.[156]

Legal unification or harmonization projects have a different market and look out for other spoils. In another modality of innocence, they pursue the question of whether the comparative method can identify a Common Core of legal principles that would lend itself to the harmonization of, say, European private law.

Regardless of the market, purpose or orientation, mainstream comparatists routinely inscribe into the foreign the legal matrix of the Western 'own' (or self). Textbook authors, such as the ones mentioned above, *innocently* believe, for example:

> [I]t is important for American law students to develop a more refined appreciation of the ways in which Soviet law is still 'Western' as an understanding of its distinctiveness.[157]

And most scholars agree that, for all their differences, at least two of the Western legal families, civil and common law, 'have one important trait in common. They are all thoroughly secularized; norms as well as

---

155 Palmer 'From Lerotholi to Lando,' 267.

156 Glendon, Mary Ann, Gordon, Michael W. and Osakwe, Christopher (1985) *Comparative Legal Traditions. Text, Materials and Case*, St. Paul: West Publishing, xvii – emphasis added.

157 *Ibid.*, xviii.

procedures have shed all sacral characteristics. The "legal formalism" ... which pervades all of Western legal families can serve a variety of regimes and ideological ends.'[158] Whether socialist law should be included in the West, remains a matter of controversy.[159] In his monumental *Law and Revolution*, Harold Berman operates quite forcefully with the concept of the 'West' as 'a cultural term' designating 'a community' characterized by 'both a historical structure and a structured history.'[160] In the same vein, comparatists make sure they do not 'dwell too much on the detailed differences in legal classifications.'[161] While they disagree on the number of distinguishing features of Western law – offering one (Ehrmann), four (Berman), nine (Sawer) or more features – and on whether to look for single criteria or an aggregate legal style, that is 'the totality of features which flesh out a distinctive form of legal system,'[162] they do agree on the existence of the Western law, legal family, system or tradition and its unproblematic utility for comparative study.

To disrupt this perspectival dominance and to break the (unconscious) spell of the Western common/civil law culture, *distancing/differencing* calls on the comparatist to decenter her worldview and to consciously establish subjectivity and context in the comparative space, that is, to take into account the observer's perspective. Only then *may* the comparatist *be able* to transgress the borders and the pull of the familiar/accustomed/own system and experience and perceive the differences 'out there.' Transcending the borders of the cognitive and the interpretative order of the self/own is not an easy thing to do and success is not guaranteed. The rationalist and the relativist both address this problem with rigor but fail to produce a convincing solution:

> The rigorous rationalist who relies on conceptual or evolutionary functional universals is prone to give her world-view and norms, her language and biases only a different label. In the end, she may bring home from her comparative enterprise nothing but dead facts and living errors, the progeny of ethnocentrism. The rigorous relativist who naively deludes herself into believing that cultural baggage and identities can be dropped at will, is prone to

---

[158] Ehrmann *Comparative Legal Cultures*, 17.

[159] For references see Glendon et al. *Comparative Legal Traditions*, 15.

[160] Berman, Harold J. (1983) *Law and Revolution: The Formation of the Western Legal Tradition*, Cambridge, MA: Harvard University Press, 17.

[161] Sawer, Geoffrey (1975) 'The Western Conception of Law' in David et al. *International Encyclopedia of Comparative Law*, Vol. II, Tübingen and The Hague: Mohr Siebeck, Chapter 1, § II.

[162] Zweigert and Kötz *Introduction*, 61–65.

> oscillate between ventriloquism and mystification. As a cultural ventriloquist, she would reproduce ethnocentrism under the guise of a pseudo-authentic understanding. As a cultural immigrant she might over-identify with the mystified new way and thereby be unable or unwilling to relate anything her sympathetic eye happens upon in travel to what she learns at home.[163]

Instead, comparatists have to learn to navigate the divide between the foreign and the familiar. Their learning process can be fortunate if they achieve a mix of 'long-distance mind reading'[164] and close-up description. Success or failure can be measured against the awareness that comparison is a construction and the caution not to cannibalize difference by exposing foreign laws and reducing their singularity.[165]

D/d are prerequisites of the work of cultural translation.[166] They challenge comparatists' claims to neutrality (of methods and criteria applied) and universality (of theoretical categories and concepts used) as well as the comparatist's independence from context and perspective. Cultural translation also dismisses the notion, entertained by orthodox comparatists, that the categories and concepts they use to classify and compare new/strange phenomena have nothing whatsoever to do with the socio-cultural environment they were trained and work in.[167]

D/d as crucial, constitutive elements of translation – to see, read, and interpret the way things are in their own terms – invite the comparatist to embark upon a demanding and exciting, intellectual enterprise that appears to be (yet, strictly speaking, is not) paradoxical. This enterprise begins with a critique of the assumption that comparison along the lines drawn by the cognitive patterns of one's own – really our? – Western culture or, for that matter, any other particular culture, comes 'naturally.' Because of this one might want to question why a textbook for *Comparative* Law, written to be used in one of the North-American law schools, *needs* to anticipate the viewpoint of the American trained lawyer. Or why textbooks excel in the universalization of the Western particular and stabilize its hegemony by making sure that Western legal families/ traditions etc. come first without so much as even mentioning the

---

163 Frankenberg 'Critical Comparisons,' 415.

164 I borrow this expression from Geertz 'Thick Description,' 14.

165 See also Geertz 'Thick Description,' 14; Legrand 'Siting Foreign Law,' 600–601.

166 Geertz 'Thick Description,' 3–30.

167 Frankenberg 'Critical Comparison,' 414, also regarding the following. See also Geertz *The Interpretation of Cultures*; Wong, David (2006) *Natural Moralities. A Defense of Pluralistic Relativism*, Oxford: Oxford University Press.

problem of ethnocentrism. Authors seem to hope their work is – somehow, maybe magically – purged from perspectival distortion, ideological misreading and the cannibalization of difference, if only guided by what they believe is a neutral referent, whereas it is easy to see that the 'idea,' 'development' or 'function' of law, or more abstractly a 'social problem' functioning as *tertium comparationis*, as long as they are constructed within the Western (or civil/common law) matrix, are anything but neutral. They are 'constructs derived from Western legal discourse' applied to the study of non-Western law; 'these alien conceptual paradigms will influence the way in which we interpret the data we observe,'[168] that is to say, they represent the non-Western laws and traditions as subaltern to the West – as same, similar or derived from or with differences in detail compared to common or civil law.

When integrated into legal comparison, *d/d* help recognize the co-existence of the familiar/self and the foreign/other[169] in the same comparative space. They foreclose any easy retreat to the land of virtuous study, where 'pure' science and methods reign and legal comparison can be believed to be unproblematic. For they make the foreign/other highly visible and point to the ethical and political ramifications of the other's co-presence in the very space where comparatists do their work.

---

[168] Ainsworth 'Categories and Culture,' 23.

[169] See Shilliam, Robert (2006) 'The "other" in Classical Political Theory: Re-contextualizing the Cosmopolitan/Communitarian debate' in Jahn, Beate ed. *Classical Theory in International Relations*, Cambridge: Cambridge University Press, 207.

4. Orientalizing comparative law's occident

Mainstream and non-mainstream approaches to comparative legal studies are charted here, simplified for argument and contrast, by means of a 'grid' that conjoins internally related styles in distinct 'tracks.' The tracks re-present a (necessarily sketchy and incomplete) disciplinary map,[1] not a geography, which gives an overview of the intellectual landscape by visualizing the patterns of comparative rhetoric and practice. 'Tracking down' the diverse methods and theories as well as (and more importantly) the ethics and politics of comparative styles is meant to bring to the fore their situatedness[2] and context.

This way, the critical analysis of comparative law tunes into methodological debates in ethnography and anthropology and turns them on the operations of *distancing* and *differencing* (*d/d*). Thereby familiar comparative legal projects are treated like strange, some even exotic, practices[3] so as to both provincialize their generalizing and universalistic rhetoric and subvert their disciplinary hegemony.

1. THE SILENCE OF THE LAMBS

Mainstream comparatists consider 'good comparative practice' to be based on scientific method, touched up with theory. Ethics and politics seem to be anathema to them. Despite their focus on method, they demonstrate a remarkable unconcern about methodological questions that have plagued the neighboring sciences and have been discussed longer

[1] On mapping, disciplinary topography, and geographical imaginations, see Gregory, Derek (1994) *Geographical Imaginations*, Oxford: Basil Blackwell.

[2] See Said, Edward (1984) 'Traveling Theory' in *The World, the Text and the Critic*, London: Faber & Faber, 226.

[3] For a similar attempt at de-familiarizing, see Frankenberg, Günter (2007) 'How to Do Projects with Comparative Law – Notes of an Expedition to the Common Core' in Bussani, Mauro and Mattei, Ugo eds *Opening Up European Law*, Bern: Stämpfli, 17.

than Karl Marx's and Friedrich Engel's *The German Ideology* (1844/1845). Naïve assumptions of objectivity, neutrality, reliable information and truth reveal an astonishing aloofness from methodological and epistemological battles, which have been waged in disciplines with a 'natural' affinity to comparative law (in particular, history and anthropology, philosophy, sociology and legal theory).[4] These debates open up access from method to ethics and politics, but comparatists, in a state of denial,[5] cultivate their preoccupation with method and, along with it, the ambivalent legacy of scientism.[6]

Denial and silence encompass the internal, systematic relation between knowledge and power, that is, the political impact or agenda of comparative practice, and the circumstance that the co-presence of the foreign in the comparative space has ethical implications. A few examples discussed in the previous chapter could be repeated here. Taxonomies are presented as strictly scientific, with no political strings attached. Unification of law is introduced as a goal without political agenda or subtext.[7] Searching for Common Cores (say, of European contract, tort and property law) is promulgated as an enterprise to obtain 'reliable information' – disconnected from politics.[8] Whereas one of the leading textbooks cautiously indicates that the resources of comparing laws and legal systems 'can be used for a wide variety of practical and scholarly purposes,'[9] others present theories and methods, sources and concepts, functions and

---

[4] Regarding the positivism dispute and other controversies about method in the social sciences, see Davis Frisby's enlightening introduction to the English translation in: Adorno, Theodor W. et al. eds (1976) *The Positivist Dispute in German Sociology*, New York: Harper & Row. See also Giddens, Anthony ed. (1974) *Positivism and Sociology*, London: Ashgate and Wellmer, Albrecht (1971) *Critical Theory of Society*, New York: Herder & Herder. Comparatists could also have found the nineteenth century debates about method instructive: Menger, Carl (1963/1883) *Problems of Economics and Sociology*, Urbana: University of Illinois Press.

[5] The leading textbook still: Zweigert and Kötz (1998) *An Introduction to Comparative Law*, 3rd ed., Oxford: Clarendon Press, has nothing to say about positivism and anti-positivism in its chapters on theory and method.

[6] See Bannister, Robert (1987) *Sociology and Scientism*, Chapel Hill, NC: University of North Carolina Press.

[7] Zweigert and Kötz *Introduction*, 24–30.

[8] Bussani and Mattei have always insisted on the search for reliable information as the primary goal of their project. See Bussani and Mattei 'Preface' in *Opening Up European Law*, xvi.

[9] Schlesinger, Rudolf et al. (1998) *Comparative Law: Cases-Text-Materials*, 6th ed., New York: Foundation Press, 2.

historical developments of comparative law[10] but remain silent on ethics or politics. Similarly, the impressive *Oxford Handbook*, and the otherwise context-sensitive handbook edited by Nelken and Örücü, do not include an extended discussion of ethics and politics. The textbook on *Comparative Legal Traditions*,[11] written to be used in the classroom, manages to avoid ethical and political issues with a strictly legocentric conception. The mainstream seems to be preoccupied with and possibly entangled in law as a web of rules and principles produced and processed, in all countries, by an ensemble of autonomous institutions.

2. INTRODUCING THE GRID

It may very well be that the absence of ethics, politics and of a robustly critical methodological reflection may be an imagined deficit or one that does not affect the quality of comparative practice, though I doubt it. To make sure that this critique is not attacking a chimera but addresses comparative law's dark side, which 'lurks unseen behind'[12] the mantra of comparative law as method and as science, I introduce a grid, gleaned quite eclectically from an imaginary conversation among anthropologists and literary critics.[13] For the purpose of charting distinct and connecting

---

[10] E.g. Zweigert and Kötz *Introduction*; Schlesinger *Comparative Law*.

[11] Glendon, Mary Ann et al. *Comparative Legal Traditions*, St. Paul: West Publishing.

[12] I borrow this expression from Zweigert and Kötz's *Introduction*: 'The functional approach concentrates on the real life problem which often lurks unseen behind the concepts of the national systems.'

[13] The basic framework was inspired by an imaginary conversation among ethnographers and anthropologists, in particular Douglas, Mary (1982) 'Cultural Bias' in *In the Active Voice*, New York: Routledge, 183. I am aware of the criticism launched against Douglas' grid analysis but find it helpful anyway. See also Geertz, Clifford (1968) 'Thinking as a Moral Act: Ethical Dimensions of Anthropological Fieldwork in the New States' 28 *Antioch Review*, 139–158; Geertz, Clifford (1983) *Local Knowledge – Further Essays in Interpretive Anthropology*, 3rd ed., New York: Basic Books, especially the chapters: 'Found in Translation' (36–54) and 'From the Native's Point of View: On the Nature of Anthropological Understanding' (55–70); Jameson, Frederic (1979) 'Marxism and Historicism' 11 *New Literary Library*, 41, 67–73 (concerning the interpretive dilemma); Nader, Laura (1996) 'Anthropological Inquiry into Boundaries, Power, and Knowledge' in *Naked Science. Anthropological Inquiry into Boundaries, Power, and Knowledge*, New York: Routledge, 1–13; and, most importantly, the grid developed for the ethics of ethnographic practice by Conquergood, Dwight (2003) 'Performing as a Moral Act: Ethical Dimensions of the Ethnography of

styles of comparative law as discrete 'tracks,' as well as differentiating three dimensions, which, I believe, constitute their distinctness – (1) method/theory,[14] (2) ethics and (3) politics – I submitted the imagined conversation to intense *bricolage*. This way the ethnographic categories and experience were adapted to the intercultural performance of legal comparison. Moreover, I aligned the diverse comparative methods, in each track, with corresponding ethical and political concerns.

The tracks bundle up a variety of comparative approaches, marked by their peculiar method, ethics, and politics, in one of the four quadrants. Accordingly, each track covers a spectrum of ways to perform legal comparison. Therefore, one has to concede that the grid shares the typical shortcomings of any attempt at modeling reality: it is comprehensive in scope, penurious in detail and does not do justice to all the features of the comparative practices mentioned. However, on the bright side, the grid allows for transition and transfer between the diverse tracks and therefore brings into view hybrid modalities of comparison. At the outset, the four tracks are treated as sites where constitutive comparison[15] produces, on the basis of settled knowledge and available categories, as well as from a specific perspective, commensurable 'products,' that is legal systems and norms, institutions and arguments. The styles of constitutive comparison are represented graphically as four discrete and opposed comparative practices:

The (infinite) *horizontal axis* of the grid graphically represents the operation and challenge of *distancing*[16] introduced in the previous chapter. It turns the focus on the comparatist and her position and identity as an observer, or scientist who researches the foreign. *Detachment* and *commitment* demarcate the polar extremes of her method of obtaining knowledge about novel, unfamiliar, and strange, i.e. foreign, phenomena

---

Performance' in Lincoln, Yvonna S. and Denzin, Norman K. eds *Turning Points in Qualitative Research. Tying Knots in a Handkerchief*, Lanham, MD: AltaMira Press, 397.

[14] As the grid also comprises the dimension of method, the historical schools and their methodological orientation which I presented in the previous chapter reappear now in conjunction with their ethical and political dimension. Unfortunately, some redundancy cannot be avoided.

[15] Concerning the constitutive quality of theory and the perspective of comparison as construction, see Frankenberg 'Critical Comparisons' and 'Comparing Constitutions.'

[16] See Frankenberg 'Critical Comparisons,' 413–416; and Chapter 3 in this volume. Regarding perspective and epistemology see Esquirol, Jorge (2013) 'Legal Latin Americanism' 16 *Yale Human Rights and Development Law Journal*, 145.

that are not part of the culture misleadingly referred to as 'the own.' Towards the *detachment* pole, *distancing* prompts an observer's posture and perspective, which is underscored by the claim to objective, neutral, disinterested analyses and is turned into comparative practice by integrating all (legal) phenomena into the settled knowledge. Towards the opposite pole, *commitment* is marked by the concern that the foreign be perceived and treated in comparison, out of respect or appreciation, as a phenomenon in its own right.

Detachment/commitment render *distancing* more concrete for comparative practice. Only by resisting the counterpull of both detachment and commitment, can the comparatist break away from firmly held beliefs and suspend the grasp and power of any settled (or situated) knowledges, categories, and analytics, and challenge their certainty. This way, she may be able to mediate between the perspectives of observer and participant. However, de-centering one's world-view – or perspectivity – comes neither easily nor naturally. It requires self-reflection, doubt and recognition of the other as coexisting in the same comparative space. Other phenomena – laws, legal institutions, doctrines, etc. – have to be brought into focus and analyzed without familiarizing and domesticating them. In this way, *distancing* strikes an always uncertain balance between going native and staying Western, between bleeding-heart comparison and cold-reason comparison. If this move is successful, the newly acquired knowledge can be seen in its untranslated form. The other is brought very close without becoming any less far away. It remains foreign.

The horizontal axis, delimited by the polar opposites of *detachment* and *commitment*, digresses from the standard self-descriptions, advanced by comparatists, who routinely consider their work to be objective or neutral – either explicitly or by implication when they accentuate the search for truth, more knowledge or reliable information. I find the concept of *detachment* more telling with regard to positionality, rather than objectivity or neutrality. While neutrality, disinterestedness or the absence of bias – and innocence – can hardly be claimed for comparative law (after what sociology, legal realism and critical hermeneutics discovered about preconceptions, bias, and so on), objectivity[17] entertains a complex relationship with representing reality and truth that cannot easily be paired with *commitment*.

---

[17] Derrida, Jacques (1976) *Of Grammatology*, Baltimore: Johns Hopkins University Press, 158: 'There is nothing outside of the text.' See also Glanert, Simone (2012) 'Method?' in Monateri, P.G. ed. *Methods of Comparative Law*, Cheltenham, UK and Northampton, MA, USA: Edward Elgar Publishing, 67.

The infinite vertical axis graphically represents the problem of *differencing*[18] and the difficulty of interpreting what is perceived as strange or foreign. Accordingly, *similarity/difference* poles turn the focus on how to interpret the foreign. This axis and its poles illustrate the 'tensile counterpull'[19] in interpretation generated by extreme *similarity* or *difference* orientations. By defining the vertical axis this way, I follow the semantic convention of the academic discourse of comparatists who 'argue down' identity to similarity, presumably to avoid the *aporia* of the philosophical concept of identity,[20] and, thereby, reduce the interpretive dilemma to a mere (but still significant) tension, hermeneutic problem or matter of perspective. Along this axis one comes across ethnocentrism, universalism, relativism, etc. depending on how comparatists cope with the thrust of the particularity of the own *by comparison* with the other.

The vertical axis takes on the problem that comparatists do not recognize and understand the phenomena they are about to compare 'from nowhere in particular'[21] but from the background and within the context of their legal education and experience. To paraphrase Derrida: there is nothing outside the comparison.

Similarity and *difference* denote the cognitive orientation and interpretive dilemma, when comparatists set out to investigate and evaluate how other – unfamiliar, foreign, strange, unknown – legal artifacts correspond to and compare with artifacts of their own legal culture. Within the *similarity* perspective, what appears to be foreign undergoes a process of assimilation to the 'host' culture and law and is embraced as part of the universal or general. By contrast, the *difference* approach treats the foreign in its own right as dissimilar – not as the same or similar, derived from or related to the domestic culture – and therefore privileges diversity.

In the intra-disciplinary debates[22] these polar opposites have been endlessly and not always very enlighteningly reiterated, at times under

---

[18] Frankenberg 'Critical Comparisons,' 414–416; and Chapter 3 in this volume.

[19] Conquergood 'Performing as a Moral Act,' 402.

[20] Noonan, Harold (2004) 'Identity' in *The Stanford Encyclopedia of Philosophy*, http://plato.stanford.edu/archives/win2011/entries/identity/ (last accessed 29 January 2016).

[21] Nagel, Thomas (1989) *The View from Nowhere*, Oxford: Oxford University Press.

[22] Legrand, Pierre (2007) 'The Same and the Different' in Legrand, Pierre and Munday, Roderick eds *Comparative Legal Studies: Traditions and Transitions*, Cambridge: Cambridge University Press, 240–311.

the labels of universalism/relativism or contextualism.[23] *Differencing* in interpretation, as located on the *similarity/difference* axis, calls into question the innocence of universal or general criteria and categories that suggest commonness, by placing them in, and relating them to, their respective context. Contextualization suspends the comparatist's otherwise constitutive perspective and establishes the particularity of universal criteria and categories (that come with an Anglo-European pedigree).

In combination, *similarity/difference* and *detachment/commitment* mark the border zones of two basic professional skills. *Distancing* includes the comparatist in the comparative practice and helps her bring the other very close and keep it far away. *Differencing* turns on the foreign and makes the comparatist realize that she sees the foreign from somewhere in particular. Both operations encompass the willingness and capability to cope with preconceptions and stereotypes, biases and rationalist assumptions that fall within the analytical framework and normative matrix of one's own (legal) education and experience. If successful, these cognitive operations prevent familiarizing or domesticating the foreign and hold at bay naïve and romantic imaginations thereof.

The extreme poles of both axes of the grid demarcate '"dangerous shores" to be navigated, binary oppositions to be transcended.'[24] In order to at least indicate the moment and difficulty of such navigating and transcending, the center of the grid delineates, if only tentatively, the methodological, hermeneutic, ethical and political minefield where polar opposites intersect and point toward a comparative practice that – uneasily, dialectically and dynamically – transgresses the borders and limitations, the idiosyncrasies and pitfalls marking the four discrete tracks of legal comparison. If at all possible, the transformative work would possibly have to be done jointly by dialogue, criticism and self-criticism as well as 'thick comparison.'[25]

---

23 On contextualism and relativism (versus universalism), see Tomberlin, James ed. (1999) *Philosphical Perspectives 13: Epistemology*, Oxford: Blackwell Publishing.

24 Conquergood 'Performing as a Moral Act,' 402.

25 The complexity of the hermeneutic operations required is elucidated by Geertz *Local Knowledge* and Geertz, Clifford (2000) *The Interpretation of Cultures*, 2nd ed., New York: Basic Books; Scheffer, Thomas and Niewöhner, Jörg eds (2010) *Thick Comparison. Reviving the Ethnographic Aspiration*, Leiden and Boston: Brill.

3. TRACKS AND DIMENSIONS OF COMPARATIVE LAW

The grid is applied here, to repeat, as an open-ended matrix to explore and chart different tracks or bundled-up styles, two of which construct foreign laws from the vantage point of the domestic (or rather Western) law and thus secure the dominance of the Anglo-European perspective (A. and B.). By contrast, of the two remaining ones, one embraces the foreign out of fascination with its foreignness (C.), whereas the other tends to remain distant for fear of being entrapped by ethnocentrism (D.). Neither qualifies as mainstream. (See Figure 4.1 below.)

Mapping the typical problems and pitfalls in four different tracks, with three internal dimensions each, is to show how comparative legal science not only incorporates method but also how it deals with the ethical problems of recognizing, studying and understanding the foreign, as well as how it 'anchors power,'[26] that is, how the cultural representations of the West show *themselves* by way of constitutive comparison in the mirror of what is perceived, defined and compared as unfamiliar, strange, foreign or 'other.'

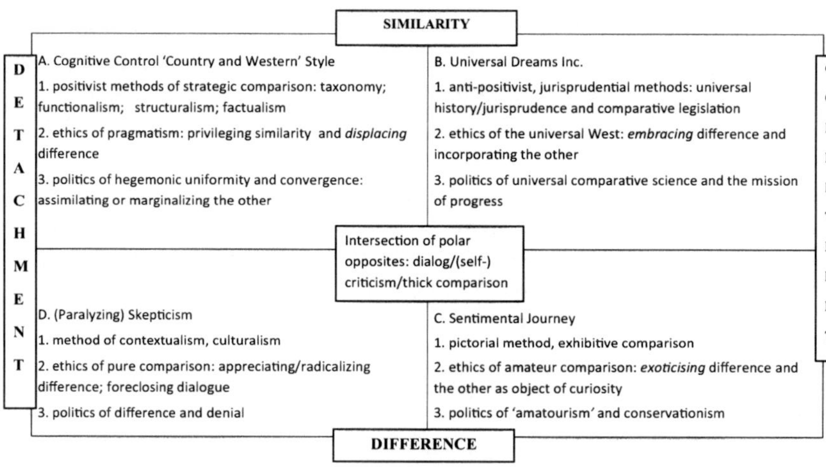

Figure 4.1 Tracks of legal comparison

[26] Nader, Laura (1996) 'Anthropological Inquiry' in Nader, Laura ed. *Naked Science*, 12. See also Legrand, Pierre (2011) 'Siting Foreign Law: How Derrida Can Help' 21 *Duke Journal of Comparative & International Law*, 595.

A. Cognitive Control 'Country and Western' Style

The comparative approaches combined in the first track are marked by the desire to establish *cognitive control.*[27] Comparison as *cognitive control*, rather than distancing and differencing, is geared toward the formalist ordering and labeling of the information attained by comparative study. The *cognitive controller* takes for granted her posture toward the foreign and has no problem with 'situated knowledges.'[28] Undaunted by the fear of ethnocentrism and therefore without *differencing/ distancing*, *cognitive control* relies on interpreting information, often randomly gleaned from limited data, from the unquestioned vantage point of one's own legal experience. These methodological operations are based on a specific formalist understanding of law, which reduces law to legal rules and rules to their propositional content. As a result comparative law has a strategic orientation buffered by the comparatist's good conscience that her practice of positing the 'home' law as normal, natural, and standard, and othering the rest, passes as objective:

> There exist today two groups of legal systems that have had wide influence throughout the world, both are of European origin. One is the civil law, the other the common law ... *In addition*, there are other legal systems such as Islamic law, Hindu law, Chinese law and others which developed outside the realm of civil law and common law.[29]

The *cognitive control* track is more or less coextensive with the dominant variety of post-World War II 'applied comparative law' and covers a wide range of approaches, notably taxonomy, functionalism, structuralism and factualism. They all feature the combination of a detached (objectivist) scientific attitude with a more or less distinctive similarity-orientation in interpretation. The alliance of *similarity* and *detachment* lends itself to a preference for establishing order and sustaining Western hegemony by relegating what is different to the margins.

---

[27] The concept was introduced in 'Critical Comparisons,' 416–426.

[28] See Haraway, Donna (1988) 'Situated Knowledges: The Science Question in Feminism and the Privilege of Partial Perspective' 14 *Feminist Studies*, 575.

[29] Liebesny, Herbert (1981) *Foreign Legal Systems: A Comparative Analysis*, 4th ed., Washington, DC: George Washington University Press, 1–2 – emphasis added; for an illustration of cognitive, see Twining, William (2007) 'Globalisation and Comparative Law' in Nelken, David and Örücü, Esin eds *Comparative Law. A Handbook*, Portland: Hart Publishing, 75–77; and Twining 'Comparative Law and Legal Theory,' 21.

Schlesinger et al. begin (and end) their textbook by applying the comparative method to domestic (US) problems. Throughout their book, the authors stress the importance of the *case* as law's crucial and constitutive unit and keep the focus on legal techniques of problem solving.[30] By introducing the U.S. constitutional system first, Murphy and Tanenhaus[31] similarly establish the presence and authority of their 'own' system and culture. They underscore its hegemony by introducing nine out of eleven chapters with examples of the jurisdiction of the U.S. Supreme Court. Glendon et al. reduce their *comparative legal traditions*, at the outset, to the common law and civil law tradition. They add socialist law not as a counter-hegemonic force or element of legal pluralism but [to] bring and keep it very close rather than keeping it far away: 'When judged by the character of its infrastructure and methodology the socialist legal system is deeply rooted in the civil law tradition.'[32] Even socialist law's peculiar political-ideological character does not establish its 'form of secular theology' instead affirms the superiority of the Western 'clear separation' of morality, politics and religion. Barton et al. promise a journey to the 'Law in Radically Different Cultures,' however, they de-radicalize their enterprise, from the very beginning, by setting up the Western concept of law as their framework for comparison.[33]

The method of cognitive control

On the level of *method*, *cognitive controllers* demonstrate a marked lack of concern for history and philosophy as well as *naïveté* regarding their Anglo-Eurocentrism. They replace rigorous theoretical and methodological reflection[34] with common sense. In consequence, their comparative practice comes across, as if from nowhere and without perspective,

---

30 Schlesinger et al. *Comparative Law*.

31 Murphy, Walter F. and Tanenhaus, Joseph (1977) *Comparative Constitutional Law. Cases and Commentaries*, New York: St. Martin's Press.

32 Glendon et al. *Comparative Legal Traditions*, 673.

33 Barton et al. *Law in Radically Different Cultures*, 1.

34 See Michaels, Ralf (2006) 'The Functional Method' in *Oxford Handbook of Comparative Law*, 340–341. Peters, Anne and Schwenke, Heiner (2000) 'Comparative Law Beyond Post-Modernism' 49 *International and Comparative Law Quarterly*, 800, criticize the theoretical deficit and methodological disdain of functionalism.

as a quasi-natural must:[35] 'In fact all methods of jurisprudence *must* be comparative ... [T]he methods of the jurist *must* have a basis in comparison.'[36]

Following William Twining's ironic characterization of the many approaches that are 'over-concerned with the domestic law of [European] "parent" nation states,'[37] I characterize *cognitive control* as the 'Country and Western' style, introduced here as a collective singular for mainly post-World War II taxonomies, classifications of the world's legal systems and functionalist and structuralist comparative analyses. They are partners under the umbrella of the presumption of similitude. The other law is registered on the same legal family or system by taxonomies, or is qualified as functionally similar in terms of social problems and legal solutions or as sharing similar legal formants or a Common Core.

And the non-adaptable laws and legal practices are relegated to the margin – as other laws, systems or radically different legal regimes, or as being different in detail. Thus, the difficulties of cultural translation and the conundrum of positionality and perspective are vividly played down, if not completely disregarded.

Generally speaking, *cognitive control* operates within the framework of a non-reflected and 'far too global typology,'[38] in particular the binary distinction between relevant or principal[39] and (by implication or through explicit treatment in treatises and standard textbooks) 'not so relevant' legal families or styles. To list a few examples: René David and John Brierley reserve roughly 450 pages of their *Major Legal Systems in the World Today* for Romano-Germanic, Anglo-American common law and socialist law; however, they dedicate only 170 pages to a variety of 'other conceptions' (Muslim law, laws of India, the Far East, Africa and

---

35 'Just as no individual can claim to be wise by himself, no legal system can be regarded as so advanced that it has little to gain from the study of foreign schools of thought.' Tunc, André (1977) 'Foreword' in von Mehren, Arthur and Gordley, James eds *The Civil Law System*, 2nd ed., Boston: Little, Brown & Co, ix.

36 Pound, Roscoe (1957) 'Foreword' in von Mehren, Arthur *The Civil Law System*, vii–viii – emphasis added. See also Cappelletti, Mauro (1978) 'Preface' in Merryman, John H. and Clark, David S. eds *Comparative Law: Western European and Latin American Legal Systems: Cases and Materials*, Indianapolis: Bobbs-Merrill, vii. For more recent statements see Gaubert 'Method?,' 67.

37 Twining 'Comparative Law and Legal Theory.'

38 Jameson 'Marxism and Historicism,' 60.

39 Merryman and Clark (*Legal Systems*, xxvii) are pitching 'The Three Principal Traditions' against the 'Major Religious and Non-Western Legal Traditions.'

Malagasy). By the same token, Zweigert and Kötz treat the Romanistic, Germanic and Anglo-American Legal Families quite elaborately but devote not more than half a dozen pages to the laws of Africa – under the heading 'The Spread of the Common Law Throughout the World' – and merely two pages to Latin America to illustrate 'The Reception of the Civil Code.'[40]

Ethics of similarity-pragmatism

The controller dismisses or plays down bias, preconceptions and pre-understandings and does not recognize the presence of the foreign in the comparative space:

> If the picture presented by a scholar is colored by his background or education, international collaboration will correct it.[41]

In one fell swoop *cognitive control* comparatists constitute their science, overdetermined in advance by a Western epistemic and ethical framework, which, in consequence, generates similarity writ large and differences in detail.

The ethical dimension[42] in the *cognitive control* track is shaped by the professional value-system of the pragmatic taxonomist, cartographer or functionalist.[43] It shows quite strongly the moral deficit that comes with the routine management of similarities. Due to the naïve assumption of a detached posture and the barely questioned similarity-perspective, the comparatist becomes an accomplice of her own legal system, education and practice:

---

[40] David, René and Brierley, John E.C. (1978) *Major Legal Systems in the World Today*, 2nd ed., New York: Simon & Schuster; Zweigert and Kötz *Introduction*. Critical: Menski, Werner (2006) *Comparative Law in a Global Context. The Legal Systems of Asia and Africa*, 2nd ed., Cambridge: Cambridge University Press. For a different approach see, e.g., Bareto, José-Manuel ed. (2013) *Human Rights from a Third World Perspective: Critique, History and International Law*, Cambridge: Cambridge University Press; and Twining, William ed. (2009) *Human Rights, Southern Voices: Francis Deng, Abdullai A-Na'im, Yash Gai and Upendra Baxi*, Cambridge: Cambridge University Press.

[41] Rabel, Ernst (1951) 'Deutsches und Amerikanisches Recht' 16 *Zeitschrift für ausländisches und internationales Privatrecht*, 359.

[42] As regards the ethics of comparative law, see Cotterell, Roger (2007) 'Is It So Bad to Be Different?' in Nelken and Örücü *Comparative Law*, 145–148.

[43] Zweigert and Kötz *Introduction*, 40–41; Schwarz-Liebermann von Wahlendorf, Hans-Albrecht (1978) *Droit Comparé – Théorie Générale et Principes*, Paris: Librairie Générale de Droit et de Jurisprudence, 213: 'Le choix des références et leur présentation doivent toujours obéir à l'éthique de la recherche.'

> [b]oth as professionals and as leaders in the public and private sectors, lawyers in the West participate in a continual institutional reconstruction of the *relevant* world. ... [T]heir *relevant* world embraces both the Common Law and the Civil Law ...[44]

They meet and recognize a foreign law on an equal footing and compare it as a phenomenon in its own right *only* if its pedigree distinguishes it as a member or close relative of the Anglo-European civil-common law family. Otherwise, the *really* 'other' laws are neglected or selectively recognized ('radically different'), treated with mild or not so mild disdain ('other'), dismissed ('non-Western') or treated as inferior ('primitive') and granted, at best, an outward show of respect[45] if called for by pragmatic concerns:

> [a]ll other [non-Western] systems, no more than survivors from the past, will ultimately disappear with the passing of time and the progress of civilization.[46]

In a later edition, the authors qualify this bold and, one is tempted to add, foolish statement and argue, looking back at the 'three families just described,' that is, Romano-Germanic law, common law and socialist law:

> Some (!) even hold the view that all other systems, no more than survivors of the past, will ultimately disappear with the passing of time and the progress of civilization. This attitude however proceeds from a rather naïve sense of superiority and is really no more than a hypothesis. It does not acknowledge an observable reality in the world.[47]

Based on said dichotomies, foreign laws and legal systems – labeled as like or unlike, derived from or antagonistic to – invariably get a second-class (if any) ticket to, and an inferior status in, the pertinent world of comparative law. The charge that mainstream comparative law treats the foreign as marginal, or even with disdain, is generally dismissed or not taken seriously. For it is not a universal sense of justice which guides the *cognitive controller* in seeking 'grand similarities' and

---

[44] Cappelletti 'Preface,' vii – emphasis added.

[45] Whitman, James Q. (2000) 'Enforcing Civility and Respect: Three Societies' 109 *Yale Law Journal*, 1279, 1291. See also Lave, Jean (1996) 'The Savagery of the Domestic Mind' in Nader ed. *Naked Science*, 87.

[46] David and Brierley *Major Legal Systems in the World*, 26.

[47] *Ibid.*, 27.

allowing for national 'differences in detail,'[48] but rather a distinct unitary purpose that becomes blatantly manifest in methodological instructions that reveal also the ethical deficit of similarity-pragmatism:

> [T]he comparatist can rest content if his researches through all the relevant material lead to the conclusion that the systems he has compared reach the same or similar practical results, but if he finds that there are great differences or indeed diametrically opposite results, he should be put on notice and go back to check again whether the terms in which he posed his original question were indeed purely functional, and whether he has spread the net of his researches quite wide enough.[49]

The politics of *cognitive control*

Cognitive control is also internally connected with a unitary project. The connection becomes manifest in the political dimension of this track. The taxonomist, functionalist, structuralist and factualist comparatists *appear* politically agnostic, because they concentrate on classifications, problems/functions, structures/formants or facts. However, the diverse analytics share a style that can be characterized as *strategic* comparison: It underscores the hegemony of Western law, i.e. the legal regimes of capitalist societies, and reiterates the political-ideological antagonism between Western/capitalist law[50] and other, in particular, socialist law. While the analytical criteria and categories appear politically neutral on their conceptual surface, their strategic design and geopolitical impact is revealed as they are applied in comparative practice: Anglo-European law, common or civil, is generally presented as mature, secular, more dynamic or rationally superior to Eastern, African or Asian law. Against the backdrop of global economic commerce, the comparatist assimilates laws that appear deviant, strange, unfamiliar and foreign to the 'own,' familiar law – its institutions, norms and doctrines – as far as they can be adapted to it and then fitted into its doctrinal structure and logic.

---

48 Zweigert and Kötz *Introduction*, 3.

49 *Ibid.*, 31. See also Zweigert (1973) 'Die "Praesumptio Similitudinis" als Grundsatzvermutung rechtsvergleichender Methode' in Rotondi, Mario ed. *Inchieste di Diritto Comparato – Scopi e Metodi di Diritto Comparato*, Padua: CEDAM, 735.

50 The concept of a *Western* legal tradition, system or law has been introduced or used, for example, by Berman, Harold (1983) *Law and Revolution: The Formation of the Western Legal Tradition*, Cambridge, MA: Harvard University Press; Smith, Joseph C. and Weisstub, David N. (1983) *The Western Idea of Law*, London: Butterworths; Glendon et al. *Comparative Legal Traditions*.

Contrary to claims or the attire of political agnosticism, the functionalist modality of legal comparison operates on the basis of an imaginary non-Western – immature, inferior, failed – other which is in need of development, stability or sophistication. This is particularly true for the works of the activist functionalists of the 'Law and Development Movement.'[51] However, the legal 're-activists' among comparative functionalists also have a political agenda. It is more hidden in their moderate proposals for law reform as adaptation of the legal system to the demands of the socio-economic environment.[52]

Even if the comparatist bent on *cognitive control* pretends not to mind the political utility of her research, this does not render dichotomies, taxonomies or classifications politically harmless:

> Classifications are enforced in an effort to stabilize power, to filter information, ration it, limit access.[53]

> Polar social categorization is a political relation since high and low categories of thinking and thinkers are not equal or symmetrical.[54]

Any comparative-legal taxonomy, accompanied by a characterization of the classified items, 'is far from innocent.'[55] Whatever instruments and categories the comparatist applies to arrange and put labels on the legal systems and families of the world, and however she defines social problems as common to all societies and evaluates the legal solutions provided by different legal systems, she always establishes order and reinforces the dominant narrative which sustains the regime of power/knowledge that is already in place[56] – and holds the high ground by virtue of the power of definition and the production of inferior others.

---

[51] See Merryman, John (1977) 'Comparative Law and Social Change: On the Origins, Style, Decline and Revival of the Law and Development Movement' 25 *American Journal of Comparative Law*, 457; Trubek, David and Santos, Alvaro eds (2006) *The New Law and Economic Development: A Critical Appraisal*, Cambridge: Cambridge University Press.

[52] Zweigert and Kötz *Introduction*, 27–31; Kahn-Freund, Otto (1966) 'Comparative Law as an Academic Subject' 82 *Law Quarterly Review*, 40.

[53] Douglas 'Cultural Bias,' 192.

[54] Lave 'The Savagery,' 100.

[55] Jameson 'Marxism and Historicism,' 59.

[56] Foucault, Michel (1980) *Power/Knowledge. Selected Interviews and Other Writings 1972–1977*, New York: Vintage.

Thus, the binary distinctions of civil and common law v. other legal systems, advanced/modern v. primitive/traditional legal systems, or secular v. religious legal systems[57] etc. have to be decoded as conceptual devices to stabilize the hegemony of Western law. Unless submitted to critique, the conceptual apparatus immunizes the always unmarked position of the West against doubt and questioning. A comparative style which pitches peripheral or 'primitive' legal orders against 'civilized' or 'advanced' ones, operates in the service of the hegemonic logic of the center, ratifies the (neo-)liberal paradigm, by globalizing Western and displacing non-Western law.[58]

Not unrelated to this (more or less hidden) agenda, some comparatists have quite openly propagated political projects. For example, the eminent scholar Ernst Rabel supported German enterprises after World War I in no uncertain terms. Realizing the need for compensation for loss suffered, his functionalist method was to provide competitive advantages for the German economy and German enterprises by improving the law and increasing 'the store of solutions.' On a more patriotic note he added:

> The *reconstruction of the fatherland* and its strengthening vis-à-vis the outside world require a sharpened perception of the events of the world. The new tasks must also find the lawyers *armed.*[59]

It is only more recently, that authors moving along the *cognitive control* track have supported – albeit in denial[60] – projects of unification or

[57] See only the tables of content in Merryman and Clark, David and Brierley, and Zweigert and Kötz; Gordon et al. *Comparative Legal Traditions*. See also Cappelletti, Mauro and Gordley, James and Johnson, Earl (1975) *Toward Equal Justice: A Comparative Study of Legal Aid in Modern Societies*, Milan: Giuffrè and Dobbs Ferry, NY: Oceana Publications.

[58] Critical: Menski *Comparative Law in a Global Context*; Sack, Peter and Aleck, Jonathan eds (1992) *Law and Anthropology*, New York: New York University Press; Baxi, Upendra (1999) 'Voices of Suffering, Fragmented Universality, and the Future of Human Rights' in Weston, B.H. and Marks, Susan eds *The Future of International Human Rights*, Ardsley, NY: Transnational Publishers, 101.

[59] Rabel, Ernst (1958) *Das Recht des Warenkaufs*, 2 vols., Tübingen: Mohr Siebeck, 27, 44–48 – emphasis added.

[60] Bussani and Mattei, the heads of the *Common Core* group, insisted on the *academic* orientation of their project, though, as part of building a common European legal culture.

harmonization[61] in Europe and elsewhere along with the imperatives of market economies: 'If the *rules* of ... two countries are already similar ... it should be no obstacle to their unification or harmonization that the legal *principles* involved come ultimately from different sources.'[62]

It is hard to overlook the political implications of such projects:

> Participants in the market need to know what their own and their contract partner's potential or actual liabilities are, to be able to obtain reliable and cost-effective security and to enjoy a secure basis for dealing with the myriad problems of contract failure. Both Groups warmly endorse the Commission in its use of a wide concept of contract law in its Communication.[63]

> The person who looks, not only at his own, but also at the surrounding laws, broadens the range of possible debate. In writing about different laws he undertakes work which is fundamentally no different from that on his own legal system, so long as the systems are equal in their basic values, in the quality of their legal method, and have continuously learned from one another.[64]

The agenda pursued here is neither politically agnostic nor aims at restoring the 'sense of universalism' René David[65] had in mind, but is meant to facilitate economic transactions, to implement supranational political integration, and, as far as Anglo-European law takes the lead, to sustain its political-legal hegemony, however modest the contribution of comparative law might be. The politics of *cognitive control* 'Country and Western' style rely on a legal-positivist ideology to validate the imperatives of economic-financial globalization from the vantage point of

---

61 These projects should be differentiated one from the other. See Rosett, Arthur (1992) 'Unification, Harmonization, Codification, and Reform in International Commercial Law' 40 *American Journal of Comparative Law*, 683; Watt, Gary (2012) 'Comparison as Deep Appreciation' in Monateri *Methods of Comparative Law*, 82, 96–99.

62 Watson, Alan (1974) *Legal Transplants*, Athens, GA: University of Georgia Press, 96–97. Gordley 'Mapping Private Law,' 61: 'The Trento Common Core Project is an ambitious search for unity in private law. [It is designed to] produce reliable information – which may provide useful for harmonisation.'

63 von Bar, Christian et al. (2002) 'Communication on European Contract Law: Joint Response of the Commission on European Contract Law and the Study Group on a European Civil Code' 10 *European Review of Private Law*, 183.

64 von Bar, Christian (1998) *The Common European Law of Torts*, Oxford: Oxford University Press, xxiii.

65 David and Brierley *Major Legal Systems in the World*, 16.

comparative law.[66] In this manner, *cognitive controllers*, primarily taxonomists, functionalists and factualists, play their part in 'the cultural politics of the world.'[67] If they try to come over as political agnostics, they apparently do so because of their mantra, 'only knowledge,'[68] but contrary to their program.

Agnosticism is hardly a striking feature of the members of the Common Core Project. For they always come with a gently toned down reformist agenda that complements and contradicts the seemingly empirical and non-political cartography they claim to have in mind. To quote one of their godfathers first:

> Those who compare legal systems are always asked about the purpose of such comparisons. The idea seems to be that the study of foreign legal systems is a legitimate enterprise only if it results in proposals for the reform of domestic law.[69]
>
> The 'Common Core' Project *has been requested* to apply its methodologies of factual approach and dissociation of legal formants to the results of [the] 'legislative activity' [sponsored by the European Commission], in order to assess the operational impact such Principles [of European Contract Law] might have on legal outcomes in the different European legal cultures.[70]

The leaders of the group made sure the Common Core Project would not be understood as an attempt to force the private law systems of the EU member-states into the Procrustean bed of harmonization:

> In using at the beginning of our journey the metaphor of cartography we have certainly tried to convey a message of neutrality and skepticism, locating our comparative work in the domain of the 'is' rather than of the 'ought.'
>
> [T]he 'common core' research *may be a useful instrument for legal harmonization*, in the sense that it provides *reliable* data to be used in devising new common solutions that may prove workable in practice. Be that as it may, the latter goal has nothing to do with the common core research in itself, which is devoted to produce *reliable* information, *whatever its policy use may be*.[71]

---

66 Menski *Comparative Law in a Global Context*, 47.

67 Lave 'The Savagery,' 100.

68 Bussani and Mattei 'Preface,' xvi.

69 Sacco 'Legal Formants,' 1–2.

70 Bussani and Mattei 'Preface,' ix – emphasis added.

71 Bussani and Mattei 'Preface: The Context,' 4 – emphasis added; Bussani, Mauro (1998) 'Current Trends in European Comparative Law: The Common Core Approach' 78 *Hastings International and Comparative Law Review*, 787.

Other influential members admitted what appears to be quite obvious: 'The Trento Common Core Project is an ambitious search for unity in private law.'[72] Similarly, a protagonist of a different European (torts) Common Core project found:

> [T]o think in a European fashion means first to stress the common characteristics, secondly, to understand national laws as reactions to developments in neighbouring countries, and thirdly, to tackle historical coincidence and rough edges, which, in view of the process of European unification, can be ground down without substantial loss.[73]

That certainly qualifies as a political project, too.

So, the modest claim that by searching for and digging out the Common Core (of contract, tort and property law in the member-states of the union) all they want is to 'obtain at least the main lines of a *reliable* geographical 'map' of the law of Europe'[74] appears like a rather empty gesture. The strategies of producing reliable information and gaining more knowledge 'whatever its policy use may be,' point toward the false modesty of a comparative enterprise whose members have yet to question their mantras – 'only knowledge' and 'reliable information' – and to energetically consider the political context (convergence, harmonization of European law) of their work.

Nonetheless, the political undercurrent of the Common Core should be distinguished from the straightforwardly political agendas of the *modernization* strategies in the 1960s and 1970s as well as the rule of law programs (ROL) in the context of political and economic development.[75]

---

72 James Gordley, one of the leading members of the Trento Group, admitted to this more demanding goal: Gordley, James (2000) 'Mapping Private Law' in Bussani and Mattei *Making European Law: Essays on the Common Core*, 61.

73 Von Bar, Christian (1998) *The Common European Law of Torts*, Oxford: Oxford University Press, xxiii.

74 Bussani, Mauro and Mattei, Ugo (1997) 'The Common Core Approach to European Private Law' 3 *Columbia Journal of European Law*, 339, 340; Bussani, Mauro and Mattei, Ugo eds (2003) *The Common Core of European Private Law. Essays on the Project*, The Hague: Kluwer; Frankenberg, Günter (2007) 'How to Do Projects with Comparative Law. Notes of an Expedition to the Common Core' in Bussani and Mattei *Opening Up European Law*, 17–48.

75 Garth, Bryant G. and Dezalay, Yves eds (2002) *Global Prescriptions: The Production, Exportation, and Importation of a New Legal Orthodoxy*, Ann Arbor: University of Michigan Press; Trubek and Santos *The New Law and Economic Development*.

While the Common Core research can be aligned with political convergence projects, ROL and related programs are *designed* to export law-rule and strengthen the role of law in the political and economic development of countries, primarily from the periphery, and to initiate law reforms through development agencies. Moreover, unlike ROL programs, the Common Core can hardly be accused of naïvely strengthening authoritarian regimes[76] or 'charting the fragile path of progress.'[77]

B. Universal Dreams Inc.

In the founding period of the discipline, long before today's triumph of the *cognitive controller's* global positivism, the comparatists' similarity-orientation in interpretation was underscored by enthusiastic commitment to the vision of a united world law or the project of a universal history of law, a universal (comparative) science or universally shared legal experience. As was shown above, the combination, within the universalistic framework, inspired different but internally related projects. In German academia, philosophical speculation and universal legal history[78] continued the tradition of Hegel and his disciple, Eduard Gans, whereas the influential founders of the discipline in France, Raymond Saleilles and Edouard Lambert, shared and proliferated the jurisprudential dream of a '*droit commun législatif*.'[79] Both schools represent, not all that distantly, anti-positivist styles related to comparative legal studies one might trace back to Montesquieu:

---

[76] See Peerenboom, Randall ed. (2004) *Asian Discourses of Rule of Law: Theories and Implementation of Rule of Law in Twelve Asian Countries, France and the U.S.*, New York: Routledge.

[77] E.g. Trebilcock, Michael J. and Daniels, Ron eds (2008) *Rule of Law Reform and Development: Charting the Fragile Path of Progress*, Cheltenham, UK and Northampton, MA, USA: Edward Elgar Publishing.

[78] Gans, *Naturrecht und Universalrechtsgeschichte*; see Vogenauer, Stefan (2012) 'Rechtsgeschichte und Rechtsvergleichung um 1900' 76 *Rabels Zeitschrift für ausländisches und internationales Privatrecht/The Rabel Journal of Comparative and International Private Law*, 1122, 1125.

[79] Jamin, Christophe (2002) 'Saleilles' and Lambert's Old Dream Revisited' 50 *American Journal of Comparative Law*, 701.

> [E]ach diversity is *uniformity*, each change is *constancy* ... Before laws were made, there were relations of possible justice ... We must therefore acknowledge relations of justice antecedent to the positive law by which they are established.[80]

More recently, comparative historical studies, shifting the focus on 'transplants'[81] and the 'exchange between traditions,'[82] on intercultural communication and evolution,[83] and globalization or calls for a 'comparative jurisprudence,'[84] have picked up and carried the banner of Universal Dreams Inc. Their universalisms come with less hyperbole and lean toward pedagogical instruction. However modestly they may be framed, they invariably incorporate the Western perspective and construct the world from *there*, based on the allegedly universal character of comparative law,[85] its method or its rights and law-rule orientation:

> Many of our constitutional rights and values – liberty, equal protection of the law, due process, freedom of expression – reflect not only specific decisions made in the United States, but also widely shared commitments of many Western democracies.[86]

---

80 Baron de Montesquieu, Charles de Secondat (1989/1748) *The Spirit of Laws*, Cambridge: Cambridge University Press (excerpts from his reflections preceding the Laws of Nature).

81 See, in particular, Watson, Alan (1993) *Legal Transplant*, 2nd ed., Athens, GA: University of Georgia Press.

82 Glenn, H. Patrick (2007) *Legal Traditions of the World*, 3rd ed., Oxford: Oxford University Press, 31.

83 Scollon, Ron and Wong Scollon, Suzanne (1995) *Intercultural Communication. A Discourse Approach*, Cambridge, MA: Basil Blackwell; Watson, Alan (1985) *The Evolution of Western Private Law*, Baltimore: The Johns Hopkins University Press. Critical of the evolution paradigm: Sack and Aleck 'Introduction' in *Law and Anthropology*, xiii, xvii.

84 Ewald, William (1995a) 'Comparative Jurisprudence (I): What Was It Like to Try a Rat?' 143 *University of Pennsylvania Law Review*, 1888; and Ewald (1995b) 'Comparative Jurisprudence (II): The Logic of Legal Transplants' 43 *American Journal of Comparative Law*, 489; see also Zweigert, Konrad (1949/50) 'Rechtsvergleichung als universale Interpretationsmethode' 15 *Rabels Zeitschrift für Rechtsvergleichung*, 5.

85 Kötz, Hein (1982) 'Neue Aufgaben der Rechtsvergleichung' 104 *Österreichische Juristische Blätter*, 355.

86 Jackson, Vicki (2004) 'Yes Please, I'd Love to Talk with You: The Court Has Learned from the World Before. It Should Continue to Do So' *Legal Affairs* http://www.legalaffairs.org/issues/July-August-2004/feature_jackson_julaug04.msp (last accessed 24 September 2015).

The method of Universal Dreams Inc.

The projects of the *belle époque* concurred in the attempt to correct the shortcomings of the classical nineteenth-century methodological orientation. Comparatists moved away from conceptual jurisprudence and a mode of reasoning that tried to imitate the laws of geometry; they relied on philosophical speculation, historical analysis and anthropological studies, instead.[87]

More recent endeavors follow this turn to ideas – to philosophy and history – that is complemented by a turn to jurisprudence, regardless of whether comparison is geared toward exploring philosophical foundations and principles[88] or searching for a neo-Aristotelian natural justice that 'everywhere has the same force,'[89] constructing *un droit commun législatif* or recapturing philosophical-theoretical reflection.[90]

The methodological pitfall of comparatists associated with *Universal Dreams Inc.* is not their enthusiasm (unless reduced to a superficial gloss), but the disposition to disregard diversity, the lack of attention to context and, in consequence, the tendency to register and ratify the Western particular, without cross-cultural reflection and justification of this 'extrapolation,' as universal.[91] The prototypical Anglo-European universalist does not realize that she cannot see the whole picture except in and through her own – Western – window because the universal does not exist independently from the particular perspective from which it is seen.[92]

Regardless of these problems and the discrepancy between philosophical speculation and the scientifically reasoned elaboration of legislation, comparative law's universalists, also those propagating a normative theory, have to assume that, *first*, there is a common framework for

---

[87] Saleilles, Raymond (1891) 'Le droit commercial comparé – Contribution à l'étude des méthodes juridiques' 5 *Annales de droit commercial*, 227; Jamin 'Old Dream Revisited,' 704–708.

[88] Del Vecchio, Giorgio (1909) *Sull'idea di una scienza del diritto universale comparat*, Rome: Fratelli Boca, 31–37; Ewald 'Comparative Jurisprudence (I),' 1896.

[89] Aristotle (2009) *The Nicomachean Ethics*, Oxford: Oxford University Press, Book V.

[90] Ewald 'Comparative Jurisprudence (I)' and 'Comparative Jurisprudence (II).'

[91] Critical: Panikkar, Raimon (1982) 'Is the Notion of Human Rights a Western Concept?' in 30 *Diogenes*, 75, 84: 'No concept as such is universal. Each concept is primarily valid where it was conceived. If we want to extend its validity beyond its own context we shall have to justify the extrapolation.'

[92] *Ibid.*

comparison – natural law, universal history, a sense of universal justice, etc. Otherwise they could not propagate comparative law as the 'universal method of interpretation.'[93] And, *second*, they have to assume that the phenomena under comparative scrutiny are essentially similar,[94] or else it would not make sense to claim:

> [c]omparativism must be at the heart of all judicial activity if law is to embody principles that are universal rather than purely domestic or even 'European.'[95]

With caution, Ruti Teitel introduces, for comparative constitutional law, a dialogical method, which both criticizes and echoes, albeit faintly, the universal dream as the possibility of 'cross-fertilization:'

> Comparative exchange is not bound in path-dependent or hierarchic ways. Rather, it poses a comity-based 'transjudicial' enterprise – a decentered view of constitutional practices deriving from pluralist sources, with the possibility of 'cross-fertilization'.[96]

Hence, in terms of method, over-generalization and amnesia of the particular context are the main pitfalls of *Universal Dreams Inc*. Comparatists of this brand operate somewhat like lawyers. They use comparison, for example, to legitimate their argument that a *particular* interpretation, say of a human rights norm, captures its universal spirit or is universally applicable.[97]

The ethics of Universal Dreams Inc.

Universal Dreams Inc. is almost by definition an approach to legal comparison which features ethics. The protagonists recognize that the co-presences of the foreign in the comparative space raises ethical concerns. However, they do not recognize their 'own' law's particularity and relate it, by comparison, to that of the foreign but produce instead varieties of universalism, which, each in its own way, melt down particularity. The other is integrated by sleight of hand into the concept

93 Zweigert 'Rechtsvergleichung als universale Interpretationsmethode,' 5.

94 Jameson 'Marxism and Historicism,' 43–49; Conquergood 'Performing as a Moral Act,' 404–405.

95 Nelken and Örücü *Comparative Law*, 37.

96 Teitel, Ruti (2004) 'Book Review: Comparative Constitutional Law in a Global Age' 117 *Harvard Law Review*, 2570, 2586.

97 See McCrudden, Christopher (2007) 'Judicial Comparativism and Human Rights' in Nelken and Örücü *Comparative Legal Studies*, 371.

of a universal history of law or universal jurisprudence.[98] Or its peculiarity disappears behind law's universal horizon.[99]

Universalistic comparison fails insofar as it makes the other banal by presupposing *in advance* what comparative study, if performed well, could ultimately demonstrate. As a result, *Universal Dreams Inc.*, rather than innocently *describing* the other,[100] operates with projections of the particular legal (predominantly Western) self onto the rest of the world: the universal history and *Weltrecht* take for granted the centrality of European law. The *droit commun législatif* takes its departure from civil law and returns there. In René David's taxonomy French/German civil and English common law play a pivotal role as the dominant regime in the concert of their major legal systems. UNIDROIT principles and Common Cores present shrunk versions of a universalism that take their cue from Western (contract, tort, etc.) law.

Therefore, Charles Taylor's critique of philosophical 'universalism as an ultimately confused and hypocritical position'[101] also applies to comparative law. By trivializing and normalizing[102] difference, the comparatist's admirable enthusiasm falls short of recognizing otherness on its own terms. The 'radically different'[103] is likely to suffocate in the gentle embrace of Anglo-European universalism.

The politics of Universal Dreams Inc.

The political dimension of *Universal Dreams Inc.* contains an intra-disciplinary project and a more comprehensive, extra-disciplinary agenda. With respect to the academic discipline of comparative law, the founding generations resumed the program of their nineteenth-century predecessors

---

98 See the works of Gans and Kohler of the German school, Saleilles and Lambert of the French school of founders of the discipline; Jamin 'Saleille's and Lambert's Old Dream Revisited'; and Vogenauer 'Rechtsgeschichte und Rechtsvergleichung'.

99 David and Brierley *Major Legal Systems in the World.*

100 Also Said, Edward (1978) *Orientalism*, London: Penguin, 149: 'Comparison is rarely descriptive; most often it is both evaluative and expository.'

101 Taylor, Charles (2002) 'The Politics of Recognition' in Gutmann, Amy ed. *Multiculturalism and 'The Politics of Recognition'*, Princeton: Princeton University Press, 25, 43–44.

102 For a critical application of normalization in comparative law, see Berman, N. (1997) 'Aftershocks: Exoticization, Normalization and the Hermeneutic Compulsion' *Utah Law Review*, 281.

103 See Barton, *Law in Radically Different Cultures.*

and sought to dignify comparative law as a science.[104] Depending on their location, institutional affiliation and study and research interest, comparative law was elevated to the level of universal (general) jurisprudence or a markedly historical or ethnological jurisprudence (Gans, Post, Kohler).[105] The most prominent French authors (Saleilles, Lambert) gave the discipline a more practical and contemporary focus as *legislation comparée* or *école de l'exegèse* when they challenged classical theories and methods of interpretation.[106]

The different jurisprudential agendas were soon dismissed as a 'beautiful dream,'[107] inspiring for the reconstruction of past traditions and serving at best as the handmaiden of the preference for comparative law as part of positive law, but little else.[108] It was in the aftermath of the Paris Congress that positivism began to win recognition, and after World War II it also prevailed in comparative law,[109] exorcising history and speculation from the discipline and paving the way for the pragmatic turn to a jejune 'applied comparative law.'

The broader, political agenda of comparative law came with a reformist (or meliorist) program and an enthusiasm for unified law.[110] The rhetoric echoed the dreams and idealism of the founding generation:

> [d]ivergences in laws cause other divergences that generate … misunderstanding and conflicts among nations which end with blood and desolation.[111] [On a somewhat more realistic note Edouard Lambert added:] [T]he essential

---

[104] The different projects are analysed by Vogenauer 'Rechtsgeschichte und Rechtsvergleichung.'

[105] Kohler, Josef (1885) *Das Recht als Kulturerscheinung. Einleitung in die vergleichende Rechtswissenschaft*, Würzburg: Stahel. See also Kötz, Hein (1999) 'Comparative Law in Germany Today' 51 *Révue internationale de droit comparé*, 753.

[106] See Vogenauer 'Rechtsgeschichte und Rechtsvergleichung', 1125–1143; Jamin 'Old Dream Revisited.'

[107] For references see Vogenauer 'Rechtsgeschichte und Rechtsvergleichung,' 1144.

[108] Rabel *Aufgabe und Notwendigkeit.*

[109] Lambert, Édouard (1905/1978) 'Conception générale, définition, méthode et histoire du droit comparé' in Zweigert and Puttfarken *Rechtsvergleichung*, 32.

[110] Gutteridge, Harold (1949) *Comparative Law: An Introduction to the Comparative Method of Legal Study and Research*, 2nd ed., Cambridge: Cambridge University Press, 147 and 154–156.

[111] Lepaulle, Pierre (1922) 'The Function of Comparative Law. With a Critique of Sociological Jurisprudence' 35 *Harvard Law Review*, 838, 857.

> mission of comparative law is one of economic peacemaking, the realization of an international economic entente.[112]

Once inscribed in the development of modern law and its political-economic context, the hyperbole of universalism, peculiar to early *Universal Dreams Inc.*, and the mission its members assign to comparative law lose their political innocence. They reappear there, maybe unwittingly, as normative reconstructions of the colonialist-imperialist world and add another chapter to the 'white mythologies'[113] that rely on generally unquestioned, culturally embedded assumptions:

> [I]n 1900 the approach of comparative law was based on two understandings that were so obvious that they were never really spelled out. The first one was that law, as understood in the west, was a sign of civilization. ... The second understanding was that civilization was mainly European (with an extension to America, due to early European emigration and settlement). To make it simple, at the beginning of the twentieth century, civilization was considered as being mainly Western, white and Christian.[114]

Therefore universal jurisprudence, universal history and more recent projects cannot be taken at face value as innocuous dreams, but have to be submitted to a critical reading that elucidates the underlying perspective, the structures of center and periphery[115] and demystifies the admittedly fascinating narratives. For the old narratives came with a dark side: the jurisprudential silence about nationalism and colonialism.

More recent narratives with a universalistic twist shifted the accent and their political agenda from constructing a world law, universal jurisprudence or law-making to more practical purposes, like broadening the horizon of students, de-provincializing the minds of lawyers, assisting the

---

112 Lambert, quoted by Jamin 'Old Dream Revisited,' 715.

113 Young, Robert (1990) *White Mythologies*, New York: Routledge; see also Baxi, Upendra (2002) *The Future of Human Rights*, Oxford: Oxford University Press, 51; and Mamdani, Mahmood (1995) *Citizen and Subject: Contemporary Africa and the Legacy of Late Colonialism*, Princeton: Princeton University Press.

114 Dupré, Cathérine (2002) 'The Perspective of Law Importation – The Hungarian Experience' in Harding, Andrew and Örücü, Esin eds (2002) *Comparative Law in the 21st Century*, London: Kluwer, 267, 269; see also Menski 'Comparative Law in a Global Context,' 46.

115 See for instance Nader, Laura (1997) 'Controlling Processes – Tracing the Dynamic Components of Power' 38 *Current Anthropology*, 711; Baxi *The Future of Human Rights*, 117.

development of countries, overcoming nationalism,[116] and propagating a 'transnational legal practice.'[117] Thus, *Universal Dreams Inc.* remained normative, but toned town its explicitly universal claims:

> Comparative law offers the law student a whole new dimension: from it he can learn to respect the special legal cultures of other people, he will understand his own law better, he can develop critical standards which might lead to its improvement, and he will learn how rules of law are conditioned by social facts and what different forms they can take.[118]

> [W]e look over the fence of our neighbor in pursuit of the common fate: to identify and grasp the human nature; indeed, to share the human destiny and to unite the human forces.[119]

With a stronger normative accent, H. Patrick Glenn considers 'comparing laws ... fundamental in the process of globalization and in the pursuit of peaceful relations between peoples' and, similarly, Paul Roberts holds that comparative law may be able to demonstrate 'that there is something that can be done by the international community in response to genocide, crimes against humanity and other massive, state-sponsored violations of fundamental human rights ...'[120]

Despite their political pedagogy or practical orientation, latter day universalists neither call into question the embedded assumptions about

---

[116] See, for example, Großfeld, Bernhard (1984) *Macht und Ohnmacht der Rechtsvergleichung*, Tübingen: Mohr Siebeck, 14–16; Constantinesco, Leontin-Jean (1971) *Rechtsvergleichung I*, Köln: Heymann; Ancel, Marc (1961) 'Valeur actuelle des études de droit comparé' in Nadelmann, Kurt, von Mehren, Arthur and Hazard, John eds *Legal Essays in Honour of Hessel E. Yntema*, Leyden: A.W. Sythoff.

[117] Glenn, H. Patrick (2001) 'Comparative Law and Legal Practice: On Removing the Borders' 75 *Tulane Law Review*, 977, 980–988.

[118] Zweigert and Kötz *Introduction*, 21; also Harding, Andrew and Leyland, Peter (2007) 'Comparative Law in Constitutional Contexts' in Nelken and Örücü *Comparative Law*, 313, 332.

[119] Thus spoke Konstantinos Kerameus, the President of the Association, in his Opening Address at the XVIIIth Congress of the International Academy of Comparative Law, 16–22 July 2006.

[120] Glenn, H. Patrick (2007) 'Com-paring' in Nelken and Örücü *Comparative Law*, 93 and Roberts, Paul (2007) 'Comparative Law for International Criminal Justice' in Nelken and Örücü *Comparative Law*, 346; also see Nelken, David 'Comparative Law and Comparative Legal Studies' in Nelken and Örücü *Comparative Law*, 13–14.

law[121] nor the underlying hegemonic (Western) presuppositions that are exported as concepts of law, law-rule and jurisprudence to other countries, courtesy of the comparative method, which enables us (!) to 'better represent our legal culture outside' (i.e. in other contexts and countries) and 'make our legal culture shine.'[122]

C. Sentimental Journey

Diametrically opposed to the influential cognitive control project and its sober style, where confidence in the hegemonic message abounds, and in contrast to *Universal Dreams Inc.*, which conjoins a minority faction of the discourse still subscribing, albeit with a different accent, to the once glorious jurisprudential mission of the discipline, fewer comparatists inhabit the quadrant demarcated by *commitment/difference.* From afar, they appear like sentimental travelers – the last amateurs[123] touring the field of comparative law (therefore: *amatourism*), quite different from the taxonomist/functionalist/structuralist/factualist mainstream's spirit that testifies to seasoned and influential professionals. Despite their small number and marginal role they do not come with a Cinderella complex. By contrast, they represent the congenial commitment to respecting – at times essentializing – difference.

Again, Montesquieu may be called as a witness of the (in his case, prolific) amateurism and as a source of inspiration for latter-day traveler-comparatists. In fact, *The Spirit of Laws* is replete with short vignettes of foreign countries and peoples, with bizarre observations ('I have observed the outmost part of a sheep's tongue.') and odd inferences (relating, for instance, the laws to the sobriety of the people, or asserting that the English are 'apt to commit suicide most unaccountably') as well as other items the traveler, upon her return, likes to exhibit.[124]

---

[121] Muir Watt, Horatia (2006) 'Globalization and Comparative Law' in Reimann and Zimmermann *Handbook of Comparative Law*, 579, 590; Legrand, Pierre (1997) 'The Impossibility of Legal Transplants' 4 *Maastricht Journal of European & Comparative Law*, 111.

[122] Großfeld *Macht und Ohnmacht*, 195. He adds that jurists trained in comparative law can be better 'placed' internationally. See also Murphy, Walter (1981) 'The Diminishing World of Western Law' 16 *Texas International Law Journal*, 1.

[123] In her article 'Encountering Amateurism' in *Rethinking the Masters* Annelise Riles is – understandably – torn between an admiration for and critique of Wigmore's amateurish comparative approach.

[124] Montesquieu *The Spirit of Laws*, 57–58 (China), 104 (India), 103, 105 and 107.

The sentimental traveler's method

As regards their *method, amatour*-comparatists[125] roam the field of anthropology but tend to eschew the anthropologist's methodological and theoretical overhead.[126] Instead, they travel with camera and treasure box to capture, collect and bring home impressions from the 'Panorama of the World's Legal Systems'[127] or 'a more sophisticated 'Cook's tour' of the great legal families of the world – as if one has been upgraded from an ordinary package tour to a luxury cruise ship with a more sophisticated guide to the standard sights.'[128]

The travelers' methodological sophistication ranges from Montesquieu's rather demanding multi-tasking, demonstrated in *The Spirit of the Laws*, to the entertaining vignettes written by writer Sybille Bedford in her *Traveller's Report* describing court procedures in five different European countries,[129] to what can be characterized as 'juxtaposition-plus'[130] as well as an attitude that Pierre Lepaulle once observed: that most American lawyers 'see in [comparative law] nothing more than an amusing puzzle, the chance to satisfy an idle curiosity.'[131]

John Wigmore found a middle ground. With his pictorial method he charted sixteen legal systems and combined comments and pictures in a delightful documentation:

---

125 Montesquieu would have to be credited with a more complex mix of historical analyses, naturalist inferences, and philosophical ideas.

126 Bernard, H. Russell ed. (1998) *Handbook of Methods in Cultural Anthropology*, Lanham, MD: AltaMira Press; Geertz *The Interpretation of Cultures*; Rosaldo, Renato (1993) *Culture & Truth: The Remaking of Social Analysis*, Boston: Beacon Press.

127 Wigmore, John H. (1928) *Panorama of the World's Legal System*, St. Paul: West Publishing; Wigmore, John H. (1931) 'Jottings on Comparative Legal Ideas and Institutions' 6 *Tulane Law Review*, 48.

128 Twining, William et al. (2006) 'A Fresh Start for Comparative Legal Studies? A Collective Review of Patrick Glenn's *Legal Traditions of the World*, 2nd ed., 1 *Journal of Comparative Law*, 100–176.

129 Bedford, Sybille (1961) *The Faces of Justice. A Traveller's Report*, New York: Simon & Schuster.

130 Frankenberg 'Critical Comparisons,' 411, 429–434 regarding the juxtaposing of legal systems and more or less elaborate comments.

131 Lepaulle 'The Function of Comparative Law,' 838; similarly, Escarra, Jean (1933) 'The Aims of Comparative Law' 7 *Temple Law Quarterly*, 296. John Merryman criticizes a widespread notion of comparative law as 'an esoteric and relatively undynamic specialty.' For a critique see also Legrand, Pierre (2001) 'The Return of the Repressed: Moving Comparative Legal Studies beyond Pleasure' 75 *Tulane Law Review*, 1033.

> If we are ever to interpret fully the cold written records of the world's legal systems, other than our own of today, must we not first seek to restore, in the mind's eye, the environment in which the several peoples lived and moved and had their being, and the setting of the distinctive events and traits in the history of their law?[132]

Whereas curiosity and, in particular, Wigmore's distinction of more legal systems than today's standard textbooks usually have on offer, are laudable, another aspect of this approach remains problematic: the essentializing representation of the other as exotic or, in terms of a more recent textbook, 'radically different.'[133] Quite telling and adequate with regard to this feature of *exhibitive comparison* is the reference to 'Wigmore's Treasure Box.'[134] Wigmore's panorama is indeed reminiscent of Mussorgsky's magnificent 'Pictures at an Exhibition' or a slide-show accompanied by learned commentaries. It epitomizes exhibitive comparison, a modality critics also detected in H. Patrick Glenn's *Legal Traditions of the World*.[135] While it is true that Glenn juxtaposes seven traditions, he also elaborately analyzes their complexity and interdependence.[136] Thus, he presents definitely more than a treasure box.

The ethics of amateurism

Amatourists are committed to the difference of the other, which they explore not infrequently through immersion from the arm-chair. Such commitment grows out of a 'fascination with the exotic, primitive, culturally remote'[137] – now and then inspired by the idea that comparative law should be pleasure. It is the normative pitfall of the amateur that she is committed to the quite different other[138] but indulges in its conspicuous exhibition and consumption. She wants to be both Claude Lévi-Strauss and the indigenous people he visited and researched.

---

132 Wigmore *Panorama*, 3.

133 See Barton et al. *Law in Radically Different Cultures*.

134 Riles, Annelise (1999) 'Wigmore's Treasure Box: Comparative Law in the Era of Information' 40 *Harvard International Law Journal*, 221.

135 See the critical comments collected in Legrand 'A Fresh Start for Comparative Legal Studies?'

136 Glenn *Legal Traditions of the World*, 357.

137 Conquergood 'Performing as a Moral Act', 405. Exoticization as a critical practice in comparative law is demonstrated by Berman 'Aftershocks.'

138 Wigmore 'Jottings', 51. In this text, Wigmore characterized, however, comparative law (and also his comparative style) as 'the tracing of an identical or similar idea or institution through all or many systems, with a view to discovering its differences and likenesses in various systems, the reasons for those variations, and the nature and limits of the inherent and invariable idea.'

From the outset, her romantic involvement and exoticizing perception of foreign laws and legal institutions is informed by their appearance as quite different artifacts.[139] This way, comparatists run the risk of closing the doors of comprehension[140] and avoiding comparison. It is in this way that so-called comparative studies 'resemble curio postcards, souvenirs, trophies brought back from the tour for display cases. Instead of bringing us into genuine contact (and risk) with the [laws] of strangers, [comparisons] in this mode bring back museum exhibits, mute and staring.'[141] On closer scrutiny, a sentimental approach to, and romantic notion of, exotic laws and legal practices reveal yet another problematic side. What seems attractive in the *amatourist's* gaze is likely to be rejected as a candidate for integration in the domestic legal order.

The politics of amateurism

Amatourism does not come with a clear political message or mission. Therefore, it is not easy to identify a political project underneath or behind the exhibitive style. Wigmore mentions in passing a 'better understanding' of the 'spirit' of the different legal systems and his aim to 'understand better the spirit and the atmosphere in which disputes were settled, laws were debated, codes enacted, and justice dispensed.'[142] This pedagogical message corresponds to the appreciation of diversity.

Beyond that, there is no indication of a specific political agenda, like working toward world peace, facilitating economic transactions or, at least, qualifying law students for international jobs. The *Panorama of the World's Legal Systems* appears like the charming and interesting lecture series which exposes and exoticises items – in particular, edifices, records and 'men of law' – which merely illustrate without requiring the reader to become fluent in the different culture. From this as well as the general appreciation of difference one might infer that the *amatourist*, if pressed, would opt for a policy of cultural conservation.

D. Skepticism

The diverse group of approaches and authors one could co-register in the *detachment/difference* track represents varieties of comparative-legal

---

139 E.g. Barton et al. *Law in Radically Different Cultures*. Berman's 'Aftershocks' would advise one to perform the countermove of normalizing the exotic.

140 Jameson 'Marxism and Historicism,' 43.

141 Conquergood 'Performing as a Moral Act,' 405 – I changed the original text and replaced 'performances' with 'comparisons,' and 'lives' with 'laws.'

142 Wigmore *Panorama*, 3.

skepticism. They range from appreciation of the other (foreign laws, legal practices and institutions) as deserving respect and equal treatment[143] via doubt (whether unique cultures can possibly be compared) to a certain paralysis that forestalls a comparative view and evaluation altogether. Though divided internally,[144] the group's common programmatic platform would be to disturb the good conscience or even (in the case of the more ambitious and optimistic members) redirect the course of the mainstream, and prevent a person's particular legal experience from masquerading as the universally legitimate and applicable, hegemonic legal system, culture or practice:

> [c]an the comparatist ever be objective or does he not come to the act of comparison as an 'encumbered self' so that whatever exists 'out there' can only be 'known' through the filter of the comparatist's own cognitive processes and will accordingly find itself being inevitably distorted along the way'? In other words, 'cultural familiarity and respectable theory' would help but would never be enough to avoid the projection by the comparatist of his own background?[145]

---

[143] From the vantage point of a 'cultural theory' of law. See Legrand, Pierre (1999) *Fragments on Law-as-Culture*, Deventer: Tjeenk Willink.

[144] For a rather random sample of skeptics and an incomplete panorama, see Baxi *The Future of Human Rights*, 46; and Baxi (2003) 'The Colonialist Heritage' in Legrand and Munday *Comparative Legal Studies*, 46; Berman 'Aftershocks'; Frankenberg 'Critical Comparisons' and Frankenberg (1997) 'Stranger than Paradise: Identity and Politics in Comparative Law' 2 *Utah Law Review*, 259; Kennedy, David (2003) 'The Methods and the Politics of Comparative Law' in Legrand and Munday *Comparative Legal Studies*, 345; Legrand, Pierre (2006) 'Antivonbar' 1 *Journal of Comparative Law*, 13 and Legrand 'The Same and the Different', 240; Monateri, Pier G. (2000) 'Black Gaius: A Multicultural Quest for the "Western Legal Tradition"' 51 *Hastings Law Journal*, 479; Muir Watt, Horatia (2000) 'La fonction subversive du droit comparé' 52 *Revue International du Droit Comparé*, 503; Nelken 'Comparative Law and Legal Studies' in Nelken and Örücü *Comparative Law*, 3; Lasser, Mitchel (2003) 'The Question of Understanding' in Legrand and Munday *Comparative Legal Studies*, 197; Mattei, Ugo (2003) 'A Theory of Imperial Law: A Study of U.S. Hegemony and the Latin American Resistance' 10 *Indiana Journal of Global Legal Studies*, 383; Twining *Human Rights, Southern Voices* and *Twining* 'Globalisation.'

[145] Legrand, Pierre (1999) 'John Henry Merryman and Comparative Legal Studies: A Dialogue' 47 *American Journal of Comparative Law*, 54 (Legrand put this question to Merryman who responded: 'Of course. Does anyone really suppose otherwise?').

Method of skepticism

Skeptics appear to concentrate their energies on systematic doubt: they critique mainstream methodology and problems of understanding foreign law, they find problematic how to construct the object of analysis and comparison, and which methods to select.[146] Method (and theory) is the most important dimension of the skeptical track. Language and translation are considered to be risky operations:

> Our knowledge is limited, for complete understanding of a foreign legal institution is almost impossible to attain. Our vision is culturally blinkered, our expertise often built on sand.[147]

To perceive and appreciate the difference of the foreign without 'othering' it presupposes methodological sensitivity and consideration of context; these properties of 'good comparative practice' often result in critiques of mainstream methodology[148] which may anger other (less skeptical) crits.[149]

Moreover, there is the problem of complexity Rodolfo Sacco tried to tackle and reduce with his analysis of 'legal formants:'

> [T]he recognition of the multiplicity of legal formants and of the complexity with each of them result in an enormous problematization of the notion of 'understanding' a foreign legal system, thereby placing the comparatist in a serious quandary. Given the multiplicity of players in a foreign system, why should she focus her analysis … on judges, as opposed to legislators, attorneys or clients? […]
>
> If the point of comparative law is 'understanding', that is, if the point is to seek not so much 'law in books' or even 'law in action', but, to use William Ewald's elegant phrase, 'law in minds,' whose mind should we have in mind?[150]

---

[146] See Lasser, Mitchel (2003) 'The Question of Understanding' in Legrand and Munday *Comparative Legal Studies*, 197, 212–216.

[147] Großfeld, Bernhard (1990) *The Strength and Weakness of Comparative Law*, Oxford: Oxford University Press, 38.

[148] Frankenberg 'Critical Comparisons'; Legrand 'The Same and the Different.'

[149] Kennedy 'The Methods and the Politics.'

[150] Lasser 'The Question of Understanding,' 214–215, referring to Ewald 'Comparative Jurisprudence (I),' 1889, 2111.

Contextualism contravenes the formalist assumption that perfect comparison and, similarly, the easy transfer of norms are possible.[151] In consequence, skeptics in the *detachment/difference* field appear estranged from comparative law tracks where taxonomies, functional requirements, similarities and universals are routinely constructed from a Western perspective. In fact, they rather avoid comparison altogether so as not to run head on into a methodological ambush or the ideological trap of ethnocentrism. In stark contrast to the members of *Universal Dreams Inc.* whose constitutive comparison embraces (and sometimes chokes) the other as part of the universal defined in terms of the particular (Western) self, radical skeptics prefer not to risk encounters with the other, both in comparison as on the pathways of transfer, so as to avoid mainstreaming the other.

Ethics of skepticism

Skeptics realize that legal comparison is not only a methodological operation but, more specifically, a performance, and this performance is risky because of the presence of the foreign in the comparative space. They rightly assume that the reciprocity between the known and the foreign (or, self and other)[152] is asymmetrical. Therefore, it constitutes an ethical challenge for comparative legal studies.

If comparatists do not believe they can 'understand' the foreign and grasp the unique experience of cultures, or if they do not see a way to avoid ethnocentric comparison, skeptics may become champions of radical versions of *detachment/difference*. They tend to shy away from the ethical problems of comparison and, as a precaution or out of conviction, rather forestall the conversation with the other than draw the unknown/foreign into an asymmetrical conversation (comparison) with the known/self.

By contrast, moderate skeptics appear to be more confident or maybe their pragmatic comparative sense tells them that a 'rosy methodology' (which is not so rosy), if applied with rigor, may help them 'gain access

---

[151] Grosswald Curran, Vivian (1998) 'Cultural Immersion, Difference and Categories in US Comparative Law' 46 *American Journal of Comparative Law*, 43, 45 and 49; Legrand 'The Impossibility of Transplants'; Frankenberg, Günter (2013) *Order from Transfer. Comparative Constitutional Design and Legal Culture*, Cheltenham, UK and Northampton, MA, USA: Edward Elgar Publishing.

[152] Bauman, Zygmunt (1993) *Postmodern Ethics*, Oxford: Blackwell; Young, Iris Marion (1997) 'Asymmetrical Reciprocity. On Moral Respect, Wonder, and Enlarged Thought' 3 *Constellations. An International Journal of Critical and Democratic Theory*, 340, 362.

to the conceptual framework of foreign legal systems by studying and reproducing their varied discursive characteristics.'[153] Some believe they might be or may become 'skilled cultural navigators'[154] if only they try hard enough and remain circumspect on the intercultural plane. In the end, they may avoid the traps and fallacies of hegemonic and ethnocentric comparison. They can be distinguished from the tragic skeptic by their (romantic) calls for a communicative ethic of empathy or intercultural dialog.[155] They take the chance of an 'imaginative immersion in the foreign cultural context.'[156] These attempts contaminate the purity of skepticism and give up systematic doubt but actually 'do' comparative law and can always correct their performance.

Politics of skepticism

Despite their internal diversity on methodological-theoretical grounds, skeptics share what one might characterize as a politics of tragic denial. They are motivated by three concerns. First, they believe that designations and classification are not guiltless but are internally related to structures of power and sustain hegemony, in particular when allied with archetypical figures, like the primitive society. Second, they argue, with good cause, that comparisons are almost never merely descriptive but more often both evaluative, prescriptive and/or expository;[157] and, third, they claim that the real-existing divergence in the world of legal systems, families, and traditions requires a strict focus on difference rather than the move to transplants, convergence or uniformization.[158]

The politics of diversity, unless connected with denial, may target the cultural-legal preservation of what is perceived as different. Granting the

---

153 Lasser 'The Question of Understanding,' 223.

154 Ballard, Roger ed. (1994) *Desh pardesh: The South Asian Presence in Britain*, London: Hurst & Co; Menski, Werner (2002) 'Immigration and Multiculturalism in Britain: New Issues in Research and Policy' in *KIAPS: Bulletin of Asia-Pacific Studies*, 43.

155 I adopted and applied the difference between tragic and romantic legal narratives in Frankenberg (2014) 'Human Rights and the "Belief" in a Just World' 12 *International Journal of Constitutional Law*, 35.

156 Grosswald Curran 'Cultural Immersion.' See also Baer, Susanne (2004) 'Verfassungsvergleich und reflexive Methode: Interkulturelle und intersubjektive Kompetenz' 64 *Zeitschrift für ausländisches öffentliches Recht und Völkerrecht*, 735.

157 See Douglas 'Cultural Bias'; Said *Orientalism*, 149.

158 Legrand, Pierre (1996) 'European Legal Systems Are Not Converging' 45 *The International and Comparative Law Quarterly*, 52; Frankenberg 'Critical Comparisons' and 'Constitutions as Commodities.'

other equality of status and differential treatment is a commendable guiding maxim for comparative studies. Conservationism, however, may lean toward the amateur's romanticism and, as a result, discredit this maxim.

Still, the dominant tracks of comparative law – *grands systémes*, 'Grands Récits Universals' and 'Country and Western' micro-studies – are mainly challenged from skeptical positions. That could be a good starting point for a heterodox practice that prevents comparative law from becoming a 'convenience of the powerful.'[159]

[159] Baxi, Upendra (2003) 'The Colonialist Heritage' in Legrand and Munday *Comparative Legal Studies*, 46.

5. Muslim veiling: critique of a comparative discourse

1. COMPARING THE VISUALITY OF DRESS

After my critique of disciplinary practices concerning methods and aims, and then the ethics and politics of comparative law, I now turn from the cognitive to the visual and shift the focus from scholarly debates on similarity/difference to the controversy concerning Muslim veiling.[1] In this controversy, the actors – in particular courts, lawyers, legislators, and legal commentators – have to negotiate diversity and navigate normative pluralism in a practical context.[2]

The grid is applied once again to test its plausibility and use-value for a critical analysis of the various tracks of the juridical veiling discourse. Special attention will be paid to the way the diversity of modest dress worn by Muslim women and girls is translated into *legal arguments* and how this translation contributes to the social construction of the veiled woman as 'other.'

How does this discursive field relate, and actually compare to, comparative law? First, the debates, decisions, and regulations concerning *how* to dress 'properly' – as teacher, student or trial witness – and *where* dress codes apply – in schools, universities and courtrooms, at the workplace, in public places, etc. – operate with normative concepts, notably rights and duties. In fact, the participants in the discourse, more often than not, resort to a legalistic language that provides an impoverished understanding of the competing motives, perspectives and sartorial styles by reducing the garment to its attributed symbolic meanings and

---

1 Due to a lack of specific sartorial competence concerning Muslim dress, I treat as variations of veiling and modest dress, and distinguish when necessary: *hijāb*, *niqāb*, *burqa* or *shador*, which cover in different ways the female head, neck, face or full body respectively.

2 In this chapter I draw, in particular, on the work of Alia Al-Saji, Ratna Kapur and Saba Mahmood. I am also indebted to discussions with Claudia Baumann, Asmaa El Idrissi, Lena-Maria Möller and Intisar Rabb and the students attending my research seminar at Sciences-po.

framing the fundamental conflict as one of religion versus the state's (or a government's) duty to protect public order, social peace, public security, etc.

Second, the various styles of Muslim dress are comparatively evaluated and their legality judged according to what kind of Muslim dress is worn; where it is worn – in institutional settings, like courts, governments, and parliaments, in the public sphere or at home; and by whom – school teacher, student, court judge, etc. So the discourse on Muslim dress is *comparative* in several respects. Openly or implicitly, supporters and critics alike pass judgment on veiling. The comparative operation routinely takes the 'Western'[3] (secular/civilized/normal/own, etc.) position and cultural-legal experience as points of departure. While this position determines interpretation (*similarity/difference*) and perspective (*detachment/commitment*), it remains unmarked in the comparative operation. Very much like *cognitive control* in comparative law, it also serves as a point of return. Thus, the comparison of dress confirms Western standards and aesthetics of clothing.

The grid is used to track down the strands of the discourse, and identify and distinguish the main legal arguments concerning Islamic dress as well as the perceptions they translate into law. The focus will be directed at the headscarf (*hijāb*), face-veil (*niqāb*) and full-body veil (*burqa*), which dominate the juridical discourse as far as it is concerned with veiling:

> Though the word *hijāb* derives from the Arabic word for 'barrier' or 'veil' … and its primary reference is to the curtain that separates men and women in prayer … a *hijāb* is a type of kerchief and not a veil, though revealingly the debate in France focused on … *le voile* (veil) when referring explicitly to the *hijāb*. Of course there are also headscarves that serve as veils to cover the face, such as the two-piece *al-amira* veil and the *khimar,* or even the eyes with a fabric mesh, such as the *burqa*. However, *hijābs* are not technically veils … The *hijāb* should also not be equated with the *jilbab*, the long flowing robe that the Koran requires women and their daughters to draw close around them so that they may be both recognized but not molested, or the *chador* worn in Iran that is really a headdress extended over the whole body but leaving the

[3] The 'West' (or 'Western') is regarded and used here as neither a geopolitical trope nor a homogenous social-cultural context but a contested concept and terrain where, especially, political-legal, cultural-social discourses intersect.

> face exposed. The *niqab* (a head veil covering the face except for the eyes, as well as the *dupatta*) is also technically just a headscarf but it covers the face.[4]

Whereas this quote illustrates a remarkable diversity in styles that come under the heading of veiling and require distinction, the comparative discourse on Muslim dress differs from the academic discourse on comparative law in several respects. First, Islam, its (presumed) dress code, and the covered Muslim woman have been cast in the ongoing debates as today's paradigmatic other:

> Religion has also become the primary, overarching frame through which the 'Islamic' world has become viewed. And leaders in America and elsewhere have frequently engaged with Islam in ways that are reductionist and simplistic, often casting it as authoritarian and in opposition to the West and Western values …
>
> The image of the veiled woman has been displaced on to a cultural divide along which many global conversations about women's rights take place, and where culture is something invariably associated with the 'native' other. … The image of the veiled woman has come to inhabit our imaginations in ways that are totalizing of the culture and its treatment of women.[5]

Consequently, the styles[6] of veiling (rather unlike foreign laws that are usually submitted to legal comparison) incite discomfort and anxiety, stimulate – often camouflaged – cultural curiosity and sexual fantasies. That is why the legal discourse appears to be obsessed with the Muslim veil, whereas other forms of covering, the turban for instance, or religious symbols worn as part of the dress, like the habit of nuns, the kippah or crucifix, are mentioned, if at all, only in passing.

Second, the emotions Muslim dress evokes in the observer are all but routinely translated into and camouflaged by political statements, official legal opinions, and legalistic media op-eds from Norway to Western

---

4 Adelman, Howard (2008) 'Rights and the *Hijāb*: Rationality and Discourse in the Public Sphere' 8 *Human Rights & Human Welfare*, 43, 45 (citations omitted).

5 Kapur, Ratna (2002) 'Un-Veiling Women's Rights in the "War on Terrorism"' 9 *Duke Journal of Gender Law & Policy*, 211, 215, 217. See also Ghazal Read, Jen'nan and Bartkowski, John P. (2000) 'To Veil or Not to Veil? A Case Study of Identity Negotiation among Muslim Women in Austin, Texas' 14 *Gender & Society*, 395–417.

6 Sandikci, Özlem and Ger, Güliz (2010) 'Veiling in Style: How Does a Stigmatized Practice Become Fashionable?' 37 *Journal of Consumer Research*, 15.

Australia and Florida to Istanbul.[7] So the discourse on veiling is a result of transfers: the perception of the veil generates a mix of emotions that are translated into the legal language and return as legislative decisions (bans), court rulings, and authoritative legal opinions. These transfers, so it seems, are particularly resistant to empirical evidence, like the diverse motives women have to veil, and intensely uninterested in listening to what Muslim girls and women have to say. The reason may be that veiling calls on the observer to account for his erotic and other fantasies and rethink both religion and his/her secular world.[8]

Third, and maybe more significantly, as distinct from the scholarly discourse on comparative law, the debates about veiling deal with and are ignited by *visual* phenomena: 'The sheer symbolism of the veil brings the woman visibly into the public sphere.'[9] Paradoxically, the other who inhabits the same political sphere – and also comparative space – becomes highly visible by her covering and produces a vision that is constitutive of the self-other relation. The co-presence of the Muslim woman is not only conceptually verified (as Oriental, foreigner, etc.) but visually represented through her embodied practice and style of dress. No wonder then that legal judgment is not only marginally but crucially influenced by the visibility and conspicuousness of *hijāb*, *niqāb* and, especially, the *burqa.*

---

[7] From the rapidly burgeoning literature, see only Adelman, 'Rights and the Hijāb'; Benhabib, Seyla (2004) *The Rights of Others. Aliens, Residents, and Citizens*, Cambridge: Cambridge University Press; Keaton, Trica D. (2006) *Muslim Girls and the Other France: Race, Identity Politics & Social Exclusion*, Bloomington: Indiana University Press; McGoldrick, Dominic (2006) *Human Rights and Religion: The Islamic Headscarf Debate*, Portland: Hart Publishers; and Ferrari, Alessandro and Pastorelli, Sabrina eds (2013) *The Burqa Affair Across Europe*, Farnham: Ashgate.

[8] For a differentiated answer to the question whether critique is secular, see Mahmood, Saba (2009) 'Religious Reason and Secular Affect: An Incommensurable Divide?' in Asad, Talal, Brown, Wendy, Butler, Judith and Mahmood, Saba eds *Is Critique Secular? Blasphemy, Injury, and Free Speech*, Berkeley: University of California Press, 64.

[9] Kapur 'Un-Veiling Women's Rights,' 218; see also the informative and engaging article by Al-Saji, Alia (2010) 'The Racialization of Muslim Veils: A Philosophical Analysis' 36 *Philosophy and Social Criticism*, 875.

2. APPLYING THE GRID TO MUSLIM VEILING

To apply a grid developed for language and meaning to sartorial styles therefore presupposes that its basic framework is sensitized and adapted to the conspicuous visuality of Muslim dress:

> Vision is as important as language in mediating social relations, and it is not reducible to language, or sign, or to discourse. Pictures want equal rights with language, not to be turned into language.[10]

In order to capture the specificity of the veil's visual impact, I used the basic coordinates of the grid to chart four discrete perceptions and interpretations of the veil that are translated into legal arguments (see Figure 5.1 below). The interpretive axis (*similarity/difference*) and the axis designating perspective and positionality (*detachment/commitment*) have been expanded to include visual aspects. This way I tried to connect legal reasoning by judges, legal scholars, governments and parliaments, who compared veiling to what they considered normal/legal/constitutional and different/similar, with images of the Muslim woman embedded in their law texts.[11]

The 'tracking' illustrates how the two main tracks, on the *similarity*-level, establish a dualistic, basically Western matrix according to which the practice of covering (A.) violates the public order, public safety or republican, secular principles or (B.) suppresses the veiled woman, and in each case warrants intervention. By contrast, the tracks on the *difference*-level dissent from the mainstream and pursue the strategy of (C.) exoticization or (D.) skepticism, and both allow for a broader margin of toleration and, for different reasons, do not advocate intervention.

The grid appears to cover almost all pertinent legal opinions on veiling. However, the four tracks are representative rather than comprehensive, they only comprise a fairly wide spectrum ranging from justifying interventions on behalf of order, security or human rights to the preference for non-intervention informed by fascination with the oriental or doubt regarding the normative matrix of Western law.

More significantly, the shift from the analysis of academic schools of comparative thought to the comparative critique of the legal and political

---

[10] Mitchell, William J.T. (2005) *What Do Pictures Want? The Lives and Loves of Images*, Chicago: University of Chicago Press, 47.

[11] The mapping of the selected materials is tentative and not representative with regard to any legal system or even the case law of a given court.

arguments that constitute the veil-discourse called for a modification of the descriptions of the three internal dimensions of the quadrants.

The dimension of *method* no longer denotes a strictly methodological approach to comparative research but a method of legal reasoning. The reasoning concentrates on and comparatively evaluates the *conspicuousness* of Islamic dress and its deviance from Western sartorial styles that are considered, often by implication, to be 'normal.'

The dimension of *ethics* is constituted by the intensely visible co-existence of the covered woman – perceived and constructed as other – in the same life-world and comparative space (society, republic, state, public sphere, classroom, etc.). As numerous laws, court decisions, and comments show, the other is under constant scrutiny – legal, political and otherwise. It remains to be seen whether the legal discourse complies with the ethics of comparison that would require recognition of the foreign/other as an equal cohabitant of this space and of her dress as not only an element of political semiotics but also a garment.

In the discourse on veiling the dimension of *politics* is coextensive with the space demarcated by prohibition/toleration and intervention/non-intervention. Generally, limits to toleration will correspond to the range of interventionist policies, whereas acceptance or appreciation of the veil informs non-intervention.

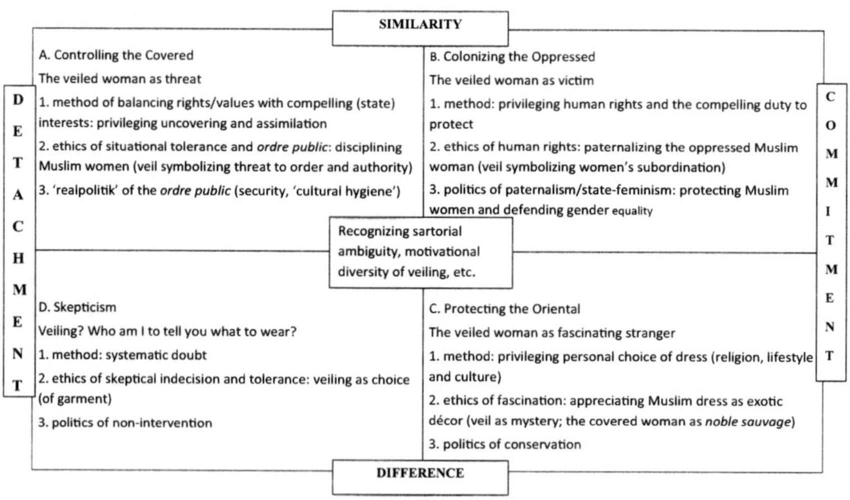

Figure 5.1 The grid applied to Muslim veiling

3. CONTROLLING THE COVERED WOMAN

Those who argue for control of covered Muslim girls and women generally perceive their veiling as a threat. As with the scholarly legal comparison characterized above as cognitive control, the *controllers* reappear in the controversies about Islamic dress. They are no less geared toward order and security and on sustaining the hegemony of the culture and world where veiling is considered strange or unusual because it deviates from sartorial standards. Here, the (visual) control track follows to a certain extent the well-known logic of the debates on public safety and security[12] and 'militant democracy.' It is triggered by the perception of a phenomenon (the veil) or practice (covering) as a *threat*: the teacher wearing a *hijāb* is regarded as threatening the social harmony in schools and, by the same token, the authority of the state which guarantees the proper functioning of public institutions. Worn in public, the modest dress of Muslim girls and women conspicuously challenges Western behavioral forms, cultural norms and social values. In France and the pre-Erdogan Turkey, the argument gets a political twist: the veil violating *laïcité*.

Basically, the threat stems from a religion – Islam – which breeds, among hundreds of millions of peaceful believers, radical crusaders who fight a holy war against the West and do not hesitate to commit terrorist acts. The short circuit from Islam to terrorism is discussed by András Sajó in his comment on the controversy about the Danish cartoons:

> [T]he cartoons indicate a truly unpleasant *factual* connection … between terrorism and a very successful version of Islam … If the criticism of religion is successfully recategorized as racism, then that means … that you cannot criticize religious terrorism, even though religion *really* does have its finger in the terrorism pie.[13]

In a second step, the perception of danger (to public peace, authority or whatever) then releases the standard arguments, instruments, and measures to outlaw potentially dangerous behavior:

---

[12] Frankenberg, Günter (2014) *Political Technology and the Erosion of the Rule of Law: Normalizing the State of Exception*, Cheltenham, UK and Northampton, MA, USA: Edward Elgar Publishing.

[13] Sajó, András (2007) 'Free Speech, Religion and the Right to Caricature' in Sajó, András ed. *Censorial Sensitivities: Free Speech and Religion in a Fundamentalist World*, Utrecht: Eleven International Publishing, 288.

> The defence of the public order … makes it possible to proscribe conduct which directly runs counter to rules that are essential to the republican social covenant.[14]

The measures aim to establish control and discipline over the covered person – her body and mind – and vindicate the endangered authority, institution or principle. The official reaction demands that the covered uncover.

Exercised by legislatures and courts, agencies and agents of the state, the concept of control of the visual comprises diverse measures: prohibiting teachers or students from wearing scarves and veils in schools or universities; banning Islamic dress from the public sphere; implementing a no-veil policy for exercise of public functions or in public settings, like schools, court procedures. Exercising control over the visibility of the veil in public relegates it to the private sphere: on a case-by-case basis, it may be allowed in non-state public settings (supermarket) where there is no authority to be threatened.

Method of Visual Control

The arguments in parliamentary or court decisions usually differ in terms of their generality or specificity. Bans can be general or restricted to areas or functions, laws can be sweeping or ad hoc, court decisions narrowly framed or overly broad. Whatever the form and scope, legal justifications of veil-control are internally connected. They transform discomfort with the *hijāb,* more so the *niqāb* (not even mentioning the *burqa*), and the religion it visualizes, into a threat to public order that has to be averted.

'Public order' comes in different conceptual guises. German police law defines it as the ensemble of (non-legal) norms that are non-renounceable for peaceful coexistence in society. Because of its blatant indeterminacy and, more so, because it privileges the moral economy of a society's majority, courts and commentators, if possible, prefer to avoid the concept.[15] In the French context, the term *ordre public* neither comes with precise contours nor the spirit of minority protection. It may refer to

---

[14] Explanatory Memorandum of the French 'Burka Ban' (2004) quoted in *S.A.S. v. France*, European Court of Human Rights (ECtHR), Decision of 1 July 2014, Application No. 43835/11, para. 25.

[15] It has seen a renaissance, though, in German constitutional jurisprudence. Regarding the *öffentliche Ordnung* as an indeterminate concept: Gusy, Christoph (2014) *Polizeirecht*, 9th ed., Tübingen: Mohr Siebeck.

'all institutions and agents that are part of the state and which the state controls,' 'to any area of shared space' or 'to anything that affects the common weal.'[16] In this quadrant it lends itself to framing the veiling conflict as one 'between secular necessity and religious threat'[17] based on the dichotomy of a secular worldview and religious fundamentalism or extremism.

The argumentative technique to solve this constellation of conflicts resembles the standard manner of balancing. The rights of the Muslim woman to religious freedom and self-expression are weighed against principles, like neutrality, separation of state and religion, radicalized to the conception of *laïcité*, or, in a courtroom setting, fair trial; and also against values, like social peace and harmony in schools, public safety or the effective functioning of the administration of justice or highway security.

Balancing, however, has always been under attack by scholars who make the criticism that it lacks precision and predictability and that the discretion granted to judges compromises the promise of fairness and justice.[18] The method of balancing is even more precarious in the context of religion and religious freedom in two regards. First, it routinely operates with criteria, like the seriousness, sincerity, and non-capriciousness of belief, in order to bring the *forum internum* within the legal review exercised by courts.[19] As far as the dress code is concerned, many courts therefore require a show of proof that its regulations are authoritative and observed as binding.

Second, the balancing is (or can be) pre-structured by the notion of religion as a mere belief that is a private matter of choice.[20] As a result, a religion and religious dress, which are hardly compatible with secular Western civilization, come with a disadvantage to the forum of balancing, where they encounter absolutes, like *laïcité*, indeterminate concepts, like public order, or incommensurable concepts, like security. Consequently,

16 Adelman, 'Rights and the Hijāb,' 56 seq. See also Bowen, John R. (2006) *Why the French Don't Like Headscarves: Islam, the State, and Public Space*, Princeton: Princeton University Press.

17 Mahmood, 'Religious Reason and Secular Affect,' 65.

18 For critiques of balancing, see Kennedy, Duncan (2002) 'The Critique of Rights in Critical Legal Studies' in Brown, Wendy and Halley, Janet eds *Left Legalism/Left Critique*, Durham: Duke University Press, 178; Michaelson, Christopher (2006) 'Balancing Civil Liberties Against National Security? A Critique of Counterterrorism Rhetoric' 29 *UNSW Law Journal*, 1.

19 See Supreme Court of Canada in *R. v. NS*, 2012 SCC 72 [2012] 3 SCR 726 and the court decisions discussed below.

20 Mahmood 'Religious Reason and Secular Affect.'

the decisionism or arbitrariness which is always contained in the balancing method already can be tipped, by sleight of hand, in favor of one or the other state interest or public concern and distinguished as 'compelling.' The following court decisions illustrate how the method of prestructured balancing operates in veiling cases.

Ludin was the first of the two headscarf cases decided by the German Federal Constitutional Court (FCC)[21] and could be expected to balance Ms. Ludin's right as a schoolteacher to freedom of religious expression against the principle of neutrality and that state's duty to protect the rights of pupils and their parents to a 'neutral' classroom setting based on their negative freedom of religion. As a matter of fact, the FCC's Second Senate started from a narrow interpretation of the headscarf:[22]

> Aside from the wish to respect the regulations of a dress-code founded in *religion* and felt to be binding, [veiling] can also be interpreted as [the wearer's desire] to adhere to the *traditions* of the society of origin.

For no good reason (provided by Ms. Ludin's reputation or performance as a teacher), the Court went on to open up the panorama of threat and risk:

> Recently, [the veil] is seen as a *political symbol* of Islamic *fundamentalism*, expressing delimitation to values of the Western society, like individual self-determination and especially the emancipation of the woman.

In a return to its *Crucifix* case decided in 1995, the Court then clarified that 'tolerating the dress of teachers … which *is to be* interpreted as religiously motivated cannot be equated with a directive of the State to mount religious symbols in classrooms' and that the daily encounter with a teacher in a headscarf does not negatively influence or indoctrinate pupils. After having declared a Bavarian law unconstitutional, which had mandated the mounting of crucifixes in elementary school classrooms,

---

[21] Federal Constitutional Court (FCC), Decision of 24 September 2003 *Ludin* 108 *Entscheidungen des Bundesverfassungsgerichts*, 282. On the legal controversy about veiling in Germany: Sacksofsky, Ute (2008) 'Religion and Equality in Germany: The Headscarf Debate from a Constitutional Perspective' in Schiek, Dagmar and Chege, Victoria eds *European Union Non-Discrimination Law: Comparative Perspectives on Multidimensional Equality Law*, London: Taylor & Francis, 353. See also Kahn, Robert A. (2007) 'The Headscarf as Threat: A Comparison of German and U.S. Legal Discourses' 40 *Vanderbilt Journal of Transnational Law*, 417.

[22] The following quotations are taken from *Ludin*, no. 50–51, 54. See also Sacksofsky, Ute (2015) 'Glaubensfreiheit' 789 *Merkur*, 54–64.

the Court felt justified in indicating a narrow, but not prohibitive, stance on teachers' religious dress.

The Court's majority held, with a restrictive interpretation of the rationale adopted by the European Court of Human Rights (ECtHR),[23] that states could not exclude religious symbols from the classroom with a blanket ban and required that they constitute a threat to school peace. Somewhat surprisingly, rather than actually deciding the *Ludin* case by constitutional balancing, the majority argued that a ban on religious symbols from classrooms required a statutory basis that would meet the constitutional standards, in particular, the principle of proportionality. And since school education, within the vertical distribution of legislative competences, is not a federal but a state matter, the Court deferred the decision to the state legislatures, whether to issue such a ban and how to frame it.

By contrast, the dissenting minority of the Second Senate concentrated on a teacher's status as a civil servant and the restrictions of her rights. The judges proceeded to balance Ms. Ludin's rights and, not surprisingly, found them deficient and not weighty enough to outbalance her duties as civil servant. The lengthy considerations on her status as civil servant clearly pre-structured the outcome: that teachers in public schools have no right to veil.

As could have been expected, several states (*Länder*) of the Federal Republic of Germany felt encouraged by this decision and came forth with statutory bans of religious symbols to protect the state's neutrality in classrooms and other public institutions. Most of them were fairly broadly worded and did not require evidence that the religious symbols could plausibly be said to pose a concrete danger to school peace. In many of the state statutes on veiling, the concept of abstract danger that comes with a low probability threshold looms dark in the background.

In a decision of 2015, the First Senate of the German Constitutional Court corrected the tendency to ban veiling (and other religious symbols) with fairly broadly worded statutes and incidentally revised *Ludin* without explicitly overruling it.[24] In a decision that was culturally sensitive and mindful of the gender aspect, the Court's majority considered the Muslim headscarf (*hijāb*) a garment which, depending on the social context, may have religious connotations. The majority also

---

[23] ECtHR, Decision of 15 February 2001 *Dahlab v. Switzerland*, Application No. 42393/98.

[24] Technically, the Court issued two (connected) rulings: FCC, Decision of 27 January 2015, 1 BvR 471/10 and 1 BvR 1181/10. In the following I refer to both cases jointly as a connected ruling.

recognized that there are 'diverse possibilities of interpretation' regarding the motives of girls and women to wear headscarves.[25] In the crucial passages, the Court conceded that while interventions to protect public interests are, by themselves, legitimate they need to be interpreted restrictively as far as religious freedom is concerned:

> [So the Court struck down as disproportionate and therefore unconstitutional] the general prohibition of religious statements by one's external appearance, already on account of the *merely abstract* qualification to endanger school peace or the State's neutrality in a school open to all denominations, if this behavior can be plausibly attributed to religious command understood as binding.[26]

The loopy wording camouflages the critique of *Ludin* and guides the reader cautiously from the former doctrine of 'religious symbol = unclear and abstract danger' to the novel doctrine requiring evidence that a religious symbol or garment brings or may bring forth controversy and concretely endanger school peace. In a concession to the old doctrine (possibly also to some of its own judges and parts of the general public) the majority made allowance for a situation of conflict. The judges considered the possibility of concrete danger, in case the external appearance of teachers led or significantly contributed to an actual disturbance of the school peace or the state's neutrality. They argued that such a situation should be handled by the school first.

The ruling refers to 'the *visibility* of religious convictions and practices of dress' that could trigger a controversial discussion about 'the correct religious behavior.'[27] With admirable clarity, the Court concluded, thinning out the ties between religious dress and security:

> Wearing an Islamic headscarf regularly does not substantiate a sufficiently concrete danger. Wearing this headdress, all by itself, does not have a soliciting or even proselytizing effect.[28]

In the Unites States, *Freeman v. Florida*, a *niqāb* case, received considerable attention.[29] A Muslim woman's driver's license was revoked after

---

[25] *Ibid.* at no. 94 and 100.

[26] *Ibid.* at no. 101.

[27] *Ibid.* at no. 113 – emphasis added.

[28] *Ibid.* at no. 116.

[29] Florida Circuit Court, Decision of 6 June 2003 *Freeman v. Florida*, No. 2002-CA-2828, 2003 WL 21338619. For a comparative view of *Ludin* and *Freeman* see Kahn 'The Headscarf as Threat,' 153 and also Moore, Kathleen M.

she had refused, appealing to her right to religious freedom, to be re-photographed for her license without her *niqāb*, a veil covering her face without her eyes. The *Freeman* Court followed – religiously, one might be tempted to add – the balancing procedure. It began with probing the sincerity of belief and continued with hearing (controversial) expert testimony on the necessity of veiling pursuant to the Islamic religion.[30] In a next step, the Court examined whether the appellant 'could show a substantial burden on the free exercise of her religion.' In the end the Court allowed her to wear a headscarf but subordinated her veiling practice to 'society's need to identify people as quickly as possible in situations in which safety and security could be at risk' and found, on balance, the state's interest in public safety compelling.

In *The Queen v. D (R)*, an equally prominent *niqāb* case in Great Britain, the judge used the balancing method in a manner that compares to the *Freeman* ruling. The judge first set the *niqāb* worn 'for religious reasons' by a prosecution witness during court proceedings against the principle of fair trial. The latter, he argued, included above all the need to see the face of a witness during testimony. Second, he weighed the 'deleterious effects … of broader societal harms' and the 'harm done by limiting the witness's sincerely held religious practice' on the one hand against 'preventing a serious risk to trial fairness' on the other. In the end, the Court tipped the balance in favor of the interests of the administration of justice, the jurors, the general public and democratic society.[31] The judge's argument rested primarily on the principle of proportionality. The proportionality test obliged the Court to consider a less intrusive but equally effective way of 'enabling the Court to conduct the proceedings fairly and effectively in the interest of all parties.'[32]

In 2014, the ECtHR had to decide whether the French '*Burqa* Ban' of 2010 violated the *European Convention on Human Rights*. The ban prohibited women, girls and, theoretically, other persons from wearing

---

(2007) 'Visible through the Veil: The Regulation of Islam in American Law' 68 *Sociology of Religion*, 237, 246–248.

[30] As in other cases, law experts affirm the strong basis for the headscarf in Islamic law but denied it for veiling.

[31] Decision of 16 September 2013 *The Queen v. D (R)*, Judge P. Murphy, 24. For a comparable reasoning see ECtHR, Decision of 1 July 1997 *Kalaç v. Turkey*, Application No. 20704/92, no. 27, also in 27 EHRR 552 and ECtHR, Decision of 10 November 2005 *Şahin v. Turkey*, Application No. 44774/98, unreported, no. 105; European Commission of Human Rights (ECmHR), Decision of 12 March 1981 *Ahmad v. United Kingdom*, no. 11, also in 4 EHRR 126.

[32] *The Queen v. D (R)*, 34.

the *burqa* or any garment concealing the face in the public sphere, comprising 'public highways and any places for the public or assigned to a public service': 'No one may, in public places, wear clothing that is designed to conceal the face.'[33]

Interestingly enough, the law of 2010 followed the French law of 2004, which had banned 'conspicuous religious signs in public schools,' and also a general interdiction of veiling in schools issued by the Minister of Education in 1994, 'interpreting every case of the veil as *ostentatoire* (conspicuous) in itself.'[34] The *Conseil d'État*, as before in the first *foulard* controversy in 1989, referred to the 1905 law on *laïcité* and emphasized the students' freedom of conscience and their right to wear religious symbols as long as this did not amount to proselytism.

In *S.A.S. v. France*, the ECtHR accompanied the French Government and *Assemblée Nationale* and went down a different road to *laïcité*. The ensemble of French commissions and institutions had previously dignified the social construction of normal dress as a 'right' of the majority to meet unconcealed women and other persons in public. To reach that result, in a series of what appear like balancing moves, the Court went down the list of possible justifications for prohibiting women from wearing a full-body veil – duress, oppression, public safety – and found them invariably wanting – not 'necessary in a democratic society … within the meaning of Articles 8 and 9 of the Convention.'

In its final and crucial turn, the ruling then extended the scope of the *European Convention on Human Rights*:

> [The ECtHR examined a concern] it has found legitimate: to ensure the observance of the minimum requirements of life in society as part of the 'protection of the rights and freedoms of others.'[35]

The Court abstained from an open (one could also say, fair) balancing, because it found satisfaction in the observation, from its Strasbourg vantage point, 'that this is an aim to which *the authorities* have given much weight.' This observation predetermined the ultimate outcome and pre-structured the decision to justify the blanket ban insofar as it seeks to guarantee the conditions of 'living together.' In a long passage, the Court, after claiming to probe the ban's proportionality, revealed the grotesque extent of the pre-structuring. It merely reiterated critiques of the ban (it

---

[33] Decision of 1 July 2014 *S.A.S. v. France*, Application No. 43835/11; Section 1 and 2 of Law No. 2010-1192.

[34] Al-Saji 'The Racialization of Muslim Veils,' 876, 879.

[35] *S.A.S. v. France*, no. 140.

held to be unfounded, of course) and then concluded with an about-turn conspicuous in a high court set up to protect human rights:

> It can thus be said that the question whether or not it should be permitted to wear the full-face veil in public places constitutes a *choice of society*. [And that] in such circumstances the Court has a duty to exercise a degree of restraint in its review of Convention compliance, since that review will lead it to assess a balance that has been struck by means of a democratic process within the society in question.[36]

Restraint and the 'margin of appreciation'[37] compromised even the mere pretense of balancing. Jointly they permitted the majority of the Grand Chamber to reverse the conventional reading (not only) of this rights convention. The reasoning, its logic rather, betrays that to begin with the Court ensured the possibility of limiting the 'rights in question' and then left a little space for their guarantee – all of this to avert the abstract threat, emanating from a miserably small number of fully covered women in France called by the ECtHR somewhat sheepishly 'the society in question.'

The Ethics of Visual Control

The *ethical* dimension of comparing dress is principally constituted, to repeat, by the presence and coexistence of the other in the same space, and the challenge to share this space. An ethical approach to comparing dress codes would demand that an unusually or conspicuously dressed other be recognized as equal and her dress seen and comparatively evaluated as a garment, and not always immediately reduced to its symbolic meaning. Once perceived and interpreted as a symbol (and a dangerous one at that), the headscarf and other styles of modest dress can be regarded not only as unusual or atypical within a given societal context but as 'ostentatious' and threatening one or the other aspect of order or being 'at odds with the values of the Republic.'[38]

---

[36] *Ibid.*, no. 153–154 – emphasis added.

[37] For a friendlier, one is inclined to say, apologetic appreciation of the ECtHR's jurisdiction and its practice of respecting a 'margin of appreciation,' that is discretion, on the part of the states: Nigro, Raffaella (2010) 'The Margin of Appreciation Doctrine and the Case-Law of the European Court on Human Rights on the Islamic Veil' 11 *Human Rights Review*, 531.

[38] Report 'On the wearing of the full-face veil on national territory' quoted in *S.A.S. v. France*, 15.

Consequently, an 'ostentatious' embodied practice is shifted from an ethics of recognition to one of selective or situational toleration. In consequence, the principles and rationales of toleration – securing peaceful coexistence, respecting difference, appreciating difference as valuable[39] – have to negotiate their force and scope with political demands that conspicuous dress be submitted to control and, in case of doubt, proscribed. Modest dress worn by Muslim women can be tolerated, in the sartorial police's narrow view, only within limits drawn by the intensity of the threat and according to what the situation may require. Hence, the limits of freedom and style are demarcated less by ethical or legal concerns than by official perceptions of risk and danger. In (non-Muslim) societies where veiling is common or not all that unusual, modest dress will therefore be tolerated for strategic rather than normative reasons, because a ban would very likely be disobeyed and threaten peaceful coexistence. In (non-Muslim) societies where veiling is uncommon, the 'margin of appreciation' can therefore be wider and defined in more generous, normative terms, as long as the risk is officially assessed as low.

Accordingly, the FCC decided in its second headscarf ruling (2015) that a teacher is entitled to wear a Muslim *hijāb* because it (a) constitutes a 'weak' religious symbol, in comparison with the crucifix, and (b) poses only the abstract (statistical, temporally remote) risk of controversy.[40] In *Freeman*, the District Court found that forcing the Muslim woman to comply with the photograph requirements for obtaining a driving license places 'no substantial burden upon her exercise of religion' because she was not required to 'engage in conduct that [her] religion forbids' and therefore confirmed the decision of the Circuit Court.[41] The latter had held that the state interest in highway safety was 'compelling' and suggested in an *obiter dictum* that the covered woman might contemplate terrorist acts from under her *niqāb*:

> It would be foolish not to recognize that there are new threats to public safety, including both foreign and national *terrorism*.[42]

---

[39] See the different models or rationales of tolerance analyzed by Forst, Rainer (2004) 'Limits of Toleration' 11 *Constellations. An International Journal of Critical and Democratic Theory*, 312; Forst, Rainer (2007) 'Toleration' in *Stanford Encyclopedia of Philosophy*, http://plato.stanford.edu/entries/toleration (last accessed 29 January 2016).

[40] FCC, Decision of 27 January 2015.

[41] The District Court of Appeal of the State of Florida, Case No. 5 D03-2296, 13 February 2006.

[42] The Circuit Court for Orange County.

In *The Queen v. D (R)*, the judge mentioned risks and, if only in passing, that the *niqāb* could be 'abused as disguise, to facilitate impersonation or for some other improper purpose.' The judge saw no threat there because

> [t]hat kind of case would pose no real problem. The Court would be justified in taking immediate steps to protect the integrity of its proceedings.' [The Court] should then decide the question before it on the basis of a universally applicable legal principle, and not on the basis of a subjective assessment of the motives of a particular defendant.[43]

These principles – in particular rule of law, open justice, fair trial, right to manifest one's religion – he used as the normative basis to carefully carve out the legal requirements for limiting the manifestation of religion, starting with 'national security, public safety, the prevention of disorder and crime, and the protection of the rights and freedoms of others.'[44] Ultimately, he proposed to adopt the least restrictive approach consistent with fair proceedings and allowed for a private identification procedure of a trial witness. After that the defendant was free to wear the *niqāb* during trial, because he saw no risk there.

In all these cases (and also in the legislative decisions the courts had to deal with), *control* of the covered woman was based on ethics of *situational tolerance*. Depending on the risk or danger assessment as to possible controversies in schools, possible dangers for the authority of the state or trial procedures, or as regards secret support for terrorism, the ethics of situational or selective tolerance produced a diversity of legal responses, which invariably at least considered and weighed the legal protection of a minority or an individual over against security and other interests.

By contrast, *S.A.S. v. France* supports a different view by agencies of government and finally also the human rights high court. In a dramatic change of the ethical perspective, the other, member of a minuscule minority, is set against the dominant moral majority, the ethical self/own. From the very beginning of the political process, throughout the legal proceedings, and finally the structure of the court's ruling, the veiled woman and rights-holder did not stand a fair chance to explicate her motives, let alone win 'her' case.

Other countries, which like France had to deal with a significant nationalist-xenophobic political party, as for instance Belgium and the Netherlands, followed the French initiative to organize the exodus of

---

43 *The Queen v. D (R)*, 7.

44 *Ibid.*, 19.

Muslim girls and women 'from the subservience of the full-face veil.' While the commissions and the *Conseil d'État* studied 'the possible legal grounds for banning the full veil,' their recommendations and the resolution of the National Assembly – and also the European Court's decision – testify to a lack of interest in hearing the voices from the suburban margins and an intense silence about the protection of minorities or tolerance of 'deviant' behavior, nonhazardous one would think. Instead, the French brand of a militant republican secularism, *laïcité*, triumphed, paradoxically even in neighboring constitutional monarchies. Without any prior risk assessment, the ethics of limited tolerance was swept away by the ethics of paranoia (like in the *Freeman* decision):

> The voluntary and systematic concealment of the face is problematic because it is quite simply incompatible with the fundamental requirements of 'living together' in French society. … Moreover, this form of public confinement, even in cases where it is voluntary or accepted, clearly contravenes the principle of respect for the dignity of the person. In addition, it is not only about the dignity of the individual who is confined in this manner, but also the dignity of others who share the same public space and who are treated as individuals from whom one must be protected by the refusal of any exchange, even if only *visual*.[45]

The combination of the *visibility* of dress and the *invisibility* of its wearer, one has to conclude, triggered the multi-institutional 'defense of the public order' and led to the invocation of 'the Republican social covenant.'[46] The covered other is not tolerated, even if she coexists in the same lifeworld and an 'objective observer' might find her strange but non-threatening.

The Politics of Visual Control

The politics of control are typically supported by advocates of intervention. They argue for order, discipline and unveiling. Regarding Islamic dress, Muslim women, and Islam, control of their visibility contains two internally related political agendas.[47] The first political project, squarely located on the *detachment/similarity* track, caters rather directly and in a

---

[45] *Exploratory Memorandum*, contained in the '*Burqa* Ban' and crucial for the decision of the ECtHR. See *S.A.S. v. France*, no. 25.

[46] *Ibid.*

[47] E.g. Scott, Joan (2007) *The Politics of the Veil*, Princeton: Princeton University Press; Ghazal Read, Jen'nan (2007) 'Introduction: The Politics of Veiling in Comparative Perspective' 68 *Sociology of Religion*, 231.

quite worldly fashion to public safety and whatever security may call for. According to the police routines of averting danger, *hijāb, niqāb* and *burqa* are reduced from garments to symbols with mainly or exclusively political connotations, like divisiveness, anti-*laïcité*, anti-Western fundamentalism, religious extremism or even Islamic terrorism.[48] And the veiled woman finds herself branded as carrier of a dangerous symbol. Incidentally, the comparative space is redefined from 'society' or 'culture' to 'national territory,'[49] which evokes the necessity of defense against religious fundamentalism and political jihadism.

Apart from a possible impact on the relations between state and religion, concealing the face and/or body is seen as a political statement informed by, or representing, religious extremism, which raises national objections and concerns of public safety. Compared to *Ludin*'s accent on state authority and only incidental defense of Christian values, *Freeman* shifted the perspective quite openly from religion to highway safety and, without cause, to national security:

> [T]he Court agrees with the State that today it is a different world than it was 20–25 years ago. It would be foolish not to recognize that there are new threats to public safety, including both foreign and national *terrorism*.[50]

On a more mundane safety note, the ECtHR, in *Refah Partisi v. Turkey*, compared the obligation of a teacher not to wear a headscarf to the traffic law 'requiring a motorcyclist to wear a crash helmet, which in his view is incompatible with his religious duties.'[51]

The second set of strategies comprises laws and doctrines that address the more abstract threat emanating from religion. The concept of control asserts that the management of religious plurality and strangeness is geared toward sustaining order. In the name of public order or *ordre*

---

48 See Moore, 'Visible'; Allen, Anita L. (2008) 'Undressing Difference: The Hijāb in the West' 23 *Berkeley Journal of Gender, Law and Justice*, 208.

49 *Ibid.*

50 The Circuit Court for Orange County in *Freeman v. Florida* at 7 – emphasis added. See also Durham, W. Cole and Liggett, Bradley D. (2006) 'The Reaction to Islamic Terrorism and the Implications for Religious Freedom After September 11: A United States Perspective' 1 *Derecho y Religión*, 41; Kahn, 'The Headscarf as Threat,' 436–441.

51 ECtHR, Decision of 13 February 2003 *Refah Partisi et al. v. Turkey*, Applications No. 41340/98, 41342/98, 41343/98 and 41344/98, also in 37 EHRR (2003) 1 para. 92. See also Fadel, Mohammad (2012) 'Muslim Reformists, Female Citizenship and the Public Accommodation of Islam in Liberal Democracy' 5 *Politics and Religion*, 2.

public, religions and religious manifestations are submitted to an intense cultural-legal scrutiny. They receive the stamp of legal approval only if they meet certain cultural standards and remain inconspicuous.

In freedom of religion cases, courts look out for similarity with the established Western religions and churches, like centralized authority, stable organization, and formalized membership, or probe into the cultural adaptability of cult practices.[52] These mechanisms of scrutiny permit courts to identify and exclude, above all, sects, beliefs lacking 'seriousness,' commercial rather than religious organizations (*Scientology*), and culturally strange manifestations of belief (sects). The project of ordering religion, by implication, privileges the established churches and the familiar religious denominations.

In pursuit of order, judicial review of the Islamic dress code is likely to defend the authority of *laïcité* in France (and countries copying this brand of secularism), and, elsewhere, the Western, secular state and its Christian-occidental foundations against the (imagined) competition with and demands of threatening religious authorities. In *Ludin*, both the majority and the dissenting judges expressed concern, though in different ways, that school children would be exposed, in the guise of the figure of the teacher – one might say, 'the elephant in the classroom'[53] – to the authority of a foreign/strange/alien religion.[54]

Previous decisions, notably of German administrative courts, justified the prohibition of headscarves and 'surrogates,' like berets, with reference to state neutrality, 'general principles of school education' and 'Christian virtues and cultural values' laid down in state constitutions, like reverence for God, respect for human dignity and toleration.[55]

In *S.A.S. v. France*, the Grand Chamber's majority overruled the strong dissent by two female judges and 'restrict[ed] the reach of pluralism' by sanctioning a blanket ban that 'prevents certain women from expressing their personality and their beliefs' for the sake of 'the ground rule of

---

[52] See, e.g., Supreme Court of Canada in *R. v. NS*, 2012 SCC 72 [2012] 3 S.C.R. 726; *The Queen v. D (R)*; and the jurisprudence of the German FCC (2005) in von Mangoldt, Herrmann, Klein, Friedrich and Starck, Christian eds (2005) *Kommentar zum Grundgesetz*, München: Franz Vahlen, Art. 4.

[53] 'To borrow and adapt slightly a phrase currently in vogue, the *niqāb* has become the "elephant in the courtroom",' *The Queen v. D (R)*, 5.

[54] *Ludin*, 306; see also two decisions of the ECtHR, sanctioning the logic of the French veil-bans: ECtHR, Decisions of 4 December 2008 *Dogru v. France*, Application No. 27058/05 and *Kervanci v. France*, Application No. 31645/04.

[55] E.g. Federal Administrative High Court (2004) Decision 2 Ca 45/03, 24 June 2004, *Neue Juristische Wochenschrift*, 3581.

communication and more broadly the requirements of "living together".'[56] Both the reasoning of the Court and the 'explanatory memorandum' of the National Assembly situate the '*Burqa* Ban' in a normative no-man's land between the two projects described here. They combine an imagined threat to *l'ordre public* with shielding the quasi-religion of *laïcité*:

> The defence of the public order is not confined to the preservation of tranquility, public health or safety. It also makes it possible to proscribe conduct which directly runs counter to rules that are essential to the Republican covenant ...[57]

Before *S.A.S. v. France*, the ECtHR and other courts demonstrated on several occasions that they privileged the decision of one or the other authority establishing order. In *Karaduman v. Turkey*, the European Commission on Human Rights (ECmHR) held that a university graduate had no right to obtain a provisional certificate because she would not submit to being photographed, as required by university rules, with an uncovered head. The Commission found no merit in her claim based on Article 9 but referred to the applicant's choice of study at a secular university and found her status 'naturally implied submission to certain rules.'[58] Similarly, the House of Lords refused to allow *Shabina Begum* to wear a *jilbab* (covering most of the body but not the face) in school and argued that she was aware of the school uniform policy when she chose this school.[59] In *Dahlab v. Switzlerland*, the ECtHR followed the Swiss High Court and privileged order in the guise of the school's denominational neutrality. In *Şahin v. Turkey*, the 'ECtHR endorsed the national authorities' view of the headscarf as antithetical to ... secularism.'[60]

In cases concerning teachers or public officials, courts also confront the rights claim with the professional duty of the individual.[61] Teachers are widely considered to be representatives of the state or school authority and therefore bound, as civil servants in particular, to observe the requirements of neutrality and moderation, which implies a *devoir de reserve*, that is, an obligation to restrain one's behavior.

---

56 *S.A.S. v. France*, no. 153.

57 *Ibid.*, no. 25.

58 *Karaduman v. Turkey* [1993] 74 DR 93, 101.

59 *Begum v. Headteacher and Governors of Denbigh High School* [2006] UKHL 15; [2007] 1 AC 100 – emphasis added.

60 Vakulenko, Anastasia (2007) 'Islamic Dress in Human Rights Jurisprudence: A Critique of Current Trends' 7 *Human Rights Law Review*, 717, 719.

61 For a strong version of this argument see the dissenting vote in *Ludin*.

It is interesting to note that in all these cases (and actually in most others) none of the Muslim women or girls was charged with proselytizing religion, being sympathizers of militant fundamentalism or members of jihadist groups.[62] In *Ludin*, the claimant had been teaching without reproach for years. In *Dahlab*, the ECtHR confirmed the integrity of the veiled woman, but expressed its unfounded and strangely contradictory view that '[i]t cannot be denied that the wearing of a headscarf might have some proselytizing effect, seeing that it appears to be imposed on women by a precept which is laid down in the Koran ...'[63]

The incriminated embodied practices were in no way concretely threatening. They challenged rules, an established practice or the authorities only in a very abstract, intangible manner, that is, in the imagination of principals, school boards and courts. One may infer that the girls and women's lifestyle, professional practice or other behavior simply did not make a difference in the eyes of the judges:

> [W]hile the veil is *hypervisible* [as a cultural barrier] Muslim women 'behind the veil' are not merely invisible to the western judges' scrutiny, but are *made invisible* as subjects.[64]

Not only were they, when wearing modest dress, not recognized as *equals* in the same comparative space, they were also, for all legal intents and purposes, de-subjectified and transformed from legal subjects into objects of legal regulation.

One is tempted to assume that these non-persons, according to the ECtHR case law, had to unveil because the *hijāb* and, more so, *niqāb* and *burqa* attracted attention, were taken personally from the Western point of view for they symbolized anti-Western behavior and sartorial practices and/or concealed a potentially dangerous mind-set. For that reason the 2004 ban stated that it was forbidden in public schools to wear signs or forms of dress with which students manifest their religious affiliation 'conspicuously':

> *Dans les écoles, les collèges et les lycées publics, le port de signes ou tenues par lesquels les élevès manifestent* ostensiblement *une appartenance religieuse est interdit.*[65]

---

[62] In *Ludin* it was officially confirmed that the claimant had been teaching without reproach for years.

[63] *Dahlab v. Switzerland.*

[64] See also Al-Saji 'The Racialization of Muslim Veils,' 886.

[65] *Loi* No. 2004-22, 15 March 2004, *Journal Officiel de la République Française*, 17 March 2004 – emphasis added.

Other religious symbols do not call for intervention insofar as they are inconspicuous or culturally familiar and do not represent a threatening manifestation of affiliation and loyalty to a religious authority that might compete with the secular powers that be. Another reason for tolerance and non-intervention could be that the religions and their faithful respect the 'structured absence' of religion in the secular public space.[66]

4. COLONIZING THE OPPRESSED MUSLIM WOMAN

The combination of *similarity* as the dominant interpretive orientation with a peculiar type of *commitment* in perspective unites the *colonizers* in the second quadrant. They locate every veiled Muslim woman in, preferably, Afghanistan, perceive her as victim, and set out to free her from the 'totalized Taliban' wherever that may be. They pretend to redirect attention away from the threatened or disturbed system and institution, state, society, school, social climate, etc., and their functional requirements, and then turn it on the woman or girl kept in a status of subjugation by tradition, religion, family, and male kin. '[T]he *hijab* is an identity marker for oppression and inequality of women under Islam.'[67]

> For many ardent feminists who uphold the French tradition of equal rights, the *foulard* was perceived as a symbol of paternalism, of patriarchy, of Muslim male oppression of women (*la femme soumise*), a means to control women's bodies and identities.[68]

On a more restrained note, some describe the article of clothing as 'a visible sign of separation and of difference.'[69] *Colonizers* usually overstate oppression and neither differentiate between choice, habit, and command nor recognize in sufficient detail the diverse motivations

---

[66] Therefore the French ban is directed against 'ostensible' (conspicuous) religious symbols in public places and respectfully retreats from violence, duress, and repression against women in the private sphere. See also Al-Saji 'The Racialization of Muslim Veils,' 881.

[67] McGoldrick *Human Rights and Religion*, 13, 265; Adelman 'Rights and the Hijāb,' 48.

[68] *Ibid.*

[69] Jack Straw, then leader of the House of Commons, in October 2006, quoted by Vakulenko, 'Islamic Dress in Human Rights Jurisprudence.'

women have to dress modestly – protection, privacy in public, presentation, piety, persecution, etc.[70] And they abstain from interpreting a highly complex act of identity construction and cultural negotiation and thus avoid what judging the dress code and liberating the wearers would actually compel them to do: listen to what they have to say about their sartorial practice[71] and then distinguish autonomy, resistance, and submission as well as questions of style, religion, tradition, family values, etc.[72]

In 1989, as if negatively commemorating the glorified *Déclaration des droits* of 200 years ago, three Muslim girls were expelled from their school outside Paris for wearing a headscarf. Had the girls been heard, Seyla Benhabib argues, 'it would have become clear that the meaning of wearing the scarf itself was changing from being a religious act to one of cultural defiance and increasing politicization.'[73] The first *foulard* crisis in France could have instructed officials and the general public that veiling resists any easy reduction of complexity. However, it did not.

The *colonizers*' track of the discourse unites diverse lines of reasoning that converge in two respects. First, the protagonists perceive scarf/veil/*burqa* as symbols of subordination or suppression.[74] Thus, they reanimate the colonial trope of 'the oppressed Muslim woman.' Second, informed by this perception, colonizers legitimize their rescue mission – as today's

---

[70] Empirical information is available: Keaton *Muslim Girls and the Other France*; Mahmood, Saba (2004) *The Politics of Piety: The Islamic Revival and the Feminist Subject*, Princeton: Princeton University Press; Ahmed *Women and Gender in Islam*; Read and Bartkowski 'To Veil or Not to Veil,' 396 with further references.

[71] The French Stasi commission heard 100 persons during their consideration but only two veiled women. Alain Touraine, one of its members, reported that the commission had decided early on not to hear veiled women. See Al-Saji 'The Racialization of Muslim Veils,' 901 [n. 93].

[72] For example, feeling proximate to one's God or culture, expressing sexual unavailability, religious modesty, defiant political identity, obedience or disobedience to parents, practising one's understanding of the Qu'ran, etc. See Mahmood *The Politics of Piety*; Ghazal Read, Jen'nan and Bartkowski, John P. (2000) 'To Veil or Not to Veil? A Case Study of Identity Negotiation among Muslim Women in Austin, Texas' 14 *Gender & Society*, 395; Ahmed, Leila (2011) *A Quiet Revolution. The Veil's Resurgence, from the Middle East to America*, New Haven: Yale University Press; Sandikci and Ger 'Veiling in Style'.

[73] Benhabib *The Rights of Others*, 191–192.

[74] Ghazal Read 'Introduction,' 232; see Adelman *Rights and the Hijāb*, 43; and Al-Saji 'The Racialization of Muslim Veils,' 875.

not all too 'gentle civilizers'[75] – with recourse to human rights and, this way, recapture the echo of *Universal Dreams Inc.*

Feminist critics tended to focus on dignity and gender equality. Courts, notably the ECtHR, complemented and still complement the universalistic human rights narrative by an often dominant and decisive story about order and rules, originating from a local, regional or national authority, reminiscent of the *controllers'* approach. Whereas gender oppression translates the sexual aspect of (un-)veiling into law, bans focus – in the name of *laïcité* and safety – on its political symbolism.

The Colonizers' Method

In terms of method, *colonizers* adhere to *Universal Dreams Inc.* and, consequently, opt for balancing rights, values, and interests to find out and designate whichever is (or are) pre-veiling. There are different brands of universalists, though, who significantly shift the accent of their legal reasoning and re-gauge the balance depending on their political program.

In the context of *control*, 'compelling interests' on the part of the state, society or single institution, because of the threatened authority and security imperative in play, routinely outweigh individual rights. By contrast, *colonizers* frame the wearing of modest dress as a human rights issue[76] and, in consequence, almost invariably take their cue from freedom of religion, at times complemented by dignity and, more often, gender equality. While many propagate the human rights rhetoric, only a few, notably Kenneth Roth, director of Human Rights Watch, *unequivocally privilege* the rights perspective. He straddled the Muslim-woman-as-victim trap and denounced the French headscarf ban as 'an unwarranted infringement on the right to religious practice':

> Under international law, states can only limit religious practices when there is a compelling public safety reason, when the manifestation of religious beliefs would impinge on the rights of others, or when it serves a legitimate educational function (such as prohibiting practices that preclude student-teacher interaction).[77]

---

[75] Koskenniemi, Martti (2001) *The Gentle Civilizer of Nations. The Rise and Fall of International Law 1870-1960*, Cambridge: Cambridge University Press.

[76] For a thorough critique of this aspect of the discourse see Vakulenko 'Islamic Dress in Human Rights Jurisprudence.'

[77] Human Rights Watch (2004) 'France: Headscarf Ban Violates Religious Freedom by Disproportionately Affecting Muslim Girls, Proposed Law Is Discriminatory' (New York, 27 February), http://www.hrw.org/english/docs/2004/

Similarly, the journal *Law Teacher* defended the human right to veiling:

> This paper argues that the case law and the state's position with regard to the religious clothing resulted to the disrespect of the manifestation of the individual's religious beliefs which relegate them to the private sphere only. People should enjoy their freedom of religion and should wear the religious dress of their choice in any place they want.[78]

Generally, *colonizers* quickly take the next step and shift the scrutiny from rights to the *nature* of the Muslim dress, they perceive and interpret as a sign of oppression:

> [The headscarf] appears to be imposed on women by a precept which is laid down in the Koran and which … is hard to square with the principle of gender equality.[79]

This view was supported by the *Communiqué de l'Association Femmes Publiques* of 2003 condemning 'this visible symbol of the submission of women.' And, incidentally, by the magazine *Elle*, otherwise not at the forefront of feminist criticism, which issued a petition against wearing *un voile* and depicted it as symbolizing 'intolerable discrimination' as a 'visible symbol of submission of women in public.'[80]

Courts can be expected to have a different take than women's magazines and feminist organizations. Yet, in its case law, the ECtHR follows a similar route. It generally neither elaborates the individualist human rights perspective nor takes into consideration the veiled women's agency and choice. *Dahlab v. Switzerland* concerned a school teacher who, after five years of work, was ordered to remove her headscarf. The ECtHR found her complaint, based on Art. 9 of the Convention (religious freedom), without substance and sustained the decision of the Swiss Federal Court which expressed

> no doubt that the appellant wears the headscarf and loose-fitting clothes not for aesthetic reasons but in order to obey a religious precept which she derives from … the Koran … and which … is hard to square with the principle of gender equality.[81]

02/26/france7666.htm (last accessed 24 September 2015). See also Vakulenko 'Islamic Dress in Human Rights Jurisprudence.'

[78] *Law Teacher*, http://www.lawteacher.net/free-law-essays/human-rights/freedom-of-religion-in-general.php (last accessed 24 September 2015).

[79] ECtHR in *Dahlab v. Switzerland* 2001-V 447.

[80] See Adelman 'Rights and the Hijāb,' 48.

[81] *Dahlab v. Switzerland* 2001-V 447.

Once the victim status has been confirmed, the Court uses the trope of oppression as a stepping stone to establish the necessity of protection and give reasons for the legality of presumably protective measures taken by the state. This way the woman's *right* to gender equality is transformed into a *duty* (of the legislator, courts, etc.) to *shield* her and *produce* gender equality. In stark contrast to the legal action taken by veiled women in *defense* of their dress, the judges sanction the unveiling ordered by law, decree or administrative decision.[82]

A slightly different method to reduce the normative impact of rights consists in *mentioning only in passing*, almost as an *obiter dictum*, gender equality and other human rights, like dignity, and 'contextualizing' the prohibition of veiling. This means that courts exercise restraint and sanction the position of the national or local authority, against whose anti-veiling measure the veiled woman had brought the charge of religious and gender discrimination. Alternatively, they may impose the duty to self-restraint on teachers and others exercising a public function, thus curbing their rights claim. In *Şahin v. Turkey*, the ECtHR argued state intervention was legitimate 'to place restrictions on freedom to manifest one's religion or belief in order to reconcile the interests of the various groups and ensure that everyone's beliefs are respected.'[83] In this manner, the ECtHR, in *Şahin v. Turkey*, put the contested ban of headscarves in public universities 'in its legal and social context', that is, the Turkish Republic's longstanding commitment to secularism and *gender equality*, on the one hand, and the 'backdrop of burgeoning extremist currents, on the other.'[84]

The human rights jurisprudence neither reflects upon the internal, asymmetric reciprocity between human rights and the duty to protect, which predetermines the outcome of the balancing, nor the selectivity with regard to the diverse motives of veiling. Wearing a *hijāb* or *niqāb* *can* be plausibly framed, in human rights terms, as expressing (also or mainly) a person's freedom to dress in public or freedom of conscience and having a strong dignity component. Therefore one wonders (or not) that this practice can be banned from schools, other public settings and

---

[82] Ahmed, Leila (1992) *Women and Gender in Islam: Historical Roots of a Modern Debate*, New Haven: Yale University Press; and Ahmed, Leila *A Quiet Revolution*. See also Fanon, Frantz (1965) *A Dying Colonialism*, New York: Grove Press; and Said, Edward (1979) *Orientalism*, New York: Random House.

[83] *Şahin v. Turkey* [2007] 44 EHRR 5.

[84] *Ibid.* See also Marshall, Jill (2005) 'Freedom of Religious Expression and Gender Equality: Sahin v. Turkey' 69 *Modern Law Review*, 452–461; see also Vakulenko 'Islamic Dress in Human Rights Jurisprudence,' 719.

'public places' in the broadest sense with the blessing of human rights courts.[85] This may mean that modest dress loses out, not only to public order and safety but also to trivia, like school uniforms. The pivotal aspects that decide whether a rights claim wins or loses, seem to be how the balancing contest is structured, whether or not the woman or girl is heard, and whether her oppression overwrites and disqualifies her testimony.

Rescue Ethics of Unveiling

Human rights law might be expected to cater naturally to and bolster the ethical dimension. In point of fact, the equal station of the other in the comparative space could easily be ascertained by the right to equal treatment and, more specifically, gender equality or a right to difference and human dignity. Yet, 'the moralistic fervor of the debate'[86] admits of no recognition of difference. Again, within the *colonizers'* track we have to distinguish feminist critics in the broadest sense[87] and official representatives of state paternalism, which at times comes in the guise of 'state feminism.' (The radicalized *colonizers* will be introduced separately as *Apocalyptic Crusaders* in the next section.)

The ethical problem begins with the silence of the victims not (only) in their homes but in the discourse of those who claim to liberate them from religious coercion, familial constraints and male suppression. It is remarkable that neither critical feminists bent on liberating the oppressed nor state or judicial paternalists let the covered speak for themselves.[88] Instead they rely on the voices of dubious crown witnesses for their always already marked position: that veiling is the victims' dress code and signifies oppression and subjugation.

Some of the feminist critics of the Muslim dress code address the ambivalence of modest dress but do not bypass its 'heavy sexual

---

[85] One of the notable exceptions is the 2015 headscarf decision of the German FCC.

[86] Vakulenko 'Islamic Dress in Human Rights Jurisprudence,' 720.

[87] It has to be noted, though, that it was not only the French *foulard* and *burqa* controversies in 1989, 1994, 2004 and since 2010 that polarized the feminists. See Al-Saji 'The Racialization of Muslim Veils'; Delphy, Christine (2004) 'Une Affaire Française' in Nordmann, Charlotte ed. *Le foulard islamique en questions*, Paris: Éditions Amsterdam, 64; Scott *The Politics of the Veil*, 21–41.

[88] See Al-Saji 'The Racialization of Muslim Veils.'

significance' and 'the ambivalent separation between the sexes' in Arab countries and communities:[89]

> [S]egregation by means of the veil was only the completion of an already ambivalent separation between the sexes ... Public sexual harassment seems to reinforce the non-veiled woman's ambivalence about her body, making her powerless in the face of unwelcome intrusions. The problem does not exist for veiled women, since adopting the veil was meant to shield them from such sexual approaches...[90]

Feminists also stress the multiplicity of veiled sexuality and bodies over against the wide-spread notion of a monolithic embodied practice:

> Although I believe that the rhetoric of the veil seeks to construct a monolithic female sexuality for its followers, I do not think that upon closer inspection, the community of the veiled reveals any such single construction. Veiled sexuality, it seems to me, reveals a multiplicity that is beyond the feminist's wildest expectations.[91]

While this statement expresses solidarity, treats the veiled woman as inhabiting the same comparative space on an equal station and respects difference, other feminists have denied teenage girls the right to choose to wear a *hijāb*:

> Feminists as well as non-feminists often assume that veiling is in and of itself an inherently oppressive practice. Many view it like domestic violence: just as staying with an abuser seems beyond comprehension, so does 'choosing' to veil. Women are seen as brainwashed or coerced, and the veil is seen as a key emblem of this oppression.[92]

As a consequence, the discourse of this track dresses for the celebration of universalism with its reference to gender equality. At the end of the day it subscribes to the *ethics* of paternalism. Rather than following the

---

[89] Seen 'from the complicated perspective of an Arab feminist': Abu-Odeh, Lama (1992) 'Post-Colonial Feminism and the Veil: Considering the Differences' 26 *New England Law Review*, 1527.

[90] *Ibid.*, 1529–1530.

[91] *Ibid.*, 1535.

[92] Hirschman, Nancy J. (1998) 'Western Feminism, Eastern Veiling, and the Question of Free Agency' 5 *Constellations. An International Journal of Critical and Democratic Theory*, 345, 349; see also El Habti, Raja (2004) 'Laicité, Women's Rights, and the Headscarf Issue in France' *The Veil Controversy: International Perspectives on Religion in Public Life*, Brooking's Institute, 19 April 2004.

(statist) logic of public safety, though, its rights rhetoric is covered with a protective lacquer and supported by an occasionally state-feminist rationale.

Undoubtedly, there is sufficient empirical evidence for gender oppression.[93] However, the *topos* becomes problematic once it is overstated, generalized and focused on the Muslim other. If one assumes that *all* covered women are victims, then the diversity of motivations to dress modestly is reduced to religion, tradition and family as sources of coercion. And if all covered women are suppressed, by implication, skin-showing comes across as a mark of liberation. Incidentally, the Western sartorial style is upgraded also in a normative sense as secular and normal, which also means that forms of self-restraint and submission exercised by subjects in the West, like diet, dress and physical exercise, can pass unnoticed. With *burqa* bans and other veiling prohibitions the *colonizer* sends out the ethical message: Dress like one of us!

In the *colonizer's* gaze, veiling cannot possibly be registered as protecting a subjective space or marking an 'elsewhere' that displaces the power of the hegemonic culture, its beauty criteria and loyalty claims. As an upshot, the covered woman has to uncover to gain entry to the universal community of unfettered human rights-holders. In this vein, the Dutch right-wing 'Party for Freedom' justified its draft bill to prohibit the *niqāb* in public with ending the 'social pressure' their social environment exerts on veiled girls and women.[94] Similarly, the French ban on headscarves in public schools (*hijāb*), and on face-veils (*niqāb*) and full-face veils (*burqa*) in the public sphere were supported by a *mélange* of secularist and republican, feminist and islamophobic arguments:

> Certainly, one can hope that the prohibition of the Islamic veil in school will be dissuasive and that many young women will find in the application of this law a way to escape the social pressure more or less against their will.[95]

---

[93] For the debate and empirical studies, see Ahmed *Women and Gender*; Callaway, Barbara and Creevey, Lucy (1994) *The Heritage of Islam: Women, Religion and Politics in Africa*, Boulder: Lynne Rienner Publishers; Read and Bartkowski 'To Veil or Not to Veil?'.

[94] Moors, Annelies (2009) 'The Dutch and the Face-Veil: The Politics of Discomfort' 17 *Social Anthropology/Anthropologie Sociale*, 393, 402.

[95] Madelin, Alain (French politician and former minister) in *Le Monde*, 5 February 2004. The ECtHR – unlike the somewhat reality-blind *Conseil constitutionnel* – was well aware of the islamophobia accompanying the '*Burqa* Ban.'

According to the *political* agenda underlying the reasoning of liberation, public veiling is officially banned in the exercise of the state's and primarily the courts' responsibility to protect Muslim women's human rights. The paternalism that aligns rights universalism and the liberation program draws its justification from a vision of double victimization. Because of their religion and religious dress Muslim women are held to be stigmatized in the public sphere and young Muslim girls especially in schools. What is more, they are believed to be branded by having to wear a symbol of ideologies of oppression. The standard argument runs like this: The state, the school principal and the courts cannot 'tolerate that girls ... are systematically indoctrinated to accept that women are subordinate and can be suppressed by adults.'[96]

Premised on a highly ambiguous notion of the public,[97] human rights law and state-feminism converge in the rationale of banning *public* veiling, as if oppression stopped at the entrance to the private sphere, to 'de-Talibanize' the suburbs and inner cities. These politics defend, from the vantage point of republican secularism, the Western concept of privatized religious practices and the code of non-conspicuous dress, as universally acceptable expressions of modern life and they contribute to the narrative of the world within which the West is anchored as the firm, normative center:

> If you support secularity, you support liberty; that is freedom from the disciplines and shackles of religion ... you stand for the constructions of a space for citizens where all men, and especially all women, can be united, whatever their belief or faith.[98]

Such a political program combines the denial of Muslim women and their complex identity construction with a reductionist understanding of

---

[96] Siim, Birte and Skjeie, Hege (2008) 'Tracks, Intersections and Dead Ends: Multicultural Challenges to State Feminism in Denmark and Norway' 8 *Ethnicities*, 322, 330. See also Coene, Gily and Longman, Chia eds (2010) *Féminisme et multiculturalisme. Les paradoxes de débat*, Frankfurt: Peter Lang.

[97] 'Public' may refer to institutions, agencies and agents of the state, shared space of groups of people (workplace) or open space for the population in general (public fora, shopping malls), non-secret information or matters affecting the common weal.

[98] Lévy, Bernard Henry (2004) 'Off with Their Headscarves,' *The Guardian*, 1 February 2004; for background analyses of the islamophobia in European countries: Bowen, *Why the French Don't Like Headscarves*; Ferrari and Pastorelli, *The Burqa Affair*.

their practices of dress.[99] While secularism is celebrated as the only path to individual liberation,[100] Islam remains in the shadow as a religion that is incompatible with democracy, human rights, and Western civilization. To sustain a universalism premised on 'our' particular ideas and ideologies, the 'other' women have to be disciplined through human rights.[101] Consequently, veiling and opposition on the part of Muslim women against veiling bans cannot be 'seen as a subject who takes up and constitutes [her]self through that oppression'[102] but are likely to be dismissed as yet a further sign of oppression:

> The politicians claimed they were liberating us; what they've done is to exclude us from the social sphere. Before this law, I never asked myself whether I'd be able to make it to a café or collect documents from a town hall. One politician in favor of the ban said *niqābs* were 'walking prisons.' Well, that's exactly where we've been stuck by this law.[103]

In *S.A.S. v. France*, the ECtHR stalled the political project of Muslim women's liberation through gender equality. Instead, the Court included in the Republican compact containing the conditions of 'living together' a peculiar ideal of femininity. It implies the availability of the female face to the male gaze.[104] The Court defended the 'right' of the unconcealed others to see and communicate with whomever they chose in public places.

---

[99] See Reece, Debra (1996) 'Covering and Communication: The Symbolism of Dress among Muslim Women' 7 *Howard Journal of Communications*, 35; and Moore 'Visible'. Critical perspectives are offered by the contributions in Coene and Longman *Féminisme and multiculturalisme*. On identity negotiation: Read and Bartkowski 'To Veil or Not to Veil?,' 397, 401.

[100] See Ahmed *Women and Gender*; Müge Coçek, Fatma and Balaghi, Shiva eds (1994) *Reconstructing Gender in the Middle East: Tradition, Identity and Power*, New York: Columbia University Press; Macdonald, Myra (2006) 'Muslim Women and the Veil' 6 *Feminist Media Studies*, 7.

[101] Kapur, Ratna (2012) 'Un-veiling Equality: Disciplining the "Other" Woman through Human Rights Discourse' in Emon, Anver M., Ellis, Marc S. and Glahn, Benjamin eds *Islamic Law and International Human Rights Law*, Oxford: Oxford University Press, 265.

[102] Al-Saji 'The Racialization of Muslim Veils,' 885.

[103] Comment by a veiled woman on the French full-face ban, in Chrisafis, Angelique (2011) 'France's Burqa Ban: Women are "Effectively Under House-Arrest",' *The Guardian*, 19 September 2011, http://www.theguardian.com/world/2011/sep/19/battle-for-the-burqa (last accessed 24 September 2015).

[104] On colonial feminism: Ahmed *Women and Gender*, 151; Al-Saji 'The Racialization of Muslim Veils,' 888; and Talpade Mohanty, Chandra (2003)

5. APOCALYPTIC CRUSADERS: A HYBRID OF CONTROLLING AND COLONIZING

On the border of the tracks defined by *controllers* and *colonizers*, some of the mis-readers of Samuel Huntington's *Clash of Civilizations*[105] – '*Apocalyptic crusaders*'[106] – wage a rhetorical war against veiling, which echoes the *colonizers'* distorted claims to be liberating the oppressed and amplifies the *controllers'* security alarm. Both tracks give distinction to the *crusaders'* rejection of veiling and their unquestioning celebration of the sartorial self. Against the backdrop of apocalyptic scenarios, in which the warriors anticipate the nemesis of the West and Western secularism in the clash with Islam, the self-anointed *crusaders*[107] radicalize pessimism concerning integration of the Muslim other. They exaggerate the *controllers'* safety and order concerns and turn into cultural antipathy their discomfort with a religion and its dress code that they find strange and wholly unacceptable. The *crusaders'* rhetoric deserves special analytical attention because it constitutes a hybrid discourse that draws on the two main tracks described above and throws into relief their respective problematic orientations. Moreover, its moral-political absolutism transgresses the boundaries of a rights discourse and therefore has to be distinguished from court rulings.[108]

'Under Western Eyes: Feminist Scholarship and Colonial Discourses' in Talpade Mohanty, Chandra ed. *Feminism Without Borders: Decolonizing Theory, Practicing Solidarity*, Durham, NC: Duke University Press, 17–42.

[105] They appear to have registered the title, but not read the analysis: Huntington, Samuel (1998) *The Clash of Civilizations and the Remaking of World Order*, New York: Simon & Schuster.

[106] They are mostly self-styled experts on veiling (intellectuals) and the media; not the courts, though.

[107] E.g. Schwarzer, Alice ed. (2002) *Die Gotteskrieger und die falsche Toleranz*, Köln: Kiepenheuer & Witsch; Schwarzer, Alice ed. (2010) *Die große Verschleierung. Für Integration, gegen Islamismus*, Köln: Kiepenheuer & Witsch; and Lévy 'Off with Their Headscarves.' For a distanced view: Laborde, Cécile (2008) *Critical Republicanism: The Hijab-Debate and Political Philosophy*, Oxford: Oxford University Press; Winter, Bronwyn (2008) *Hijab and the Republic. Uncovering the French Headscarf Debate*, Syracuse: Syracuse University Press.

[108] Documented by their manifesto-style pamphlets and dramatizing rhetoric. E.g. Schwarzer *Die große Verschleierung*; Lévy 'Off with Their Headscarves'; Badinter, Élisabeth et al. (1989) 'Profs, ne capitulons pas!' *Le Nouvel Observateur*, 2 November 1989, 58–59.

Their polarizing crusade is energized by the preconception of Islam as a (the only?) religion oppressing women, constituting a threat to the civilized world[109] as well as a 'fundamental case of arrested human development.'[110] *Crusaders* demonize *hijāb*, *niqāb* and, notably, *burqa* as symbols of a cultural-religious pathology that epitomizes the irrational.[111]

Crusaders' Method of Militancy

Their *method* of reasoning, if one may call it that, evokes the balancing which was mentioned and criticized above. For it demonstrates an arrogant preference for the militant manifesto-style rhetoric that needs no structured argumentation. They appeal to the 'self-evident' truth of Western ideas, values and principles, not even camouflaged in universalistic terms:

> [T]here is, by *current Western* standards and possibilities, something lacking in the lives of most Middle Eastern women, whatever satisfactions and positive features these lives may contain ...[112]

A self-righteous sense of purpose replaces the already slack discipline of reasoning and allows *crusaders* to deny that choice and agency might be hidden under the veil. The denial of free will on the part of women and girls wearing modest dress justifies their exclusion:

> *Tolérer le foulard islamique, ce n'est pas accueillir un être libre (en l'occurrence une jeune fille), c'est ouvrir la porte à ceux qui ont décidé, une fois pour toutes et sans discussions, de lui faire plier l'échine.*[113]

---

109 Said, Edward (1997) *Covering Islam. How the Media and the Experts Determine How We See the Rest of the World*, New York: Vintage; Said, Edward *Orientalism*; Esposito, John (1992) *The Islamic Threat: Myth or Reality?*, Oxford: Oxford University Press.

110 A qualification originally made by Ernest Renan; see Said, *Covering Islam*, 135, 137.

111 Badinter, Élisabeth (2002) 'Der verschleierte Verstand' in Schwarzer ed. *Die Gotteskrieger*, 139.

112 Beck, Lois and Keddi, Nikki (1978) *Women in the Muslim World*, Cambridge, MA: Harvard University Press, 18 – emphasis added.

113 'Tolerating the Islamic veil does not mean welcoming a free human being (in this case of a young girl), it means opening the door to those who have decided, once and for all, and without discussion, to let her bend her back.' Badinter, Élisabeth et al. (1989) 'Profs, ne capitulons pas!' *Le Nouvel Observateur*, 2 November 1989, 58–59.

By absolutely prioritizing the political-cultural imperatives of secularism, regardless of their pedigree, *crusaders* campaign for a total ban on veiling in public. And they do not temper their aim by even the pretense of balancing. By the same token, they assess neither the gender subtext nor the racist implications[114] of their rhetoric and agenda. Since the internal reciprocity of female covering and uncovering in public remain unthematized, those crusading against veiling cannot be expected to 'agree that if a law banning extremes of prudery is on the cards, so, too, should a ban on extreme displays of female flesh.'[115]

Crusaders' Ethics

Disturbed by the Muslim women's mimicry, the humorless guardian angels of secular-republican virtues propagate an *ethics* of zero tolerance for veiling.[116] They rally to the battle cry 'Off with Their Headscarves',[117] which deepens the self/other rift. Against the backdrop of an apocalyptic confrontation between the enlightened Occident and the dark forces of the Orient, they defend the Western normative order and culture and decry 'false tolerance' on the part of the liberal, moderate defenders or merely selective tolerators of veiling. In their brave old world, darkness, opaqueness, and covering cannot be put up with. Religious, ethnic and cultural diversity is (to be) eliminated from the unified space of the republic. The absolutism of the following statement mirrors the revolutionary spirit of the *Loi le Chapelier* with an assimilationist twist. Its uni-culturalism negates today's multi-ethnic, multi-cultural reality of France (and other immigration countries):

> If you support secularity, you support liberty; that is, freedom from the disciplines and shackles of religion. It also means that you support maintaining a distance between all spiritual or community affiliation in the public arena, thus making all equal and the same in civil life. If you stand for secularity, you stand for the construction of a space for citizens where all men, and especially women, can be united, whatever their belief or their faith.[118]

---

114 See Al-Saji 'The Racialization of Muslim Veils.'

115 *The Guardian*, 1 February 2004, http://www.theguardian.com/world/2004/feb/01/france.schoolsworldwide (last accessed 24 September 2015).

116 See Schwarzer *Die Gotteskrieger*; Schwarzer *Die große Verschleierung*.

117 Lévy 'Off with Their Headscarves.'

118 *Ibid.*

The visibility of the veil demonstrates *ostensiblement* that the covered Muslim woman chooses to be sexually unavailable and *therefore* deviates from Western sartorial conventions and also from established ways to show resistance to or compliance with religion, family, and culture. The combination of visibility and invisibility, demonstration and withdrawal evokes in *crusaders* a fear of otherness and the irresistible desire to uncover. On the grounds of absolutist standards of secularism those who are veiled are denied access to and equal status in the normally dressed community, unless they comply with the imperative to take off whatever conceals their face or hides their hair and body.[119]

The *crusaders'* ethical predisposition is animated by the explosive concoction of feminist or secularist liberation fantasies combined with a republican modernization agenda and an islamophobic imaginary, which radicalizes the colonial obsession with unveiling, uncovering and unmasking.[120] This *mélange* limits knowledge of and, most likely, any interest in the empirical Muslim woman. What is more, it deepens the polarity between self and other and, as an upshot, ends the multi-religious and multi-ethnic dialog before it has even begun.

Politics of Anti-Veiling Crusading

As regards their politics, *crusaders* pursue their agenda to ban the Islamic dress code more openly than participants of the legal discourse. They step up the security program (marking the track of visual *control*) and claim to continue the fight against female/sexual oppression that they believe justifies paternalist interventions of the *colonizers'* track.[121] *Hijāb*, *niqāb* and *burqa* they take to be uniforms of God's subversive warriors or 'soldiers of green fascism'[122] and read religious-political statements into the style of dress.

Crusaders fear not only for the state's authority, (French) *laïcité* and secularism in general, but they also see Western civilization as being at

[119] Lévy 'Off with Their Headscarves'; Badinter, Élisabeth (2009) 'Adresse à celles qui portent volontairement la burqa,' *Le Nouvel Observateur*, 9 July 2009, 26. See also Yeğenoğlu, Meyda (1998) *Colonial Fantasies. Towards a Feminist Reading of Orientalism*, Cambridge: Cambridge University Press, 50.

[120] Macdonald 'Muslim Women,' 9; Yeğenoğlu *Colonial Fantasies*, 12.

[121] Badinter 'Profs, ne capitulons pas!.' See also Juergensmeyer, Mark (1993) *The New Cold War? Religious Nationalism Confronts the Secular State*, Berkeley: University of California Press.

[122] The terminology was used by Schwarzer, Badinter and other intellectuals, see only Schwarzer *Die Gotteskrieger*.

risk. In their eyes, modest Islamic dress is a marker of fundamentalist anti-modern ultra-religiosity and family values, if not militant, *jihadi* terrorism. The politics of crusading recasts some of *Universal Dreams Inc.*'s victims as warriors, others as recalcitrant defenders of a traditional, backward life-style, and dramatizes as a real danger what *visual control* considers a potential risk:

> [Whoever wears *hijāb* and *niqāb* might] pretend to ascribe to religious beliefs in order to carry out activities that would threaten lives.[123]

Paradoxically, *crusaders* stir up the very divisiveness (brought on by religion) they firmly believe is admitted to public schools and other institutions by those who wear or tolerate Islamic dress. From the partly militant reactions to veil-bans in European countries one may infer that religious fanaticism is not exorcised but proliferated instead.

Moreover, *crusaders* carry their program beyond the limits of *Realpolitik* and liberation concerns by treating veiling also as expression of a social pathology that cannot be tolerated: 'To me, the full veil, the covered face, it's a woman in a portable coffin.'[124] In their alarmist pamphlets, some Cassandras warn of a '*Munich de l'école républicaine*,' reject the right to difference for what they call 'slavery,'[125] and therefore call upon the public – or at least, the media and academics – not to capitulate.[126]

With this battle-call the remnants of rationalist secular discipline and republican spirit that can be found in tracks I and II, go awry.[127] Driven by the self-certitude of secular egoistic cadres of a new republicanism, neo-colonial and sexual fantasies about what might lurk behind the veil can take the lead. The intense, negative fascination with veiling often slips into a 'pathological antipathy.'[128] In the end, the security and rescue

123 Judge Thorpe in *Freeman v. Florida*, 7. See also Fanon *A Dying Colonialism*, 61, concerning the veil and strategies of subversion in the Algerian liberation movement.

124 Gérin, André, Communist Member of Parliament, quoted by Bolderson, Claire (2010) 'Behind France's Islamic Veil,' *BBC News*, 8 April 2010.

125 Badinter 'Profs, ne capitulons pas!'; Critical: Bilge, Sirma (2010) 'Beyond Subordination vs. Resistance. An Intersectional Approach to the Agency of Veiled Women' 31 *Journal of Intercultural Studies*, 9.

126 Badinter 'Profs, ne capitulons pas!.'

127 For a critique of the crusades against veiling see Kapur 'Un-Veiling Women's Rights.'

128 Macdonald *Muslim Women*, 7, 9; similar, Yeğenoğlu *Colonial Fantasies*, 12.

program is escalated to one of social-cultural hygiene geared toward conquering the covered woman and unveiling her in the public sphere. In Charles Dickens' words: she ought to be 'civilized out of existence.'[129] After 'Algeria Unveiled!'[130] *crusaders* propagate today's neo-colonial project which commands: 'Unveil the Republique!'[131] and brings to mind the political doctrine of the French colonial administration in Algeria:

> If we want to destroy the structure of Algerian society, its capacity for resistance, we must first of all conquer the women; we must go and find them behind the veil where they hide themselves ...[132]

It is interesting to note that the *crusaders* target their unveiling campaign against a minority, while they seem to have no or fewer objections to 'under cover' secret services and government operations being removed from public scrutiny. *Crusaders* should put down *The Clash of Civilizations* and read Benjamin Franklin instead:

> Savages we call them, because their manners differ from ours, which we think the perfection of civility; they think the same of theirs.[133]

6. CONSERVING THE ORIENTAL

The combination of *commitment* in perspective with sensitivity to *difference* evolves from fascination with strangeness and the culturally remote. The *traveler* perceives the *hijāb* and *niqāb* as neither symbolizing a threat to public safety or order nor symbolizing oppression. On the contrary, she relishes the strangeness *controllers* register as dangerous and *colonizers* record as suppressive, because she does not share the discomfort with veiling and Islam. *Travelers* disregard any symbolic connotations and

---

[129] In his cynical description of the American Indians: Dickens, Charles (1853) 'The Noble Savage' in Harlow, Barbara and Carter, Mia eds (2003) *Archives of Empire Volume II. The Scramble for Africa*, Durham, NC: Duke University Press, 134.

[130] Fanon *A Dying Colonialism*, 35.

[131] See Chatterjee, Partha (1986) *Nationalist Thought and the Colonial World: A Derivative Discourse,* London: Zed Books; and Yeğenoğlu *Colonial Fantasies*.

[132] Quoted by Fanon *A Dying Colonialism*, 38.

[133] Franklin, Benjamin (1782–1783) 'Remarks Concerning the Savages in North America' in Ketcham, Ralph L. ed. (2003) *The Political Thought of Benjamin Franklin*, Indianapolis: Hackett, 368.

appreciate the veil as what it originally is – an article of clothing. At least they tone down the symbolism from politics to culture.

Method of Orientalizing

Travelers do not balance rights and duties. They see, are impressed and *expose* what strikes their fancy as exotic. Where *colonizers* are prone to naturalize and *controllers* tend to demonize the veil, *travelers* are inclined to essentialize it as embodying the Oriental. To quote Frantz Fanon's 'Algeria Unveiled':

> For the tourist and the foreigner, the veil demarcates both Algerian society and its feminine component.[134]

Correspondingly, the Muslim woman represents to the traveler the 'noble savage.'[135] And Islam is constructed as the religious other – an unfamiliar religion with quite mysterious features, strange but equal. While putting too much emphasis on the veil, *travelers* are likely to idealize the covered woman as living in harmony with her traditional culture and family values, and may thus miss the different connotations modest dress may also have, like opposition or submission. More importantly, they might give in to romantic primitivism, which functions as a cover for the racist representation of Muslim women as naturally or culturally inferior.

In general, the ways of law are not amenable to tourism and traveling. In their doctrinal everyday, courts have to hand down plausible decisions. So they are not likely to embark upon sentimental journeys to explore the unknown. Their professional training does not qualify judges as *jouisseurs* of the exotic. Therefore, jurists (judges, lawyers, legal scholars), even if committed to difference, are called on to translate what they see into the language of rights and duties, autonomy and coercion. This is part of their normalization routine. After that translation, the veil is no longer the essential exotic but a piece of clothing (with symbolic connotations, or not) worn on account of one's own or another person's decision. Once framed in this manner, the law can deal with the practice of veiling and subsume it to freedom of expression or conscience, manifestation of belief or lifestyle, protect it as a subjective space, or

---

134 Fanon *A Dying Colonialism*, 36.

135 This trope may have first appeared in Dryden, John (1676) *The Conquest of Granada by the Spaniards*, London: Herringman. An insightful reconstruction of the myth: Ellingson, Ter (2001) *The Myth of the Noble Savage*, Berkeley: University of California Press.

prohibit it as a transgression of norms. Within its structural limits, the law's apparatus of methods and concepts can capture very well, and process, the instrumental and symbolic meaning of the veil, as we have seen above.

A British judge's instruction to a jury not only illustrates the cautious commitment to difference in a matrix offered by the rights vocabulary but also reveals insight into veiling as identity construction:

> I am sure you will have noticed that the defendant … is wearing a full face veil – it hides her face apart from a narrow slit for the eyes. … Let me begin by saying that in this country everyone is entitled to express any religious view they wish … or to express any religious view we may have in any way that we choose – that includes wearing a form of dress which a person may consider to be appropriate … I emphasise that *D* is fully entitled to dress in any way she chooses. If you have any feelings about that put them aside because they have nothing to do with the case.[136]

Travelers' Ethics

Idealizing the indigene and orientalizing the veiled Islamic woman are likely to remain the *traveler's* liabilities, unless her perception can be corrected by critical ethics. *Travelers*, the way they have been characterized here, do not merely replicate the colonizing gaze and project. They have no (or do not admit to having a) desire to liberate and unveil. This detached attitude allows them to be committed to an ethics of difference, which is a necessary condition for moving beyond abstract formal egalitarianism toward appreciating the other as valuable. It all depends on whether the *traveler* likes to share the inner city or their workplace with veiled women – and not out of curiosity or because they create an exotic atmosphere.[137]

In the absence of an ethics of difference, the *hijāb, niqāb* and *burqa* are culturalized as exotic items and flattened to fit into the Western *traveler's* treasure box – rather than being perceived as visual aspects of a complex image management, identity construction and coping strategies, prompted by a minority religion and family tradition, oppression (based on tradition, religion or patriarchy) or subversive contestations of

---

[136] The defendant stood trial on charges of witness intimidation, see above *The Queen v. D (R)*. The judge upheld a ruling that *(D)* could stand trial wearing a full face veil but had to remove it while giving evidence.

[137] See also Said, *Orientalism*; and Berman, Nathaniel (1997) 'Aftershocks: Exoticization, Normalization and the Hermeneutic Compulsion' *Utah Law Review*, 281.

power and stereotypes. Once orientalized, headscarves and veils function in a paradoxical way as an imaginary anchor for the European self. Thus, the Muslim other confirms the Western identity.[138]

Politics of Orientalizing

Travelers committed to *difference* neither openly subscribe to a political project nor do their arguments betray sympathy with a pronounced political agenda, say of liberation or civilizing. Their political common denominator can best be described as non-intervention, punctured by conservationist interferences. Aside from that, they travel without a cause and have no problem with offering protection to the varieties of modest dress. As their perception remains superficial, they do not probe the motivational depths of veiling but appreciate its aesthetics as religious, ethnic or feminine chic.

There are some dispersed, idiosyncratic voices, with little purchase, that are committed to difference but transgress the limits of non-intervention. In particular Islamic law seems to inspire fantasies of legal transfer. The Archbishop of Canterbury found it 'irresistible to recognize elements of the Sharia in the common law' for the sake of social cohesion.[139] Possibly thereby inspired, a Swiss professor favored accommodating Swiss law to the Sharia:

> Legal pluralism is more a question of introducing in some areas of the law mechanisms that take into account cultural *idiosyncracies* … I think some people … are embedded in their culture and I don't think you can force them to change their identity politics.[140]

On a similar but distinctly more problematic note, a Frankfurt judge informed a Moroccan woman in a divorce trial that it was not unusual in her home culture for a husband to exercise his right to cane his wife and it therefore could not be held against him as a reason for divorce.[141] The judge's understanding of what she superficially considered to be an authentic rule or practice under Islamic law did not survive the appeal.

---

[138] Brennan, Teresa (1993) *History After Lacan*, London: Routledge.

[139] *BBC News*, 7 February 2008, http://news.bbc.co.uk/2/hi/7232661.stm (last accessed 21 September 2015).

[140] Giordano, C. quoted by Stephens, Thomas (2009) 'There's no place for Sharia in Switzerland,' http://origin.swissinfo.ch/eng/-there-s-no-place-for-sharia-in-switzerland-/7147982 (last accessed 24 September 2015) – emphasis added.

[141] See Medic, Veit and Reimann, Anna 'Justifying Marital Violence: A German Judge Cites Koran in Divorce Case,' *Spiegel online*, 21 March 2007,

Established Western legal procedures and routines are not amenable to preserve the exotic or naïvely import the laws of other cultures.

7. SKEPTICISM BETWEEN CRITIQUE AND RELATIVISM

The *skeptic* is generally believed to remain on the sidelines. Her way of obtaining knowledge through systematic doubt comes across as indecisiveness, whereas it may only be caution or careful scrutiny. In the context of comparing dress codes, *skeptics* stay detached from the heated controversies and do not take a stand; also they privilege difference. All the same, they distrust their ability to bring the other close enough for a good view, while at the same time, keeping it – veiling, the covered woman and Islam – far enough away to avoid domesticating and 'civilizing' it.

In the ongoing veiling debates, the *skeptic* is uneasily situated between being fascinated and feeling threatened, between the apologists of order and the visionaries of a multi-religious and multi-ethnic society. The *skeptic* shares neither the *traveler's naïveté* nor the *colonizer's* sense of purpose. And she does not feel threatened by what is conspicuously visible and invisible. The skeptical position can best be paraphrased by the question: 'Who are we to tell them what to wear?'

Hijāb, *niqāb* and *burqa* provoke secularist observers to evaluate the embodied practice that strikes them as strange. There are few who waver and resist that provocation and can be listed in the track of sartorial *skepticism*. There are fewer still in judicial discourse, which is geared toward deciding cases rather than indulging in systematic doubt.

The *skeptic's* questioning attitude makes her perceptive of what others, notably, *crusaders*, are unable to see:

> Religious dress, along with organizational affiliations, serves as an important individual marker or visual cue that helps to promote conceptions of self-identification as it simultaneously preserves group cohesion.[142]

---

http://www.spiegel.de/international/germany/justifying-marital-violence-a-german-judge-cites-koran-in-divorce-case-a-473017.html (last accessed 24 September 2015).

142 Moore, *Visible*, 239; Peek, Lori Ann (2005) *The Identity of Crisis: Muslim-Americans After 9/11*, Ph.D. Dissertation, Boulder: Department of Sociology, University of Colorado. See also Sandikci and Ger, *Veiling in Style*, 21–29 about covering choices and practices.

> What critics of Islam fail to understand is that when they see a young woman in a *hijāb* she may have chosen the garment as a mark of her defiant political identity and also as a way of regaining control over her body.[143]

Method of Doubt

The *skeptical* method features systematic doubt, a questioning attitude toward knowledge, beliefs, and perception.[144] For the purpose of this grid and the comparison of contributions to the discourse on veiling, I introduce the *skeptic* as the representative of doubt. She is critical of the three other styles or tracks (plus the crusaders) because their protagonists believe their *general* picture of veiling, and their assumptions about why women wear veils, are right. By contrast, *skeptics* give *crusaders*, *controllers* and *colonizers* a good dressing down (!) and approach the practice of veiling from the perspective of cultural relativism and recognition of diversity. Therefore *skeptics* are appalled by the *crusaders'* prescriptive ardor and cultural-political absolutism. Not even in their wildest dreams would skeptics join their campaign, because they know from insider portraits or assume from experience that Muslim women's motivations to dress modestly vary dramatically and that *hijāb* and *niqāb have a diversity of meanings within Muslim society, and within Muslim communities in the diaspora, and are differently interpreted from an Anglo-European or Middle Eastern perspective.*

Detachment prevents them also from embracing the *traveler's* conservationist perspective; and their *difference* orientation blocks fantasies of disciplining or colonizing. Rather than advocating that Muslim women and girls unveil (for whatever purpose), *skeptics* hesitate to advocate anything at all as they navigate the terrain of normative pluralism.

The following comment could qualify as a skeptical position, insofar as it lists the diversity of practices and avoids a prescriptive statement:

---

143 Alibhai-Brown, Yasmin (2001) *WHO do WE THINK we ARE*, London: Penguin Books, 246; quoted with approval in House of Lords, Decision of 22 March 2006 *R Begum v. Denbigh High School* no. 94–95 and *The Queen v. D (R)*, 28. Similarly, Supreme Court of Canada, Decision of 20 December 2012 *R. v. NS*, 2012 SCC 72 [2012] 3 S.C.R. 726. See also, Read and Bartkowski 'To Veil or Not to Veil?' and Abu-Lughod, Lila (1986) *Veiled Sentiments*, Berkeley: University of California – concerning women's different motivations in veiling.

144 See Burnyeat, Myles ed. (1983) *The Skeptical Tradition*, Chicago: University of Chicago; Klein, Peter (2010) 'Skepticism' in *Stanford Encyclopedia of Philosophy*, http://plato.stanford.edu/entries/skepticism (last accessed 24 September 2015).

> 'Veiling' has a complex history. Many Muslim women cover themselves as an affirmation of cultural identification with a rich and varied tradition. For others, wearing a headdress or veil is a modern feminist statement. In some contexts, the veil clearly marginalizes women in society. In others, a headscarf de-marginalizes and expresses liberation from colonial legacies. To preserve their sexual identity, some wear a headscarf to avert the male gaze. Others do so as a sign of rank and nuanced social status. What women wear on their heads and bodies is always intimately connected with notions of the self, the body and community and the cultural construction of identity, privacy and space.[145]

With regard to veiling and its connotations, *skeptical* positions can be located, in terms of method, between a hermeneutics of suspicion and one of fascination. The concentration on negotiating differences helps avoid a positive political agenda and opens up the space for critique:

> It should be noted that these different senses of veiling are not exhaustive of its possibilities, nor are all manifestations of veiled subjectivity necessarily subversive or feminist.[146]

Where some skeptics may waver and endlessly agonize over what to do, courts have to come down with rulings that say 'what the law is.' Similarly, legal commentators evaluate laws or court decisions and rarely avoid the prescriptive moment. Almost as a rule they conclude what legislators should have done, how judges should have decided a case or could have produced a better argument at least. That is why, in the legal discourse, straightforwardly skeptical statements are the exception. The routine of silencing doubt demands judges appear secure and decisive as well as to hide their doubts – or rather translate them into apodictic comments. If they are uncertain about the right answer to a case, they can always fall back on a variety of options to camouflage their skepticism, if that is what it is. First, they may refer to an outside expert to answer the question they feel uncertain about. In *The Queen v. D (R)* the judge put the question whether Muslim women are obliged to wear a *niqāb* before the Muslim Council in Britain:

> *'Does a Muslim woman have to wear a Hijab?'*

---

[145] Adelman 'Rights and the Hijab,' 48; El Guindi, Fatwa (1999) *Veil: Modesty, Privacy and Resistance*, New York et al.: Bloomsbury Academic – challenging the 'simplistic assumption that veiling is largely about modesty and seclusion, honor and shame.'; and Abu-Lughod *Veiled Sentiments*.

[146] Al-Saji 'The Racialization of Muslim Veils,' 893.

> A central principle of the Holy Qu'ran is that 'there is no compulsion in religion' … It is thus up to us autonomous beings to contemplate and evaluate the merits of these teachings. Hence, although *Hijab* is certainly an integral part of the overall Islamic dress code, it is not for anyone to force it upon another human being.[147]

While expert evidence is quite common, deferring to local, regional or national authorities is not, at least outside the scope of the right to manifest one's religion.[148] This technique becomes dubious when, as in the veiling jurisprudence of the ECtHR, the other authority is actually the party challenged by the lawsuit.[149] In *Ludin*, the German FCC did not acquiesce in the school administration's arguments but delegated the decision to prohibit or allow teachers to wear a headscarf to the regional legislators.[150] The ECtHR regularly invokes the margin of appreciation of the local authorities, submits to school, university or other regulations and limits the Convention's freedom of religious expression.[151] In *Şahin v. Turkey*, the ECtHR found the Vice Chancellor's circular prohibiting headscarves in the university 'justified.'[152]

Similarly, in *Shabina Begum v. Denbigh High School*, the House of Lords overruled the decision of the Court of Appeal which had delegated to the school authority the responsibility for deciding the pivotal substantive issue of whether the school girl's modest dress (*jilbab*) had to be reconciled with the school uniform regulations. Whereas the Court recognized a legitimate 'area of judgment,' the Lords argued in a similar fashion that

> [i]n applying the principles of *Şahin v. Turkey* the justification must be sought *at the local level* and it is there that an area of judgment, comparable to the margin of appreciation, must be allowed to the school.[153]

---

[147] *The Queen v. D (R)*, 8.

[148] See Vakulenko 'Islamic Dress in Human Rights Jurisprudence,' 721–725.

[149] *Begum v. Denbigh High School* [2005] EWCA Civ. 199; [2005] 2 All ER 369.

[150] See, in particular, *Ludin*.

[151] See also *S.A.S. v. France*.

[152] *Şahin v. Turkey* [2007] 44 EHRR 5; see also *Dogru v. France* and *Kervanci v. France* Applications No. 27058/05 and 31645/04, judgment of 10 November 2005.

[153] *R (on the application of SB) v. Headteacher and Governors of Denbigh High School* [2005] EWCA Civ. 199; [2005] 2 All ER 369, Lord Bingham, no. 64 – emphasis added.

In *Denbigh*, Lord Bingham believed it would be 'irresponsible of any court, lacking the experience, background and detailed knowledge of the head teacher, staff and governors, to overrule their judgment on a matter as sensitive as this.'[154] Lord Hoffmann concurred that the school was 'in the best position to weigh and consider ... its wish to avoid clothes which were perceived by some Muslims (rightly or wrongly) as signifying adherence to an extremist vision of the Muslim religion and to protect girls against external pressures.'[155]

Whereas this deferral appears to be a feature of the ECtHR case law on veiling, the avoidance of difficult issues with a 'retreat to procedure' is not.[156] The (normalizing) turn to procedure provides courts with the opportunity to abstain from deciding a case on its merits and instead discuss rules of admissibility.[157] Recently, the ECtHR declared inadmissible three applications filed by parents whose daughters were not allowed to wear veils in public schools. The Court recognized the crucial role of the state in matters concerning religion and found the prohibition of conspicuous religious symbols justified by the neutrality and impartiality of the state.[158] Those decisions also illustrate another technique of not addressing difficult questions. The ECtHR considered unfounded the claims that the Islamic veil ban might discriminate against a religion.

It is not at all clear whether the courts' position in these cases can be qualified as skeptical; they might very well be simply avoiding political controversy (on the part of the states) or be taking the easy way out of the backdoor. With that in mind one could read the opinion of the *Conseil d'État* regarding the first of three French *foulard* controversies as a skeptical comment, at least as expressing doubt. With reference to the 1905 law on *laïcité*:

---

[154] *Denbigh High School*; Vakulenko 'Islamic Veiling in Human Rights Jurisprudence,' 723 seq.

[155] *R (on the application of SB) v. Headteacher and Governors of Denbigh High School* [2005] EWCA Civ. 199; [2005] 2 All ER 369, no. 65. Critical: Davies, Gareth (2007) 'The House of Lords and Religious Clothing in *Begum v. Headteacher and Governors of Denbigh High School*' 13 *European Public Law*, 423.

[156] See Lord Bingham's opinion, as part of the House of Lord's judgment in *Denbigh*, no. 30.

[157] In *Karaduman v. Turkey* the university graduate claiming a breach of Art. 9 of the ECtHR did not pass the admissibility stage; the ECtHR interpreted para. 1 of Art. 9 narrowly and also touched on the applicant's choice to study at a secular university, which 'naturally' implied acquiescence to certain rules.

[158] For references see Nigro 'The Margin of Appreciation,' 539.

> The Republic assures freedom of conscience. It guarantees the free exercise of [religious beliefs] subject only to the restrictions to be found in the following regulations issued in the interests of public order ...[159]

The *Conseil d'État* held that students' freedom of conscience should be respected and that the girls, therefore, had the right to wear religious symbols, unless this would take the form of proselytism.[160] Similarly, the German FCC argued in the second decision on veiling:

> The merely visual perceptibility [of the headscarf] has to be tolerated in schools as a consequence of the individual exercise of rights, as otherwise there is no constitutional claim to be untroubled by the perception of other religious convictions or worldviews.[161]

Ethics and Politics of Skepticism

Ethically, *skeptics* also doubt what the right normative position should be. Caution prepares them to treat unfamiliar phenomena, however strange they may be, as different but, to begin with, on an equal footing. Since they distrust both the zeal of radical secularist *crusaders* and the *controllers'* policing routine, *skeptics* are disposed to accept a *droit à la difference* because it goes along with their questioning attitude. Moreover, a focus on difference works as an antidote against domestication of what appear to be strange practices of dress. And it certainly does not rule out criticism.

Skeptics' ethical disposition does not lend itself – at least not easily – to pursuing a political agenda or mission. Their politics is one of non-intervention, because they generally respect a person's or a group's uniqueness rather than imposing their own concept of a good life or dress code. They prefer not to probe into the motives women have to veil or not to veil.

Skeptics do not address the question whether the full veil protects a subjective space in public or functions like a 'portable seclusion,' 'mobile

---

[159] *Loi du 9 décembre 1905 concernant la séparation des Églises et de l'État, Journal Officiel de la République Francaise, publiée 11 décembre 1905*; Al-Saji 'The Racialization of Muslim Veils,' 896 with further references.

[160] *Conseil d'État* quoted by Al-Saji 'The Racialization of Muslim Veils,' 879.

[161] The second headscarf decision of the FCC [2015], no. 117. See also Sacksofsky 'Glaubensfreiheit.'

prison' or a 'kind of body bag for the living,'[162] whether 'veiling can provide the place within which a certain sense of bodily self is formed, allowing participation and mobility in public places without contradiction [of] conventions of modesty, community and custom,' or 'provides the very means for women's self-constitution as pious subjects;'[163] or whether the practice of covering is dictated by an oppressive religion, clan or husband.

> By pointing to the multiplicity of meanings which veiling can take and its implication in subject-formation in different Muslim and western contexts, my aim is to indicate the complexity of the question without assigning any one meaning, liberatory or oppressive, to veiling. There is neither an essence to veils, nor is veiling easily reducible to any one dimension of sense.[164]

As far as a *skeptic* is concerned, *controllers*, *colonizers* and *travelers* all *may* have a point but, more importantly, she considers those positions and attitudes also basically flawed. The *skeptic* does not share the *controller's* vision of threat, the liberator's paternalism of the *colonizer* (and false universalism) or the *traveler's* naïveté. Because of her restraint in passing judgment and her different orientation in interpreting the semiotics of modest dress, a *skeptic* finds the *crusaders'* obsession and rhetoric particularly appalling, because their absolutism masks a lack of introspection and sensitivity to context. The *skeptic* may or may not share the other protagonists' strong discomfort and may feel uneasy about certain forms of veiling. That uneasiness would still not translate into prohibitive measures and more sweeping political anti-veiling programs.

Furthermore, the skeptic's self-critical and questioning attitude extends to the problem of how to bring about the social and cultural integration of religions, religious groups, and (religious) practices in secular societies. *Skepticism* probes the religious core of secularism, especially the French version of the republican-secular ideology. Surveying French Muslim hostility and other forms of alienation throughout Europe, an observer concluded, on a skeptical note:

---

[162] See Al-Saji 'The Racialization of Muslim Veils,' 892. Frantz Fanon analyzes the dialectic of veiling and unveiling and how the latter may immobilize previously veiled women in *A Dying Colonialism*, 59. See also Kapur 'Un-Veiling Women's Rights,' 216.

[163] *Ibid.* Referring to Mahmood *The Politics of Piety*; and Abu-Lughod, Lila (2002) 'Do Muslim Women Really Need Saving? Anthropological Reflections on Cultural Relativism and Its Others' 104 *American Anthropologist*, 783, 785.

[164] Al-Saji 'The Racialization of Muslim Veils,' 875, 893.

> [T]hey are certainly signs of a great social transformation whose outcome is unclear but whose dangerous potential is all too visible. And frighteningly, despite the desire of many reasonable people in France to find peaceful and reasonable accommodation, no one seems to know how to stop the worst case from developing.[165]

The prototypical *skeptic* is likely to agree that 'the underlying issue is not primarily one of rights but of alienation that finds membership in the modern state to be inadequate and unfulfilling.'[166] And she would seriously doubt whether legislative bans or administrative measures (by school principals) will help to find answers to the complex problems of integration in immigration societies.[167] Skepticism and systematic doubt do not flourish in times like the present that appear to 'require certainty and judgment rather than critical rethinking of secular goods.'[168]

8. CONCLUDING NOTES: THE COMPLEX NORMATIVE MATRIX OF DRESS

Putting the veiling discourse 'on the grid' is meant to elucidate the legal implications of interventions for or against veiling and to disrupt the construction of the stereotypical image of the veil, Islamic woman and Islam. The quadrants of the grid help distinguish, I believe, the various perspectives, whose confluence forms the comparative-legal composite of 'the veiled woman.' With their focus on the foreign dress code, each track reduces, from a peculiar angle determined by positional detachment or commitment and an interpretive orientation toward similarity (assimilation) or difference (diversity), the complex identity construction Muslim women are forced to undertake especially in Western societies. As a result, the grid analysis shows how veiled women are represented, in the normative and comparative discourses, quite paradoxically as the carrier of a threatening symbol or even a dangerous *actor* hiding a politically extremist mind-set, on the one hand, and the *victim* of oppression, on the other. The contradiction of granting and denying her agency is camouflaged as far as the veil controversy is concerned by the antagonistic

---

[165] Bell, David A. (2007) 'Veil of Tears' in *The New Republic*, 5 March 2007.

[166] Adelman 'Human Rights and the Hijab,' 62.

[167] Klausen, Jytte (2005) *The Challenge of Islam: Politics and Religion in Western Europe*, Oxford: Oxford University Press; and Klausen, Jytte (2006) 'The Islamic Challenge: Politics and Religion in Western Europe' *The Berlin Journal*, 50.

[168] Mahmood 'Religious Reason and Secular Affect,' 65.

imperatives of public safety and order, the duty to liberate and protect the oppressed woman.[169] This incongruity seems to pass unnoticed in mainstream tracks A and B. That is why judges challenge veiling, unfazed by the paradox, as a matter of 'choice' or 'free will' 'dictated' by religion and claim that a veil ban would be the best way of protecting girls from 'external pressures.'[170] Tracks C and D show that the difference orientation, including a *right* to difference, generally does not have much purchase in those controversies. Many participants consider veiling strange, unusual or coercive and find modest dress, even *hijāb*, conspicuous. Yet, they have no qualms about translating their discomfort and ignorance into strategies of control or liberation in Western terms.

The grid provides a heuristic device to chart and deconstruct the dichotomization of the secular/modern West versus the religious/traditional East (in hiding) and turn the critical scrutiny on the ethnocentric subtext of the discourse, which affirms the superiority of Western secularism/modernism, its management of (privatized) beliefs and sartorial styles and, by implication, the inferiority of the embodied practice of veiling. It also questions, by implication, the liberatory meaning of skin showing. The Western identity of superiority would be undermined if we acknowledged that 'we have our own form of compulsory feminine dress': 'the nearly compulsory baring of skin.'[171] '[W]e need fundamentalism, indeed, we project and produce it elsewhere, to represent ourselves as free.'[172]

The comparative analysis sheds light on the problematic – constitutive – role of law and legal language in spelling out *emotions*, in particular, aversion, anxiety or fascination, as well as *perceptions* of the covered woman and the veiling practice, and then transferring them into legal forms (ban, court decision) and arguments (doctrine, commentary). These forms and arguments reveal how a vision pre-structured by ethnocentric habit and prejudice is replicated by pre-structured legal reasoning and that vision is not a simple recording device: 'We learn to see'[173] and we

[169] This conceptualization is submitted to critique by Mahmood *ibid.*

[170] *Denbigh High School*, no. 18, 65 – emphasis added; Vakulenko 'Islamic Dress in Human Rights Jurisprudence,' 723–727.

[171] Brown, Wendy (2006) *Regulating Aversion: Tolerance in the Age of Identity and Empire*, Princeton: Princeton University Press, 176, 189. See also Mahmood, Saba (2006) 'Secularism, Hermeneutics and Empire: The Politics of Islamic Reformation' 18 *Public Culture*, 323, 344.

[172] Brown *Regulating Aversion*, 189.

[173] Merleau-Ponty, Maurice (2013) *Phenomenology of Perception*, London: Routledge.

think we see what we see. Vision is habitual, structured, and constitutive: to the Western gaze the veil is hypervisible, whereas Muslim men see it but may not register it as strange or *ostensible*.

Participants in the veil discourse authorize their perception of Muslim dress with scenarios of danger, oppression or deviance which are intensified by a lack of familiarity with Islam and Muslim women's motivations to dress the way they dress and conceal their hair, face or body. To change these observations, more than a cognitive approach is called for. To end this authorization, the Western (male) gaze has to be turned on itself – on the paradoxical interpretation of *hijāb* and *niqāb* as threatening/submissive, exotic/pathological as well as the construction of religion as (Western) life's and law's other.

Piercing the veil of ignorance and clearing the fog of emotions might help to recognize the various reasons,[174] empirical rather than imaginary, Muslim women have for modest dress. According to what is known or knowable, comparative statements better allow for obedience and resistance, subordination and self-assertion, heteronomy and autonomy, modesty and pride, quietism and politics, religion and lifestyle, honor and chic – and then cope with the complex normative matrix of dress.

Legal and ethical comparisons of the other, judged from the vantage point of the unmarked, often implicit Western secular self, are interlaced with fear, aversion and discomfort. Therefore, fresh knowledge alone will generate neither an undistorted evaluation of Islam and its dress code nor an 'uncoercive contact'[175] with covered Muslim women. A thought experiment, relating modest dress to Western sartorial styles and embodied practices, might help though. For starters, one could imagine Britney Spears or Miley Cyrus wearing *hijāb* or *niqāb*. That might call to mind 'the myriad of practices that Western women are involved in … which can be seen as deeply patriarchal'[176] and cast doubt on the gender-liberating effect of skin-showing.

---

[174] For evidence of the motivational diversity see Hirschman 'Western Feminism, Eastern Veiling,' 360; Reece 'Covering and Communication'; Coene and Longman *Féminisme et multiculturalisme*; Wadud, Amina (2006) *Inside the Gender Jihad. Women's Reform in Islam*, London: Oneworld Publications; Mahmood *The Politics of Piety*; Open Society Foundations ed. (2011) *Unveiling the Truth: Why 32 Muslim Women Wear the Full-Face Veil in France*, New York: Open Society Foundations, http://www.opensocietyfoundations.org/sites/default/files/a-unveiling-the-truth-20100510_0.pdf (last accessed 21 September 2015).

[175] Said *Covering Islam*, 167

[176] Hirschman 'Western Feminism, Eastern Veiling,' 360; Pedwell, Carolyn (2010) *Feminism, Culture and Embodied Practice: The Rhetorics of Comparison*, London: Routledge, 85–106.

In a second thought experiment, the apocalypse or 'new cold war' of the religions has to be suspended, at least for the time being. Even toned down to a return of the religious, *crusaders* might still find this phenomenon alarming. *Controllers* might still suspect it to threaten danger, provided they assumed that a return of the religious could not be kept under a tight security lid. However, by listening to the always already contingent and situated other voices, they could hear the polyphony of arguments to dress modestly and, more importantly, the echo of 'the awareness of what is missing'[177] in the realm of secular reason. '[P]recisely because veiling is 'other' to most Westerners, it might reveal aspects of the West to which Westerners are often blind.'[178] Notably, the paradoxical opaqueness of enlightened secular reason in its relation to religion and also the disciplinary mechanisms, denying girls and women autonomy also in Western societies.[179]

If the *crusaders* and other agents of public safety turned their attention from veiled women to armed men (some veiled, others not), from garments to caliphates, ultra-religiosity, murder, gangs of terror, etc.; if the *amatourists* laid to rest the *noble sauvage* stereotype; if the *universalists* accounted for motivational variety and the *crusaders* looked into their own discomfort and concepts of freedom and happiness not exhausted by liberal notions of agency[180] – then the monologs comparing dress codes might end up in the delirious diversity of voices at the crossroads of, perchance, *similarity/difference* and *detachment/commitment*.

---

177 Habermas, Jürgen (2010) *An Awareness of What is Missing: Faith and Reason in a Post-Secular Age*, Cambridge, MA: Polity Press.

178 Hirschman 'Western Feminism, Eastern Veiling.'

179 Duits, Linda and van Zoonen, Liesbet (2006) 'Headscarves and Porno-Chic: Disciplining Girls' Bodies in the European Multicultural Society' 13 *European Journal of Women's Studies*, 103.

180 Kapur, Ratna (2013) 'In the Aftermath of Critique We Are Not in Epistemic Free Fall: Human Rights, the Subaltern Subject, and Non-liberal Search for Freedom and Happiness,' unpublished manuscript on file with author.

PART III

Comparing human rights narratives

6. Human rights and narratives of justification

1. LOOKING AT THE BRIGHT AND DARK SIDES OF HUMAN RIGHTS

Human rights law has had an astounding career, not only as a globally available vocabulary but also because it offers a set of narratives for exposing the scandals of abuse of power and miserable living conditions, asserting a certain legal status for the individual, and capturing peoples' struggles for justice, as well as offering the vision of a better world. Some of these narratives are presented[1] here as another field of comparative legal study.

In this chapter, I take a look at and compare diverse human rights narratives. The romantic picture of human rights narratives will be confronted here with a more pragmatic and skeptical assessment, in order to disrupt their routinization and, by the same token, to defend their polemical origins. These considerations are not meant to downplay the positive effects of human rights law and activism. I merely intend to unsettle the political routines of human rights policies and put into perspective the moral high ground of normativist projects.

Against the backdrop of the career of human rights as a *lingua franca* for the translation of human misery into legal entitlements, comparing human rights narratives might seem, *prima facie*, futile – a venture that is likely to produce just another story, this time, at best, with a comparative twist. Nevertheless, I follow this path, not at all because I hope to return with a comprehensive analysis of human rights law, something like the 'ultimate story.' I simply want to discuss in comparative perspective diverse approaches to human rights law, distinguish and then connect them, especially with regard to their focus, structure and their – romantic

---

[1] For the following I draw on my article Frankenberg, Günter (2014) 'Human Rights and the "Belief" in a Just World' 12 *International Journal of Constitutional Law*, 35.

or tragic – modality. This way the operations of distancing and differencing that I introduced above are applied and tested again, now to compare human rights narratives and, hopefully, prepare the ground for a thicker description.[2] First, the concept of (legal) narrative is introduced; then I discuss how human rights narratives cope with contingency as narratives of justification, before diverse approaches to human rights law are finally presented in the light of their critiques.

2. LEGAL NARRATIVES: COMING TO TERMS WITH CONTINGENCY

A narrative may be tentatively defined as a story created in a constructive format as a work of writing, speech, pictures, etc. that describes a sequence of fictional or non-fictional events, thus joining description, explanation, and argumentation as a further rhetorical mode of discourse. In the social and legal sciences, the understanding of narrative[3] has been influenced by the assumption, elaborated in narrative psychology, that human beings give their life sense and meaning by rendering their experience in the form of a story. The point of departure is not the collection of facts but the embeddedness of the narrating subject in space and time. While, in psychology, the biographical story functions as a construction of the self,[4] in historiography, the social sciences, and literary theory the narrative style – allowing a historical, political or social event to develop as is expected from a story – may be regarded as

---

[2] See Scheffer, Thomas and Niewöhner, Jörg eds (2010) *Thick Comparison. Reviving the Ethnographic Aspiration*, Leiden and Boston: Brill. See, in particular, the editors' insightful introduction, 1–16. The concept of thick(er) comparison is, of course, indebted to Geertz, Clifford (1973) *The Interpretation of Cultures*, New York: Basic Books, Chapter 1; and also to Moore, Sally Falk (2005) 'Comparisons: Possible and Impossible' 324 *Annual Review of Anthropology*, 1; and Yengoyan, Aram A. ed. (2006) *Modes of Comparison. Theory/ Practice*, Michigan: University of Michigan Press.

[3] For a brief discussion of the meanings of narrative see Ducrot, Oswald and Todorov, Tzvetan (1983) 'Narrative' in *Encyclopedic Dictionary of the Sciences of Language*, Baltimore and London: Johns Hopkins University Press, 297–299.

[4] See Dennett, Daniel C. (1992) 'The Self as Center of Narrative Gravity' in Kessel, F., Cole, P. and Johnson, D. eds *Self and Consciousness: Multiple Perspectives*, Hillsdale, NJ: Erlbaum, 103.

a reaction to the linguistic turn informed by postmodern theories.[5] In one of the most influential manifestoes, Hayden White characterizes narrativity as 'a discourse that feigns the world speak itself and speak itself as a story.'[6]

Narrativity is not believed to be a property of law. The law is subject to and the subject of narratives and produces narratives of its own but still seems to resist narrativity. The resistance is structural insofar as the formalist concept of law is based upon law's separation from anything like fiction, history or literature. For stories relate, establish connections, provide context, whereas law is grounded on unrelatedness. The resistance is also political and has to do with authority and legitimacy. Where stories are or pretend to be specific, the law claims generality; where stories are about concrete events and real persons, law's authority is premised on abstractions and distance. That is why narrativity might undermine the force of law, its counterfactual magic. And it might reveal law's secret: that it operates with fictions and presumptions.

Not only the mainstream citadels of law but also the critics' smaller camps withstood the influx of the narrative style, until scholars and lawyers, legislators and judges came to realize that narrativity offers a language to communicate explanations and justifications and helps to cope with contingency. Critics found the narrative style useful to transmit a critical perspective.[7] They recognized that narratives have *always already* been present in the law or that they have used legal storytelling as more authentic, concrete and embodied than legal analysis, syllogism

---

5 Concerning the intense and controversial debate about narrative and narrativity, see Lévi-Strauss, Claude (1966) *The Savage Mind*, Chicago: University of Chicago Press; Lukács, Georg (2005) 'Narrate or Describe' in his *Writer and Critic and Other Essays*, Lincoln: Universe Inc., 110 seq.; Ricœur, Paul (1980) 'Narrative Time' 7 *Critical Inquiry*, 169 seq. See also Hübner, Kurt (1985) *Die Wahrheit des Mythos*, München: C.H. Beck, 357.

6 White, Hayden (1990) 'The Value of Narrativity in the Representation of Reality' in White, Hayden ed. *The Content of the Form. Narrative Discourse and Historical Representation*, Baltimore: Johns Hopkins University Press, 1, 2, 21.

7 See, in general, Weisberg, Richard (1984) *The Failure of the Word*, New Haven: Yale University Press; and Brooks, Peter and Gewirtz, Paul eds (1996) *Law's Stories. Narrative and Rhetoric in the Law*, New Haven: Yale University Press. Lopez, Gerald (1984) 'Lay Lawyering' 31 *UCLA Law Review*, 1, introducing story-telling as an element of human problem-solving by lawyers. In Patricia Williams' (1991) autobiographical essay, *The Alchemy of Race and Rights*, Cambridge, MA: Harvard University Press, she presents, in a narrative style, the intersection of race, gender and class. David Kennedy uses a distinctly and provocatively narrative style in (2004) *The Dark Sides of Virtue. Reassessing*

or deduction. Legal narrations, critical or not, began to be understood as attempts to map out, from the perspective of the here and now, a coherent or plausible story about a series of disparate past events.

Like narrations in the everyday world or in other sciences, legal science stories establish a relationship between why, or at least how, something happened and turned into a memorable event (deserving critique), and what will come of it. Routinely courts state 'the facts of a case' as a story. Similarly, theoretical and doctrinal legal narratives try to come to terms with contingency by embedding singular events or facts in a historical or logical connection. This connection may be a systematic scheme or ideological pattern, such as stories of 'generations of human rights,'[8] their migration[9] and transfer.[10] Especially, the continuous flow of constitutional or legal history lends itself to narrative corroboration:

> Our Constitution is a covenant running from the first generation of Americans to us and then to future generations. It is a coherent succession.[11]

Strong narrative components of the law have always been, albeit not always duly recognized, the story of the case at hand interwoven with the precedent or rule and the courts' attempts to present their opinion as part of 'seamless webs of arguments':[12]

International Humanitarianism, Princeton: Princeton University Press (particularly: the chapters 'Spring Break' and 'Autumn Weekend'). See also Charlesworth, Hilary (1999) 'Feminist Methods in International Law' 93 *American Journal of International Law*, 379, 381, exploring the 'silences of international law.'

[8] E.g. Tomuschat, Christian (2008) *Human Rights: Between Idealism and Realism*, Oxford: Oxford University Press, 26–29.

[9] The consecutive waves of transnational migration of fundamental rights are analyzed by Kadelbach, Stefan (2012) 'The Territoriality and Migration of Fundamental Rights' in Handl, Günther, Zekoll, Joachim and Zumbansen, Peer eds *Beyond Territoriality – Transnational Legal Authority in an Age of Globalization*, Leiden: M. Nijhoff Publishers, 295–324.

[10] Concerning constitutional transfer and experimentalism: Frankenberg, Günter (2013) 'Constitutions as Commodities. Notes on a Theory of Transfer' in Frankenberg, Günter ed. *Order from Transfer. Comparative Constitutional Design and Legal Culture*, Cheltenham, UK and Northampton, MA, USA: Edward Elgar Publishing, 1; and Frankenberg, Günter (2013) 'Constitutional Transfers and Experiments in the 19th Century' in *Order from Transfer*, Cheltenham, UK and Northampton, MA, USA: Edward Elgar Publishing, 279.

[11] Justice Souter (1992) *Planned Parenthood v. Casey*, 505 U.S., 833, 837.

[12] Brooks, Peter (1996) 'The Law as Narrative and Rhetoric' in Brooks and Gewirtz *Law's Stories*, 14, 21.

> Liberty finds no refuge in a jurisprudence of doubt. *Yet 19 years after our holding* that the Constitution protects a woman's right to terminate her pregnancy in its early stages, 410 *Roe v. Wade* 113 (1973), that definition is still questioned ... *Our cases* recognize 'the right of the individual, married or single, to be free from unwarranted governmental intrusion' ... *Our precedents* have respected the private realm of family life ...[13]

Legal narratives also come as legislative commentary accompanying and explaining the official purpose of statutes, or are encapsulated, at times elaborated in the preambles of constitutions.[14] They differ from ordinary stories, though. While the use value of the latter depend on their informational content, suspense, entertainment, moral uplift, etc., law's narratives require a coherent, or at least plausible, structure provided by reasoned doctrinal elaboration, a chain of precedents, etc. to lend credence or to the counterfactual meaning and rationality to its authoritative message.[15]

3. HUMAN RIGHTS AS NARRATIVES OF JUSTIFICATION

Human rights narratives are peculiar in that they are cast in a language of entitlement as regards their bearers and of responsibility as regards states', international and national institutions' and courts' duty to provide for their protection. Both entitlement and responsibility also imply exoneration and justification:

> [W]hat is not in is out. To prohibit abuse is to authorize whatever does not constitute abuse. ... With rights come rationales for setting them aside.'[16]

---

13 *Planned Parenthood v. Casey*, 505 U.S., 833 (1992) – emphasis added.

14 E.g. the preambles of the constitutions of Bolivia (2009), China (1982), East Timor (2002), Vietnam (1992), South Africa (1996) and Myanmar (2008).

15 In recent years, narrative approaches have left behind these conventions and moved from persuasion through the force of logic to emotive, intuitive, aesthetic and other forms of persuasion, which question received wisdom, definitions and presuppositions.

16 Marks, Susan (2012) 'Human Rights in Disastrous Times' in Crawford, James and Koskenniemi, Martti eds *The Cambridge Companion to International Law*, Cambridge: Cambridge University Press, 309, 320.

Thereby, human rights have become central to justificatory arguments for all incidents of injustice, most dramatically genocide and ethnic 'cleansing,' war and military intervention.[17] In fact, human rights law offers an array of stories, justifying, for instance, organized (state) violence: in the international context, this invokes the doctrine of just war, humanitarian intervention and, more recently, the responsibility to protect.[18] In the domestic context, lawyers came to the defense of the rights of 'innocent victims' in 'ticking bomb' situations by legitimizing 'rescue torture' and the intercepting and downing of 'renegade aircraft' hijacked by terrorists.[19] One may safely conclude that justification of violence cuts across the various types of legal narratives.

In everyday usage, justification refers to a dimension of social interaction, namely the way in which a participant or advocate, from the first person perspective, defends her actions or decisions, standards or beliefs to others so as to make them (appear) 'right' or at least 'acceptable.' The impression of commonness wanes once different sciences come forward with their peculiar meanings of justification.[20] The term is anything but unequivocal, even if we disregard the technicians' concept of alignment, the religious connotation of the forgiveness of sins, the psychological usage of justification as one of the mechanisms of defense,[21] and its narrow notion in criminal jurisprudence as a defense to criminal charges or exemption from criminal liability.

In political-legal contexts, justification usually responds to a real or imaginary challenge (caused or constituted by injustice) and gives reasons in an elaborate, story-like way. A justifier tries to render acceptable actions, decisions, beliefs or programs that deviate from a

---

[17] *Ibid*; and Berman, Nathaniel (2004) 'Privileging Combat? Contemporary Conflict and the Legal Construction of War' 43 *Columbia Journal of Transnational Law*, 1; Kennedy, David (2006) *Of War and Law*, Princeton: Princeton University Press.

[18] See Orford, Anne (2003) *Reading Humanitarian Intervention. Human Rights and the Use of Force in International Law*, Cambridge: Cambridge University Press; Orford, Anne (2011) *International Authority and the Responsibility to Protect*, Cambridge: Cambridge University Press; and Kennedy *Of War and Law*.

[19] See Frankenberg, Günter (2014) *Political Technology and the Erosion of the Rule of Law. Normalizing the State of Exception*, Cheltenham, UK and Northampton, MA, USA: Edward Elgar Publishing, Chapter VII.

[20] See Boltanski, Luc and Thevenot, Laurent (2006) *On Justification: Economies of Worth*, Princeton: Princeton University Press.

[21] Freud, Anna (1937) *The Ego and the Mechanisms of Defense*, London: Hogarth.

given standard, break a promise, or disappoint the expectation of justice (otherwise it would suffice to explain the way things turned out). Justification is meant to alleviate dissatisfaction or curb disobedience, and, quite often, prevent or settle a controversy by 'explaining away' a cognitive, normative or emotional dissonance. In this vein, the US and UK governments tried to justify their violation of international law in Iraq, committed by ordering the military invasion without a clear and present mandate from the UN Security Council but fabricating the story of 'weapons of mass destruction' (WMD) stockpiled there and threatening humanity:

> The purpose of … Resolution [1441] was to disarm Iraq of its weapons of mass destruction … My second purpose today is to provide you with additional information, to share with you what the United States knows about Iraq's weapons of mass destruction …[22]

> Regime change in Iraq would be a wonderful thing. That is not the purpose of our action; our purpose is to disarm Iraq of weapons of mass destruction …[23]

Legal (and also human rights) justification figures as a crucial element of conflict management and coping with contingency, that is, ordering the world, by communicating a normative point of view. Narratives of justification bestow what is narrated with an authoritative meaning and legitimizing force: *just* war, *humanitarian* intervention, *civilizing* mission, *rescue* torture, detaining *illegal* combatants, war on *terror*, etc., are some of the concepts that are elevated by their sound of *rightfulness*.

What then needs to be justified in law and politics? Generally speaking, the operation of making something just is provoked by a why-question and based on a comparison requiring that a certain asymmetry be 'explained away.' Regarding the burden of justification two ideal-typical situations can be distinguished:

(1) If something – an action, event or state of being – is *clearly unjust*, the difference between the way things are and the way they should be needs to be 'explained away' contrary to the evidence of injustice. In such situations, typically presented as *extreme* cases or *exceptions* to the rule, justificatory narratives elaborate why injustice is necessary or has to be tolerated for the time being in the name of a higher value or interest

---

[22] E.g. US Secretary of State Colin Powell, addressing the UN Security Council, on 5 February 2003.

[23] Prime Minister Tony Blair, Answer to Parliamentary Question, 29 June 2011, www.publications.parliament.uk/pa/cm200102/cmhansrd/vo020924/debtext/20924-05.htm (last accessed 22 September 2015).

(often located outside the law). Accordingly, the infamous *Enabling Act* and the *Decree for the Protection of People and State*, which suspended the 1918 *Weimar Constitution* and paved the way for establishing the Nazi regime, were declared to remedy 'the distress of the people' and to 'stave off communist violence.'[24] Frequently, the occupation of foreign territories, unless claimed to be 'devoid of all civil inhabitants,'[25] and their exploitation have been legitimized by one or the other 'mission' to defend human rights.

Executors of the dictatorship of the proletariat had regular, if implicit, recourse to their superior insight into the scriptures of Marxism-Leninism or, more abstractly, the 'scientific laws of socialism.' History, class and the requirements of the revolution transcended what the individual might consider hcr right or legitimate interest.

Camouflaging blatant injustice has its risks. The more justificatory narratives contradict what is evident and diverge from expectations of justice or perpetuate themselves with scant empirical content or other compensation the more they lose their purchase and have to be backed by a show of force or an actual implementation of force.

(2) The comparison of the way things are with how they should be becomes more complex and entails more sophisticated techniques of argumentative justification if the shades are grey: if something *may arguably* be considered *unfair* or *illegal* because it deviates from or violates a given normative (or human rights) standard and/or disappoints reasonable expectations. Justificatory narratives may then try to bridge the gap between the 'is' and the 'ought' and clear some action, decision or event of blame by offering a justifying storyline: a person admits that *in this one* case justice was miscarried and the mistake will be corrected on appeal; another claims that *the law* provided for an *exception*; or someone promises that the disadvantaged will be duly *compensated*.

Accordingly, politicians (and their legal advisors) will justify secret government practices, if they cannot be condoned routinely, by arguing that, as a matter of constitutional law, an executive privilege shields them

---

[24] *Reichsgesetzblatt* [law gazette of the German Reich], Vol. I, 28 February 1933, 83 and *Reichsgesetzblatt*, Vol. I, 24 March 1933, 141.

[25] By way of justification the Pilgrims counterfactually spread the tale of the emptiness of the land they were out to settle and reduced the few native American present to 'savage and brutish men … little otherwise than wild beasts,' who could be 'discounted' normatively speaking – Bradford, William (1967) *Of Plymouth Plantation*, New York: Modern Library, 25 seq.

from any obligation to disclose information.[26] They may claim to be exempt from criminal prosecution or refer to 'implied powers' that come with the office or function.[27]

Beneficiaries of a given distribution of goods or entitlements tend to vindicate their benefits as obtained 'of right' or 'within the law.' To veil the lack of legitimacy or the impression of unfairness, legislators (or any elite) taking over, without authorization, the constituent power, are likely to invoke a special mission (see above) and think of compensating those excluded:

> [The deputies] entrusted with legislative power, will seize constituent power on behalf of the nation even in the absence of any explicit charge to do so, in this revolutionary usurpation of power, the gap in legitimacy will be filled by presenting the people with the tables of the essential rights, under the title of '*Declaration of Rights*'.[28]

Human rights stories come with different layers or rather modalities of justification, some normalizing them, others turning them into ideology or myth or instrumentalizing them as benchmarks for judging other societies and polities. Finally, with the proliferation of the human rights language as a global idiom military commanders have also learned to dress up any military action in terms of justice and human rights:

> [J]ustice has become, in all Western countries, one of the tests that any proposed military strategy has to meet … moral theory has been incorporated into war-making as a real constraint on when and how wars are fought.[29]

---

26 With this argument, the Nixon Administration sought to prevent further publication of the Pentagon Papers, which revealed the genealogy of the Vietnam War and the systematic disinformation of the American public about the war by US Governments. See *New York Times Co. v. U.S.* 403 U.S. 713 (1971).

27 Still instructive are the legal arguments of the President's defenders in the Watergate Scandal. See Friedman, Leon and Levantrosser, William F. eds (1992) *Watergate and Afterward – The Legacy of Richard M. Nixon*, Westport, CT: Greenwood Press.

28 Baker, Keith (1992) 'The Idea of a Declaration of Rights' in van Kley, Dale ed. *The French Idea of Freedom*, Stanford: Stanford University Press, 169.

29 Walzer, Michael (2004) *Arguing about War*, New Haven: Yale University Press, 12; see also Kennedy, *The Dark Sides*, 287, 289, who argues that humanitarian norms have been 'metabolised into the routines of the US Navy.'

4. NARRATIVES OF NORMALIZATION: LAW-RULE AS ORDER

The narratives collected under this heading are internally related to one another by privileging a focus on order and the guarantor of rights regimes. They integrate human rights into the different conceptual and functional versions of law-rule that are geared toward limiting the authority of government and, paradoxically relying on the common violator of human rights – the state – whose strength seems crucial for the protection of human rights: '[T]he strength of the state can alone secure the liberty of its members.'[30]

Two strands of the discourse will be introduced and distinguished: legal normalization first; and ideology in the next section. Legal professionals take the routines of law-rule for granted. They do not question the normalizing effects they have. Against the tragedy contained in human rights law, they adopt a pithy attitude.

Submitting Reality to the Language and Routines of Law-Rule

Human rights come with a loss. To paraphrase Clifford Geertz: whatever it is that human rights law is after, it is not the whole story.[31] In the light of the routines and standard procedures of law-rule, human rights law *cannot* possibly be after the whole story. It contains mechanisms that re-present, re-construct and transform reality in a specific way: they *normalize* it.

As human rights intervene in the way things are and translate conflicts into the world of entitlements and obligations, they not only reflect 'practical attitudes toward the management of controversy'[32] but also focus on legally relevant aspects and information and present a distorted picture of reality. Legal methods, argumentative techniques, and procedural requirements filter, reduce complexity and recycle what initially appears to be the whole story. The protagonists of the rights discourse reiterate the story of normalization, encapsulated in human rights cases, as the natural course of events.

---

[30] Rousseau, Jean Jacques (1950) *The Social Contract and Discourses*, New York: Dutton, 52.

[31] Geertz, Clifford (1983) 'Local Knowledge: Fact and Law in Comparative Perspective' in Geertz, Clifford ed. *Local Knowledge: Further Essays in Interpretive Anthropology*, New York: Basic Books, 167, 173.

[32] *Ibid.*

In terms of *method*, human rights law stays firmly within the framework of (modern) regimes of law-rule. To handle controversies it has to frame them as *rights* conflicts first. Consequently, human rights law presents as a given, as an unproblematic necessity, the standard requirement: Individuals have to translate their grievance into *legal terms* and recode their suffering as illegal or violating their *right*; they have to act the role and obey the script of a *claimant*, to say 'that's my right' – rather than: 'that's my interest, need or suffering.' Furthermore, they must direct any rights claim to the legal apparatus and staff (courts, human rights commissions), and follow the rules of the established rituals, hoping their complaint will then and there be properly dealt with.

Deferral and Displacement

Any person claiming her (or other people's) human rights initially experiences the way her conflict is *removed* from the everyday to the halls of justice and processed there by gowned officials, speaking a foreign language and acting at a slow pace, thereby bringing up aspects not anticipated and omitting others one may have considered crucial. Legal professionals take all this for granted; they have been trained to accept the transformation, dislocation and displacement as required by legal method or procedure. General systems-theory considers these aspects of normalization a necessary consequence of functional differentiation (see above cognitive control).

The professional discourse accepts, feeds into and does anything but criticize what is described here as *normalization*: the metamorphosis of a 'real life' conflict into a 'case' and the translation of the grievance into the legal vocabulary; the displacement of the conflict to the fora of legal institutions (courts, law firms, etc.) where they are deferred according to institutional capacity, priority schedules, and workload (see the next chapter).

A rights conflict, *translated*, *dislocated* and *deferred* in this way, can hardly be expected to be solved quickly, predictably and to the claimant's satisfaction. Therefore, the fairly long wait for justice and the experience of injustice needs to be justified or camouflaged. Professional narratives book these limitations and failures of the administration of justice as the inevitable price to be paid for regulated and civilized conflict management and argue that, on balance, the benefits of the professional and institutional application of human rights under the terms and procedures of law regularly, at least in most cases, outweigh the costs. So, the justificatory tale becomes one of economy and necessity.

Selectivity

The constant selection of information joins *dislocation* (or displacement) and *deferral* as a further facet of normalization. Part of the brightness of human rights law, complementing the story of its civilizing mission, stems from the promise that all the significant conflicts can be brought under the umbrella of human rights law and are covered by the rights vocabulary. Human rights law's ordering of the world carries with it the promise that all situations and problems are covered by rights:

> We, the people of South Africa, … adopt this Constitution … so as to … heal the divisions of the past and establish a society based on democratic values, social justice and human rights …[33]

> The General Assembly proclaims this Universal Declaration of Human Rights as a common standard of achievement for all peoples and all nations.[34]

Tales of law's and, in particular, human rights law's comprehensive grasp of the complexity and richness of life and, in the process of application, of 'all the relevant factors' of a case are vulnerable to two charges, though: they miss the *specificity* of each conflict – the singularity of the individual with her identity, needs and life situation – and also the structural and strategic *selectivity* of human rights law, its legislation as well as its application.

As regards legislation, parliaments have demonstrated a preference for *ad hoc* decisions and limiting rights (quite often for the sake of national security) rather than extending them. Their human rights law is remarkable but anything but comprehensive. Likewise, courts adjudicate under considerable constraints in terms of time and institutional resources, fine-tuned by a network of mechanisms of selectivity, which undermine the chances of human rights claims being heard thoroughly, if at all, and judged in all relevant respects. Mechanisms of selectivity are, to name only a few, admissibility thresholds, deals and plea-bargaining in criminal trials, the politics of granting or denying *certiorari*, and the subsidiary character of constitutional review.

These procedural and substantive restrictions suggest that human rights law not only promises more than, due to its structures, it can possibly deliver[35] but has also disempowering side-effects, by dint of its elements

---

[33] *Constitution of the Republic of South Africa* (1996), Preamble.

[34] *Universal Declaration of Human Rights* (1948), Preamble.

[35] This can be said about any counterfactual norms and is therefore a rather trivial statement.

of normalization, that are usually overlooked, adjusted or 'explained away' when professionals talk about their work. Theoretical (jurisprudential and sociological) narratives legitimize the negative side-effects of the standard methods of application as inherent necessities of ordering society, reduction of complexity, or legitimation by procedure.[36]

Alienation

Human rights have the reputation of incarnating the core components of humanist ethics. Therefore, to argue that they have alienating effects, must appear counterintuitive. And yet, alienation,[37] at least the aspects of *estrangement* and *separation*, apply to both the rights discourse and the rights practice. First, the notion of the rights-holder introduces a 'thin' personality, as will be shown in more detail in the next chapter.[38] The rights-holder seems to be a person out of context:

> Poverty offers a good example of the underlying problem. Lack of assets in the midst of a society of riches based on property rights makes the poor feel 'excluded, shunned, scorned, by everyone.' The recognition offered by the abstract right to property, by the potential to hold property, is clearly inadequate.[39]

The alienating effect can be seen more clearly, if one takes into consideration the aspects of deferral and displacement of human rights law, which relegates rights-holders to the role of intimidated and rather

---

[36] One of the central concepts of systems theory; see Luhmann, Niklas (2000) *Vertrauen. Ein Mechanismus der Reduktion sozialer Komplexität*, Stuttgart: UTB; and Luhmann, Niklas (1985) *A Sociological Theory of Law*, London: Routledge and Kegan Paul.

[37] See Schacht, Richard (1970) *Alienation*, Garden City: Doubleday; Mészáros, István (2006) *Marx's Theory of Alienation*, London: Merlin Press; and Jaeggi, Rahel (2005) *Entfremdung. Zur Aktualität eines sozialphilosophischen Problems*, Frankfurt: Campus.

[38] In the normative discourse, human rights are defined as 'weapons' or 'trumps' in the hands of the individual rights-holder. They are said to override any competing political, economic or other concerns. Such definitions accept as normal the circumstance that the personal is faded out and treated as an incidence of the universal. See, for example, Dworkin, Ronald (1978) *Taking Rights Seriously*, London: G. Duckworth & Co.

[39] Douzinas *Human Rights and Empire*, 40, referring to Hegel, Georg F.W. (1983) *Philosophie des Rechts: Die Vorlesung von 1819/20*, Frankfurt: Suhrkamp.

ignorant bystanders who observe the automatic functioning of a well-oiled, complex legal machinery.[40] While the conflict is removed from the everyday of experience, the claimants, unless commanding a modicum of legal training, will hardly be able to avoid feeling dispossessed of what had once been their conflict – a feeling that may very well be described as alienation. They experience the normalizing juridification as a separation from their original plea and plight and see themselves placed in a relation of unrelatedness.[41]

How normalization erodes the ethical basis of a human right will be discussed in the next chapter with regard to access to justice. Here, I concentrate on the way asylum cases are judicially processed and how the right to asylum has been eroded in post-World War II Germany.

Originally asylum evolved from the (non-legal) duty of hospitality.[42] During the nineteenth century, when the system of nation-states developed, asylum for political refugees was regarded as an instrument of foreign policy. To prevent the disturbance of good neighborly relations by citizens seeking refuge abroad and claiming to be politically persecuted, states mutually tolerated the institution and practice of asylum. For reasons of foreign policy, asylum was separated (and alienated) from the asylum seeker's charge against her country – political persecution.

Against the background of totalitarian atrocities, the asylum rationale shifted in the twentieth century from foreign affairs to ethics and philosophy and then to *Realpolitik*. Hannah Arendt and other authors held asylum to be the ultimate 'right to have rights' and the only *genuine* human right.[43] It received a programmatic, albeit somewhat enigmatic, juristic wording in Article 14 of the Universal Declaration: 'Everyone has the right to seek and to enjoy in other countries asylum from persecution.' One year later and for the first time in constitutional history, the German Basic Law, in its original version of 1949, elevated asylum to a

---

[40] Niklas Luhmann analyzed and interpreted this dark side as 'legitimation by procedure' in his (2001) *Legitimation durch Verfahren*, 6th ed., Frankfurt: Suhrkamp; Niklas Luhmann *A Sociological Theory of Law*. See Machura, Stefan (1997) 'The Individual in the Shadow of Powerful Institutions' in Röhl, Klaus F. and Machura, Stefan eds *Procedural Justice*, Aldershot: Ashgate, 181.

[41] Jaeggi *Entfremdung*, 53 with reference to Isaiah Berlin's concept of positive freedom.

[42] Derrida, Jacques and Dufourmantelle, Anne (2000) *Of Hospitality: Cultural Memory in the Present*, Stanford: Stanford University.

[43] Arendt, Hannah (1966) *The Origins of Totalitarianism*, New York and San Diego: Harcourt Brace & World, in the chapter 'The Perplexities of the Rights of Man,' 290 seq.; see also Benhabib, Seyla (2004) *The Rights of Others. Aliens, Residents, and Citizens*, Cambridge: Cambridge University Press, 56 seq.

human right – according to Ronald Dworkin's theory: a 'trump' in the hands of those who are victims of political persecution.

In the course of its further doctrinal progress on the path of law in West Germany, asylum's gold – the *right* – turned, in a perverse sort of alchemy, into lead.[44] The ethical basis of the human right was sustained as long as refugees came from Germany's East; at any rate, they were considered *by law* German nationals or ethnic Germans, so asylum was actually superseded by (re)patriation. The real downfall of the human right began, and the asylum seekers' legal recognition became distinctly more hesitant and selective, when socialists and communists persecuted by the Pinochet regime knocked on German doors in the early 1970s. Some courts then required a 'no violence' test, others restricted asylum, in a similar turn to the nineteenth century, to 'democratic protesters' or 'politically engaged citizens.'[45] In addition, courts changed the burden of proof and shifted the right one more notch away from the reality of refugees. Asylum seekers, in particular torture victims, had to prove a 'political motivation to persecute' on the part of their persecutors. The Federal Administrative Court argued:

> A persecution for political reasons crucially depends on the motives underlying the infringements by the state … and … requires in each case clarification of the purpose a police measure or criminal prosecution serves. [Consequently, the right to asylum] offers protection neither against any excess of state power nor any disregard of human dignity [such as torture, but requires in addition the showing of] … political motives of the state abusing its power.[46]

Once the number of refugees increased dramatically to over 100,000 per year in the 1990s, and their appearance differed considerably in terms of color, habit and religion from what was familiar, ethical and human rights concerns were lowered significantly. German courts and administrative agencies adapted their reading of the right to asylum to the debates on the global plane.[47] They separated their decisions even more from the facts presented by the asylum seekers and privileged blatantly political, social and economic considerations (social costs, limits of integration, harmonization of asylum laws within the European Union) at the expense

---

44 The metaphor I borrow from Geertz 'Local Knowledge,' 182.

45 Decisions of the Federal Administrative Court – 67 *BVerwGE*, 195/202.

46 Federal Constitutional Court of Germany – 67 *BVerfGE* 184/189 and 193.

47 For a critical analysis of the global debates: Cheah, Pheng (2006) *Inhuman Conditions: On Cosmopolitanism and Human Rights*, Cambridge: Harvard University Press.

of asylum's ethical foundation as a human right. Since then, the asylum guarantee has been devalued, step by step, from a 'trump card' to a vocabulary that has to compete with others on the same plane, such as security, fiscal policy, demography or European integration.

Reducing the Imaginative Space and Strategic Options

Once people realize that to dress their interest in, or demand for, whatever they need as a right, say, to free speech, health, a safe work place, access to justice or equal pay, is to give their agenda the strongest possible setting, they will translate their experience of what they deem unjust, arbitrary, or degrading into legal claims of right – to reveal the scandal of the way things are and to seek redress for their grievances. As a matter of consequence, the focus on the grammar and vocabulary of rights narrows the imaginative space of emancipation to the world of law and rights and marginalizes or negates other vocabularies and strategies, like the vocabulary of duties and responsibilities, of basic needs or interests, or, in particular, strategies relying on collective commitment[48] and it tends to de-politicize the conflict at hand.

David Kennedy takes the right to development as an example to illustrate this problematic aspect of human rights law. He focuses on the ambivalent consequences, which is to say, the dark side, once concerns about global poverty are mainly raised in terms of a human right:

> [E]nergy and resources are drawn to developing a literature and an institutional practice at the international level of a particular sort. Efforts that cannot be articulated in these terms seem less legitimate, less practical, less worth the effort.[49]

Narratives justifying a right to development systematically overlook or play down the fact that activists concerned about poverty are increasingly drawn into (a) endless debates about a series of legal quandaries: right of whom, against whom, remedying poverty how, to be implemented in what way and by which institutions, and so forth, and (b) into institutional projects of codification, monitoring, and reporting that are quite familiar from other human rights efforts. Meanwhile, other endeavors that human rights narratives neither cover nor criticize because they insulate the economy and politics from law are strengthened. In the end '[i]nternational economic policy … is taken over by neo-liberal players

[48] Kennedy *The Dark Sides*, 108 seq.
[49] *Ibid.*

who do not see development as a special problem' affecting or causing global poverty. One may infer that human rights law requires a narrative of justification insofar as it narrows the imaginative space of emancipation.

Normalization as De-Politicization

Aside from limiting the imaginative space, the normalizing interventions of human rights have political implications also in other respects. As a rule, narratives of human rights – with their dominant message that legal formalization warrants the neutrality of procedures and outcomes – appear to privilege legal over political aspects and legislation over application.

This implies that political concerns can only be introduced into the legislative process where they are deliberated and then either filtered out as not relevant (or rather, not representing an important social interest or value) or transposed to the level of a *right that is given priority* over other interests. Such transformation establishes a human right in its general and abstract legal existence and purges it from its underlying political or other rationales.

The second part of the story concentrates on the application of rights. From a normative point of view, this operation is described as reasoned elaboration in a particular case guided by legal method. If we are to believe the standard narratives, judicial decisions are generally believed to merely translate *lege artis*, that is by way of syllogism, balancing, interpretation or other legal techniques, a legislative (or contractual) rights program. This narrative has been challenged by numerous realist, sociological, critical, and political theories of law.[50] To these theories and critiques I want to add only one aspect: privileging the legislative production of human rights over their judicial application is prone to miss the power strategies that are shifted to the conflict over definitions (of rights).

Again, the fall of the Germany asylum guarantee would be instructive about how the normalizing discourse de-politicizes conflicts.[51] In the following I focus, however, on the prohibition of torture as it opens up the terrain for different strategies of de-politicization.

---

[50] For an overview see Frankenberg, Günter (1988/1989) 'Down by Law: Irony, Seriousness, and Reason' 83 *North Western University Law Review*, 360; Douzinas *Human Rights and Empire*, Chapter 8.

[51] And it will be instructive to see how the law of the member-states of the European Union and union law deal with the present refugee crisis.

The 1948 *Universal Declaration on Human Rights*, similarly the 1950 *European Convention on Human Rights*, strictly and absolutely, commands in Art. 5: 'No one shall be subjected to torture or cruel, inhuman or degrading treatment or punishment.' The 1984 *Convention against Torture and Other Cruel, Inhuman or Degrading Treatment or Punishment*[52] attempted to move beyond the generalized vocabulary of 'the language of Eden'[53] by offering a fairly detailed definition:

> [T]he term torture means any act by which severe pain or suffering, whether physical or mental, is intentionally inflicted on a person for such purposes as obtaining from him or a third person information or a confession, punishing him for an act he or a third person committed or is suspected of having committed, or intimidating or coercing him or a third person, or for any reason based on discrimination of any kind, when such pain or suffering is inflicted by or at the instigation or with the consent or acquiescence of a public official or other person acting in an official capacity. It does not include pain or suffering arising only from, inherent in or incidental to lawful sanctions.

The document anticipated that readers (especially states) might look for loopholes:

> No exceptional circumstances whatsoever, whether a state of war or a threat of war, internal political instability or any other public emergency, may be invoked as a justification of torture.[54]

No sooner had this definition been laid down than an endless series of semantic battles began, motivated by unabashedly political concerns. Early on, the US Government, Congress as well as the Administration, submitted a number of provisos to the Convention's definition and, in the process, reduced the rather strictly defined interdict to a flexible standard. These definitional moves appear to be designed to cover past and ongoing CIA and military interrogation methods that qualify as torture.[55]

Political battles over the semantics of torture, facilitated by its polysemy, came to a head during the Bush/Cheney Administration. A new narrative of justification was introduced: the responsibility to protect a

---

[52] Adopted by the General Assembly Resolution 39/46 of 10 December 1984.

[53] Peters, Edward (1985) *Torture*, London: Basil Blackwell.

[54] Art. 1 and 2 of the *Convention against Torture*.

[55] See only Sands, Philippe (2004) *Torture Team. Rumsfeld's Memo and the Betrayal of American Values*, London: Palgrave Macmillan; and Levinson, Sanford ed. (2004) *Torture: A Collection*, New York.

society from terrorist attacks, derived from an always available, extended security *dispositif*:

> 'National security' has been the privileged term giving the state discretion to override policies and human rights when it feels threatened by real or imaginary enemies. But Western states have not replaced national with 'human' security as the basis for engagement in world politics, 'a conception more attentive to the concerns and insecurities of persons and people.'[56]

The duty to provide security, i.e. to protect, served as a vehicle for putting the adversary of human rights, the state, in a concrete conflict alongside the rights-holders and shifted from a vertical to a horizontal understanding of human rights. In the name of security, the commanders and practitioners of torture methods, before and more so after 9/11, claimed authority to conduct more aggressive interrogation methods than were legally permitted.[57] This way, the US Assistant Attorney-General, Jay Bybee, 'defined down' torture as:

> [E]xtreme acts … of an intensity akin to that which accompanies serious physical injury such as death or organ failure … [b]ecause the acts inflicting torture are extreme, there is [a] significant range of acts that, though they might constitute cruel, inhuman, or degrading treatment or punishment, fail to rise to the level of torture.[58]

Members of the administration and the military were instructed by government memoranda that torturing terrorists in captivity abroad 'may be justified' and international laws against torture 'may be unconstitutional if applied to interrogations.'[59]

A memo from 2002 issued by the Justice Department held, among others, that (a) the President's inherent authority must be construed as overriding the prohibition against torture, (b) 'it is difficult to take a specific act out of context and conclude that the act in isolation would

56 Douzinas, *Human Rights and Empire*, 184 referring to Falk, Richard (2004) *The Declining World Order: America's Imperial Geopolitics*, London and New York: Routledge, 11, 16. See also Orford, Anne (2011) *International Authority and the Responsibility to Protect*, Cambridge: Cambridge University Press.

57 For a detailed analysis see Sands *Torture Team*; and Frankenberg *Political Technology*, Chapter VII.

58 Quoted by Eaves, Elizabeth (2004) 'Defining Deviancy Down,' *Harper's Magazine*, 6 September 2004, 81 seq.

59 Priest, Dana and Smith, R. Jeffrey (2004) 'Memo Offered Justification for Use of Torture,' *Washington Post*, 8 June 2004, A01.

constitute torture,' (c) '[f]or purely mental pain or suffering to amount to torture, it must result in significant psychological harm of significant duration, e.g. lasting for months or even years,' and (d) that 'harm[ing] an enemy combatant during an interrogation in a manner that might arguably violate criminal prohibition' would be justified if done 'in order to prevent further attacks on the United States by the al Qaeda terrorist network.'[60]

The US Government complemented these politics of definition by intensely exploiting the polysemy of torture. The agencies resorted to euphemism and cynicism, dodging the 't-word' by officially talking about 'extreme prison conditions', 'disadvantageous' or 'full coercive treatment,' 'torture lite' or 'extra encouragement' in interrogation situations. In a further political move, the government outflanked the formalized human right by informal security practices well-known today as 'torture by proxy' and 'offshore torture'. In keeping with the logic of outsourcing,[61] political office-holders, military commanders, and secret service agents sought to sidestep the charge of human rights violations. They delegated the application of violence to proxyholders – countries and subcontracted private agencies – well known for brutal interrogation techniques.

From these semantic battles and strategies to camouflage torture practices one may infer that a strict human right interdict does not put to rest the politics of organized cruelty. On the contrary, the stricter the prohibition, the more it will provoke governmental opposition, because an absolute prohibition escapes 'the familiar dynamic of rights and state power, in which the recognition of a right is also, and arguably more importantly, an acknowledgment of state power.'[62]

5. HUMAN RIGHTS AS POSITIVE IDEOLOGY

The political ideologue presents human rights as part and parcel of a project of positive ideology and gives the tragic a programmatic twist. In

---

[60] *Ibid.* See also Sands *Torture Team*; and Lazreg, Marnia (2008) *Torture and the Twilight of Empire*, Princeton: Princeton University Press.

[61] Mayer, Jane (2005) 'Outsourcing Torture,' *The New Yorker*, 14 February 2005, 81, 106. See also Frankenberg, Günter (2008) 'Torture and Taboo: An Essay Comparing Paradigms of Organized Cruelty' 56 *American Journal of Comparative Law*, 403 with further references.

[62] Parry, John (2005) 'The Shape of Modern Torture: Extraordinary Rendition and Ghost Detainees' 6 *Melbourne Journal of International Law*, 516, 520.

this context, ideology connotes the way its addressees (are made to) see reality. The term comes with a long conceptual history and a package of meanings. To actually 'work' and be successful an ideology 'must have at least enough cognitive content to help organize the practical lives of human beings.'[63] The more the descriptions of society and the justification of a system, say, in a constitution or declaration of independence, diverge from the experienced reality and are 'accomplished with false consciousness' (Friedrich Engels),[64] the more they become negative ideology – ignoble lies to deceive those who 'excel at what they wish to believe.'[65] Still, the ideology of human rights as a set of interpretive ideas and beliefs – true or false – captures the belief in the power of these rights to order the world and correct injustice.

Theories of human rights qualify as ideologies insofar as they contain 'prepackaged units of interpretation'[66] ordering the world and shaping the vision of how the world is or, rather, should be seen. These packages contain, in particular, programmatic visions (aims) and interpretations of past experiences and actions (justifications). They are offered either by a dominant class or elite or by the non-dominant class or their advocates as mobilizing messages to persuade the recipients to look at things and understand reality from the offered point of view, for instance, as violations of human rights that can be adjusted, redressed, and healed by having recourse to human rights.

As far as rights-stories contain or imply a *developmental scheme* or program of action, they correspond to the style of a *positive* (political) ideology. This style is epitomized, in particular but not exclusively, by socialist and some postcolonial constitutions which outline and project how society *should* work and which goals should be achieved. Their tone is one of mobilization against enemies or adverse circumstances:[67]

---

[63] For an overview of the complex discourse on ideology and the possible meanings of ideology, see Eagleton, Terry (2007) *Ideology. An Introduction*, London and New York: Verso, 1, 27.

[64] Eyerman, Ron (1981) 'False Consciousness and Ideology in Marxist Thought' 24 *Acta Sociologica*, 43, 56.

[65] Jost, John T.T., Ledgerwood, Alison and Hardin, Curtis D. (2008) 'Shared Reality, System Justification and the Relational Basis of Ideological Beliefs' 2 *Social and Personality Psychology Compass*, 171.

[66] *Ibid.*

[67] For a thoughtful, critical analysis see Mutua, Makau Wa (1995/1996) 'The Ideology of Human Rights' 36 *Virginia Journal of International Law*, 589; see also Koskenniemi, Martti (1990) 'The Politics of International Law' 1 *European Journal of International Law*, 4.

> *El pueblo boliviano … desde la profundidad de la historia, inspirado en las luchas del pasado, en la sublevación anticolonial … construimos un nuevo estado.*[68]

> The Chinese people must fight against those forces and elements, both at home and abroad, that are hostile to China's socialist system and try to undermine it.[69]

Since human rights law has replaced the exhausted natural rights tradition, it was linked to one or the other political agenda: Western anti-communism and Eastern anti-imperialism, first; later, foreign aid/development and the promotion of democracy; and more recently humanitarian interventions and neo-liberal restructuring of economies. Accordingly, 'the holy trinity' of liberalism, democracy and human rights[70] has been said to serve as the 'West's ideology, the credo of a new world order,'[71] its neo-liberal agenda[72] and its ideological subtext.

What is more, human rights became a 'bargaining chip' in trade, aid, diplomatic and other international relations as well as a platform for world-wide involvement in domestic affairs; they were 'hijacked by governments for a moral-sounding policy.'[73] Ritually, political leaders, traditionally in Russia, China and peripheral countries, like Cuba, have to respond to queries (from Western politicians) regarding the human-rights situation in their country before the delegations then go ahead with concluding economic deals or sitting down for dinner. In the context of foreign policy, national interests, economic intentions, and ideological hegemony are reconstructed in human rights terms.[74]

---

68 'The Bolivian people … from the depth of their history, inspired by the struggles of the past, in the indigenous anti-colonial uprising … We build a new State.' *Constitution of the Republic of Bolivia* 2009, Preamble.

69 *Constitution of the People's Republic of China* 1988, amended on 14 March 2004, Preamble.

70 Mutua 'The Ideology of Human Rights,' 589, 601.

71 Douzinas *Human Rights and Empire*, 32 seq.

72 From the vast literature, see only the critical interventions: Chomsky, Noam (1999) *Profit over People. Neoliberalism and Global Order*, New York: Seven Stories Press; Stiglitz, Joseph (2002) *Globalization and its Discontents*, New York: W.W. Norton; and Brown, Wendy (2015) *Undoing the Demos: Neoliberalism's Stealth Revolution*, Cambridge, MA: MIT Press.

73 Douzinas *Human Rights and Empire*, 32.

74 See only Brysk, Alison (2000) *Global Good Samaritans – Human Rights as Foreign Policy*, Oxford: Oxford University Press; and Chomsky, Noam (1978) *'Human Rights' and American Foreign Policy*, Nottingham: Spokesman Books.

Meanwhile, even the organizers of sports events have adopted the human rights terminology. Russian anti-gay laws banning the 'propaganda of nontraditional sexual relations to minors' and, incidentally disregarding a ruling of the European Court of Human Rights,[75] provoked protest against the 2014 Winter Olympics in Sochi. However, once again, and in contrast to the boycott of South African sports events during the *Apartheid* era, the indomitable opportunism of the International Olympic Committee prevailed.

Putting human rights into commission for foreign and other policy lets their fragrance of transcendence – transcending first and foremost national interests, that is – evaporate. Today's examples follow an ignoble series of historical justifications of military interventions by substantiating or indicating a mission:

> [T]he intervenors, when challenged, always resort to a moral justification – natural law and Christianity in the sixteenth century, the civilizing mission in the nineteenth century, and human rights and democracy in the late twentieth and twenty-first centuries.[76]

One wonders what the mission of FIFA, the world football association, or the International Olympic Committee might be, though.

6. HUMAN RIGHTS: NARRATIVES OF THEIR UNIVERSAL NATURE

In academia, narratives of justification are worlds apart, it seems, and follow a different path. They present and set the normative standards for the way things ought to be and they no longer, or do not always, strictly compare the 'is' with an 'ought', but initiate a philosophical or jurisprudential project of reasoned elaboration, which is internally related to the style of legal comparison introduced above as Universal Dreams Inc.

---

75 In *Alekseyev v. Russia*, 21 October 2010, the Court held that banning gay pride rallies violates Articles 11 and 14 of the European Convention on Human Rights.

76 Wallerstein, Immanuel (2006) *European Universalism: The Rhetoric of Power*, New York: The New Press, 27; Anghie, Antony (2005) *Imperialism, Sovereignty, and the Making of International Law*, Cambridge: Cambridge University Press; Koskenniemi, Martti (2001) *The Gentle Civilizer of Nations*, Cambridge: Cambridge University Press.

In stark contrast to the professional-technical and ideological-mobilizing discourses, the universalistic debates on human rights shift the accent from order, control and strategy to the victims of injustice and, this way, to those who should actually benefit from human rights. Regardless of their internal differences, the various normative projects come with a vision. Human rights documents and philosophical (liberal) publicists, lawyers and activists promise to lead the willing to (or at least work with them for) a world where rights guarantee that conflicts are solved civilly, wars are waged justly, trials are fair, children grow up not suffering privations, women receive equal pay, the police no longer profile racially, persons with disabilities participate fully in all spheres of life, and even the interests of future generations command adequate concern and respect, and so forth (see Universal Dreams Inc. above).

In consequence, there is hardly any other field or discipline of law that has generated more theoretical energy and doctrinal reasoning, political-legal rhetoric, literature inspired by activism, and also critical thought and commentary, than human rights. Libraries testify to an abundance of treatises and articles, pamphlets and resolutions that, in turn, document enthusiasm and disappointment, skepticism and pragmatism.[77]

From the activists' perspective, human rights turned into a global currency or *lingua franca*. Their story became one of success,[78] the more individuals, groups, and even government officials realized that resorting to rights claims – in spite of their limitations and exceptions – may be the best way to buttress and dress up their stakes in a conflict. As inventions of reason and justice, human rights are reputed to incarnate the good in an evil world. As spoils of the suppressed classes and discriminated

---

[77] From the vast critical literature, see Alston, Philip and Mégret, Fred eds (2011) *The United Nations and Human Rights: A Critical Appraisal*, Oxford: Oxford University Press; Kennedy, David *The Dark Sides*; Marks 'Human Rights in Disastrous Times'; Knop, Karen ed. (2004) *Gender and Human Rights*, Oxford: Oxford University Press.

[78] Karen Engle (1992) 'International Human Rights and Feminism: When Discourses Meet' 13 *Michigan Journal of International Law*, 517 calls them, more cautiously, 'affirmative approaches.' Anne Orford stresses that the 'human rights discourse has been extremely effective at maintaining public awareness of the treatment of detainees [in] the infamous Woomera Immigration Reception and Processing Center' located in the Simpson Desert in Australia – see Orford, Anne (2007) 'Biopolitics and the Tragic Subject' in Dauphinee, Elizabeth and Masters, Cristina eds *The Logics of Biopower and the War on Terror*, London: Palgrave Macmillan, 207, 211.

minorities, they symbolize that the struggle against tyranny and for egalitarian causes can be and has been successful. As reflections of humans' modern experience and predicament, they mirror evolution and progress. This overall optimistic picture characterizes the *romantic* narrative of human rights.[79] Telling the human rights story as a drama of redemption, or at least occasional reconciliation, draws its liberating appeal from the widespread proliferation of human rights, not only as a globally available language for the translation of any kind of human injury, misery and misrecognition, but also as globally implementable instruments for the struggle against those conditions.

Their discourse is strictly normative, either philosophical or legal-doctrinal. Whether profoundly philosophical or blandly legal-doctrinal, the basic structure invariably runs like this: *A* (the rights-holder) has a *right* to *X* (freedom, support, etc.) *against B* (the respondent who has a correlative duty) *by virtue of Y* (the justificatory basis for or ground of the entitlement).[80] Legal-doctrinal narratives usually have no major problem finding a statutory, constitutional, international legal or other basis for a human right, but must pay attention to all the other elements of the structure, in particular to the preconditions and limitations of a human right, and often have to address the question of enforcement, too. In stark contrast, philosophical narratives are preoccupied with the 'human' and the 'by virtue of.' They qualify as foundational stories.

Outside their narrow technical application, human rights narratives often start from past memories of injustice, fear and oppression.[81] In the mode of normative construction, visions of the human being and society, of needs and interests are translated into possibly more coherent,

---

[79] I borrow the categories and in particular the distinction between a romantic and a tragic narrative from Frye, Northrop (1957) *The Anatomy of Criticism*, Princeton: Princeton Press; and White, Hayden (1990) 'Narrativity in the Representation of Reality' in White, Hayden ed. *The Content of the Form. Narrative Discourse and Historical Representation*, Baltimore: Johns Hopkins University Press, 1.

[80] See Gewirth, Alan (1986) 'Are There Absolute Rights?' in Waldron, Jeremy ed. *Theories of Rights*, Oxford: Oxford University Press, 91, 93.

[81] Günther, Klaus (1999) 'Human Rights and Political Culture' in Alston, Philip ed. *The EU and Human Rights*, Oxford: Oxford University Press, 117, 126.

well-grounded principles of justice[82] and human rights[83] primarily guaranteeing dignity,[84] integrity, autonomy and equality. The critical project consists in (and is often limited to) confronting a bad reality with rights that point toward a better world. The normative discourse focuses on victims of practices and conditions of injustice against which authors bring to bear the counterfactual force of human rights to redress all grievances.

As distinct from stories informed by a practical purpose as ideologies or stories of normalization, normative narratives invariably claim to take human rights seriously and concentrate on the systematic rational elucidation of normative propositions, ideas and beliefs. It is virtually impossible to recount here the richness and variety of minimalist or maximalist, individualist or collectivist, ethical/moral or political-legal, universalist or relativist stories elaborating human rights as situated on national, transnational or international planes, with or without a 'freestanding moral normativity' – developed from basic needs or interests, informed by a 'global public reason', based on an 'overlapping consensus' or emanating from discursive procedures.

Just as little do I want to participate or take sides in the 'race to the bottom,' to wit, the search for the ultimate and most fundamental of all human rights. The list is already long (enough): it contains the 'right to have rights' (Hannah Arendt), the 'right to equal concern and respect' (Ronald Dworkin) and dignity (Pico della Mirandola), the equi-original concept of private and political autonomy (Jürgen Habermas) and the 'right to justification' (Rainer Forst); the right to membership in a

---

[82] To name only the most illustrious that cover a variety of approaches within the liberal paradigm: Rawls, John (1971) *A Theory of Justice*, Cambridge, MA: Harvard University Press; Habermas, Jürgen (1996) *Between Facts and Norms: Contributions to a Discourse Theory of Law and Democracy*, Cambridge, MA: Blackwell Publishers; Scanlon, Thomas (1998) *What We Owe to Each Other*, Cambridge: Cambridge University Press; Buchanan, Allan (2004) *Justice, Legitimacy, and Self-Determination. Moral Foundations for International Law*, Oxford: Oxford University Press; and Forst, Rainer (2007) *Das Recht auf Rechtfertigung. Elemente einer konstruktivistischen Theorie der Gerechtigkeit*, Frankfurt: Suhrkamp.

[83] See Waldron *Theories of Rights*; Pogge, Thomas (2002) *World Poverty and Human Rights*, Cambridge: Cambridge University Press; Nickel, James (2006) *Making Sense of Human Rights*, 2nd ed., Oxford: Oxford University Press; Griffin, James (2008) *On Human Rights*, Oxford: Oxford University Press.

[84] Dupré, Cathérine (2013) 'Human Dignity in Europe: A Foundational Constitutional Principle' 19 *European Public Law*, 319.

political society (Joshua Cohen), the right to enjoy minimal conditions of a good life (John Tasioulas) and freedom from fear (Franz L. Neumann).

In general, philosophers and scholars of jurisprudence alike embrace a romantic discourse and expect to transcend the world of sorry experiences. They construct the justification for human rights on diverse foundations: the common humanity or membership of the human race; humans' shared rationality; or, somewhat more modestly, membership in a legally constituted community (nation, state).

In a second step, they translate their intention to ameliorate the way things are into a theoretical (or doctrinal) vocabulary with a fundamental or natural rights tone to ascertain that human rights are understood as neither accidental nor conventional entitlements. Some authors and documents also hold out hope for a more general liberation and reconciliation in a world whose fairness, they claim, hinges upon rights.

These narratives and the human rights law they have helped to emerge, profile and proliferate on the domestic and international planes, are appreciated as 'a search for absolutes in a world whose complexity has created the danger of unfettered relativism, ... bureaucratic abuse'[85] and arbitrary power, as well as a search for limits to cost–benefit calculations, administrative or managerial discretion and the cyclical fluctuations of political preferences. The appreciation of human rights constructions has to be qualified insofar as the normative discourse is geared toward legitimizing the political-social status quo or covering up the rifts in the texture of society. As far as that is the case

> [t]he discourse of universal human rights ... presents a fantasy scenario in which society and the individual are perceived as whole, as non-split. In this fantasy, society is understood as something that can be rationally organized, as a community that can become non-conflictual if only it respects 'human rights.'[86]

Most of the normative theories stress the universal nature of human rights, which usually comes with the promise of a comprehensive problem solution. Reasoned elaboration, philosophical or doctrinal, suggests or promises that human rights law covers *all* situations and *all relevant* problems, wherever they may arise. In this vein, some authors in the field of human rights agonize over perfecting the method of their

---

[85] Koskenniemi, Martti (2010) 'Human Rights Mainstreaming as a Strategy for Institutional Power' 1 *Humanity*, 47.

[86] Salecl, Renata (1994) *The Spoils of Freedom. Psychoanalysis and Feminism after the Fall of Socialism*, London: Routledge, 127.

application, while others elaborate 'systems' of rights.[87] Normative theories with a romantic twist will prefer to uphold the story of human rights' comprehensive and universal reach by either downplaying (justifying) selectivity as a *singular* bad practice not compromising the universal ideal or *counterfactually* neutralizing the selectivity of normalization.

The universal reach and claim come at a cost, though. The particularity of the individual complaint is never completely exhausted but taken as an *instance* – technically, a concrete controversy – to be fitted and dealt with in the all-encompassing universal scheme. And this way, many aspects the individual may find crucial get lost in translation. Or worse, the universal grasp, to preserve its allure, denies the Eurocentric particularity of the human rights corpus and denies its cultural specificity, which can be traced back to liberal constitutionalism and diverse constitutional documents. At this corner of the project, human rights law has to thwart the attacks of cultural relativists.[88] Richard Rorty challenged the idea that human rights can be supported philosophically by good reasons, like the truth of moral intuitions or claims to knowledge about the nature of human beings, and he criticizes the idealizing vocabulary. Instead, he argues that the emergence of the human rights culture owes nothing to increased moral knowledge and everything to 'hearing sad and sentimental stories.' He proposes to discontinue the rationalist project of reasoned elaboration, and the attempt to found culture on nature and moral obligation on knowledge of transcultural universals, and concentrate energies on manipulating sentiments, i.e. developing empathy,[89] in order to ultimately come up with a good answer to the question why we should care about other people's misery or happiness.[90]

---

87 Habermas *Beyond Facts and Norms*.

88 Rorty, Richard (1993) 'Human Rights, Rationality, and Sentimentality' in Shute, Stephen and Hurley, Susan eds *On Human Rights*, New York: Basic Books, 111; Donnelly, Jack (1984) 'Cultural Relativism and Universal Human Rights' 6 *Human Rights Quarterly*, 400.

89 Rorty 'Human Rights, Rationality, and Sentimentality,' 117–119. In the same vein: Baier, Annette (1991) *A Progress of Sentiments*, Cambridge: Cambridge University Press. She proposes a move from obligation to trust.

90 See Frankenberg, Günter (1996) 'Why Care? The Trouble with Social Rights' 17 *Cardozo Law Review*, 1365.

7. HUMAN RIGHTS NARRATIVES AS MYTHOLOGY

Narratives of human rights may also follow the grammar and share some structural features of what appears to be a modern mythology. They shift the accent on the story about what human rights are supposed to achieve – redemption and order – and give a primary place to imagination rather than the institutional setting, like courts or due process. Their message is ambivalent, it may propagate radical reforms as well as protection of the status quo.

Similar to myths,[91] as the term is (possibly with simplification) used here, human rights narratives are 'words with power.'[92] They rely on a method which establishes a connection between human existence and human suffering. Mythical human rights stories span tales of justification that construct, first, a comprehensive narrative connection of disparate (past) events; second, advance claims concerning the validity of the narrative of legitimate entitlement, occasionally with transcendent underpinning, religious or otherwise; and third, have a political-educational agenda of how things legitimately should be, often, but not necessarily, couched in a vision of progress and redemption.[93] By removing human rights from their all-too earthly moorings, these three aspects may legitimize the defense of the status quo or call for its reform or amelioration. Aside from the fascination with the juridical, I believe the affinity to myth accounts for the peculiar purchase of and redemptive power ascribed to mythical human rights narratives.

Structural Connection of Disparate Events

Reading mythical narratives of justification from a structural point of view, they are distinguished by an *internal connection*. Like any other good story, they have a beginning, albeit mysterious and dark, and an end, however temporary and elusive. More importantly, they construct, or let the reader/listener imagine, a plausible transition from beginning to

---

[91] From the vast body of literature, see Barthes, Roland (1957) *Mythologies*, Paris: Seuil; Lévi-Strauss, *The Savage Mind*; Lévi-Strauss, Claude (1963) *Totemism*, Boston: Beacon Press; and Blumenberg, Hans (1979) *Arbeit am Mythos*, Frankfurt: Suhrkamp.

[92] See Frye, Northrop (1992) *Words with Power. Being the Second Study of the Bible and Literature*, New York: Mariner Books.

[93] For a fascinating analysis of US mythology, see Slotkin, Richard (1973) *Regeneration through Violence. The Mythology of the American Frontier, 1600–1860*, Middletown, CT: Wesleyan University Press.

closure, which creates a developmental connection between singular, contingent events or a systematic or logical link between various, disparate facts or concepts. As against merely factual accounts, such narratives attempt to capture and direct the listener's or reader's attention through complex clusters of facts by couching what is narrated in a not too thin description, however brief it may be, and a convincing interpretation whose persuasive power hinges also upon their appeal to emotions (empathy). More often than not, these narratives contain gaps and dark passages, though, they may try to hide. And they represent, almost invariably, the conflicting voices of autonomy and authority, and oscillate between an apology for the way things are and a utopian[94] other.

Tales from constitutional mythology most effectively start with a momentous decision on the part of the rulers (like the *Edict of Nantes* or the *Convocation of the General Estates*) or a dramatic act of liberation or protest on the part of the ruled as a founding moment (like the *Boston Tea Party*, *Simon Bolivar's* crusade or *Gandhi's* anticolonial demonstration) or triggering the process of foundation of a polity (the *Convention* in Philadelphia). For example, the narrative structure of stories about the French Revolution spans a series of events. They arguably begin with the *Convocation of the General Estates*, are then dramatized by the presentation of the *cahiers de doléances*, the Women's March on Versailles and the Storming of the Bastille. In retrospect, justificatory narratives connect these moments and reconstruct a plausible flow of events to the moment of closure. Depending on the perspective or agenda, the closure may be moved to the end of the revolutionary movement: its transformation into a rights revolution.[95] Or, its authoritative representation may be in the most concise and abstract form as pure script in three consecutive, solemnly sealed documents. These documents re-constituted the French polity, if only briefly, as constitutional monarchy (1791), revolutionary regime (1793) and Directorate (1795). When told in this manner, the story incidentally legitimizes a considerable amount of violent acts, terror even, and, in the end, the restorative move to empire and Bonapartism guaranteeing stability.

---

[94] See Koskenniemi, Martti (2005) *From Apology to Utopia. The Structure of International Legal Argument*, 2nd ed., Cambridge: Cambridge University Press.

[95] For a most informative narrative of the various constitutional projects see Gauchet, Marcel (1989) *La Révolution des droits de l'homme*, Paris: Gallimard; Fitzsimmons, Michael P. (1994) *The Remaking of France. The National Assembly and the Constitution of 1791*, Cambridge: Cambridge University Press – he gives a detailed account of the debates in the National Assembly 1789–1791.

While the French Revolution, more than the anti-colonial uprising and constitutional revolution in the United States, was to become paradigmatic for later mythical narratives of liberation, it allowed for a variety of internal structural connections, beginning with the revolution and first successful slave revolt in Saint-Domingue (Haiti) from 1791 to 1804,[96] followed by, *ex negativo*, the political restoration in nineteenth-century Europe.

Decolonization and liberation movements in the former colonies and the 'Velvet Revolution' in Eastern Europe produced waves of constitution-making, not necessarily following the path of (liberal) rights constitutionalism. Yet, some of the more recent constitutional documents have adopted the mythical narrative style by undertaking in their preambles to connect the different historical moments and draw a line from the mythical founding of the polity to its present state of tranquility and success, after having banned the furies of imperialist occupation and war.[97]

Claim to Validity

Similar to myths, legal narratives of justification have idealizing and fictitious moments, and come with a claim to validity concerning some legitimate entitlement, in particular of the authors and the message. Manifesto constitutions,[98] for example, base their claim to validity routinely on common knowledge, a shared experience or what is considered to be evident: 'That all men are by nature equally free and independent, and have certain inherent rights' (1776, *Virginia Bill of Rights*),[99] that 'public calamities and … the corruption of governments' are caused by 'the ignorance, neglect, or contempt of rights of man' (1789, *French Déclaration*).

---

[96] See James, Cyril L.R. (1938) *The Black Jacobins. Toussaint l'Ouverture and the San Domingo Revolution*, London: Secker and Warburg; and Marks 'Human Rights in Disastrous Times.'

[97] E.g. the constitutions of Bolivia (2009), China (1982), Croatia (1990), East Timor (2002), Myanmar (2008) and Vietnam (1992).

[98] Frankenberg, Günter (2000) 'The Return of the Contract: Problems and Pitfalls of European Constitutionalism' 3 *European Law Journal*, 257; and Frankenberg 'Constitutions as Commodities.'

[99] In a similar tone and rhetoric, the authors of the *Liberian Declaration of Independence* (1847) presented their narrative of liberation and, incidentally, a different version of 'the country which gave them no protection' – a story usually not told by the US Founding Fathers. See Huberich, Charles H. (1947) *The Political and Legislative History of Liberia*, New York: Central Book Co.

Having formally established their legitimate authority as 'Representatives of the United States of America,' the framers of the *US Declaration of Independence* underscored their legitimate entitlement to 'declare the causes which impel them to the separation' with (a) an elaborated story, listing the abuses committed by the tyrannical British monarch, (b) necessity ('when it becomes *necessary* for one people to dissolve the political bands'), (c) 'the laws of nature and of nature's God'[100] and, most significantly, (d) the truth as the basis of the legitimacy of their narrative: 'We hold these truths to be self-evident, that all men are created equal …'

The Declaration's validity claim, based on a differentiated justification, not only legitimized secession but also, by its remarkable silence over the existence of Native Americans, the colonists' right to colonize America. At one of their prominent beginnings and one of their first colonial encounters, we might conclude, the mythical story of human rights already had a colonial bias legitimizing predators' raids.

A different normative narrative technique is brought into play when validity claims are derived from presumably superior knowledge provided, for example, by an authoritative theory (of history, society, revolution, etc.) transcending the horizontal plane of society and justifying violence in the name of science, politics (progress), culture, class or religion.[101] Cases in point are the socialist cadres imagining (and convincing themselves of) their privileged insight into the 'laws of socialism' as laid down in Marx's historical materialism and Lenin's theory of revolution and also, in China, Mao Zedong's Thought and the mythical 'Three Represents' today.[102] Their narratives justify the exclusion, suppression, at times even physical extinction, of large parts of the

---

[100] A Declaration by the Representatives of the United States of America in General Congress Assembled, July 4, 1779 – emphasis added.

[101] See, for example, justifications of violence, brutality and subjugation in the name of racial superiority: Esposito, Roberto (2008) *Biopolitics and Philosophy*, University of Minnesota; or religion: Appleby, R. Scott (2000) *The Ambivalence of the Sacred: Religion, Violence, and Reconciliation*, Lanham: Rowman & Littlefield; Pape, Robert (2006) *Dying to Win: The Strategic Logic of Suicide Terrorism*, New York: Random House.

[102] This trinity is generally credited to General Secretary Jiang Zemin's concept of the Communist Party (2002) representing the developmental needs of China's advanced productive capacity, the progressive direction of its advanced culture, and the fundamental interests of the broad majority of the people of all nationalities in China.

population for the sake of what is claimed to be a valid purpose, like progress, social peace or proletarian internationalism.[103]

Structurally speaking, like socialism's 'red engineers'[104] and cadres, capitalism's white experts and political technicians,[105] because they modify or sidestep the rule of the people through their agency and expertise, have to adjust technocracy or expert rule to the standards of democracy. The authority and superior legitimacy of knowledge, in the context of expert rule, reappears under the guise of the metaphysics of 'inherent necessities and practical constraints,' which in non-socialist democracies become the functional equivalent of the 'laws of socialism.'

Protest movements, as distinct from ruling elites, may take their claims to the streets and resort to narratives that invoke the traditional right to resistance, but will more frequently underscore the validity of their programs and projects with references to a shared experience of discrimination or oppression that violates written or unwritten norms of humanity – in particular human rights laid down in constitutions and international pacts. Their legitimate entitlement, though related to their experience and interests, may also be based on authoritative texts, like UN conventions on rights or national constitutions.

Political-Educational Agenda

Legal narratives of justification share with certain myths a *political-educational agenda*. Their *Volkspädagogik* or political pedagogic consists in interpreting and suggesting *how to cope with* a problematic situation. These stories – a rather heterogeneous body of writings consisting of documents, historical and theoretical tracts, pamphlets, constitutional texts and commentaries, and international pacts – produce knowledge by narration in order to *instruct* their readers, thus introducing a political and pedagogical register.[106]

---

[103] For an overview over such narratives, see the contributions to Jouannet, Emmanuelle and Motoc, Iulia eds (2012) *Internationalist Doctrines During the Years of Real Communism in Europe*, Paris: Société de législation comparée.

[104] The term is borrowed from Andreas, Joel (2009) *The Rise of the Red Engineers. The Cultural Revolution and the Origins of China's New Class*, Stanford: Stanford University Press.

[105] Frankenberg *Political Technology*, Chapter I; Kennedy, David (2005) 'Challenging Expert Rule: The Politics of Global Governance' 27 *Sydney Journal of International Law*, 5.

[106] Insofar as human rights stories combine their legal message with a political project, they are vulnerable to legal and political demands that may be addressed to a regime to redeem a given promise. Consequently, a justificatory

In accordance with the educational register, the authors of the *US Declaration of Independence* addressed 'the candid world.' Then, in a brilliant moment of justificatory political pedagogy, they reiterated 'the history of repeated injuries and usurpations' on the part of the King of Great Britain (conspicuously – and with an eye to the future – bypassing the not all that innocent Westminster Parliament) and 'the barbarous acts' committed by the monarch, described in a legal turn as 'disregard and contempt for human rights.' So instructed, the colonialists were expected to mobilize for, and join, the war of secession. And the 'candid world' abroad was called on to empathize with and possibly support this venture.

The educational agenda of the French revolutionaries in 1789 implied awareness of rights and duties and 'maintenance of the constitution' so as to enable and motivate the people to compare the acts of the legislative and executive power 'at any moment with the objects and purposes of all political institutions.' This combination of rights optimism and political pedagogy provided a pattern numerous drafters of constitutions and rights declarations later found it irresistible to copy. The *Universal Declaration of Human Rights* followed the pedagogical register insofar as it propagates 'teaching and education to promote respect for these rights and freedoms.' It also offered a matrix for legal narratives by re-imagining the cold brutality and mass murders of Fascism and Stalinism as 'disregard and contempt for human rights [that] have resulted in barbarous acts' and stating as its normative project 'that human rights should be protected by the rule of law.' In the end, the *Universal Declaration* proclaims a vague benchmark for progress: 'a common standard of achievement for all peoples and nations.' The underlying and somewhat surprising political purpose is relegated to a subordinate clause, namely to prevent 'recourse … to rebellion against tyranny and oppression.'

In the same vein, albeit in a different style and written with different motives, the authors of past and present socialist constitutions have adopted the vocabulary and followed the grammar of narratives of justification, first and foremost, in lengthy preambles idealizing, particularly, history and the leading role of the party. Thus, the preamble of the Chinese Constitution instructs 'the people of all nationalities in China'

---

story of how rights work and the way things are may come into conflict with new justificatory claims of how they should work. Such a conflict may build up considerable tension, lead to disillusionment and the delegitimation of an old normative regime, and set in motion a dynamic, which, in the course of events, may create a new or reform the old one.

about the 'glorious revolutionary tradition' and the 'successes ... in economic development.' Then it goes on to interpret the way things are in China today as achievements credited to the theoretical authorities and the Communist Party. Finally, the text of the preamble shifts from imagining the past to projecting the future by formulating the 'task of the nation ... to concentrate its efforts on socialist modernization along the road of Chinese-Style socialism.' Interestingly enough, no mention is made of the 'Great Leap Forward' (1958–1963) and of the 'Cultural Revolution' (1966–1976). Both events would have blemished the glorious tradition and also have defeated any educational purpose the authors of the Chinese preamble may have had in mind.

8. COMPARATIVE REMARKS

Development and Sources

Human rights narratives moved from naturalism (natural rights and evidence) and traditionalism (immemorial rights of Englishmen) to positivism (constitutional rights, rights laid down in national, regional and international documents). They changed the notion of the sources of these rights, how rights come into the world and can be recognized as such. The journey went from revelation and evidence, tradition and practice, to contractarian theories and, finally, the consent of the governed. Along that path from religion to democracy, as their foundations were secularized, they began to share properties of a modern mythology, replacing the ancient gods and heroes by more up-to-date, secular authorities.

Authority and Promise

Depending on the historical-political context, either the vanguard party, an authoritative theory, managerial expertise, the constitution or human rights resolutions are expected to control the latter-day furies, turn chaos into order, and guarantee redemption from the world's misery. In combining dramatic, mythical and ideological rhetorical elements, narratives of justification intervene in the obstinate world of facts as apologetic or utopian imaginations of the real.[107]

[107] Geertz 'Local Knowledge,' 173.

Language and Modality

They oscillate 'between a language of imagination and one of decision'[108] to form, thereby, a more or less determinate sense of justice concerning the way things are and should be. This much can be learned from comparing the diverse narratives, and especially the recent discourse on torture: human rights narratives construct reality as tragedy (destruction of the human being) or romance (rescue victim in distress). Whether they lean toward banning the latter-day furies with myth and pedagogy or favor the more programmatic style of positive ideology, the different narratives, at the end of the day when the violation of human rights turns into a legal controversy, cannot but normalize whatever they deal with. They translate real life into law, and transform conflicts, needs, demands, etc. into 'cases.' Thus, human rights are included in the interplay of legal concepts, syllogisms, and balancing. They become a vocabulary and, however dignified the cause may be, they are forced into a competition with other vocabularies.

While modernist, normative, romantic narratives stress the emancipatory, empowering and liberating effects this language has or may have, other narrators look at human rights from a more realistic or pessimistic perspective and argue that their success comes at a price. They challenge the romantic stories and employ reality as *tragedy*, setting narrow and unreliable limits for what can be aspired to in the quest for security and the pursuit of happiness in this world. Or else their narrative comes across as *satire* and a drama of non-redemption. Tragedy and satire presuppose a pessimistic perspective and skeptical attitude. Accordingly, the tragic discourse would, for example, point to the co-presence and rise of human rights and (modern) torture throughout the twentieth century[109] and, more generally, the contrast between 'the celebratory and self-congratulatory rhetoric of human rights and the perception of the world's reality.'[110] In the spirit of tragedy, one might criticize the absolutism of

---

108 *Ibid.* 174.

109 Hannah Arendt distinguished the twentieth century as 'the century of human rights.' See Arendt *The Origins of Totalitarianism*, 290 seq. Nevertheless, the very same century witnessed the triumph of modern practices of torture; see Frankenberg, Günter *Political Technology*, Chapter VII with further references.

110 Mégret, Frédéric 'That Springbreak Feeling. Pragmatism, Irony and Belief in the Age of Human Rights' – paper presented in December 2009 (unpublished, on file with author).

the human rights rhetoric[111] or its ambivalence,[112] its surplus value or strategic advantage over other competing – political, economic, etc. – vocabularies,[113] or, on the basis of realistic accounts, the ineffectiveness of human rights treaties in changing the behavior of states for the better.[114]

Authorship and Narrative

Whatever arguments critics and meta-critics produced, they were unable to black out the prospect of human rights law's redemption from tyranny and misery, which is at the heart of romance or reconciliation, if only after trials and tribulations. Notwithstanding these critiques, the romantic, normative point of view of human rights law has been progressively anchored in human rights treaties and defended by human rights institutions. The evermore burgeoning human rights literature testifies to the proliferation of human rights. Maybe there is more to be said about the liberal point of view.

As a matter of fact, human rights law contains many stories that may be told as an antidote against romantic hyperbole. Torture is only one case in point but an important one. It radically and irrevocably marks the moment when the narrator is silenced. Then and there, all justifying, mythologizing, ideologizing and normalizing ends, because torture destroys the very humanity and thereby bares the core of *any* human rights narrative – the individual's authorship of her life history. This internal connection between human rights and biographical authorship

---

111 Regarding the topos of human rights fundamentalism, see Günther, Klaus (1994) 'Diskurstheorie des Rechts oder Naturrecht in diskurstheoretischem Gewande?' *Kritische Justiz*, 470.

112 Kennedy *The Dark Sides.*

113 Koskenniemi 'The Fate of Public International Law: Between Technique and Politics'; Kennedy, *The Dark Sides*; and Frankenberg, Günter (2004) 'Ambivalenzen zivilgesellschaftlicher Praxis' *Kritische Justiz*, 21. For other skeptical views see Campbell, Tom, Ewing, K.D. and Tomkins, Adam eds (2001) *Sceptical Essays on Human Rights*, Oxford: Oxford University Press.

114 On the basis of her quantitative study, Hathaway, Oona (2002) 'Do Human Rights Treaties Make a Difference?' 111 *Yale Law Journal*, 1870, concludes that despite the progressive ratification of human rights treaties (and increased human rights advocacy by NGOs) violations appear to have increased. Non-compliance with treaty obligations (except for the Genocide Convention) appears to be common and not infrequently treaty ratification is associated with worse practices, in particular due to weakly enforced and/or monitored human rights.

(rather than individualism and agency) needs to be cast as tragedy and defended against all odds and mobilized against all attempts to defend, define 'down', vindicate, justify or cover up organized brutality. Once this connection is recognized as constituting the narrativity of human rights law, it can be re-imagined as a point of departure for the resistance to normalization and ideology.

7. 'Before the Law': the discourse about 'access to justice'[1]

> Before the law sits a gatekeeper. To this gatekeeper comes a man from the country who asks to gain entry into the law. But the gatekeeper says that he cannot grant him entry at the moment. The man thinks about it and then asks if he will be allowed to come in later on. 'It is possible,' says the gatekeeper, 'but not now.'[2]

1. 'BEFORE THE LAW'

The topic and quotation demarcate a Bermuda triangle of sorts, where the belief in a just world gets lost. Superficially, one might say the triangle is formed by, first, the demand for *access*. That would be the door or gate, like the one in Kafka's parable. Second, there are those who seek access to justice, who are not always directly addressed or specified in the access-to-justice literature – like the man from the country who waits and yearns for justice, and believes he deserves to be granted access to the Law. He represents all men and women from the country. Then, third, there is *justic*e, of course. It is accompanied by the endless debate about what Law's purpose and the goal of our search should be. We imagine the end somewhere behind the gate, possibly in the third room later mentioned by Kafka's doorkeeper. It may be the Law or justice – or both.

In the beginning, the man from the country cannot see the third room, let alone others further back, in the shadow of darkness. In the end, he only perceives an illumination which breaks blindingly out of the

[1] Based on lectures at the Perugia Roundtable and the Melbourne University School of Law in 2015. I am indebted to Maria Rosaria Marella, Giovanni Marini and Anne Orford for inviting me to present these ideas. I am grateful to all participants for valuable comments.

[2] Kafka, Franz (1971) 'Before the Law' in Kafka, Franz ed. *Collected Stories*, New York: Schocken; see also Derrida, Jacques (1971) 'Before the Law' in Derrida, Jacques ed. *Acts of Literature*, London: Routledge, 181.

gateway. Almost blind, the countryman believes he sees a shining, which could have been the Law. Or the onset of death. He will never find out which.

2. ACCESS AND GATEKEEPERS

On closer scrutiny, and with insights gleaned from comparative analysis, the picture changes somewhat. To return to the theme of *access*: Whose, or which, admission, entry, ingress or entrance is the man from the country (and we) looking for? This seems to be a strange question because, browsing the access-to-justice literature, there is mention of many roads within the different legal regimes that lead to basically *one* entry for everyone: the *general* possibility, provided almost everywhere, that legal remedy may be obtained from institutions of law for grievances brought before them.[3] And then, once there has been due process, one may have and experience justice in the end.

The access-seeker is surprised, however, to meet a gatekeeper who controls the gateway to the Law, the stairway to justice. The porter watches the door behind which the Law and justice can only be surmised as long as they remain invisible: a doorman, usher or, maybe, a bouncer. He (in Kafka's elliptic story not a she) makes the access-seeker wait; suspends his desire to gain entry. Actually, he offers the man from the country the chance to try to get inside, while warning him: '[T]ake note: I am powerful. And I am only the lowest-ranking gatekeeper.' So there are more. And they are more powerful because they can make others wait without as much as even appearing. The countryman (and we others) learn that whoever wants to have access (to justice) needs to deal with the many gatekeepers' powers.

In the Kafkaesque world of grey subalternity and cold bureaucracy, the gatekeeper sits before the Law and poses irrelevant questions. In the everyday of law-rule, whatever its label may be – *Rechtsstaat*, *état de droit*, *estado de derecho* or rule of law – there is a plurality of gatekeepers, and they sit in the middle, somewhat elevated, and speak. They ask questions that are, one assumes, pertinent, and they want information, one hopes, that is relevant to the cause – pertinent and relevant to being granted or denied access. Less metaphorically, judges,

---

3 Cappelletti, Mauro ed. (1978) *Access to Justice*, Milan: Giuffrè Editore; a critical perspective is supplied by Rhode, Deborah L. (2005) *Access to Justice*, Oxford: Oxford University Press.

courts or court-like institutions specifically empowered to exercise judicial review probe into the *admissibility* of a cause. They test, for instance, whether we-from-the-country have standing and the right to sue. If they are persuaded we do, they may elevate our grievance to the status of a *case*. Jurists know this and consider it part of their normal routine. Yet, access is never unmediated, never immediate.

3. SEEKING ACCESS TO JUSTICE

Then there are those who *seek* access to justice. *We*-from-the-country ask to be granted entry. However, we are not alone. There are also highwaymen, who like to see themselves as 'servants of justice.' They are generally referred to as lawyers or attorneys. Or as solicitors, which sounds much more comforting and endearing. They claim – and are paid – to assist those before the Law, who search for justice, to be admitted, granted entry. It is their job to deal with the gatekeepers and the guardians of the Law who are not visible from the outside, before the Law.

The ones who serve justice, or, on a more modest note, serve the Law by providing legal counsel, come in fancy outfits. They wear long black gowns, as if they are prepared to attend a funeral. To bury – what? The Law, or justice even?

In some places of law-rule, their hair and head are covered by wigs. So they look like dignitaries from a distant past or messengers from a planet far away – dinosaurs rather than servants of justice. On a more sober note one might say that their apparel distinguishes a trade that requires lawyerly dress for the Law's theater, the court-room drama. It impresses the audience, very much like the gatekeeper's fur-coat contrasts with the countryman's nondescript outfit. Lawyers prefer to see themselves as midwives of access to justice. And expensive midwives they are, more often than not.

Whatever those lawyers may say, there is no easy, no safe and no direct access to the Law. To reach the Law is always a possibility, which keeps up our hopes, but it is neither immediate nor easy. To gain access takes time, money and patience. It is fraught with tribulations.

Finally, there are the law-seekers' other helpers. Generally unpaid, they hope to be rewarded, ultimately, by a good conscience or the blessing of altruism. More directly, their efforts are squared by public interest donations. As a rule they come in groups – NGOs, foundations, agencies – or are sent by institutions and initiatives programmatically geared toward opening the channels of the rule of law, lending assistance, providing legal aid. They furnish expertise and information, reports and *pro bono* lawyerly assistance. Or they gather and show, at the least, statistical data concerning access and its denial, which means encouragement at the beginning and sorry comfort in the end.

4. JUSTICE OR THE LAW: THE TRAGEDY

Which justice? Or which Law? (Assuming that they are synonymous). This is another, even stranger question, one would think, because, turning again to the access-to-justice literature, there seems to be only one justice/Law: the *general* one, the universally recognized (notion of) justice or rule of law. And this amounts to the general possibility of pursuing, obtaining and savoring the justice provided by law-rule.

Justice, explained Derrida, is 'that which must not wait … [however] remains, is yet to come.'[4] Closer to the spirit of the access-to-justice discourse and in a less post-modern vocabulary, one might say that justice is always *in the process of coming*. Other authors circumscribe justice as fairness[5] or, with less philosophical sophistication, as the way things should be – or what we deeply believe the world is (or should be) like.[6]

In Kafka's story justice, or rather the Law, is not specified. It could be that the countryman comes with a property claim. He could also have been summoned to testify as a witness or defend himself. But would he have waited for that? More likely, a grievance brought him *before the Law*, and he hopes for justice. There seems to be a problem with the Law, though. Kafka suggests, by the gatekeeper's attire, that the countryman, while waiting in front of the gate exclusively reserved for him, seeks access to the wrong law, the city's Law. City would then figure as the *other* and her law as the *foreign*.

'Before the Law' is a metaphor for the human tragedy. It invokes the elusiveness of justice and that it is wrong to believe a just world can be had. Psychologists tell us – with empirical support – that the belief in justice and a fair world 'is one of the most basic and also one of the most

---

4 Derrida, Jacques (1990) 'Force of Law. The "Mystical Foundation of Authority"' 11 *Cardozo Law Review*, 920, 969.

5 Rawls, John (1971) *A Theory of Justice*, Cambridge: Harvard University Press.

6 For the concepts of justification and normalization I draw on my article, Frankenberg, Günter (2014) 'Human rights and the "Belief" in a Just World' 12 *International Journal of Constitutional Law*, 35.

fundamentally deluded characteristics of the human brain.'[7] Our desire for justice, we learn, is so strong that victims of injustice, unless they are masochists who relish suffering, will protect this desire by denying or minimizing the unfairness they experience, or by believing that 'these injustices are en route to being amended, or that they are counterbalanced by greater benefits, or that they are inevitable.'[8] Or worse: by attributing to *themselves* all the problems that may have caused the injustice. Similarly, in Kafka's *The Trial*,[9] Joseph K. curses the fate for which he believes he is responsible.[10] By the same token, the man from the country 'curses his bad luck, in his early years boldly and loudly, later, as he grows old, he only grumbles to himself.'[11]

5. RECODING TRAGEDY AS COMEDY

Yet, we humans (from the country or from wherever we may live) cannot bear our ill fate and therefore recode *tragedy*[12] as *comedy*. Rather than resigning ourselves to the conditions we live and labor under, which offer somber reconciliations with our fate at best, we hope for a small triumph over our (unfair) world and the prospect of temporary reconciliation and

---

[7] Merrill Block, Stefan (2009) *The Story of Forgetting*, London: Faber & Faber, 197.

[8] Eagleton, Terry (2007) *Ideology. An Introduction*, London and New York: Verso, 27.

[9] Kafka, Franz (1999) *The Trial*, New York: Schocken.

[10] According to Claudia Dalbert's analysis of empirical studies concerning their own or observed experience of injustice: (1996) *Über den Umgang mit Ungerechtigkeit. Eine psychologische Analyse*, Bern: Huber; based on Melvin J. Lerner's just-world hypothesis, in his (1970) 'The Desire for Justice and Reactions to Victims' in Macauley, J. and Berkowitz, L. eds *Altruism and Helping Behaviour*, New York: Academic Press, 205–229; for an overview of justice-related research, see Lerner, Melvin J. (2003) 'The Justice Motive: Where Social Psychologists Found It, How They Lost It, and Why They May Not Find It Again' 7 *Personality & Social Psychology Review*, 388.

[11] Kafka 'Before the Law.'

[12] I borrow the categories of tragedy and romance from Northrop Frye's and Hayden White's archetypical genres providing emplotments and rather freely transfer them from history to biography, and later to the narratives of human rights law: Frye, Northrop (1957) *The Anatomy of Criticism*, Princeton: Princeton University Press; and White, Hayden (1973) *Metahistory: The Historical Imagination in Nineteenth-Century Europe*, Baltimore: Johns Hopkins University Press.

harmony. In Kafka's story, the man from the country, instead of recognizing the tragic situation, i.e. of having to wait before the Law, studies the fleas in the gatekeeper's fur coat and asks them to help him.

Unless they are cynics not minding that a man from the country has to wait for no good reason until he dies, observers of injustice uphold their idea of hope in a just world, where access to justice is granted, by dint of narratives told from a normative point of view. They transform the somber reality before the Law into a counterfactual, *romantic* story and thus transcend the unjust experience and transform the wrong law, the law of the city, into the right one. The facts of a 'bad reality,' where vulnerable groups have no access to courts of justice or are discouraged from seeking legal redress of their grievances, and where men and women from the country die before they see the Law, are neutralized by the counterfactual force of stories their narrators find encapsulated in legal norms, principles of justice and the rule of law. They change the register from *tragedy* to a *romantic* plot and invoke salvation to descend on the bruised human spirit,[13] or rather those excluded from courts and jurisdiction, by offering rule of law, access to justice, human rights law as redemption available in an otherwise Kafkaesque world.

The rule of law promises justice, whose administration and dispensation functions as a regime. Based on that story, law-rule has had an astounding career as a globally proliferated regime of conflict management, which identifies and (as not only we-from-the-country hope) also prevents the abuse of power. From a normative point of view, law-rule offers the vision of a better world – a world where legal procedures and courts guarantee that conflicts are solved in a civil manner, trials are fair, indigenous peoples have rights, the interests of future generations command adequate legal concern, and even those not familiar with the ways of law may enjoy its blessings.

Reading the rule of law thusly as a drama of redemption or occasional reconciliation draws its romantic appeal from the view that law-rule delivers what it promises and prevents arbitrary governance and guarantees rights and justice.

Law-rule's success story and, in particular, the tale that access to justice is open to everyone, is naïvely reflected by the countryman's firm belief that 'the Law ... should be surely accessible at all times and to everyone.'[14] But he never knows (nor does the doorman) what the Law is,

13 Steiner, George (1961) *The Death of Tragedy*, New York: Alfred A. Knopf.
14 Kafka 'Before the Law.'

where and how it takes place because, in awe of the one and the other gatekeepers, he never looks inside.

Critics are inclined to picture law-rule's reality as tragedy and read it as an ideology offering an interpretive framework for an orderly world where vulnerable minorities or lower classes are kept waiting before the Law. Or they read it as a myth that is meant to domesticate the latter-day furies, such as arbitrary government, authoritarian rulers. And they may find 'Before the Law' a telling parable for the common obstacles to the access to courts. As a matter of fact, there is no regime of law-rule where admission to judicial review is not considered to be in need of reform and repair.[15]

Nevertheless, the prospect of redemption from tyranny and misery, on offer where the Law rules, can hardly be blacked out by critical narratives bringing to the fore the contrast between the celebratory rhetoric of law-rule and the sober perception of its reality; by realist or sociological accounts of law-rule not delivering what it promises; by analyses of the ambivalence of law-rule, granting access to some, systematically denying it or making it difficult for others; and by analyses of law-rule's ambivalence and unpredictability.

6. THE MANAGEMENT OF INJUSTICE

Critiques of the romantic narrative about law (and justice), its accessibility and rule may be missing the point, though. Because the *justice* as in *access-to-justice* may differ significantly from the *justice* of our 'belief' in a just world. The former can denote, depending on the context, rule of law, law, judiciary or fairness of (notably, distributive) procedures and results.

To begin with, the varieties of law-rule do not promise speedy trials, immediate justice in the broadest and most substantive sense but guarantee, more modestly, that rights-holders will be admitted to a jurisdiction and that a functioning administration of justice will be available there. Actually, the rule of law narrative is more about law in general (the system and its procedures), the access to the institutions specialized in judicial review, and the fora where justice is spoken. One might say that the discourse is rather about the access to the access of justice or the right to a day in court, which has a less romantic ring than justice *tout court* or living in a just world.

---

15 See Cappelletti *Access to Justice*.

The discourse on *access* to justice is linked, however, to the general normative discourse on *justice*. Both touch upon ground covered by narratives of justification. That means, both have to deal with the denial of access to courts and judicial review – partial or complete, temporary or for good. And both participate, therefore, in the *management of injustice* by means of narratives[16] that justify unfairness, which means management of disappointment.

In contrast to the neighboring sciences, the Law, represented by legislators, legal scholars and judges, has resisted the general trend to *narrativity*. Law, one is inclined to assume, does not want its texts to have a narrative personality of their own, for fear that narrativity might reduce law's authority.[17] Therefore, the authority of law excludes narrativity; it must remain *before* the Law, like all the stories the countryman tells to the gatekeeper.

Literary fiction has to stop *before* and *outside* Law's realm for another reason also: the Law is the subject of and is subject to stories, like Kafka's 'Before the Law' or *The Trial*, and Derrida's 'Before the Law,' court-room dramas and legal TV series. Still, narrativity has to be separated from Law's own stories and fictions. It might diminish their 'rule of distance' from the passions of the everyday, because narrative accounts *approach* the Law and make it *present* and *concrete*, like even the very condensed tragic narrative of the countryman's fate. Stories *relate*, whereas *the Law* is structured so as to remain abstract, general and unrelated.

That is why there is little room in legal education and legal practice for legal narratives (and law's narrativity), as if they would undermine the counterfactual force of law. Here and there, narrative components have been integrated in law-making and law-applying: the story of the case at hand is interwoven with the narrative line of precedents. Courts attempt to present their opinion, in the narrative style, as 'seamless webs of arguments.' Legislators reveal a certain distrust of the propositional content and casual counterfactuality of the rules they produce by introducing or relining them with explanatory stories that elaborate the purpose or programmatic context of a statute.

Legal narratives differ from ordinary stories, though. While the popularity of the latter depend on *content* (information, suspense, entertainment or moral uplift), law's authoritative narratives require a coherent or

---

[16] For a brief discussion of the meanings of narrative see Ducrot, Oswald and Todorov, Tzvetan (1983) *Encyclopedic Dictionary of the Sciences of Language*, Baltimore: Johns Hopkins University Press, 297–299.

[17] Derrida 'Before the Law,' 186, 190.

at least plausible *structure*, such as reasoned doctrinal elaboration, chain of precedents, etc., to lend credence to what the Law justifies with authority.

Justifying some unfairness, that is *injustice,* like letting the countryman wait until his death before the Law, is no easy task for legal narratives. In everyday usage, *justification* refers to a dimension of social interaction, namely the way in which somebody defends her beliefs, actions and decisions to others, from the first person perspective, so as to make them (appear) 'right' or 'acceptable.'[18] They deviate from a given standard, break a promise or disappoint an expectation (access to justice), otherwise it would suffice to *explain* the discrepancy.[19]

Legal narratives of justification cast rays of normativity – in the colors of law and, if legal norms are not available or fail, of ethics or morality – on what is narrated. Thus, they bestow the story they tell with authoritative meaning and legitimizing force as well as bequeath the story-teller authority. A military intervention is turned into a 'just war,' occupation is dignified as a 'humanitarian intervention' or 'colonizing mission.' Recently, organized cruelty condoned or executed by governments was justified as 'rescue torture.' Similarly, exclusion from access to justice is justified by narratives.

Generally speaking, the operation of giving an asymmetry of access the appearance of fairness or rightness is triggered by an unfavorable comparison: some groups gain entry, others do not or do so with difficulty, after a delay or at a higher cost. The burden of justification differs according to what has to be justified. If something is *clearly* unjust, the discrepancy between the way things are and the way they should be needs to be 'explained away' contrary to the *evidence* of injustice. 'Explaining away' is difficult, if not impossible

> where there is no access to justice [because] citizens (especially marginalized groups fear the system, see it as alien … where the system is financially inaccessible; where individuals have no lawyers; where they do not have information or knowledge of rights; or where there is a weak justice system.[20]

---

[18] See Boltanski, Luc and Thevenot, Laurent (2006) *On Justification: Economies of Worth*, Princeton: Princeton University Press; also Freud, Anna (1937) *The Ego and the Mechanisms of Defense*, London: Hogarth.

[19] As distinct from explanations, justifications are meant to alleviate dissatisfaction or curb disobedience, prevent or settle controversies by *explaining away* a cognitive dissonance, normative discrepancy or emotional or other disappointment.

[20] US Institute of Peace 'Necessary Condition: Access to Justice,' www.usip.org/guiding-principles-stabilization-and-reconstruction-the-web-version/7-rule-law/

If vulnerable groups or marginalized minorities are systematically excluded from law-rule, apologetic justifications refer to a situation of emergency or, at best, to law-rule's *development* as being in progress; or that the channels of justice are there and open but not used by those who feel excluded, which individualizes and psychologizes the asymmetry of access.

Paradoxically, the comparison of how access to justice actually works with how it should work becomes more complex and entails more sophisticated argumentative techniques of justification, if the situation (redress of grievances, right to a day in court, etc.) is considered unfair or illegal because it *arguably* deviates from or violates a given normative standard, say constitutional provisions or principles, and therefore disappoints reasonable expectations. There are legal regimes that refer to the state of exception as a legitimizing trope, which is a risky and, in the long run, costly strategy because it exchanges the cloak of law for naked politics, shifts from procedure to power. Therefore, it is more pragmatic and unobtrusive to try to bridge the gap between the 'is' and the 'ought.' Narratives of justification offer various storylines; for example, the narrators admit that *in this one case* (the case of the man from the country), access was denied but that the *mistake* will be corrected; they argue that *this* incident was an *exception* provided for by *law*; or that the disadvantaged person or group will be duly *compensated*.

Accordingly, mistakes and oversights, unfortunate exceptions and singular problems concerning access to justice are corrected or at least addressed by one or some of the following reform measures:

- improving *legal aid*, making it available to indigent persons and other vulnerable minorities, enhancing knowledge of the grievance system, or offering human rights training programs, for instance in Community Law Centers (South Africa);
- establishing *institutional reforms*, like village or community courts (Zimbabwe; Mozambique), small claims courts, legal aid boards (South Africa) or law clinics (South Africa);
- facilitating access by *technical-legal reforms*, such as easing the burden of proof, improving procedural safeguards[21] or introducing

access-justice (last accessed 16 June 2015); The Public Justice Foundation, http://publicjustice.net/what-we-do/access-justice (last accessed 17 July 2015).

[21] Aarhus 'Convention on Access to Information, Public Participation in Decision-Making and Access to Justice in Environmental Matters,' adopted 25 June 1998.

class or popular action (Brazil, Colombia, Mexico, Argentina, Chile, Ecuador);[22]
- lowering *threshold fears*[23] by requiring that lay judges participate in court decisions and that the judiciary reflect the gender and racial composition of the country.[24]

For years these proposals have been discussed nationally and on a global plane. Many of them have been translated into constitutional provisions. To give a few examples: the constitutions of Zimbabwe (1979, Nr. 69 [3]), South Africa (1996, Nr. 34 and 38)[25] and Mozambique (Art. 62) mandate (equal) access to the courts. For the future, Bolivia's 2009 Constitution promises all 'naçiones y pueblos indígena' ('all nations and indigenous peoples') access to justice and effective protection by judges and tribunals and that '[t]he State guarantees the right to due process and defense, and to plural, prompt, appropriate, free and transparent justice' (Art. 115 [2]). Ecuador's 2008 Constitution recognizes the collective interest in the protection of social rights, like the right to a healthy environment.

One should be wary, though, of the jaunty counterfactualism conveyed by constitutional provisions. They are not self-executing; their domain is promise not results. Good will and well-crafted documents alone do not certify access to justice. The value and ambivalence of reform measures have to be weighed and evaluated after they have been implemented. And the discourse on access to justice is replete with stories about enforcement deficits and problems of application. In that respect, the reports by foundations monitoring access to justice programs and, in particular, the submissions to the *Aarhus Convention Compliance Committee* are quite instructive.[26]

---

22 See Sedgwick *Guide to Class Actions in Latin America*, sedgwicklaw.com/files/Publication (last accessed 29 June 2015).

23 Inter-American Commission on Human Rights (IACHR) 'Access to Justice and Social Inclusion. The Road Towards Strengthening Democracy in Bolivia' (OEA/Ser/V/II.Doc.34), 28 June 2007.

24 See McQuoid-Mason, David (1999) 'Access to Justice in South Africa' 17 *Windsor Yearbook of Access to Justice*, 230 concerning measures to facilitate access in South Africa.

25 *Ibid.*

26 See www.unece.org/env/pp/pubcom.html (last accessed 30 June 2015). See also The World Bank (2015) *Nigeria: Access to Justice for the Poor – Implementation Status Results Report*, http://www-wds.worldbank.org/external/default/WDSContentServer/WDSP/LEG/2015/02/13/090224b082aa826c/1_0/Rendered/PDF/Nigeria000NIGE0Report000Sequence004.pdf (last accessed 30 June 2015).

7. THE NORMATIVE DISCOURSE ON ACCESS TO JUSTICE

Academic narratives of justification, while kin to constitutions in counterfactual spirit, execute a more theoretical, rather than practical agenda. They develop the normative standards for the way things *ought* to be and this includes the conditions of ingress to the courts. They no longer, or do not always, strictly compare the 'is' with an 'ought' but initiate a philosophical or jurisprudential project designed to elaborate the normative *foundation* of a *right* to access to justice, which follows the logic of other human rights (as in the Universal Dreams Inc. located in quadrant B above). The reasoning often starts from past memories of injustice and abuse of power, exclusion and discrimination. In the mode of normative construction, visions of the human being and society, of needs and interests are translated into possibly more coherent principles of justice[27] and fundamental entitlements as for instance, to repeat, dignity, integrity, autonomy, equality, and also access to justice. Most prominently, Hannah Arendt argued, when considering the plight of displaced and stateless persons, that 'the right to have rights' (her philosophical circumscription of access to justice) qualifies as the only genuine *human* right because it presupposes only the right-holders' humanity and no further qualification, like citizenship:

> We become aware of the existence of a right to have rights (and that means to live in a framework where one is judged by one's actions and opinions) and a right to belong to some kind of organized community, only when millions of people emerge who had lost and could not regain their rights ...[28]

As distinct from stories informed by a practical political-legal purpose, like reforming the administration of justice or enhancing legal aid, philosophical and jurisprudential narratives concentrate on the systematic elaboration or rational elucidation of principles and ideas that (should) guide the individual right to a day in court and to just decisions. Thus,

---

[27] For example Rawls *A Theory of Justice*; Habermas, Jürgen (1996) *Between Facts and Norms: Contributions to a Discourse Theory of Law and Democracy*, Cambridge, MA: Blackwell Publishers; Scanlon, Thomas (1998) *What We Owe to Each Other*, Cambridge: Cambridge University Press; Buchanan, Allan (2004) *Justice, Legitimacy, and Self-Determination. Moral Foundations for International Law*, Oxford: Oxford University Press.

[28] Arendt, Hannah (1949) 'Es gibt nur ein einziges Menschenrecht' 4 *Die Wandlung*, 754. See also Benhabib, Seyla (2004) *The Rights of Others: Aliens, Residents and Citizens*, Cambridge: Cambridge University Press.

access to justice or the right to a day in court, undoubtedly one of the rights considered fundamental, comes with strong normative underpinnings. As a matter of fact, the very effectiveness of human rights law hinges upon the possibility of judicial review. Therefore, from a philosophical or jurisprudential point of view, access to justice is basically called for by freedom from the deprivation of liberty or mandated by principles of equitable distribution of resources.[29]

8. ACCESS TO JUSTICE: THE NARRATIVE OF NORMALIZATION

Legal narratives of justification contain mechanisms that filter, represent, re-construct and thereby change reality. Also, the access to justice literature shows that, for structural reasons, law *cannot* be after the whole story. In fact, access to courts and judicial review appears to be a model case for that structural deficit that comes with normalization.[30] The promise of equal and unhampered access to the courts and, in the end, to justice presents a fantasy scenario. The fantasy is reflected by the countryman's belief that one day he will see *the Law*, a belief which echoes normativist theories, that 'the Law ... should be *accessible at all times* and *to everyone*;'[31] that any problem or conflict can be brought to court and will enjoy judicial review, then be solved and individual needs and expectations met; and that there is only one law, not the distinction between the law of the people from the country and the law of the people from the city or the citizens' law.

In this fantasy world, law rules, justice reigns, and people enjoy their 'right to a day in the court.'[32] And society appears rationally organized, where individuals and their actions are tuned to rules and reasons. Those living in the city and those who don't are all *in* the Law, not before the Law. That is why conflicts, the inevitable by-products of life in society,

---

[29] For normative justifications of access to justice see, e.g., Trebilcock, Michael J. and Daniels, Ronald J. (2008) *Rule of Law Reform and Development: Charting the Fragile Path of Progress*, Cheltenham, UK and Northampton, MA, USA: Edward Elgar Publishing.

[30] See Chapter 6 in this volume.

[31] Kafka 'Before the Law' – emphasis added. See also, e.g., UNDP 'Access to Justice and Rule of Law,' http://www.undp.org/content/undp/en/home/ourwork/democraticgovernance/focus_areas/focus_justice_law.html (last accessed 24 September 2015).

[32] The Public Justice Foundation, http://publicjustice.net/what-we-do/access-justice (last accessed 24 September 2015).

can be resolved civilly once the 'government of laws and not of men' has been established. This fantasy scenario mirrors, albeit in reverse, Kafka's nightmarish parable, where the seeker of access and justice ends up before the Law and suffers the full impact of *normalization*: his *case* is *delayed ad infinitum.* And he never sees the Law.

As the regulations and procedures of law-rule organize the way things are and translate conflicts into the world of rights-entitlements and legal duties, they not only reflect 'practical attitudes toward the management of controversy'[33] but also transform reality. Therefore the mechanisms at work have to be discussed again (now with regard to access to justice): how legal methods, argumentative techniques and legal procedures are deployed to filter, reduce and recycle what initially appeared to be the whole story.

Displacing and Deferring the Conflict

While modernist, romantic narratives stress the empowering and liberating effects law and access to courts may have, one has to add that law-rule comes at a cost. Lawyers and legal scholars have been trained to take for granted the requirement that reality has to be translated into law and claimants have to recode their suffering as 'illegal' or 'violating a right.' Access to justice implies that any rights claim has to be addressed to the legal apparatus and staff, where it follows the rules of the established rituals. Is that too trivial and obvious to merit attention?[34] Kafka does not seem to think so. 'Before the Law' captures the (adequately tragic) story of normalization.

Translating a problem, concern, need or issue into the legal vocabulary and submitting to legal procedures implies a double movement of *displacement* and *deferral.* Conflicts are shifted from the everyday locations where they arise – home, street, school, workplace – and transferred to official institutions and handed over to professional bodies specialized in dealing with legal conflicts. And there, in law firms, court-rooms and (human rights or other) commissions, they are invariably shelved or registered and then processed according to institutional capacity, priority schedules, workload, etc. – 'with all deliberate speed'[35]

---

[33] Geertz, Clifford (1983) 'Local Knowledge: Fact and Law in Comparative Perspective' in Geertz, Clifford ed. *Local Knowledge: Further Essays in Interpretive Anthropology*, New York: Basic Books, 173.

[34] Derrida 'Before the Law,' 186.

[35] *Brown v. Board of Education of Topeka*, 347 U.S. 483 [1954].

– and handled by the members of the legal staff, who bring to bear their professional expertise. Lawyers call this 'due process.'[36]

Thereby, conflicts may indeed be cooled down and civilized. Such civilizing means, however, that everyday conflicts are forced into the format of a case. Whatever the issue may be, it is recast in terms of rights and duties and needs, desires and interests are converted into legal entitlements – a conversion that also puts off satisfaction. While the legal discourse turns everything into a legal claim, the political-social dimension of a conflict, the personal drama also tends to get lost or obscured in translation. Justice has become a case.

Narratives of justification book these limitations and effects of the administration of justice as the inevitable price to be paid for civil(ized) conflict management; or they tell us that, on balance, the benefits of the professional and institutional application of rights under the terms and procedures of law regularly, at least in most cases, outweigh the costs. So, the justification of these aspects of normalization invokes necessity and economy.

Selecting What is Legally Relevant

Law's glamour also stems from the promise that the legal vocabulary covers the whole range of 'factors' of a conflict more adequately than any other vocabulary and there is 'due' process. Comprehensiveness is suggested by philosophical and jurisprudential stories that perfect the method of application and elaborate a 'system' of rights or stress their universal nature. The universal reach – or *framework*, as Hannah Arendt formulated it – comes at a price, though: it brings rights claims under the Western liberal-legal matrix. The specificity of the individual complaint and conflict is hardly ever *completely* recognized but, more often than not, taken as an instance that is fitted into the abstract and general conceptual framework and dealt with in the all-encompassing scheme of judicial review. Rather than dealing with the whole story, as a case is processed, courts concentrate on aspects that meet the criteria of relevance or pertinence.

As courts adjudicate under considerable constraints in terms of time and institutional resources, their work is fine-tuned by a maze of selectivity mechanisms. There are, to name only a few: the distinction between questions of fact and questions of law; admissibility thresholds;

---

[36] See Pennock, J. Roland and Chapman, John W. (1977) *Due Process*, New York: New York University Press.

the requirement of standing; the politics of granting or denying *certiorari*; the subsidiary character of constitutional review; criteria of 'relevance'; the preclusion of arguments, and so forth.[37] These formal, procedural and substantive restrictions suggest that law – and access to its courts – cannot possibly deliver what we, or the man from the country, expects. Translating his story into a crucial criterion of admissibility one might say, he does not have standing. More significantly, they metamorphose the (benign, permitting, accessible) law of the country into the (cool, austere, forbidding) *Law* of the city.

Disempowering Side-Effects: Reducing Strategic Options

By dint of its selectivity, displacement and deferral mechanisms, the law also has side-effects that are usually overlooked and adjusted: legal constraints that come with legal procedures also disempower. While Kafka concentrates on these mechanisms and the helplessness they produce, jurisprudential and theoretical narratives 'explain away' these side-effects as implied by the necessary reduction of complexity,[38] required to ease the burden for courts or guarantee legal certainty. Mechanisms of deferral and selectivity are 'difficulties the countryman has not expected.'[39] They render *the Law* inaccessible, even where it presents itself as being somehow there,[40] and they move him far away even though he is right there before the Law.

Where Kafka painfully indulges in the experience of normalization, normative theories with a romantic twist uphold undauntedly the story of law's comprehensive reach by either downplaying selectivity as a singular malpractice not compromising the rule or universal ideal that functions, theoretically at least, in the interest of everyone. Other authors base their defense of comprehensiveness on the claim that restrictions in one case are complemented in another one, which then re-presents the deficient case or has a radiating effect onto other cases.

The normalizing power of law also consists in privileging the use of a specific vocabulary and, thereby, de-privileging or even delegitimizing

---

[37] It may be interesting to note that less than 2 percent of all constitutional complaints reaching the Federal Constitutional Court of Germany turned out to be successful.

[38] One of the central concepts of systems-theory; see Luhmann, Niklas (2000) *Vertrauen. Ein Mechanismus der Reduktion sozialer Komplexität*, Stuttgart: UTB.

[39] Kafka 'Before the Law.'

[40] See Derrida 'Before the Law,' 199.

others. Once people realize that they have to dress their interest in (or demand for whatever they need as) a right, they will translate their experience of what they deem unjust, arbitrary or degrading into legal entitlements. Consequently, they concentrate on the legal grammar, vocabulary and institutions, which they believe precludes other strategic options and vocabularies.[41] They address their grievance to the law, focus on access to law and justice, very much as Kafka's man from the country waits patiently and submissively to be admitted by the gatekeeper and defers, adjourns his decision as to what else he could do to have his grievance redressed or, more generally, his problem solved.

Alienating

The idea that law rules and the suggestion that there is access to justice have a positive ring. To argue that they *alienate* runs against the tenor of the romantic discourse, our deep belief in a just world and the countryman's expectations. And yet, alienation,[42] at least the aspects of estrangement and separation apply to the discourse on access to justice and its practice as well as to the discourse on human rights.

To begin with, the notion of the legal subject as rights-holder introduces a personality estranged from her desires and emotions, isolated and separated from her community. This brings to mind the man from the country in his self-inflicted quarantine. We learn very little about his background and actual plight and do not understand what keeps him before the Law. Furthermore, the rights-holder is reduced to a point of reference where abstract entitlements and obligations intersect, whereas concrete traits and needs fade into the background. In the normative discourse, rights are defined as 'weapons' in the hands of the (otherwise disarmed) individual rights-holder. They are said to override any competing political, economic or other concerns. Such definitions accept as normal the circumstance that the personal is faded out and treated as an incidence of the universal.[43]

The alienating effect can be seen more clearly if one takes into consideration the aspects of deferral and displacement. Normally, access

---

[41] Kennedy, David (2004) *The Dark Sides of Virtue. Reassessing International Humanitarianism*, Princeton: Princeton University Press, 108 seq.

[42] See Schacht, Richard (1970) *Alienation*, Garden City: Doubleday; Jaeggi, Rahel (2005) *Entfremdung. Zur Aktualität eines sozialphilosophischen Problems*, Frankfurt: Campus.

[43] See, e.g., Dworkin, Ronald (1977) *Taking Rights Seriously*, London: G. Duckworth & Co.

and the decision about the 'case' are not denied but delayed, unless the criteria of selectivity are met. In that respect, 'Before the Law' is a story of alienation. The man from the country is kept waiting to be admitted. Having heard the doorkeeper's account of the other – more terrible – doorkeepers, he 'decides that it is better to wait until he gets permission to enter.'[44] So, he never sees the Law with his own eyes, he only knows about it from hearsay. Moreover, he does not understand its workings. Only as he is dying does he learn from the gatekeeper: 'No one else could ever be admitted here, since this gate was made only for you. I am now going to shut it.'[45]

Legal claimants who have been luckier and have been granted access, still experience alienation. They watch, mystified and intimidated, rather like ignorant bystanders, the automatic functioning of a well-oiled, complex legal machinery: how the conflict is being removed from the everyday of their experience, dissected by legal professionals whose language becomes less and less understandable, and processed in court, on ever higher and less transparent institutional levels, with ever less concern for the 'facts' of the case and the claimant's *petitum*.[46] As due process moves along, claimants are gradually dispossessed of what they once thought was their conflict.

What is more, claimants, like the countryman, are isolated, appear alone before the Law and confront the guardians as individuals: 'Everyone strives to reach the Law, so how does it happen that for all these many years no one but myself has ever begged for admittance?' the countryman asks. Romantic narratives emplot this dark side of law, the reality of normalization as romance – a romance with individualism: individual agency, individual rights. They justify normalization instead of trying to escape from it. And their narratives often stop short of narrating what it means to appear before the Law, and they do not reveal the authority that orders deferral, displacement, selectivity and alienation – *the Law*. They imagine but do not *know* justice. Very much like the gatekeeper who is a representative of the Law but has never seen it.

---

[44] Kafka 'Before the Law.'

[45] *Ibid.*

[46] The effects of legal normalization are brillantly translated into moving pictures by director Zhang Yimon (1992) 'The Story of Qiu Ju,' Hong Kong: Sil-Metropole Organisation Ltd.

9. OPTIONS TO ENJOY THE RIGHT TO A DAY IN COURT

Can normalization be resisted? It cannot, Kafka suggests, as any reader of *The Trial* would expect. Until his death, the man from the country waited to see the space or room where law happens but missed that and never experienced justice. He neither realized that the delay was ordered by the Law nor that he wasted his time and life before the wrong law, the law of the city, where men from the country cannot possibly find justice. He never understood that the doorkeeper fooled him by not denying him access but endlessly delaying the permission.

Is there a different, non-Kafkaesque path that leads from the forbidding and exclusive Law and its austere form of justice to the permitting and inclusive law and its benign justice – at least to the enjoyment of one's 'right to a day in court'? Four venues seem to be arguably open to those who believe in a just world where access to justice is granted to everyone:

1. The *voluntarist* concentrates on the gatekeeper's ambiguous message: 'If you are so drawn to the Law, just try to go in, despite my veto.' But 'be wary of the more powerful guardians.'

   This could be interpreted to mean: Go ahead, do not be afraid to supersede the gatekeeper's veto, then enter and see what happens! The justice-seeker may be in for a disappointment – or she may in fact experience law-rule at its best because justice can actually be experienced there. At any rate, she can claim to have challenged law's prohibitive and deferring authority and transfigured Kafka's 'Law' into (a more democratic) law.
2. *Normativists* follow the path of reasoned elaboration displayed by the discourse of philosophers and legal scholars. They could defend their position and double role, in a democracy, as *authors* of law and claim, as *subjects* of law, their right of access to justice. Practically, this means they would have to convince the gatekeeper (and guardians) with 'good reasons.' If that option seems to be too romantic, because all his reasoning did not help the man from the country, the normative approach could be translated into a more practical-political agenda (see the reformist below).
3. The *reformist* first accounts for the problems and obstacles in justice's way. Then, she will develop a plan and analyze which institutional, procedural and other measures it takes to grant everyone access to justice – legal aid, class action, community courts,

technical-legal reforms and so forth. Finally, she would have to persuade legislators and hope for efficient implementation. She could not be farther away from Kafka's predicament and narrative.

4. Another venue is always *critique*: It could begin with a close reading of Kafka's parable (and Derrida's lengthy interpretation), which would reveal that the gate to (even) the Law is open. So, access to justice is generally not prohibited but delayed, displaced, submitted to criteria of selection (exclusion) and fraught with risk and alienation – but also offering possibilities.

The problem might very well be the discourse, the gatekeeper's talk before the Law, which mirrors legal narratives of justification and the effects of normalization. Regarding those, Derrida might be of help. He suggests that the Law 'is not to be seen or touched but deciphered'.[47] That is what the man from the country failed to do: that is, first, before seeking access, decipher how the law presents itself, second, decode how the law justifies injustice, and, finally, see through its mechanisms of normalization as part of its management of disappointment.

---

[47] Derrida 'Before the Law,' 197.

8. Thick comparison?

How can the quite different be brought near enough and at the same time kept far away? What does it take to shuttle between detachment and commitment? How can the comparatist study the foreign without 'othering' it and cannibalizing difference? What does she have to do to avoid hegemonic comparison and establishing asymmetric relationships between the 'own' and the foreign (law, dress code, whatever)? There are no easy answers to these questions. They have plagued comparative social sciences, in particular ethnographic comparison. My basic point is that they should plague comparative law. Instead of giving answers or providing advice with these final remarks, I merely want to indicate possible venues of and approaches to comparative practice that qualify as 'thick' or 'thicker.'[1]

1. *AUFHEBUNG?* WHERE DETACHMENT/COMMITMENT AND SIMILARITY/DIFFERENCE INTERSECT

The center square of the grid appears to suggest that there is a space, where the boundaries of the four tracks meet, and that, right there, at the intersection of *similarity/difference* and *detachment/commitment*, the usual pitfalls of comparative practice can possibly be avoided. This space – square or not – seems to demarcate the very middle ground between extreme poles, common wisdom counsels to always seek. Similarly, geometry recommends cutting in half the distance between polar opposites, whereas the mindset of a mechanic is likely to somehow neutralize

[1] Comparable to Geertz's 'thick description' in anthropological studies – see Geertz, Clifford (1973) *Thick Description: The Interpretation of Cultures*, New York: Basic Books, 3–30. In this vein, William Twining provides a richer context (life, personal experience) in Twining, William ed. (2009) *Human Rights, Southern Voices: Francis Deng, Abdullai A-Na'im, Yash Gai and Upendra Baxi*, Cambridge: Cambridge University Press.

the 'tensile counter-pull'[2] of *commitment/detachment* and *similarity/difference.* Yet, (comparative) law as a social science never fared well with borrowing ideas and applying practices developed for mathematics: in their new, legal environment they were soon criticized as 'mechanical.' As a matter of fact, it is hard to imagine how the comparison of laws and legal cultures could possibly be done *more geometrico*, unless one follows the path of mechanical comparison.

On the other hand, the grid analysis advises us rather strongly not to hope and look for a terrain where oppositional or even antagonistic approaches to comparative law could intersect, where the trenches separating the country-and-western stylists, universal dreamers, *amatourists*, and skeptics are bridged or disappear by sleight of hand and their protagonists meet to casually smoke the *calumet* in methodological harmony.

To suspend the counterpull would require a cognitive operation, a dialectical move resembling Hegel's *Aufhebung* ['sublation'].[3] Nothing is lost or destroyed but raised up and preserved on a higher level (of the spiral). *Aufhebung*, in comparative practice, demanded, for example, the preservation of the Anglo-Eurocentric constellation of the pristine Western/European self and the othered foreign. It is hard to believe that self/other, once sublated, would be on a par with one another, that comparatists recognized them as equals then and let them casually enter into inter-subjective negotiations to sort out diversity and similarities in principle or detail.[4] It is not easy to see how this could come about and actually work. The critique of mainstream comparative law (misguided or unfair as it may be) renders it even less plausible that the ethnocentric constellation has to be 'preserved' at all – in whatever form and on whatever higher level.

Thus discouraged, one could turn to Edward Said for advice. He advocated a 'willed effort of overcoming distances and cultural barriers

---

[2] Conquergood, Dwight (2003) 'Performing as a Moral Act: Ethical Dimensions of the Ethnography of Performance' in Lincoln, Yvonna S. and Denzin, Norman K. eds *Turning Points in Qualitative Research: Tying Knots in a Handkerchief*, Lanham, MD: AltaMira Press, 397.

[3] See Kaufmann, Walter (1960) *Hegel: A Reinterpretation*, New York: Anchor Books, § 37.

[4] See Shilliam, Robert (2006) 'The "Other" in Classical Political Theory: Re-Contextualising the Cosmopolitan/Communitarian Debate' in Jahn, Beate ed. *Classical Theory in International Relations*, Cambridge: Cambridge University Press; and Adelman, Howard (2008) 'Rights and the *Hijab*: Rationality and Discourse in the Public Sphere' 8 *Human Rights & Human Welfare*, 43, 80.

that makes knowledge of other societies and cultures possible – and at the same time limits that knowledge.'[5] He warned, though, that it might take more than that. What could be 'more' than a willed effort? Vivian Grosswald Curran proposes, as was mentioned before, cultural immersion as the necessary (or at least a promising) effort comparatists have to make.[6] Other authors favored intercultural dialog. Yet others counsel change of the comparative style to a more interpretive anthropological or ethnographic register.[7]

Culture, context and reflexivity appear to be key elements these otherwise dissimilar projects consider crucial. I would like to add *distancing* and *differencing* in terms of method and ethics, a theory of normalization and awareness of the politics of the legal-comparative practice. The two versions of the grid analysis will serve as a matrix to identify the pitfalls to be avoided.

2. THICKER COMPARISON – 'RICHER' LAW: FROM REGULATING TO WORLD-MAKING

Any attempt at a thick, thicker or thickening comparison had better start with a richer conception of law (including legal regimes, families, systems, etc.) than is often present in the comparatists' toolkit. Comparatists interested in a thicker, that is more narrative, quality of comparison, which is open to local knowledge and context-sensitive, have to overcome the reductionism characterizing mainstream projects. I call reductionist, approaches that feature scanning the textual surface of laws and court rulings; surfing the comparative high ground over families and systems (writ large); boiling down law's events, conflicts, and practices to general functions imputed from a generalizing external perspective; or making up 'facts' for thin constructions of principles of, say, contract or tort law in a plurality of countries.

---

[5] Said, Edward (1997) *Covering Islam. How the Media and the Experts Determine How We See the Rest of the World*, New York: Vintage, 164.

[6] Grosswald Curran, Vivian (1998) 'Cultural Immersion, Difference and Categories in U.S. Comparative Law' 46 *American Journal of Comparative Law*, 43.

[7] E.g. Geertz, Clifford (1983) *Local Knowledge. Further Essays in Interpretive Anthropology*, 3rd ed., New York: Basic Books; Scheffer, Thomas and Niewöhner, Jörg (2010) *Thick Comparison: Reviving the Ethnographic Aspiration*, Leiden and Boston: Brill; Baer, Susanne (2004) 'Verfassungsvergleich und reflexive Methode: Interkulturelle und intersubjektive Kompetenz' 64 *Zeitschrift für ausländisches öffentliches Recht und Völkerrecht*, 735.

Thick (or non-Cinderella) legal comparison is interested in restoring and rehabilitating law's detail, because it needs to bring law into view instead of making it disappear behind abstract categories and concepts. So far, most taxonomies of *grands systèmes*, functional analyses, maps of principles of contract law in the member-states of the European Union, etc. have failed to re-present and transmit the richness of law's events, like legislative or judicial controversies with their cultural background as well as their political, economic and social ramifications. In contrast to thin comparison, comparatists have to demonstrate that *Burqa* bans, the opposition against them, and court decisions justifying them (or not), as well as hardly less spectacular legal controversies about abortion and more or less routine cases concerning prospect liability or hate crimes, are not just law in books and/or law in action but 'ways of world-making.'[8] The sense that law is *also* shaping a form of life and being, in turn, shaped by it, helps move comparative work beyond its at times unbearable formalism, barrenness, and mechanistic style.[9]

As distinct from doctrine, comparative law is not at all, or significantly less, geared toward decision-making. Comparatists are not obliged to constantly recapitulate the if/then structure of case law or reiterate the various 'methods' of interpretation, which are to (but do not) clear the path from statute to court decision by neutralizing extra-legal inferences. By the same token, unlike judges, lawyers or law teachers 'doing doctrine,' comparatists are under no constraint to accept and legitimize the radical dissociation of law and fact.[10] Like legal theorists, they may challenge, for instance, the criteria of admissibility and relevance, which account for the deferral of legal conflicts, law's selectivity and alienation.[11] This means that comparative law has the advantage, generally speaking,[12] that it can confront with impunity the abstract – formalist,

---

8 Goodman, Nelson (1978) *Ways of World-Making*, Indianapolis: Hackett Publishing.

9 E.g. the abstract-generalizing representation of 'major legal systems' or '*grands systèmes*' or the juxtaposition of constitutional provisions from different countries, stripped of any shred of context. See also Niewöhner, Jörg and Scheffer, Thomas (2010) 'Thicker Comparison' in Niewöhner, Jörg and Scheffer, Thomas ed. *Thick Comparison: Reviving the Ethnographic Aspiration*, 3.

10 See Geertz, Clifford (1983) 'Local Knowledge: Fact and Law in Comparative Perspective' in Geertz, Clifford ed. *Local Knowledge: Further Essays in Interpretive Anthropology*, New York: Basic Books, 167.

11 See Chapters 6 and 7 in this volume.

12 Unless, of course, comparatists are involved in legal consulting or provide expertise for concrete cases and controversies in private international law or arbitration cases.

positivist – version of law, so dominant in doctrinal legal thought, practice and education. It has more leeway as a discipline to resist normalization and critique its impact. Insofar as comparatists are not directly involved in cases and controversies, they may analyze, from a comparative perspective, how laws function as the management of disappointment.[13] They are at liberty to investigate the way that law contains other sorts of knowledge, peoples' experiences, anxieties and aspirations. In a reversal of normalization, comparative analysis has the opportunity to make law's events tangible by restoring their detail and including law's cultural 'accretions.'[14] In this fashion, law comes to be seen as a way things are – or, to be more precise: as a way law serves as a way of constructing reality. While it is true that law is constituted by and connected with norms, institutions and practical attitudes and as such has a technical dimension, it is also much more than that. Law is what Clifford Geertz called 'part of a distinctive manner of imagining the real.'[15] The legal notion of the refugee, definitions of torture, medical malpractice, the right to privacy, etc., testify to the constitutive and normalizing power of law and legal concepts to capture what we imagine being politically persecuted, suffering extreme physical and psychic brutality, practicing medicine, living in a sphere protected from public scrutiny, etc., is *like*, and transform this imagination into law.

3. REFLEXIVE COMPARISON: THE COMPARATIST

'[T]he comparative study of law cannot be a matter of reducing concrete differences to abstract commonalities.'[16] How to move beyond reductionist comparison is hard to say and even harder to do. In general, however, it seems imperative to bring the comparatist into the picture, locate her position between detachment and commitment and show how she constructs, between the poles of similarity and difference, the comparative constellation she is about to study. To begin with, comparatists have to be aware that comparison is not only done by (academic) researchers but also by actors in the field. There are legal consultants, who operate as merchants dealing in law and transferring statutes, institutions, and

---

[13] See, for example, Luhmann's theory of legitimation by (court) procedure, Luhmann, Niklas (2001) *Legitimation durch Verfahren*, Frankfurt: Suhrkamp.

[14] I take this cue from Geertz 'Local Knowledge.'

[15] *Ibid.*, 173.

[16] Goodman *Ways of World-Making*, 215.

doctrine,[17] judges, who are confronted with difference, as for instance in Muslim veiling cases, or arbitrators, who prepare settlements in trade conflicts. All of them have to perceive differences, negotiate interdependencies, and navigate hybrid normative regimes constituted by law, ethics, politics, tradition and religion.

The problem of reductionism is not that the comparative practice is quite often limited to desk research and that the comparatist constructs her comparison on the basis of her readings of first order textual sources, like statutes and cases, and second order sources, like commentaries to these statutes and cases, or of third order ones, like comparative analyses of all of these materials.[18] These readings become problematic and 'thin out' comparison, if the comparatist limits her work to scanning the surface of textual sources, juxtaposing provisions or court decisions from different legal regimes,[19] operating with abstract commonalities informed by an unshakable similarity orientation, rather than recognizing 'the irreducible nature of some cultural differences.'[20]

There is another stepping-stone on the path to a self-critical and context-sensitive style of comparison: the comparatist is *always already* anchored in a specific, particular legal tradition, culture, and experience. So, in a reflexive move, the comparison has to be turned on the comparatist. While she cannot possibly strip herself of what she learned and came to believe about her 'own' law (what I somewhat misleadingly called 'going native' before), there are several possibilities for de-familiarizing the familiar ways of law, challenge settled knowledges and, thus, hinder, suspend and, if all goes well, prevent their automatic reproduction.

A good start would be to 'weld the processes of self-knowledge, self-perception, self-understanding to those of other-knowledge, other-perception, other-understanding.'[21] Then a *critical dialog* between the familiar and the unfamiliar legal cultures could be initiated so as to stop the production – and recursive validation – of inferior others. For that to

---

[17] See Frankenberg, Günter (1997) 'Stranger than Paradise: Identity and Politics in Comparative Law' 1997 *Utah Law Review*, 259.

[18] See also Frankenberg, Günter (2006) 'Comparing Constitutions: Ideas, Ideals, and Ideology – Toward a Layered Narrative' 4 *International Journal of Constitutional Law*, 439.

[19] I prepared this argument in Frankenberg, Günter (1985) 'Critical Comparisons. Re-Thinking Comparative Law' 26 *Harvard International Law Journal*, 411.

[20] Grosswald Curran 'Cultural Immersion.'

[21] Geertz 'Local Knowledge,' 181.

happen, self-delusions about the comparatist's objectivity and the neutrality of her research and instruments – the innocence of method[22] – need to be abandoned.[23] In short, it requires a *reflexive turn* to address how one defines and where one situates the self and the foreign in the comparative space, and relates them to each other in practice, as well as a *critical turn* that scrutinizes the very act of comparing. How, for what purpose, and for whose benefit does one compare laws, dress codes or other regulations?

4. THICKER COMPARISON: CULTURE, CONTEXT, CRITIQUE, ETC.

From there it is only a short step to recognizing that comparison is not (only) a technical operation but a performative act with ethical and political implications, due to the co-presence of the foreign in the comparative space. To detect these implications, and also to uncover hidden political agendas, the comparatist's toolkit has to be checked for Anglo-Eurocentric concepts that have sustained, however marginally, Western hegemony and asymmetric center-periphery relations.

To thicken comparative studies, there is a lot one can do if one wants to turn away from the standard mode of formalistic, mechanistic comparison with its *naïveté* vis-à-vis hegemonic concepts, asymmetrical classifications, ethnocentric similarity theories. Comparatists could probe universalistic concepts to bring to the fore their (Western) particularity. This applies also to the meager universalism of *grands systèmes*. Comparatists could bear in mind that no concept as such is universal or generally applicable but requires translation. And, believe it or not, '[t]ranslations are more delicate than heart transplants.'[24] Similarly, functionalists could start to look very closely at their key concepts of function, solution, and similarity, and answer to the best of their

---

22 This means that comparatives have to familiarize themselves with the methodological and theoretical debates about 'value-free' research in the social sciences. See Chapter 3 in this volume.

23 For a strong critique (supported by Derrida) of the orthodoxy of comparative law, see Legrand, Pierre (2011) 'Siting Foreign Law: How Derrida Can Help' 21 *Duke Journal of Comparative and International Law*, 595.

24 Panikkar, Raimon (1982) 'Is the Notion of Human Rights a Western Concept?' 30 *Diogenes*, 75. The same applies to legal transfer: see Frankenberg, Günter (2013) 'Constitutions as Commodities' in Frankenberg, Günter ed. *Order from Transfer*, Cheltenham, UK and Northampton, MA, USA: Edward Elgar Publishing, 1.

knowledge how and by whom these concepts have been introduced and defined as 'common' or generally applicable, and for whom the 'better' solution they discover is really better. Taxo-comparatists might feel tempted to scrutinize their classificatory schemes and criteria and correct (unintended?) asymmetries. Factualists, in search of Common Cores, would be hard pressed to investigate how they construct, rather than innocently find, their 'facts', as well as do a close 'political' reading of their comparative practice.

Considering that comparative law is neither generally nor directly geared toward making decisions, a turn to 'thicker comparison' or a more narrative style presupposes a shift from producing results to making discoveries.[25] The comparatist would be discovering herself, her biases, pre-understandings and comparative practice, discovering new insights about her own or foreign law. To be fair one has to issue the warning: whoever ventures into the hermeneutic, ethical, and political minefield of the intercultural/contextual and transnational/local should bear in mind that thick comparison will be 'more like grasping a proverb, catching an allusion, seeing a joke – or … reading a poem – than it is like achieving communion.'[26] These difficulties should not keep the comparatist from 'focus(ing) on and explicat(ing) the production of comparability,'[27] gaining access to local knowledge, and sustaining the conversation between the familiar and the foreign.

After all, the troublesome, adventurous performance may be worth its while. A good, self-critical and context-sensitive comparative practice might get Cinderella gravid with new ideas and exciting prospects. Who would not leave behind the shallow and deceiving marriage with (anything but) 'innocent knowledge' for an alluring romance with Cinderella who, almost promiscuously, meets other laws and legal practices at eye-level and pursues a dialog with quite-different and quite-similar legal cultures on their own terms?

Critical, reflexive and context-sensitive operations – differencing and distancing, the reversal of normalization, etc. – may not suffice to

---

[25] Yengoyan, Aram A. (2006) 'Introduction' in Yengoyan, Aram A. ed. *Modes of Comparison. Theory and Practice*, Michigan: Michigan University Press, 1–30.

[26] Geertz, Clifford (1983) 'From the Native's Point of View: On the Nature of Anthropological Understanding' in Geertz, Clifford ed. *Local Knowledge: Further Essays in Interpretive Anthropology*, New York: Basic Books, 55.

[27] Niewöhner, Jörg and Scheffer, Thomas (2010) 'Thickening Comparison: On the Multiple Facets of Comparability' in Niewöhner, Jörg and Scheffer, Thomas eds *Thick Comparison: Reviving the Ethnographic Aspiration*, 1–15.

disentangle the threads of the *similarity/difference*-dilemma of interpretation and to defuse the tension between *detachment* and *commitment* in comparative legal studies.[28] But at least they keep reductionism at bay, meet the methodological, ethical and political challenges of comparative law and yield greater adventure and discovery[29] by taking comparatists to the heart of what is interpretation,[30] making them give their attention to the diverse ways of knowledge production. As comparatists grasp how complex, foreign worlds of law are put into words and compared, they could be inspired, more than anything, to tolerate ambivalence and express their will not to be governed by the conventions of comparative law.

---

28 According to Geertz, Clifford *Local Knowledge* ethnographers try to bring 'the enormously distant enormously close without becoming less far away,' 48.

29 On the same note: Moore, Sally Falk (1986) 'Legal Systems of the World' in Lipson, Leon and Wheeler, Stanton eds *Law and the Social Sciences*, New York: Russell Sage, 11.

30 See Kaplan, David A. (2012) *Ricœur's Critical Theory*, Albany: State University of New York Press.

Bibliography

Abu-Lughod, Lila (1986) *Veiled Sentiments*, Berkeley: University of California.

Abu-Lughod, Lila (2002) 'Do Muslim Women Really Need Saving? Anthropological Reflections on Cultural Relativism and Its Others', 104 *American Anthropologist*, pp. 783–790.

Abu-Odeh, Lama (1992) 'Post-Colonial Feminism and the Veil: Considering the Differences', 26 *New England Law Review*, pp. 1527–1537.

Adelman, Howard (2008) 'Rights and the *Hijāb:* Rationality and Discourse in the Public Sphere', 8 *Human Rights & Human Welfare*, pp. 43–77.

Adorno, Theodor W. et al. (ed.) (1976) *The Positivist Dispute in German Sociology*, New York: Harper & Row.

Ahmed, Leila (1992) *Women and Gender in Islam: Historical Roots of a Modern Debate*, New Haven: Yale University Press.

Ahmed, Leila (2011) *A Quiet Revolution. The Veil's Resurgence, from the Middle East to America*, New Haven: Yale University Press.

Ainsworth, Janet E. (1996) 'Categories and Culture: On the "Rectification of Names" in Comparative Law', 82 *Cornell Law Review*, pp. 19–42.

Alibhai-Brown, Yasmin (2001) *WHO do WE THINK we ARE?*, London: Penguin Books.

Allen, Anita L. (2008) 'Undressing Difference: The Hijāb in the West', 23 *Berkeley Journal of Gender, Law and Justice*, pp. 208–224.

Alston, Philip and Mégret, Fred (eds) (2011) *The United Nations and Human Rights: A Critical Appraisal*, Oxford: Oxford University Press.

Al-Jabri, Mohammed Abed (2010) *The Formation of Arab Reason: Text, Tradition and the Construction of Modernity in the Arab World*, London: I.B. Tauris.

Al-Saji, Alia (2010) 'The Racialization of Muslim Veils: A Philosophical Analysis', 36 *Philosophy and Social Criticism*, pp. 875–902.

Ancel, Marc (1961) 'Valeur actuelle des études de droit compare', in: Nadelmann, Kurt, von Mehren, Arthur and Hazard, John (eds) *Legal Essays in Honour of Hessel E. Yntema*, Leyden: A.W. Sythoff.

Andreas, Joel (2009) *The Rise of the Red Engineers. The Cultural Revolution and the Origins of China's New Class*, Stanford: Stanford University Press.

Anghie, Antony and Chimni, B.S. (2003) 'Third World Approaches to International Law and Individual Responsibility in Internal Conflict', 2 *Chinese Journal of International Law*, pp. 77–104.

Anghie, Antony (2005) *Imperialism, Sovereignty and the Making of International Law*, Cambridge: Cambridge University Press.

Appleby, R. Scott (2000) *The Ambivalence of the Sacred: Religion, Violence, and Reconciliation*, Lanham: Rowman & Littlefield.

Arendt, Hannah (1949) 'Es gibt nur ein einziges Menschenrecht', 4 *Die Wandlung*, pp. 754–770.

Arendt, Hannah (1966) *The Origins of Totalitarianism*, New York and San Diego: Harcourt Brace & World.

Arminjon, Pierre, Nolde, Boris and Wolff, Martin (1950) *Traité de droit comparé*, Paris: Librairie Générale de Droit et de Jurisprudence.

Aristotle (2009) *The Nicomachean Ethics*, Oxford: Oxford University Press.

Badinter, Élisabeth et al. (1989) 'Profs, ne capitulons pas!', *Le Nouvel Observateur*, 2 November.

Badinter, Élisabeth (2002) 'Der verschleierte Verstand', in: Schwarzer, Alice (ed.) *Die Gotteskrieger und die falsche Toleranz*, Köln: Kiepenheuer & Witsch, pp. 139–146.

Badinter, Élisabeth (2009) 'Adresse à celles qui portent volontairement la burqa', *Le Nouvel Observateur*, 9 July, p. 26.

Baer, Susanne (2004) 'Verfassungsvergleich und reflexive Methode: Interkulturelle und intersubjektive Kompetenz', 64 *Zeitschrift für ausländisches öffentliches Recht und Völkerrecht*, pp. 735–758.

Baier, Annette (1991) *A Progress of Sentiments*, Cambridge: Cambridge University Press.

Baker, Keith M. (1992) 'The Idea of a Declaration of Rights', in: van Kley, Dale (ed.) *The French Idea of Freedom. The Old Regime and the Declaration of Rights of 1789*, Stanford: Stanford University Press, pp. 169–196.

Ballard, Roger (ed.) (1994) *Desh pardesh: The South Asian Presence in Britain*, London: Hurst & Co.

Bannister, Robert (1987) *Sociology and Scientism*, Chapel Hill NC: University of North Carolina Press.

von Bar, Christian (1998) *The Common European Law of Torts*, Oxford: Oxford University Press.

von Bar, Christian, Lando, Ole and Swann, Stephen (2002) 'Communication on European Contract Law: Joint Response of the Commission on European Contract Law and the Study Group on a European Civil Code', 10 *European Review of Private Law*, pp. 183–248.

Bareto, Jose Manuel (ed.) (2013) *Human Rights from a Third World Perspective: Critique, History and International Law*, Cambridge: Cambridge University Press.

Barthes, Roland (1957) *Mythologies*, Paris: Seuil.

Barton, John H., Gibbs, James Lowell, Li, Victor H and Merryman, John Henry (1983) *Law in Radically Different Cultures*, St. Paul: West Publishing.

Bauman, Zygmunt (1993) *Postmodern Ethics*, Cambridge MA: Blackwell.

Baxi, Upendra (1999) 'Voices of Suffering, Fragmented Universality, and the Future of Human Rights' in: Weston, B.H. and Marks, Susan (eds) *The Future of International Human Rights*, Ardsley NY: Transnational Publishers, pp. 101–156.

Baxi, Upendra (2002) *The Future of Human Rights*, Oxford: Oxford University Press.

Baxi, Upendra (2003) 'The Colonialist Heritage of Comparative Law', in: Legrand, Pierre and Munday, Roderick (eds) *Comparative Legal Studies: Traditions and Transitions*, Cambridge: Cambridge University Press, pp. 46–75.

Beck, Lois and Keddi, Nikki (1978) *Women in the Muslim World*, Cambridge MA: Harvard University Press.

Beckett, Samuel (2009) 'Worstward Ho' in: *Company. Ill Seen Ill Said. Worstward Ho. Stirrings*, New York: Faber & Faber, pp. 79–104.

Bedford, Sybille (1961) *The Faces of Justice. A Traveller's Report*, New York: Simon & Schuster.

Bell, David A. (2007) 'Veil of Tears', *The New Republic*, 5 March.

Benhabib, Seyla (2004) *The Rights of Others. Aliens, Residents, and Citizens*, Cambridge: Cambridge University Press.

Benjamin, Walter (2004) 'Critique of Violence' [1921, first published in German], in: Bullock, Marcus and Jennings, Michael W. (eds) *Selected Writings Volume 1: 1913–1926*, London: Belknap Press.

Berman, Harold J. (1983) *Law and Revolution: The Formation of the Western Legal Tradition*, Cambridge MA: Harvard University Press.

Berman, Nathaniel (1997) 'Aftershocks: Exoticization, Normalization and the Hermeneutic Compulsion', *Utah Law Review*, pp. 281–286.

Berman, Nathaniel (2004) 'Privileging Combat? Contemporary Conflict and the Legal Construction of War', 43 *Columbia Journal of Transnational Law*, pp. 1–72.

Bernard, H. Russell (ed.) (1998) *Handbook of Methods in Cultural Anthropology*, Lanham MR: AltaMira Press.

Bilge, Sirma (2010) 'Beyond Subordination vs. Resistance. An Intersectional Approach to the Agency of Veiled Women', 31 *Journal of Intercultural Studie*s, pp. 9–28.

Blumenberg, Hans (1979) *Arbeit am Mythos*, Frankfurt: Suhrkamp.

Bolderson, Claire (2010) 'Behind France's Islamic Veil', *BBC News*, 8 April, http://news.bbc.co.uk/2/hi/europe/8607802.stm (last accessed 24 September 2015).

Boltanski, Luc and Thevenot, Laurent (2006) *On Justification: Economies of Worth*, Princeton: Princeton University Press.

Borges, Jorge Luis (1964) 'The Analytical Language of John Wilkins', in: Borges, Jorge Luis (ed.) *Other Inquisitions*, Austin: Texas University Press.

Bowen, John R. (2006) *Why the French Don't Like Headscarves: Islam, the State, and Public Space*, Princeton: Princeton University Press.

Bradford, William (1967) *Of Plymouth Plantation*, New York: Modern Library.

Brennan, Teresa (1993) *History After Lacan*, London: Routledge.

Brooks, Peter and Gewirtz, Paul (eds) (1996) *Law's Stories. Narrative and Rhetoric in the Law*, New Haven: Yale University Press.

Brown, Wendy and Halley, Janet (eds) (2002) *Left Legalism/Left Critique*, Durham: Duke University Press.

Brown, Wendy (2006) *Regulating Aversion: Tolerance in the Age of Identity and Empire*, Princeton: Princeton University Press.

Brown, Wendy (2015) *Undoing the Demos: Neoliberalism's Stealth Revolution*, Cambridge MA: MIT Press.

Brüggemeier, Gert and Colombi Ciacchi, Aurelia (2002) 'Common Core of European Private Law: Torts, Questionnaire on Personality Rights in European Tort Law', September, University of Bremen, pp. 1–4.

Brysk, Alison (2000) *Global Good Samaritans – Human Rights as Foreign Policy*, Oxford: Oxford University Press.

Buchanan, Allan (2004) *Justice, Legitimacy, and Self-Determination. Moral Foundations for International Law*, Oxford: Oxford University Press.

Burgess, John W. (1890/2000) *Political Science and Comparative Constitutional Law*, Getzville NY: William S. Hein & Co.

Burnyeat, Myles (ed.) (1983) *The Skeptical Tradition*, Chicago: University of Chicago.

Bussani, Mauro and Mattei, Ugo (1997) 'The Common Core Approach to European Private Law', 3 *Columbia Journal of European Law*, pp. 339–356.

Bussani, Mauro (1998) 'Current Trends in European Comparative Law: The Common Core Approach', 21 *Hastings International and Comparative Law Review*, p. 785–802.

Bussani, Mauro and Mattei, Ugo (eds) (2000) *Making European Law. Essays on the Common Core Project*, Trento: Università degli Studi.

Bussani, Mauro and Mattei, Ugo (2002) 'Preface: The Context', in: Bussani, Mauro and Mattei, Ugo (eds) *The Common Core of European Private Law. Essays on the Project*, The Hague: Kluwer, pp. 1–9.

Bussani, Mauro and Mattei, Ugo (2007) 'Preface', in: Bussani, Mauro and Mattei, Ugo (eds) *Opening Up European Law. The Common Core Project towards Eastern and South Eastern Europe*, Bern: Stämpfli Publishers, pp. xiii–xx.

Bussani, Mauro and Mattei, Ugo (eds) (2012) *The Cambridge Companion to Comparative Law*, Cambridge: Cambridge University Press.

Butler, Judith (2002) 'What is Critique? An Essay on Foucault's Virtue', in: Ingram, David (ed.) *The Political. Blackwell Readings in Continental Philosophy*, Malden and Oxford: Blackwell, pp. 212–228.

Callaway, Barbara and Creevey, Lucy (1994) *The Heritage of Islam: Women, Religion and Politics in Africa*, Boulder: Lynne Rienner Publishers.

Campbell, Tom, Ewing, K.D. and Tomkins, Adam (eds) (2001) *Sceptical Essays on Human Rights*, Oxford: Oxford University Press.

Cappelletti, Mauro, Gordley, James and Johnson, Earl (1975) *Toward Equal Justice: A Comparative Study of Legal Aid in Modern Societies*, Milan: Giuffrè and Dobbs Ferry NY: Oceana Publications.

Cappelletti, Mauro (ed.) (1978) *Access to Justice*, Milan: Giuffrè.

Cappelletti, Mauro (1978) 'Preface', in: Merryman, John H. and Clark, David S. (eds) *Comparative Law: Western European and Latin American Legal Systems: Cases and Materials*, Indianapolis: Bobbs-Merrill.

Carbonnier, Jean (2002) *Droit civil: Introduction*, 27th ed., Paris: Presses Universitaires de France.

Carozza, Paolo (1997) 'Continuity and Rupture in "New Approaches to Comparative Law"', 2 *Utah Law Review*, pp. 657–663.

Carrington, Paul (1984) 'Of Law and the River', 34 *Journal of Legal Education*, pp. 222–228.

Chakrabarty, Dipesh (2007) *Provincializing Europe. Postcolonial Thought and Historical Difference*, 2nd ed., Princeton: Princeton University Press.

Charlesworth, Hilary (1999) 'Feminist Methods in International Law', 93 *American Journal of International Law*, pp. 379–394.

Chatterjee, Partha (1986) *Nationalist Thought and the Colonial World: A Derivative Discourse*, London: Zed Books.

Cheah, Pheng (2006) *Inhuman Conditions: On Cosmopolitanism and Human Rights*, Cambridge: Harvard University Press.

Chomsky, Noam (1978) *'Human Rights' and American Foreign Policy*, Nottingham: Spokesman Books.

Chomsky, Noam (1999) *Profit over People. Neoliberalism and Global Order*, New York: Seven Stories Press.

Chrisafis, Angelique (2011) 'France's Burqa Ban: Women are "Effectively Under House-Arrest"', *The Guardian*, 19 September, http://www.theguardian.com/world/2011/sep/19/battle-for-the-burqa (last accessed 24 September 2015).

Coene, Gily and Longman, Chia (eds) (2010) *Féminisme et multiculturalisme. Les paradoxes de débat*, Frankfurt: Peter Lang.

Conquergood, Dwight (2003) 'Performing as a Moral Act: Ethical Dimensions of the Ethnography of Performance', in: Lincoln, Yvonna S. and Denzin, Norman K. (eds) *Turning Points in Qualitative Research. Tying Knots in a Handkerchief*, Lanham MD: AltaMira Press, pp. 397–414.

Constantinesco, Léontin-Jean (1971) *Rechtsvergleichung. Band I: Einführung in die Rechtsvergleichung*, Köln: Heymann.

Cotterell, Roger (2007) 'Is It So Bad to Be Different? Comparative Law and the Appreciation of Diversity' in: Nelken, David and Örücü, Esin (eds) *Comparative Law. A Handbook*, Portland: Hart Publishing, pp. 133–154.

Cover, Robert M. (1986) 'Violence and the Word', 95 *Yale Law Journal*, pp. 1601–1629.

Crane, William W. and Moses, Bernhard (1884) *Politics: An Introduction to the Study of Comparative Constitutional Law*, New York: G.P. Putnam.

Crapanzano, Vincent (1986) 'Hermes' Dilemma: The Masking of Subversion in Ethnographic Description', in: Clifford, James and Marcus, George E. (eds) *Writing Culture: The Poetics and Politics of Ethnography*, Berkeley: University of California Press, pp. 51–76.

Dalbert, Claudia (1996) *Über den Umgang mit Ungerechtigkeit. Eine psychologische Analyse*, Bern: Huber.

Damaška, Mirjan (1986) *The Faces of Justice and State Authority. A Comparative Approach to Legal Process*, New Haven: Yale University Press.

Danielsen, Dan and Engle, Karen (eds) (1994) *After Identity. A Reader in Law and Culture*, New York: Routledge.

Dannemann, Gerhard (2006) 'Comparative Law: Study of Similarities or Differences?', in: Reimann, Mathias and Zimmermann, Reinhard (eds) *The Oxford Handbook of Comparative Law*, Oxford: Oxford University Press, pp. 383–420.

David, René (1950) *Traité élémentaire de droit civil compare. Introduction à l'étude des droits étrangers et à la méthode comparative*, Paris: Librairie Générale de Droit et de Jurisprudence.

David, René (1964) *Les Grands Systèmes de Droit Contemporains (Droit Comparé)*, Paris: Librairie Dalloz.

David, René et al. (eds) (1972 seq.) *International Encyclopedia of Comparative Law*, Tübingen: Mohr Siebeck.

David, René (1972) 'Introduction', in: David et al. (eds) *International Encyclopedia of Comparative Law, The Legal Systems of the World: Their Comparison and Unification*, Vol. II, pp. 3 seq.

David, René (1978) 'Le droit comparé – Enseignement de culture générale', in: Zweigert, Konrad and Puttfarken, Hans-Jürgen (eds) *Rechtsvergleichung*, Darmstadt: Wissenschaftliche Buchgesellschaft, pp. 205–210.

David, René and Brierley, John E. (1978) *Major Legal Systems of the World Today*, 2nd ed., London: Stevens & Sons.

David, René and Brierley, John E. (1985) *Major Legal Systems of the World Today*, 3rd ed., New York: Simon & Schuster.

Davies, Gareth (2007) 'The House of Lords and Religious Clothing in *Begum v Headteacher and Governors of Denbigh High School*', 13 *European Public Law*, pp. 423–432.

De Cruz, Peter (2007) *Comparative Law in a Changing World*, 3rd ed., New York: Routledge.

Del Vecchio, Giorgio (1909) *Sull'idea di una scienza del diritto universale comparato*, Rome: Fratelli Boca.

Delphy, Christine (2004) 'Une affaire française', in: Nordmann, Charlotte (ed.) *Le foulard islamique en questions*, Paris: Éditions Amsterdam, p. 64 seq.

Dennett, Daniel C. (1992) 'The Self as Center of Narrative Gravity', in: Kessel, Frank S. and Cole, Pamela M. and Johnson, Dale L. (eds) *Self and Consciousness: Multiple Perspectives*, Hillsdale NJ: Erlbaum, pp. 103–115.

Derrida, Jacques (1971) 'Before the Law', in: Derrida, Jacques (ed.) *Acts of Literature*, London: Routledge.

Derrida, Jacques (1990) 'Force of Law. "The Mystical Foundation of Authority"', 11 *Cardozo Law Review*, pp. 920–1045.

Derrida, Jacques (1992) 'The Force of Law. The Foundation of Authority', in: Cornell, Drucilla, Rosenfeld, Michel and Carlson, David Gray (eds) *Deconstruction and the Possibility of Justice*, London: Routledge, pp. 3–67.

Derrida, Jacques (1976) *Of Grammatology*, Baltimore and London: Johns Hopkins University Press.

Derrida, Jacques and Dufourmantelle, Anne (2000) *Of Hospitality: Cultural Memory in the Present*, Stanford: Stanford University.

Dickens, Charles (1853) 'The Noble Savage', in: Harlow, Barbara and Carter, Mia (eds) [2003] *Archives of Empire Volume II. The Scramble for Africa*, Durham NC: Duke University Press, pp. 134–139.

Donnelly, Jack (1984) 'Cultural Relativism and Universal Human Rights', 6 *Human Rights Quarterly*, pp. 400–419.
Douglas, Mary (1982) 'Cultural Bias', in: Douglas, Mary (ed.) *In the Active Voice*, London: Routledge, pp. 183–254.
Douzinas, Costas (2007) *Human Rights and Empire: The Political Philosophy of Cosmopolitanism*, Abingdon: Routledge-Cavendish.
Dryden, John (1676) *The Conquest of Granada by the Spaniards*, London: Herringman.
Ducrot, Oswald and Todorov, Tzvetan (1983) *Encyclopedic Dictionary of the Sciences of Language*, Baltimore and London: Johns Hopkins University Press.
Duits, Linda and van Zoonen, Liesbet (2006) 'Headscarves and Porno-Chic: Disciplining Girls' Bodies in the European Multicultural Society', 13 *European Journal of Women's Studies*, pp. 103–117.
Dupré, Cathérine (2002) 'The Perspective of Law Importation: The Hungarian Experience', in: Harding, Andrew and Örücü, Esin (eds) *Comparative Law in the 21st Century*, London and New York: Kluwer, pp. 267 seq.
Dupré, Cathérine (2013) 'Human Dignity in Europe: A Foundational Constitutional Principle', 19 *European Public Law*, pp. 319–339.
Durham, W. Cole and Liggett, Bradley D. (2006) 'The Reaction to Islamic Terrorism and the Implications for Religious Freedom After September 11: A United States Perspective', 1 *Derecho y Religión*, pp. 41–66.
Duval Smith, Alex (2004) 'France Divided as Headscarf Ban is Set to Become Law', *The Guardian*, 1 February, http://www.theguardian.com/world/2004/feb/01/france.schoolsworldwide (last accessed 24 September 2015).
Dworkin, Ronald (1978) *Taking Rights Seriously*, Cambridge MA: Harvard University Press.
Eagleton, Terry (2007) *Ideology. An Introduction*, New ed., London and New York: Verso.
Eaves, Elizabeth (2004) 'Defining Deviancy Down', *Harper's Magazine*, 6 September, pp. 81–83.
Ehrmann, Henry W. (1976) *Comparative Legal Cultures*, Englewood Cliffs: Prentice Hall.
El Guindi, Fatwa (1999) *Veil: Modesty, Privacy and Resistance*, New York et al.: Bloomsbury Academic.
El Habti, Raja (2004) 'Laicité, Women's Rights, and the Headscarf Issue in France', in: *The Veil Controversy: International Perspectives on Religion in Public Life*, Washington DC: Brookings Institute, 19 April.
Ellingson, Ter (2001) *The Myth of the Noble Savage*, Berkeley: University of California Press.

Engle, Karen (1992) 'International Human Rights and Feminism: When Discourses Meet', 13 *Michigan Journal of International Law*, pp. 517–610.

Escarra, Jean (1933) 'The Aims of Comparative Law', 7 *Temple Law Quarterly*, pp. 296–310.

Esposito, John (1992) *The Islamic Threat: Myth or Reality?*, Oxford: Oxford University Press.

Esposito, Roberto (2008) *Biopolitics and Philosophy*, Minneapolis: University of Minnesota Press.

Esquirol, Jorge (2001) 'At the Head of the Legal Family: René David', in: Riles, Annelise (ed.) *Re-Thinking the Masters of Comparative Law*, Oxford: Hart Publishing, Ch. 8.

Esquirol, Jorge (2013) 'Legal Latin Americanism', 16 *Yale Human Rights and Development Law Journal*, p. 145.

Evans-Pritchard, Edward Evan (1965) 'The Comparative Method in Social Anthropology', in: Evans-Pritchard, Edward Evan (ed.) *The Position of Women in Primitive Societies and Other Essays in Social Anthropology*, London: Faber & Faber, pp. 13–36.

Ewald, William (1995) 'Comparative Jurisprudence (I): What Was It Like to Try a Rat?', 143 *University of Pennsylvania Law Review*, pp. 1888–2149.

Ewald, William (1995) 'Comparative Jurisprudence (II): The Logic of Legal Transplants', 43 *American Journal of Comparative Law*, pp. 489–510.

Eyerman, Ron (1981) 'False Consciousness and Ideology in Marxist Thought', 24 *Acta Sociologica*, pp. 43–56.

Fadel, Mohammad (2012) 'Muslim Reformists, Female Citizenship and the Public Accommodation of Islam in Liberal Democracy', 5 *Politics and Religion*, pp. 2–35.

Falk, Richard (2004) *The Declining World Order*, London and New York: Routledge.

Fanon, Frantz (1965) *A Dying Colonialism*, New York: Grove Press.

Fauvarque-Cosson, Bénédicte (2006) 'Development of Comparative Law in France', in: Reimann, Mathias and Zimmermann, Reinhard (eds) *The Oxford Handbook of Comparative Law*, Oxford: Oxford University Press, pp. 35–68.

Ferrari, Alessandro and Pastorelli, Sabrina (eds) (2013) *The Burqa Affair Across Europe*, Farnham: Ashgate.

Feuerbach, Anselm von (1810) *Blick auf die deutsche Rechtswissenschaft*, München: Fleischmann.

Fikentscher, Wolfgang (1995) *Modes of Thought: A Study in the Anthropology of Law and Religion*, Tübingen: Mohr Siebeck.

Fischer-Lescano, Andreas and Amstutz, Marc (eds) (2013) *Kritische Systemtheorie. Zur Evolution einer normativen Theorie*, Bielefeld: transcript.

Fitzsimmons, Michael P. (1994) *The Remaking of France. The National Assembly and the Constitution of 1791*, Cambridge: Cambridge University Press.

Fletcher, George (1998) 'Comparative Law as a Subversive Discipline', 46 *American Journal of Comparative Law*, pp. 683–700.

Forst, Rainer (2004) 'Limits of Toleration', 11 *Constellations. An International Journal of Critical and Democratic Theory*, pp. 312–325.

Forst, Rainer (2007) 'Toleration', in: *Stanford Encyclopedia of Philosophy*, plato.stanford.edu/entries/toleration (last accessed 24 September 2015).

Forst, Rainer (2007) *Das Recht auf Rechtfertigung. Elemente einer konstruktivistischen Theorie der Gerechtigkeit*, Frankfurt: Suhrkamp.

Foster, Nicholas (2007) 'Comparative Commercial Law: Rules or Context?', in: Nelken, David and Örücü, Esin (eds) *Comparative Law. A Handbook*, Portland: Hart Publishing, pp. 263–286.

Foucault, Michel (1970) *The Order of Things: An Archeology of the Human Sciences*, New York: Pantheon Books.

Foucault, Michel (1980) *Power/Knowledge: Selected Interviews and Other Writings 1972–1977*, New York: Pantheon Books.

Foucault, Michel (1997) 'What is Critique?', in: Foucault, Michel and Lotringer, Sylvère (eds) *The Politics of Truth*, Los Angeles: Semiotext(e), pp. 41–82.

Frank, Jerome (1930) *Law and the Modern Mind*, New York: Brentano's Publishing.

Frankenberg, Günter (1985) 'Critical Comparisons. Re-Thinking Comparative Law', 26 *Harvard International Law Journal*, pp. 411–456.

Frankenberg, Günter (1988/1989) 'Down by Law: Irony, Seriousness, and Reason', 83 *Northwestern University Law Review*, pp. 360–397.

Frankenberg, Günter (1996) 'Why Care? The Trouble with Social Rights', 17 *Cardozo Law Review*, pp. 1365–1390.

Frankenberg, Günter (1997) 'Stranger than Paradise: Identity and Politics in Comparative Law', *Utah Law Review*, pp. 259–274.

Frankenberg, Günter (2000) 'The Return of the Contract: Problems and Pitfalls of European Constitutionalism', 6 *European Law Journal*, pp. 257–276.

Frankenberg, Günter (2004) 'Critical Theory', in: *Max-Planck Encyclopedia of Public International Law*, http://opil.ouplaw.com/view/10.1093/law:epil/9780199231690/law-9780199231690-e693?prd=EPIL (last accessed 24 September 2015).

Frankenberg, Günter (2004) 'Ambivalenzen zivilgesellschaftlicher Praxis', *Kritische Justiz*, pp. 21–36.

Frankenberg, Günter (2006) 'Comparing Constitutions: Ideas, Ideals, and Ideology – Toward a Layered Narrative', 4 *International Journal of Constitutional Law*, pp. 439–459.

Frankenberg, Günter (2007) 'How to Do Projects with Comparative Law. Notes of an Expedition to the Common Core', in: Bussani, Mauro and Mattei, Ugo (eds) *Opening Up European Law. The Common Core Project towards Eastern and South Eastern Europe*, Bern: Stämpfli Publishers, pp. 17–47.

Frankenberg, Günter (2008) 'Torture and Taboo: An Essay Comparing Paradigms of Organized Cruelty', 56 *American Journal of Comparative Law*, pp. 403–422.

Frankenberg, Günter (2013) 'Constitutions as Commodities: Notes on a Theory of Transfer', in: Frankenberg, Günter (ed.) *Order from Transfer, Comparative Constitutional Design and Legal Culture*, Cheltenham, UK and Northampton, MA, USA: Edward Elgar Publishing, pp. 1–26.

Frankenberg, Günter (2013) 'Constitutional Transfers and Experiments in the Nineteenth Century', in: Frankenberg, Günter (ed.) *Order from Transfer, Comparative Constitutional Design and Legal Culture*, Cheltenham, UK and Northampton, MA, USA: Edward Elgar Publishing, pp. 279–305.

Frankenberg, Günter (2014) 'Human Rights and the "Belief" in a Just World', 12 *International Journal of Constitutional Law*, pp. 35–60.

Frankenberg, Günter (2014) 'The Innocence of Method – Unveiled: Comparison as an Ethical and Political Act', 9 *Journal of Comparative Law*, pp. 222–258.

Frankenberg, Günter (2014) *Political Technology and the Erosion of the Rule of Law: Normalizing the State of Exception*, Cheltenham, UK and Northampton, MA, USA: Edward Elgar Publishing.

Franklin, Benjamin (2003) 'Remarks Concerning the Savages in North America', in: Ketcham, Ralph L. (ed.) *The Political Thought of Benjamin Franklin*, Indianapolis: Hackett, pp. 368–372.

Freud, Anna (1937) *The Ego and the Mechanisms of Defense*, London: Hogarth.

Friedman, Leon and Levantrosser, William F. (eds) (1992) *Watergate and Afterward – The Legacy of Richard M. Nixon*, Westport CT: Greenwood Press.

Frug, Mary Joe (1991) *Postmodern Legal Feminism*, New York: Routledge.

Frye, Northrop (1957) *The Anatomy of Criticism*, Princeton: Princeton Press.

Frye, Northrop (1992) *Words with Power. Being the Second Study of the Bible and Literature*, New York: Mariner Books.

Gans, Eduard (2005) *Naturrecht und Universalrechtsgeschichte: Vorlesungen nach G.W.F. Hegel* [1836], Tübingen: Mohr Siebeck.

Garth, Bryant G. and Dezalay, Yves (eds) (2002) *Global Prescriptions: The Production, Exportation, and Importation of a New Legal Orthodoxy*, Ann Arbor MI: University of Michigan Press.

Gauchet, Marcel (1989) *La Révolution des droits de l'homme*, Paris: Gallimard.

Geertz, Clifford (1968) 'Thinking as a Moral Act: Ethical Dimensions of Anthropological Fieldwork in the New States', 28 *Antioch Review*, pp. 139–158.

Geertz, Clifford (1982) 'The Way We Think Now: Towards an Ethnography of Modern Thought', 35 (5) *Bulletin of the American Academy of Arts and Sciences*, pp. 14–34.

Geertz, Clifford (1983) *Local Knowledge: Further Essays in Interpretive Anthropology*, New York: Basic Books.

Geertz, Clifford (1983) 'Found in Translation', in: Geertz, Clifford (ed.) *Local Knowledge: Further Essays in Interpretive Anthropology*, New York: Basic Books, pp. 36–54.

Geertz, Clifford (1983) 'From the Native's Point Of View: On the Nature of Anthropological Understanding', in: Geertz, Clifford (ed.) *Local Knowledge: Further Essays in Interpretive Anthropology*, New York: Basic Books, pp. 55–70.

Geertz, Clifford (1983) 'Local Knowledge: Fact and Law in Comparative Perspective', in: Geertz, Clifford (ed.) *Local Knowledge: Further Essays in Interpretive Anthropology*, New York: Basic Books, pp. 167–234.

Geertz, Clifford (2000) 'Thick Description: Toward an Interpretive Theory of Culture', in: Geertz, Clifford (ed.) *The Interpretation of Cultures*, 2nd ed., New York: Basic Books.

Gewirth, Alan (1986) 'Are There Absolute Rights?', in: Waldron, Jeremy (ed.) *Theories of Rights*, Oxford: Oxford University Press, pp. 91–109.

Ghazal Read, Jen'nan and Bartkowski, John P. (2000) 'To Veil or Not to Veil? A Case Study of Identity Negotiation among Muslim Women in Austin, Texas', 14 *Gender & Society*, pp. 395–417.

Ghazal Read, Jen'nan (2007) 'Introduction: The Politics of Veiling in Comparative Perspective', 68 *Sociology of Religion*, pp. 231–236.

Gieryn, Thomas (1999) *Cultural Boundaries of Society*, Chicago: Chicago University Press.

Giddens, Anthony (ed.) (1974) *Positivism and Sociology*, London: Ashgate Publishing.

Glanert, Simone (2012) 'Method?', in: Monateri, Pier G. (ed.) *Methods of Comparative Law*, Cheltenham, UK and Northampton, MA, USA: Edward Elgar Publishing, pp. 61–81.
Glendon, Mary Ann, Gordon, Michael W. and Osakwe, Christopher (1985) *Comparative Legal Traditions. Text, Materials and Cases*, St. Paul: West Publishing.
Glenn, H. Patrick (2004) *Legal Traditions of the World*, 3rd ed., Oxford: Oxford University Press.
Glenn, H. Patrick (2006) 'Comparative Legal Families and Comparative Legal Traditions', in: Reimann, Mathias and Zimmermann, Reinhard (eds) *The Oxford Handbook of Comparative Law*, Oxford: Oxford University Press, pp. 421–440.
Glenn, H. Patrick (2007) 'Com-paring', in: Nelken, David and Örücü, Esin (eds) *Comparative Law. A Handbook*, Portland: Hart Publishing, pp. 91–108.
Goodman, Nelson (1978) *Ways of World-Making*, Indianapolis: Hackett Publishing.
Gordley, James (1998) 'Comparative Law in the United States Today: Distinctiveness, Quality, and Tradition', 46 *American Journal of Comparative Law*, pp. 607–616.
Gordley, James R. (2002) 'Mapping Private Law', in: Bussani, Mauro and Mattei, Ugo (eds) *The Common Core of European Private Law. Essays on the Project*, The Hague: Kluwer.
Graziadei, Michele (2003) 'The Functional Heritage', in: Legrand, Pierre and Munday, Roderick (eds) *Comparative Legal Studies: Traditions and Transitions*, Cambridge: Cambridge University Press, pp. 100–130.
Gregory, Derek (1994) *Geographical Imaginations*, Oxford: Basil Blackwell.
Griffin, James (2008) *On Human Rights*, Oxford: Oxford University Press.
Großfeld, Bernhard (1984) *Macht und Ohnmacht der Rechtsvergleichung*, Tübingen: Mohr Siebeck.
Großfeld, Bernhard (1990) *The Strength and Weakness of Comparative Law*, Oxford: Oxford University Press.
Grosswald Curran, Vivian (1998) 'Cultural Immersion, Difference and Categories in U.S. Comparative Law', 46 *American Journal of Comparative Law*, pp. 43–92.
Grosswald Curran, Vivian (2007) 'On the Shoulders of Schlesinger: The Common Core of European Private Law Project', in: Bussani, Mauro and Mattei, Ugo (eds) (2007) *Opening Up European Law. The Common Core Project towards Eastern and South Eastern Europe*, Bern: Stämpfli Publishers, pp. 1–16.

Günther, Klaus (1994) 'Diskurstheorie des Rechts oder Naturrecht in diskurstheoretischem Gewande?', *Kritische Justiz*, pp. 470–487.

Günther, Klaus (1999) 'Human Rights and Political Culture', in: Alston, Philip (ed.) *The EU and Human Rights*, Oxford: Oxford University Press, pp. 117–146.

Gusy, Christoph (2014) *Polizeirecht*, 9th ed., Tübingen: Mohr Siebeck.

Gutteridge, Harold (1949) *Comparative Law: An Introduction to the Comparative Method of Legal Study and Research*, 2nd ed., Cambridge: Cambridge University Press.

Habermas, Jürgen (1972) *Knowledge and Human Interests*, Boston: Beacon Press.

Habermas, Jürgen (1987) *The Theory of Communicative Action Vol. II*, Boston: Beacon Press.

Habermas, Jürgen (1988) *On the Logic of the Social Sciences*, Cambridge MA: MIT Press.

Habermas, Jürgen (1996) *Beyond Facts and Norms: Contributions to a Discourse Theory of Law and Democracy*, Cambridge MA: Blackwell Publishers.

Habermas, Jürgen (2010) *An Awareness of What is Missing: Faith and Reason in a Post-Secular Age*, Cambridge MA: Polity Press.

Halley, Janet (2006) *Split Decisions*, Princeton: Princeton University Press.

Halley, Janet and Rittich, Kerry (2010) 'Critical Directions in Comparative Family Law', 58 *American Journal of Comparative Law*, pp. 753–776.

Haraway, Donna (1988) 'Situated Knowledges: The Science Question in Feminism and the Privilege of Partial Perspective', 14 *Feminist Studies*, pp. 575–599.

Harding, Andrew and Örücü, Esin (2002) *Comparative Law in the 21st Century*, London: Kluwer Academic Publishers.

Harding, Andrew and Leyland, Peter (2007) 'Comparative Law in Constitutional Contexts', in: Nelken, David and Örcüsü, Esin (eds) (2007) *Comparative Law. A Handbook*, Portland: Hart Publishing, pp. 313–338.

Hathaway, Oona (2002) 'Do Human Rights Treaties Make a Difference?', 111 *Yale Law Journal*, pp. 1935–2042.

Hegel, Georg F.W. (1983) *Philosophie des Rechts: Die Vorlesung von 1819/20*, Frankfurt: Suhrkamp.

Hirschl, Ran (2013) 'Editorial: From Comparative Constitutional Law to Comparative Constitutional Studies', 11 *International Journal of Constitutional Law*, pp. 1–12.

Hirschman, Nancy J. (1998) 'Western Feminism, Eastern Veiling, and the Question of Free Agency', 5 *Constellations. An International Journal of Critical and Democratic Theory*, pp. 345–368.
Horkheimer, Max (1972) 'Traditional and Critical Theory', in: Horkheimer, Max (ed.) *Critical Theory. Selected Essays*, New York: Continuum Publishing Company, pp. 188–243.
Horwitz, Morton (1992) *The Transformation of American Law, 1870–1960: The Crisis of Orthodoxy*, Oxford: Oxford University Press.
Huberich, Charles H. (1947) *The Political and Legislative History of Liberia*, New York: Central Book Co.
Hübner, Kurt (1985) *Die Wahrheit des Mythos*, München: C.H. Beck.
Human Rights Watch (2004) 'France: Headscarf Ban Violates Religious Freedom by Disproportionately Affecting Muslim Girls, Proposed Law Is Discriminatory' (New York, 27 February), http://www.hrw.org/english/docs/2004/02/26/france7666.htm (last accessed 24 September 2015).
Huntington, Samuel (1998) *The Clash of Civilizations and the Remaking of World Order*, New York: Simon & Schuster.
Inter-American Commission on Human Rights (IACHR) (2007) 'Access to Justice and Social Inclusion. The Road towards Strengthening Democracy in Bolivia' (OEA/Ser/V/II.Doc June 2007).
Jackson, Vicki (2004) 'Yes Please, I'd Love to Talk with You: The Court Has Learned from the World Before. It Should Continue to Do So', *Legal Affairs*, http://www.legalaffairs.org/issues/July-August-2004/feature_jackson_julaug04.msp (last accessed 24 September 2015).
Jaeggi, Rahel (2005) *Entfremdung. Zur Aktualität eines sozialphilosophischen Problems*, Frankfurt: Campus.
Jaeggi, Rahel and Wesche, Thilo (eds) (2009) *Was ist Kritik?*, Frankfurt: Suhrkamp.
James, Cyril L.R. (1938) *The Black Jacobins. Toussaint l'Ouverture and the San Domingo Revolution*, London: Secker & Warburg.
Jameson, Frederic (1979) 'Marxism and Historicism', 11 *New Literary History*, pp. 41–73.
Jamin, Christophe (2002) 'Saleilles' and Lambert's Old Dream Revisited', 50 *American Journal of Comparative Law*, pp. 701–718.
Jost, John T.T., Ledgerwood, Alison and Hardin, Curtis D. (2008) 'Shared Reality, System Justification and the Relational Basis of Ideological Beliefs', 2 *Social and Personality Psychology Compass*, pp. 171–186.
Jouannet, Emmanuelle and Motoc, Iulia (eds) (2012) *Internationalist Doctrines During the Years of Real Communism in Europe*, Paris: Société de législation comparée.

Juergensmeyer, Mark (1993) *The New Cold War? Religious Nationalism Confronts the Secular State*, Berkeley: University of California Press.

Kadelbach, Stefan (2012) 'The Territoriality and Migration of Fundamental Rights', in: Handl, Günther, Zekoll, Joachim and Zumbansen, Peer (eds) *Beyond Territoriality – Transnational Legal Authority in an Age of Globalization*, Leiden: M. Nijhoff Publishers, pp. 295–326.

Kafka, Franz (1971) 'Before the Law', in: *Collected Stories* [1915, 'Vor dem Gesetz', in: *Selbstwehr*], New York: Schocken.

Kafka, Franz (1999) *The Trial* [1915, *Der Process*], New York: Schocken.

Kahn, Robert A. (2007) 'The Headscarf as Threat: A Comparison of German and U.S. Legal Discourses', 40 *Vanderbilt Journal of Transnational Law*, pp. 417–444.

Kahn-Freund, Otto (1966) 'Comparative Law as an Academic Subject', 82 *Law Quarterly Review*, pp. 40–61.

Kairys, David (ed.) (1980) *The Politics of Law. A Progressive Critique*, New York: Pantheon.

Kaplan, David A. (2012) *Ricœur's Critical Theory*, Albany: State University of New York Press.

Kant, Immanuel (1999) *Critique of Pure Reason* [1781], Cambridge: Cambridge University Press.

Kapur, Ratna (2002) 'Un-Veiling Women's Rights in the "War on Terrorism"', 9 *Duke Journal of Gender Law & Policy*, pp. 211–226.

Kapur, Ratna (2012) 'Un-veiling Equality: Disciplining the "Other" Woman Through Human Rights Discourse', in: Emon, Anver M., Ellis, Marc S. and Glahn, Benjamin (eds) *Islamic Law and International Human Rights Law*, Oxford: Oxford University Press, pp. 265–290.

Kapur, Ratna (2013) 'In the Aftermath of Critique We Are Not in Epistemic Free Fall: Human Rights, the Subaltern Subject, and Non-liberal Search for Freedom and Happiness' (unpublished manuscript, on file with author).

Kaufmann, Walter (1960) *Hegel: A Reinterpretation*, New York: Anchor Books.

Keaton, Trica D. (2006) *Muslim Girls and the Other France: Race, Identity Politics & Social Exclusion*, Bloomington: Indiana University Press.

Kelman, Mark (1987) *A Guide to Critical Legal Studies*, Cambridge MA: Harvard University Press.

Kennedy, David and Tennant, Chris (1994) 'New Approaches to International Law. A Bibliography', 35 *Harvard International Law Journal*, pp. 417–460.

Kennedy, David (1997) 'New Approaches to Comparative Law: Comparativism and International Governance', 2 *Utah Law Review*, pp. 545–638.

Kennedy, David (2003) 'The Methods and the Politics of Comparative Law', in: Legrand, Pierre and Munday, Roderick (eds) *Comparative Legal Studies: Traditions and Transitions*, Cambridge: Cambridge University Press, pp. 345–433.

Kennedy, David (2004) *The Dark Sides of Virtue. Reassessing International Humanitarianism*, Princeton: Princeton University Press.

Kennedy, David (2005) 'Challenging Expert Rule: The Politics of Global Governance', 27 *Sydney Law Review*, pp. 5–28.

Kennedy, David (2006) *Of War and Law*, Princeton: Princeton University Press.

Kennedy, Duncan (2002) 'The Critique of Rights in Critical Legal Studies', in: Brown, Wendy and Halley, Janet (eds) *Left Legalism/Left Critique*, Durham: Duke University Press, pp. 178–228.

Kennedy, Duncan (2006) 'Three Globalizations of Law and Legal Thought: 1850–2000', in: Trubek, David and Santos, Alvaro (eds) *The New Law and Economic Development*, Cambridge: Cambridge University Press, pp. 19–73.

Kirchheimer, Otto (1961) *Political Justice*, Princeton: Princeton University Press.

Kitagawa, Zentaro (2006) 'Comparative Law in East Asia', in: Reimann, Mathias and Zimmermann, Reinhard (eds) *The Oxford Handbook of Comparative Law*, Oxford: Oxford University Press, pp. 237–260.

Klausen, Jytte (2005) *The Challenge of Islam: Politics and Religion in Western Europe*, Oxford: Oxford University Press.

Klausen, Jytte (2006) 'The Islamic Challenge: Politics and Religion in Western Europe', 11 *Berlin Journal*, pp. 50–52.

Klein, Peter (2010) 'Skepticism' in: *Stanford Encyclopedia of Philosophy*, http://plato.stanford.edu/entries/skepticism (last accessed 24 September 2015).

Kötz, Hein (1982) 'Neue Aufgaben der Rechtsvergleichung', 104 *Juristische Blätter*, pp. 355–362.

Kötz, Hein (1998) 'Abschied von der Rechtskreislehre?', 6 *Zeitschrift für Europäisches Privatrecht*, pp. 493–505.

Kötz, Hein (1999) 'Comparative Law in Germany Today', 51 *Révue internationale de droit comparé*, pp. 753–758.

Kocourek, Albert and Wigmore, John H. (1915) *Sources of Ancient and Primitive Law*, Boston: Little, Brown & Co.

Kocourek, Albert and Wigmore, John H. (1915) *Primitive and Ancient Legal Institutions*, Boston: Little, Brown & Co.

Kohler, Josef (1885) *Das Recht als Kulturerscheinung. Einleitung in die vergleichende Rechtswissenschaft*, Würzburg: Stahel.
Kohler, Josef (1904) 'Rechtsphilosophie und Universalrechtsgeschichte', in: von Holtzendorff, Franz (ed.) *Enzyklopädie der Rechtswissenschaft*, Vol. I, 6th ed., Leipzig: Duncker & Humblot.
Kohler, Josef (1914) *Philosophy of Law*, London: Macmillan.
Kohler, Josef and Wenger, Leopold (1914) *Allgemeine Rechtsgeschichte*, Leipzig and Berlin: B.G. Teubner.
Koskenniemi, Martti (1990) 'The Politics of International Law', 1 *European Journal of International Law*, pp. 4–32.
Koskenniemi, Martti (2001) *The Gentle Civilizer of Nations. The Rise and Fall of International Law 1870–1960*, Cambridge: Cambridge University Press.
Koskenniemi, Martti (2005) *From Apology to Utopia. The Structure of International Legal Argument*, 2nd ed., re-issue with new epilogue, Cambridge: Cambridge University Press.
Koskenniemi, Martti (2007) 'The Fate of Public International Law: Between Technique and Politics', 70 *Modern Law Review*, pp. 1–30.
Koskenniemi, Martti (2010) 'Human Rights Mainstreaming as a Strategy for Institutional Power', 1 *Humanity. An International Journal of Human Rights, Humanitarianism and Development*, pp. 47–58.
Kuhn, Thomas (1970) *The Structure of Scientific Revolutions*, 2nd ed., Chicago: University of Chicago Press.
Kunze, Rolf Ulrich (2004) *Ernst Rabel und das Kaiser-Wilhelm-Institut für Ausländisches und Internationales Privatrecht 1926–1945*, Göttingen: Wallstein.
Laborde, Cécile (2008) *Critical Republicanism: The Hijab-Debate and Political Philosophy*, Oxford: Oxford University Press.
Lambert, Édouard (1905) 'Conception générale et définition de la science du droit comparé, sa méthode, son histoire; le droit comparé et l'enseignement du droit', in: Zweigert, Konrad and Puttfarken, Hans J. (eds) (1978) *Rechtsvergleichung*, Darmstadt: Wissenschaftliche Buchgesellschaft, pp. 30–51.
Lasser, Mitchel de S.-O.-l'E. (1995) 'Judicial (Self-)Portraits: Judicial Discourse in the French Legal System', 104 *Yale Law Journal*, pp. 1325–1410.
Lasser, Mitchel de S.-O.-l'E. (2003) 'The Question of Understanding', in: Legrand, Pierre and Munday, Roderick (eds) *Comparative Legal Studies: Traditions and Transitions*, Cambridge: Cambridge University Press, pp. 197–239.
Latour, Bruno (2002) *La Fabrique du Droit: Une Ethnographie du Conseil d'Etat*, Paris: La Découverte.

Lave, Jean (1996) 'The Savagery of the Domestic Mind', in: Nader, Laura (ed.) *Naked Science: Anthropological Inquiry into Boundaries, Power and Knowledge*, Abingdon and New York: Routledge, pp. 87–100.

Lazreg, Marnia (2008) *Torture and the Twilight of Empire*, Princeton: Princeton University Press.

Legrand, Pierre (1995) 'Comparative Legal Studies and the Commitment to Theory', 58 *Modern Law Review*, pp. 262–273.

Legrand, Pierre (1996) 'European Legal Systems Are Not Converging', 45 *International and Comparative Law Quarterly*, pp. 52–81.

Legrand, Pierre (1997) 'The Impossibility of Legal Transplants', 4 *Maastricht Journal of European & Comparative Law*, pp. 111–124.

Legrand, Pierre (1999) *Fragments on Law-as-Culture*, Deventer: W.E.J. Tjeenk Willink.

Legrand, Pierre (1999) 'John Henry Merryman and Comparative Legal Studies: A Dialogue', 47 *American Journal of Comparative Law*, pp. 3–66.

Legrand, Pierre (2001) 'The Return of the Repressed: Moving Comparative Legal Studies Beyond Pleasure', 75 *Tulane Law Review*, pp. 1033–1052.

Legrand, Pierre (2003) 'The Same and the Different', in: Legrand, Pierre and Munday, Roderick (eds) *Comparative Legal Studies: Traditions and Transitions*, Cambridge: Cambridge University Press, pp. 240–311.

Legrand, Pierre and Munday, Roderick (eds) (2003) *Comparative Legal Studies: Traditions and Transitions*, Cambridge: Cambridge University Press.

Legrand, Pierre (2006) 'Antivonbar', 1 *Journal of Comparative Law*, pp. 13–40.

Legrand, Pierre (2011) 'Siting Foreign Law: How Derrida Can Help', 21 *Duke Journal of Comparative & International Law*, pp. 595–630.

Leiter, Brian (2005) 'American Legal Realism', in: Edmundson, William A. and Golding, Martin P. (eds) *The Blackwell Guide to Philosophy of Law and Legal Theory*, Oxford: Blackwell, pp. 50–66.

Lepaulle, Pierre (1922) 'The Function of Comparative Law. With a Critique of Sociological Jurisprudence', 35 *Harvard Law Review*, pp. 838–858.

Lerner, Melvin J. (1970) 'The Desire for Justice and Reactions to Victims', in: Macauley, J. and Berkowitz, L. (eds) *Altruism and Helping Behaviour*, New York: Academic Press, pp. 205–230.

Lerner, Melvin J. (2003) 'The Justice Motive: Where Social Psychologists Found It, How They Lost It, and Why They May Not Find It Again', 7 *Personality & Social Psychology Review*, pp. 388–399.

Levinson, Sanford (ed.) (2004) *Torture: A Collection*, New York: Oxford University Press.

Lévi-Strauss, Claude (1963) *Totemism*, Boston: Beacon Press.

Lévi-Strauss, Claude (1966) *The Savage Mind*, Chicago: University of Chicago Press.

Lévy, Bernard Henry (2004) 'Off with Their Headscarves', *The Guardian*, 1 February.

Liddell, Henry G. and Scott, Robert (1977) *A Greek-English Lexicon*, 9th ed., Oxford: Clarendon.

Liebesny, Herbert J. (1981) *Foreign Legal Systems: A Comparative Analysis*, Washington DC: George Washington University Press.

Lopez, Gerald (1984) 'Lay Lawyering', 32 *UCLA Law Review*, pp. 1–60.

Luhmann, Niklas (2000) *Vertrauen. Ein Mechanismus der Reduktion sozialer Komplexität*, Stuttgart: UTB.

Luhmann, Niklas (2001) *Legitimation durch Verfahren*, Frankfurt: Suhrkamp.

Luhmann, Niklas (2004) *Law as a Social System*, Oxford: Oxford University Press.

Lukács, Georg (2005) 'Narrate or Describe', in: Lukács, Georg (ed.) *Writer and Critic and Other Essays*, Lincoln: Universe, Inc., pp. 110–148.

Machura, Stefan (1997) 'The Individual in the Shadow of Powerful Institutions: Niklas Luhmann's Legitimation by Procedure As Seen by Critics', in: Röhl, Klaus F. and Machura, Stefan (eds) *Procedural Justice*, Farnham: Ashgate, pp. 181–206.

Macdonald, Myra (2006) 'Muslim Women and the Veil', 6 *Feminist Media Studies*, pp. 7–23.

Mahmood, Saba (2004) *The Politics of Piety: The Islamic Revival and the Feminist Subject*, Princeton: Princeton University Press.

Mahmood, Saba (2006) 'Secularism, Hermeneutics and Empire: The Politics of Islamic Reformation', 18 *Public Culture*, pp. 323–347.

Mahmood, Saba (2009) 'Religious Reason and Secular Affect: An Incommensurable Divide?', in: Asad, Talal, Brown, Wendy, Butler, Judith and Mahmood, Saba (eds) *Is Critique Secular? Blasphemy, Injury, and Free Speech*, Berkeley: University of California Press, pp. 64–100.

Mamdani, Mahmood (1996) *Citizen and Subject: Contemporary Africa and the Legacy of Late Colonialism*, Princeton: Princeton University Press.

Mangoldt, Herrmann von, Klein, Friedrich and Starck, Christian (eds) (2005) *Kommentar zum Grundgesetz*, München: Franz Vahlen.

Marcuse, Herbert (1964) *The One-Dimensional Man. Studies in the Ideology of Advanced Industrial Society*, Boston: Beacon Press.

Marcuse, Herbert (1965) 'Repressive Tolerance', in: Marcuse, Herbert, Wolff, Robert P. and Moore, Barrington (eds) *A Critique of Pure Tolerance*, Boston: Beacon Press, pp. 81–117.
Markesinis, Basil S. (1997) *Foreign Law and Comparative Methodology*, Oxford: Hart Publishing.
Marks, Susan (2012) 'Human Rights in Disastrous Times', in: Crawford, James and Koskenniemi, Martti (eds) *The Cambridge Companion to International Law*, Cambridge: Cambridge University Press, pp. 309–326.
Marshall, Jill (2006) 'Freedom of Religious Expression and Gender Equality: Sahin v. Turkey', 69 *Modern Law Review*, pp. 452–461.
Marshall, Paul A. (ed.) (2007) *Religious Freedom in the World*, Washington DC: Rowman & Littlefield.
Mattei, Ugo (2003) 'A Theory of Imperial Law: A Study on US Hegemony and the Latin Resistance', 10 *Indiana Journal of Global Studies*, pp. 383–448.
Mattei, Ugo (2006) 'Comperative Law and Critical Legal Studies', in: Reimann, Mathias and Zimmermann, Reinhard (eds) *The Oxford Handbook of Comparative Law*, Oxford: Oxford University Press, pp. 815–836.
Mayer, Jane (2005) 'Outsourcing Torture', *The New Yorker* 14 February, http://www.newyorker.com/magazine/2005/02/14/outsourcing-torture (last accessed 24 September 2015).
McCrudden, Christopher (2007) 'Judicial Comparativism and Human Rights', in: Nelken, David and Örcüsü, Esin (eds) *Comparative Law. A Handbook*, Portland: Hart Publishing, pp. 371–398.
McGoldrick, Dominic (2006) *Human Rights and Religion: The Islamic Headscarf Debate*, Portland: Hart Publishing.
McQuoid-Mason, David (1999) 'Access to Justice in South Africa', 17 *Windsor Yearbook of Access to Justice*, pp. 230–254.
Medic, Veit and Reimann, Anna (2007) 'Justifying Marital Violence: A German Judge Cites Koran in Divorce Case', Spiegel Online 21 March, http://www.spiegel.de/international/germany/justifying-marital-violence-a-german-judge-cites-koran-in-divorce-case-a-473017.html (last accessed 24 September 2015).
Mégret, Fred (2009) 'That "Springbreak" Feeling: Pragmatism, Irony and Belief in the Age of Human Rights' (paper presented in December 2009, unpublished, on file with author).
Menger, Carl (1963) *Problems of Economics and Sociology* [1883], Urbana: University of Illinois Press.
Menski, Werner (2002) 'Immigration and Multiculturalism in Britain: New Issues in Research and Policy', 12 *KIAPS: Bulletin of Asia-Pacific Studies*, pp. 43–66.

Menski, Werner (2006) *Comparative Law in a Global Context. The Legal Systems of Asia and Africa*, Cambridge: Cambridge University Press.

Menski, Werner (2007) 'Beyond Europe', in: Nelken, David and Örcüsü, Esin (eds) *Comparative Law. A Handbook*, Portland: Hart Publishing, pp. 189–216.

Merino Acuña, Roger (2012) *Comparative Law from Below. The Construction of a Critical Project in Comparative Legal Studies*, Saarbrücken: Lambert Academic Publishing.

Merleau-Ponty, Maurice (2013) *Phenomenology of Perception*, London: Routledge.

Merrill Block, Stefan (2009) *The Story of Forgetting*, London: Faber & Faber.

Merryman, John (1977) 'Comparative Law and Social Change: On the Origins, Style, Decline & Revival of the Law and Development Movement', 25 *American Journal of Comparative Law*, pp. 457–491.

Merryman, John H. and Clark, David S. (eds) (1978) *Comparative Law: Western European and Latin American Legal Systems: Cases and Materials*, Indianapolis: Bobbs-Merrill.

Merryman, John (1999) *The Loneliness of the Comparative Lawyer*, Boston: Kluwer Law.

Merryman, John (2007) *The Civil Law Tradition: An Introduction to the Legal Systems of Europe and Latin America*, Palo Alto CA: Stanford University Press.

Messer-Davidow, Ellen, Shumway, David R. and Sylvan, David J. (1993) 'Preface', in: Messer Davidow, Ellen, Shumway, David R. and Sylvan, David J. (eds) *Knowledges. Historical and Critical Studies in Disciplinarity*, Charlottesville and London: University of Virginia Press, pp. vii seq.

Messer-Davidow, Ellen, Shumway, David R. and Sylvan, David J. (1993) 'Introduction: Disciplinary Ways of Knowing', in: Messer Davidow, Ellen, Shumway, David R. and Sylvan, David J. (eds) *Knowledges. Historical and Critical Studies in Disciplinarity*, Charlottesville and London: University of Virginia Press, pp. vii seq.

Mészáros, István (1970) *Marx's Theory of Alienation*, London: Merlin Press.

Michaels, Ralf (2001) *Common Core?* (unpublished manuscript, on file with author).

Michaels, Ralf (2002) 'Im Westen nichts Neues? 100 Jahre Pariser Kongress für Rechtsvergleichung', 66 *Rabels Zeitschrift für ausländisches und internationales Privatrecht*, pp. 97–115.

Michaels, Ralf (2006) 'The Functional Method of Comparative Law', in: Reimann, Mathias and Zimmermann, Reinhard (eds) *The Oxford*

Handbook of Comparative Law, Oxford: Oxford University Press, pp. 339–382.

Michaelson, Christopher (2006) 'Balancing Civil Liberties Against National Security? A Critique of Counterterrorism Rhetoric', 29 (2) *UNSW Law Journal*, pp. 1–21.

Mitchell, William J.T. (2005) *What Do Pictures Want? The Lives and Loves of Images*, Chicago: University of Chicago Press.

Monateri, Pier G. (1999) 'Critique et différence: Le droit comparé en Italie', 51 *Revue Internationale de Droit Comparé*, pp. 989–1002.

Monateri, Pier G. (2000) 'Black Gaius: A Quest for the Multicultural Origins of the "Western Legal Tradition"', 51 *Hastings Law Journal*, pp. 479–556.

Monateri, Pier G. (ed.) (2012) *Methods of Comparative Law*, Cheltenham, UK and Northampton, MA, USA: Edward Elgar Publishing.

Montesquieu, Charles de Secondat Baron de (1989) *The Spirit of Laws* [1748], Cambridge: Cambridge University Press.

Moore, Kathleen M. (2007) 'Visible through the Veil: The Regulation of Islam in American Law', 68 *Sociology of Religion*, pp. 237–251.

Moore, Sally Falk (1986) 'Legal Systems of the World: An Introductory Guide to Classifications, Typological Interpretations, and Bibliographical Resources' in: Lipson, Leon and Wheeler, Stanton (eds) *Law and the Social Sciences*, New York: Russell Sage, pp. 11–62.

Moore, Sally Falk (2005) 'Comparisons: Possible and Impossible', 34 *Annual Review of Anthropology*, pp. 1–11.

Moors, Annelies (2009) 'The Dutch and the Face-Veil: The Politics of Discomfort', 17 *Social Anthropology*, pp. 393–408.

Moran, Joe (2010) *Interdisciplinarity (The New Critical Idiom)*, 2nd ed., New York: Routledge.

Müge Coçek, Fatma and Balaghi, Shiva (eds) (1994) *Reconstructing Gender in the Middle East: Tradition, Identity and Power*, New York: Columbia University Press.

Muir Watt, Horatia (2000) 'La fonction subversive du droit comparé', 52 *Revue International de Droit Comparé*, pp. 503–527.

Muir Watt, Horatia (2006) 'Globalization and Comparative Law', in: Reimann, Mathias and Zimmermann, Reinhard (eds) *The Oxford Handbook of Comparative Law*, Oxford: Oxford University Press, pp. 579–608.

Murphy, Walter F. and Tanenhaus, Joseph (1977) *Comparative Constitutional Law. Cases and Commentaries*, New York: St. Martin's Press.

Murphy, Ewell (1981) 'The Diminishing World of Western Law', 16 *Texas International Law Journal*, pp. 1–10.

Mutua, Makau Wa (1995/1996) 'The Ideology of Human Rights', 36 *Virginia Journal of International Law*, pp. 589–657.

Nader, Laura (1996) 'Anthropological Inquiry into Boundaries, Power, and Knowledge', in: Nader, Laura (ed.) *Naked Science. Anthropological Inquiry into Boundaries, Power, and Knowledge*, New York: Routledge, pp. 1–27.

Nader, Laura (1997) 'Controlling Processes – Tracing the Dynamic Components of Power', 38 *Current Anthropology*, pp. 711–738.

Nagel, Thomas (1989) *The View from Nowhere*, Oxford: Oxford University Press.

Nelken, David and Örücü, Esin (eds) (2007) *Comparative Law. A Handbook*, Portland: Hart Publishing.

Nelken, David (2007) 'Comparative Law and Comparative Legal Studies', in: Nelken, David and Örcüsü, Esin (eds) *Comparative Law. A Handbook*, Portland: Hart Publishing, pp. 3–42.

Neumann, Franz (1937) 'The Change in the Function of Law in Modern Society', in: Scheuermann, William (ed.) (1996) *Rule of Law under Siege. Selected Essays of Franz Neumann and Otto Kirchheimer*, Berkeley: Berkeley University Press, pp. 101–141.

Neumann, Franz (1942) *Behemoth. The Structure and Practice of the National Socialism*, Oxford: Oxford University Press.

Nickel, James (2006) *Making Sense of Human Rights*, Oxford: Oxford University Press.

Nigro, Raffaella (2010) 'The Margin of Appreciation Doctrine and the Case-Law of the European Court on Human Rights on the Islamic Veil', 11 *Human Rights Review*, pp. 531–564.

Noonan, John T. (2002) *Persons and Masks of the Law: Cardozo, Holmes, Jefferson, and Whyte as Makers of the Masks*, Berkeley and Los Angeles: University of California Press.

Noonan, Harold (2004) 'Identity' in: *The Stanford Encyclopedia of Philosophy*, http://plato.stanford.edu/archives/win2011/entries/identity/ (last accessed 21 September 2015).

Open Society Foundations (ed.) (2011) *Unveiling the Truth: Why 32 Muslim Women Wear the Full-Face Veil in France*, New York: Open Society Foundations, http://www.opensocietyfoundations.org/sites/default/files/a-unveiling-the-truth-20100510_0.pdf (last accessed 21 September 2015).

Örücü, Esin (1999) *Critical Comparative Law: Considering Paradoxes for Legal Systems in Transition*, Deventer: Kluwer.

Örücü, Esin (2007) 'What Next in the Convergence Process in Europe?', in: Bussani, Mauro and Mattei, Ugo (eds) *Opening up European Law: the Common Core Project towards Eastern and South Eastern Europe*, Bern: Stämpfli, pp. 175–194.

Orford, Anne (2003) *Reading Humanitarian Intervention. Human Rights and the Use of Force in International Law*, Cambridge: Cambridge University Press.

Orford, Anne (2007) 'Biopolitics and the Tragic Subject of Human Rights', in: Dauphinee, Elizabeth and Masters, Cristina (eds) *The Logics of Biopower and the War on Terror: Living, Dying, Surviving*, New York: Palgrave Macmillan, pp. 205–228.

Orford, Anne (2011) *International Authority and the Responsibility to Protect*, Cambridge: Cambridge University Press.

Palmer, Vernon V. (2005) 'From Lerotholi to Lando: Some Examples of Comperative Law Methodology', 53 *American Journal of Comparative Law*, pp. 261–290.

Panikkar, Raimon (1982) 'Is the Notion of Human Rights a Western Concept?', 30 *Diogenes*, pp. 75–102.

Pape, Robert (2006) *Dying to Win: The Strategic Logic of Suicide Terrorism*, New York: Random House.

Parry, John (2005) 'The Shape of Modern Torture: Extraordinary Rendition and Ghost Detainees', 6 *Melbourne Journal of International Law*, pp. 516–533.

Peek, Lori Ann (2005) *The Identity of Crisis: Muslim-Americans After 9/11*, Ph.D. Dissertation, Department of Sociology, University of Colorado, Boulder.

Peerenboom, Randall (ed.) (2004) *Asian Discourses of Rule of Law: Theories and Implementation of Rule of Law in Twelve Asian Countries, France and the U.S.*, London and New York: Routledge.

Pedwell, Carolyn (2010) *Feminism, Culture and Embodied Practice: The Rhetorics of Comparison*, London: Routledge.

Pennock, J. Roland and Chapman, John W. (1977) *Due Process*, New York: New York University Press.

Peters, Anne and Schwenke, Heiner (2000) 'Comparative Law Beyond Post-Modernism', 49 *International and Comparative Law Quarterly*, pp. 800–834.

Peters, Edward (1985) *Torture*, Oxford and New York: Blackwell.

Pogge, Thomas (2002) *World Poverty and Human Rights*, Cambridge: Cambridge University Press.

Pound, Roscoe (1957) 'Foreword', in: von Mehren, Arthur (ed.) *The Civil Law System*, Boston: Little, Brown & Co, pp. vii–viii.

Priest, Dana and Smith, R. Jeffrey (2004) 'Memo Offered Justification for Use of Torture', *Washington Post*, 8 June, p. A01.

Pufendorf, Samuel (2009) *Two Books of the Elements of Universal Jurisprudence* [1660], Miami: Liberty Fund.

Rabel, Ernst (1951) 'Deutsches und Amerikanisches Recht', 16 *Zeitschrift für ausländisches und internationales Privatrecht*, pp. 340–359.
Rabel, Ernst (1958) *Das Recht des Warenkaufs*, 2 Vols., Tübingen: Mohr Siebeck.
Rabel, Ernst (1967) 'Aufgabe und Notwendigkeit der Rechtsvergleichung', in: Rabel, Ernst *Gesammelte Aufsätze III*, Tübingen: Mohr Siebeck.
Rawls, John (1971) *A Theory of Justice*, Cambridge MA: Harvard University Press.
Reece, Debra (1996) 'Covering and Communication: The Symbolism of Dress among Muslim Women', 7 *Howard Journal of Communications*, pp. 35–52.
Reimann, Mathias (1998) 'Stepping out of the European Shadow: Why Comparative Law in the United States Must Develop Its Own Agenda', 46 *American Journal of Comparative Law*, pp. 637–646.
Reimann, Mathias (2002) 'The Progress and Failure of Comparative Law in the Second Half of the Twentieth Century', 50 *American Journal of Comparative Law*, pp. 671–700.
Reimann, Mathias and Zimmermann, Reinhard (eds) (2006) *The Oxford Handbook of Comparative Law*, Oxford: Oxford University Press.
Reitz, John (1998) 'How to Do Comparative Law', 46 *American Journal of Comparative Law*, pp. 617–636.
Rhode, Deborah L. (2005) *Access to Justice*, Oxford: Oxford University Press.
Ricœur, Paul (1970) *Freud and Philosophy: An Essay on Interpretation*, New Haven: Yale University Press.
Ricœur, Paul (1980) 'Narrative Time', 7 *Critical Inquiry*, pp. 169–190.
Riles, Annelise (1999) 'Wigmore's Treasure Box: Comparative Law in the Era of Information', 40 *Harvard International Law Journal*, pp. 221–284.
Riles, Annelise (2001) *Rethinking the Masters of Comparative Law*, Oxford: Hart Publishing.
Riles, Annelise (2006) 'Comparative Law and Socio-Legal Studies', in: Reimann, Mathias and Zimmermann, Reinhard (eds) *The Oxford Handbook of Comparative Law*, Oxford: Oxford University Press, pp. 775–814.
Riley, Patrick (1996) *Leibniz' Universal Jurisprudence: Justice as the Charity of the Wise*, Cambridge MA: Harvard University Press.
Roberts, Paul (2007) 'Comparative Law for International Criminal Justice', in: Nelken, David and Örcüsü, Esin (eds) *Comparative Law. A Handbook*, Portland: Hart Publishing, pp. 339–370.

Rorty, Richard (1993) 'Human Rights, Rationality, and Sentimentality', in: Shute, Stephen and Hurley, Susan (eds) *On Human Rights*, New York: Basic Books, pp. 111–134.

Rorty, Richard (1995) 'Feminism, Ideology, and Deconstruction: A Pragmatist View', in: Žižek, Slavoj (ed.) *Mapping Ideology*, London and New York: Verso, pp. 227–234.

Rosaldo, Renato (1993) *Culture and Truth. The Remaking of Social Analysis*, Boston: Beacon Press.

Rosen, Lawrence (2006) *Law as Culture: An Invitation*, Princeton: Princeton University Press.

Rosett, Arthur (1992) 'Unification, Harmonization, Codification, and Reform in International Commercial Law', 40 *American Journal of Comparative Law*, pp. 683–698.

Rousseau, Jean Jacques (1950) *The Social Contract and Discourses*, New York: Dutton.

Ruskola, Teemu (2013) *Legal Orientalism – China, the United States, and Modern Law*, Cambridge MA: Harvard University Press.

Sacco, Rodolfo (1991) 'Legal Formants: A Dynamic Approach to Comparative Law', 39 *American Journal of Comparative Law*, pp. 1–34 and 343–401.

Sacco, Rodolfo (2000) 'One Hundred Years of Comparative Law', 75 *Tulane Law Review*, pp. 1159–1176.

Sacco, Rodolfo (2001) 'Diversity and Uniformity in the Law', 49 *American Journal of Comparative Law*, pp. 171–190.

Sack, Peter and Aleck, Jonathan (1992) 'Introduction', in: Sack, Peter and Aleck, Jonathan (eds) *Law and Anthropology*, New York: New York University Press, pp. xiii–xxxi.

Sacksofsky, Ute (2008) 'Religion and Equality in Germany: The Headscarf Debate from a Constitutional Perspective', in: Schiek, Dagmar and Chege, Victoria (eds) *European Union Non-Discrimination Law: Comparative Perspectives on Multidimensional Equality Law*, London: Taylor & Francis, pp. 353–370.

Sacksofsky, Ute (2015) 'Glaubensfreiheit – ein Grundrecht nur für den religiösen Mainstream?', 69 (789) *Merkur*, February, pp. 57–64.

Said, Edward (1979) *Orientalism*, New York: Random House.

Said, Edward (1984) 'Traveling Theory', in: Said, Edward (ed.) *The World, the Text and the Critic*, London: Faber & Faber, pp. 226–247.

Said, Edward (1997) *Covering Islam. How the Media and the Experts Determine How We See the Rest of the World*, New York: Vintage Books.

Sajó, András (2007) 'Free Speech, Religion and the Right to Caricature', in: Sajó, András (ed.) *Censorial Sensitivities: Free Speech and Religion in a Fundamentalist World*, Utrecht: Eleven International Publishing.

Salecl, Renata (1994) *The Spoils of Freedom. Psychoanalysis and Feminism after the Fall of Socialism*, London: Routledge.

Saleilles, Raymond (1891) 'Le droit commercial comparé – Contribution à l'étude des méthodes juridiques', 5 *Annales de droit commercial*, pp. 227 seq.

Samuel, Geoffrey (2004) 'Epistemology and Methodology of Comparative Law: Contributions from the Sciences and Social Sciences', in: van Hoecke, Mark (ed.) *Epistemology and Methodology of Comparative Law*, Oxford: Hart Publishing, pp. 35–78.

Sandikci, Özlem and Ger, Güliz (2010) 'Veiling in Style: How Does a Stigmatized Practice Become Fashionable?', 37 *Journal of Consumer Research*, pp. 15–36.

Sands, Philippe (2008) *Torture Team. Rumsfeld's Memo and the Betrayal of American Values*, London: Palgrave Macmillan.

Sawer, Geoffrey (1975) 'The Western Conception of Law', in: David et al. (eds) *International Encyclopedia of Comparative Law*, Vol. II, Tübingen and The Hague: Mohr Siebeck.

Scanlon, Thomas (1998) *What We Owe to Each Other*, Cambridge: Cambridge University Press.

Schacht, Richard (1970) *Alienation*, Garden City: Doubleday.

Scheffer, Thomas and Niewöhner, Jörg (eds) (2010) *Thick Comparison. Reviving the Ethnographic Aspiration*, Leiden and Boston: Brill.

Schlesinger, Rudolf (1968) *Formation of Contracts. A Study of the Common Core of Legal Systems*, Dobbs Ferry NY: Oceana.

Schlesinger, Rudolf (1995) 'The Past and Future of Comparative Law', 43 *American Journal of Comparative Law*, pp. 477–482.

Schlesinger, Rudolf, Baade, Hans W., Herzog, Peter E. and Wise, Edward M. (1998) *Comparative Law: Cases-Text-Materials*, 6th ed., New York: Foundation Press.

Schröder, Jan (2010) *Rechtswissenschaft in der Neuzeit*, Tübingen: Mohr Siebeck.

Schwarz-Liebermann von Wahlendorf, Hans-Albrecht (1978) *Droit Comparé – Théorie Générale et Principes*, Paris: Librairie Générale de Droit et de Jurisprudence.

Schwarzer, Alice (ed.) (2002) *Die Gotteskrieger und die falsche Toleranz*, Köln: Kiepenheuer & Witsch.

Schwarzer, Alice (ed.) (2010) *Die große Verschleierung. Für Integration, gegen Islamismus*, Köln: Kiepenheuer & Witsch.

Schwenzer, Ingeborg (2006) 'Development of Comparative Law in Germany, Switzerland, and Austria', in: Reimann, Mathias and Zimmermann, Reinhard (eds) *The Oxford Handbook of Comparative Law*, Oxford: Oxford University Press, pp. 69–106.

Scollon, Ron and Wong Scollon, Suzanne (1995) *Intercultural Communication. A Discourse Approach*, Cambridge MA: Basil Blackwell.

Scott, Joan (2007) *The Politics of the Veil*, Princeton: Princeton University Press.

Shilliam, Robert (2006) 'The "Other" in Classical Political Theory: Re-Contextualizing the Cosmopolitan/Communitarian Debate', in: Jahn, Beate (ed.) *Classical Theory in International Relations*, Cambridge: Cambridge University Press, pp. 207–232.

Siem, Mathias (2014) *Comparative Law*, Cambridge: Cambridge University Press.

Siim, Birte and Skjeie, Hege (2008) 'Tracks, Intersections and Dead Ends: Multicultural Challenges to State Feminism in Denmark and Norway', 8 *Ethnicities*, pp. 322–344.

Slotkin, Richard (1973) *Regeneration Through Violence. The Mythology of the American Frontier, 1600–1860*, Middletown CT: Wesleyan University Press.

Smith, Joseph C. and Weisstub, David N. (1983) *The Western Idea of Law*, London: Butterworths.

Smits, Jan M. (ed.) (2012) *Elgar Encyclopedia of Comparative Law*, Cheltenham, UK and Northampton, MA, USA: Edward Elgar Publishing.

Steiner, George (1961) *The Death of Tragedy*, New York: Alfred A. Knopf.

Stephens, Thomas (2009) 'There's no place for Sharia in Switzerland', http://origin.swissinfo.ch/eng/-there-s-noplace-for-sharia-in-switzerland-/7147982 (last accessed 24 September 2015).

Stiglitz, Joseph (2002) *Globalization and its Discontents*, New York: W.W. Norton.

Talpade Mohanty, Chandra (2003) *Feminism Without Borders: Decolonizing Theory, Practicing Solidarity*, Durham NC: Duke University Press.

Taylor, Charles (1992) 'The Politics of Recognition', in: Gutmann, Amy (ed.) *Multiculturalism and "The Politics of Recognition"*, Princeton: Princeton University Press, pp. 25 seq.

Teitel, Ruti (2004) 'Book Review: Comparative Constitutional Law in a Global Age', 117 *Harvard Law Review*, pp. 2570–2596.

Thomas, John Penford (1828) *A Treatise of Universal Jurisprudence*, London: Longman.

Thompson Klein, Julie (1990) *Interdisciplinarity: History, Theory & Practice*, Detroit: Wayne State University Press.

Tomberlin, James (ed.) (1999) *Philosphical Perspectives 13: Epistemology*, Oxford: Blackwell Publishing.

Tomuschat, Christian (2008) *Human Rights: Between Idealism and Realism*, Oxford: Oxford University Press.

Trebilcock, Michael J. and Daniels, Ronald J. (eds) (2008) *Rule of Law Reform and Development: Charting the Fragile Path of Progress*, Cheltenham, UK and Northampton, MA, USA: Edward Elgar Publishing.

Trubek, David and Santos, Alvaro (eds) (2006) *The New Law and Economic Development. A Critical Appraisal*, Cambridge: Cambridge University Press.

Tunc, André (1977) 'Foreword', in: von Mehren, Arthur T. and Gordley, James (eds) *The Civil Law System*, Boston: Little, Brown & Co, p. ix.

Tunc, André (1978) 'La contribution possible des études juridiques comparatives à une meilleure compréhension entre nations', in: Zweigert, Konrad and Puttfarken, Hans-Jürgen *Rechtsvergleichung*, Darmstadt: Wissenschaftliche Buchgesellschaft, pp. 282–306.

Twining, William (2000) 'Comparative Law and Legal Theory: The Country and Western Legal Tradition', in: Edge, Ian (ed.) *Comparative Law in Global Perspective*, Ardsley NY: Transnational Publishers, pp. 21–76.

Twining, William (2000) *Globalization and Legal Theory*, Cambridge: Cambridge University Press.

Twining, William et al. (2006) 'A Fresh Start for Comparative Legal Studies? A Collective Review of Patrick Glenn's *Legal Traditions of the World*, 2nd edition', 1 *Journal of Comparative Law*, pp. 100–176.

Twining, William (2007) 'Globalisation and Comparative Law', in: Nelken, David and Örücü, Esin (eds) *Comparative Law. A Handbook*, Portland: Hart Publishing, pp. 69–90.

Twining, William (ed.) (2009) *Human Rights, Southern Voices: Francis Deng, Abdullai A-Na'im, Yash Gai and Upendra Baxi*, Cambridge: Cambridge University Press.

UNDP (2011) *Access to Justice and Rule of Law*, http://www.undp.org/content/undp/en/home/ourwork/democraticgovernance/focus_areas/focus_justice_law.html (last accessed 24 September 2015).

Unger, Roberto M. (1986) *The Critical Legal Studies Movement*, Cambridge MA: Harvard University Press.

Vakulenko, Anastasia (2007) 'Islamic Dress in Human Rights Jurisprudence: A Critique of Current Trends', 7 *Human Rights Law Review*, pp. 717–739.

Vogenauer, Stefan (2006) 'Sources of Law and Legal Method' in: Reimann, Mathias and Zimmermann, Reinhard (eds) *The Oxford Handbook of Comparative Law*, Oxford: Oxford University Press, pp. 869–898.

Vogenauer, Stefan (2012) 'Rechtsgeschichte und Rechtsvergleichung um 1900', 76 *Rabels Zeitschrift für ausländisches und internationales Privatrecht*, pp. 1122–1154.

Wadud, Amina (2006) *Inside the Gender Jihad. Women's Reform in Islam*, London: Oneworld Publications.
Waldron, Jeremy (ed.) (1984) *Theories of Rights*, Oxford: Oxford University Press.
Wallerstein, Immanuel (2006) *European Universalism: The Rhetoric of Power*, New York: The New Press.
Walzer, Michael (2004) *Arguing about War*, New Haven: Yale University Press.
Watson, Alan (1974) *Legal Transplants: An Approach to Comparative Law*, Edinburgh: Scottish Academic Press.
Watson, Alan (1985) *The Evolution of Western Private Law*, Baltimore: Johns Hopkins University Press.
Watt, Gary (2012) 'Comparison as Deep Appreciation', in: Monateri, Pier G. (ed.) *Methods of Comparative Law*, Cheltenham, UK and Northampton, MA, USA: Edward Elgar Publishing, pp. 82–103.
Wellmer, Albrecht (1971) *Critical Theory of Society*, New York: Herder & Herder.
Weisberg, Richard (1984) *The Failure of the Word*, New Haven: Yale University Press.
White, Hayden (1973) *Metahistory: The Historical Imagination of the 19th-Century Europe*, Baltimore: Johns Hopkins University Press.
White, Hayden (1990) 'The Value of Narrativity in the Representation of Reality', in: White, Hayden (ed.) *The Content of the Form. Narrative Discourse and Historical Representation*, Baltimore: Johns Hopkins University Press, pp. 1–25.
Whitman, James Q. (2000) 'Enforcing Civility and Respect: Three Societies', 109 *Yale Law Journal*, pp. 1279–1398.
Wiethölter, Rudolf (1968) *Rechtswissenschaft*, Frankfurt: Fischer.
Wiethölter, Rudolf, Joerges, Christian and Zumbansen, Peer (eds) (2013) *Politische Rechtstheorie revisited. Rudolf Wiethölter zum 100. Semester*, Bremen: ZERP- Disskussionspapier No.1, University of Bremen.
Wigmore, John H. (1928) *A Panorama of the World's Legal Systems*, Vol. III, St. Paul: West Publishing Co.
Wigmore, John H. (1931) 'Jottings on Comparative Legal Ideas and Institutions', 6 *Tulane Law Review*, pp. 48–82.
Williams, Patricia (1991) *The Alchemy of Race and Rights*, Cambridge MA: Harvard University Press.
Williams, Raymond (1976) *Keywords. A Vocabulary of Culture and Society*, Oxford: Oxford University Press.
Winter, Bronwyn (2008) *Hijab and the Republic. Uncovering the French Headscarf Debate*, Syracuse: Syracuse University Press.
Wong, David (2006) *Natural Moralities. A Defense of Pluralistic Relativism*, Oxford: Oxford University Press.

World Bank (2015) *Nigeria: Access to Justice for the Poor – Implementation Status Results Report*, http://www.wds.worldbank.org/external/default/WDSContentServer/WDSP/LEG/2015/02/13/090224b082aa826c/1_0/Rendered/PDF/Nigeria000NIGE0Report000Sequence004.pdf (last accessed 24 September 2015).

Yeğenoğlu, Meyda (1998) *Colonial Fantasies. Towards a Feminist Reading of Orientalism*, Cambridge: Cambridge University Press.

Yengoyan, Aram A. (ed.) (2006) *Modes of Comparison. Theory & Practice*, Michigan: University of Michigan Press.

Young, Iris Marion (1997) 'Asymmetrical Reciprocity. On Moral Respect, Wonder, and Enlarged Thought', 3 *Constellations. An International Journal of Critical and Democratic Theory*, pp. 340–363.

Young, Robert (1990) *White Mythologies*, London and New York: Routledge.

Yu, Ganghua (2013) *Rethinking Law and Development*, New York: Routledge.

Zimmermann, Reinhard (2006) 'Comparative Law and the Europeanization of Private Law', in: Reimann, Mathias and Zimmermann, Reinhard (eds) *The Oxford Handbook of Comparative Law*, Oxford: Oxford University Press, pp. 539–578.

Zitelmann, Ernst (1888) *Die Möglichkeit eines Weltrechts*, Berlin: Duncker & Humblot.

Zumbansen, Peer (2005) 'Comparative Law's Coming of Age? Twenty Years after *Critical Comparisons*', 6 *German Law Journal*, 1073–1084.

Zumbansen, Peer (2012) 'Transnational Comparisons: Theory and Practice of Comparative Law as a Critique of Governance', *Osgoode Hall Law School Research Paper Series*, No. 1.

Zweigert, Konrad (1949/1950) 'Rechtsvergleichung als universale Interpretationsmethode', 15 *Rabels Zeitschrift für ausländisches und internationales Privatrecht*, pp. 5–21.

Zweigert, Konrad (1960) 'Zur Methode der Rechtsvergleichung', 13 *Studium Generale*, pp. 193–200.

Zweigert, Konrad (1973) 'Die "Praesumptio Similitudinis" als Grundsatzvermutung rechtsvergleichender Methode', in: Rotondi, Mario (ed.) *Inchieste di Diritto Comparato II: Scopi e Metodi di Diritto Comparato*, Padova: CEDAM, p. 735.

Zweigert, Konrad and Puttfarken, Hans-Jürgen (eds) (1978) *Rechtsvergleichung*, Darmstadt: Wissenschaftliche Buchgesellschaft.

Zweigert, Konrad and Kötz, Hein (1998) *An Introduction to Comparative Law*, 3rd ed., Oxford: Clarendon.

Index